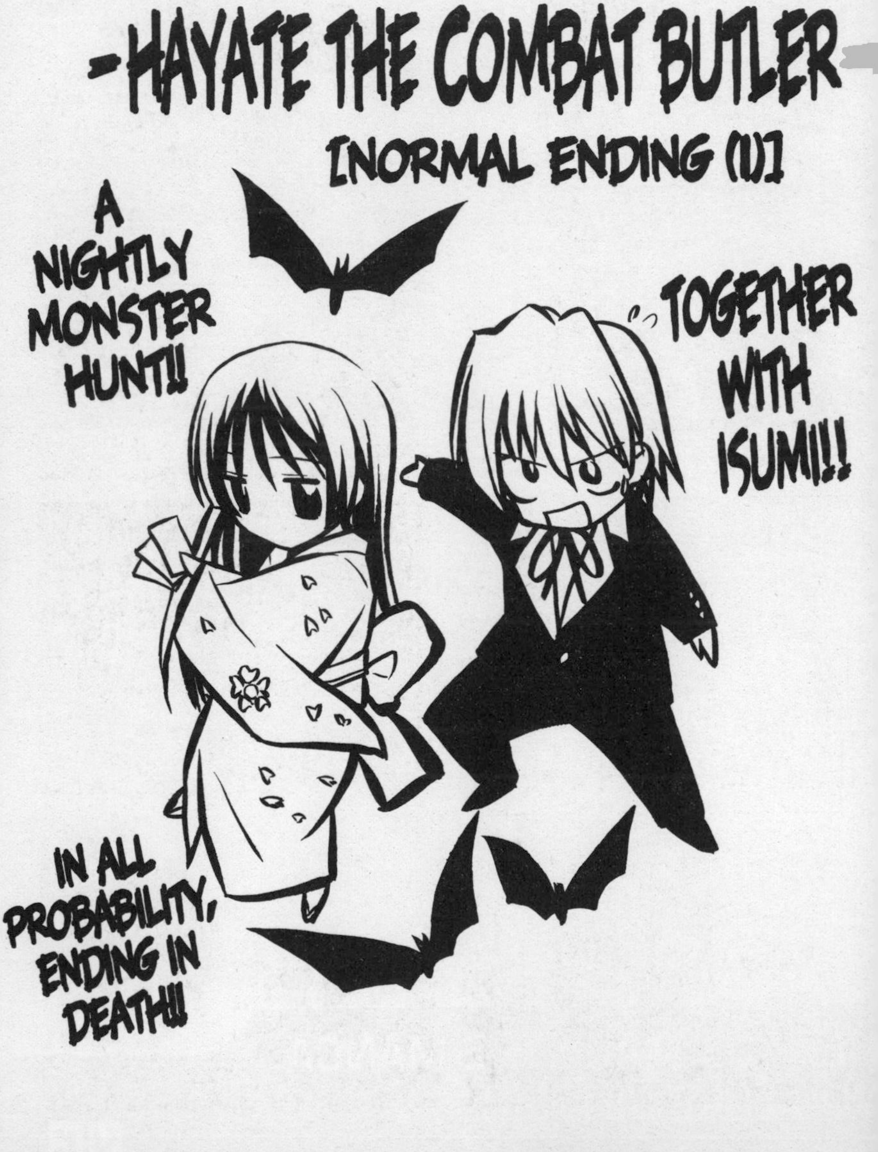
-HAYATE THE COMBAT BUTLER-
[NORMAL ENDING (1)]
TOGETHER WITH ISUMI!!
A NIGHTLY MONSTER HUNT!!
IN ALL PROBABILITY, ENDING IN DEATH!!

LOVE MANGA?
LET US KNOW WHAT YOU THINK!

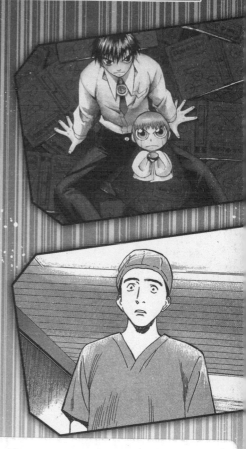

HELP US MAKE TH
YOU LOVE BETTER

Hayate the Combat Butler

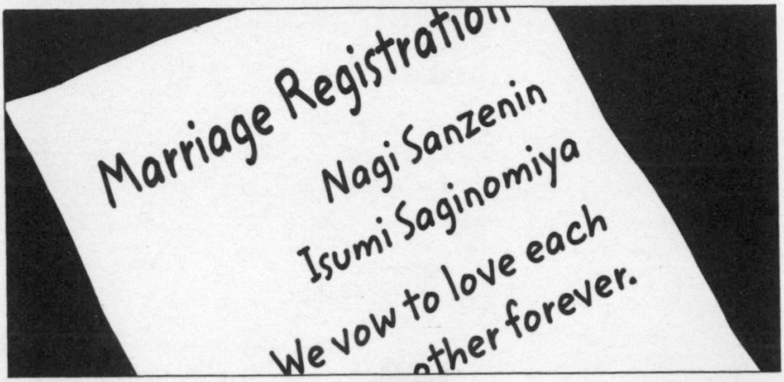
Marriage Registration
Nagi Sanzenin
Isumi Saginomiya
We vow to love each
other forever.

3

KENJIRO HATA

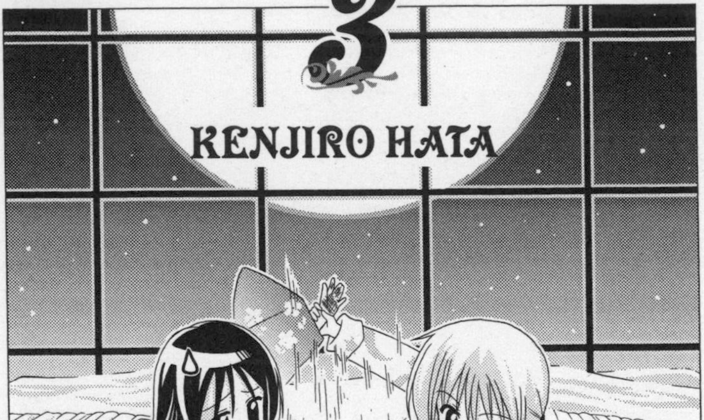

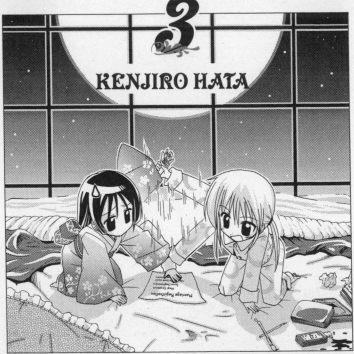

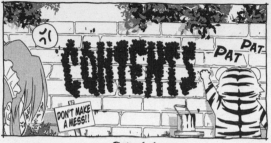

CONTENTS

Episode 1
"A Battle for Men"
5

Episode 2
"The Tokyo Underground"
21

Episode 3
"The Kingdom of Ambition"
37

Episode 4
"I Lost My Temper and Did It Because I Was Mortified About Losing to
Little Kids on the Street. But, I Have No Regrets"
53

Episode 5
"A Nuisance, Even for Peter Pan"
69

Episode 6
"Who Came Up with the Sound Effect, 'Kapok'? It's Awesome"
85

Episode 7
"I Never Had the Problem of Being Too Popular"
102

Episode 8
"I Wanted to See the Challenge of the Super Shuffle"
119

Episode 9
"By the Time Ojō-sama Cries"
135

Episode 10
"Wavering Hearts"
151

Episode 11
"I'm Hoping My Voice Will Reach You"
167

Episode 1: "A Battle for Men"

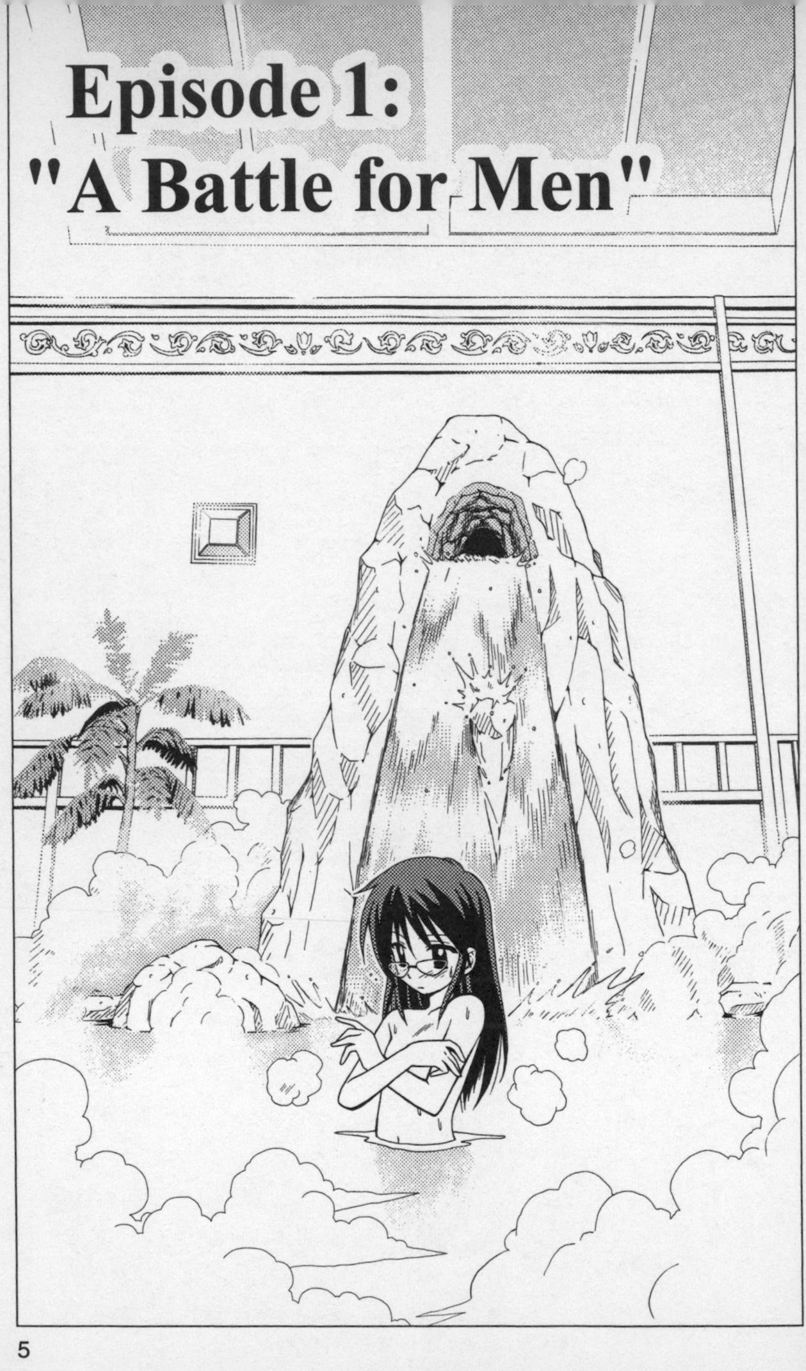

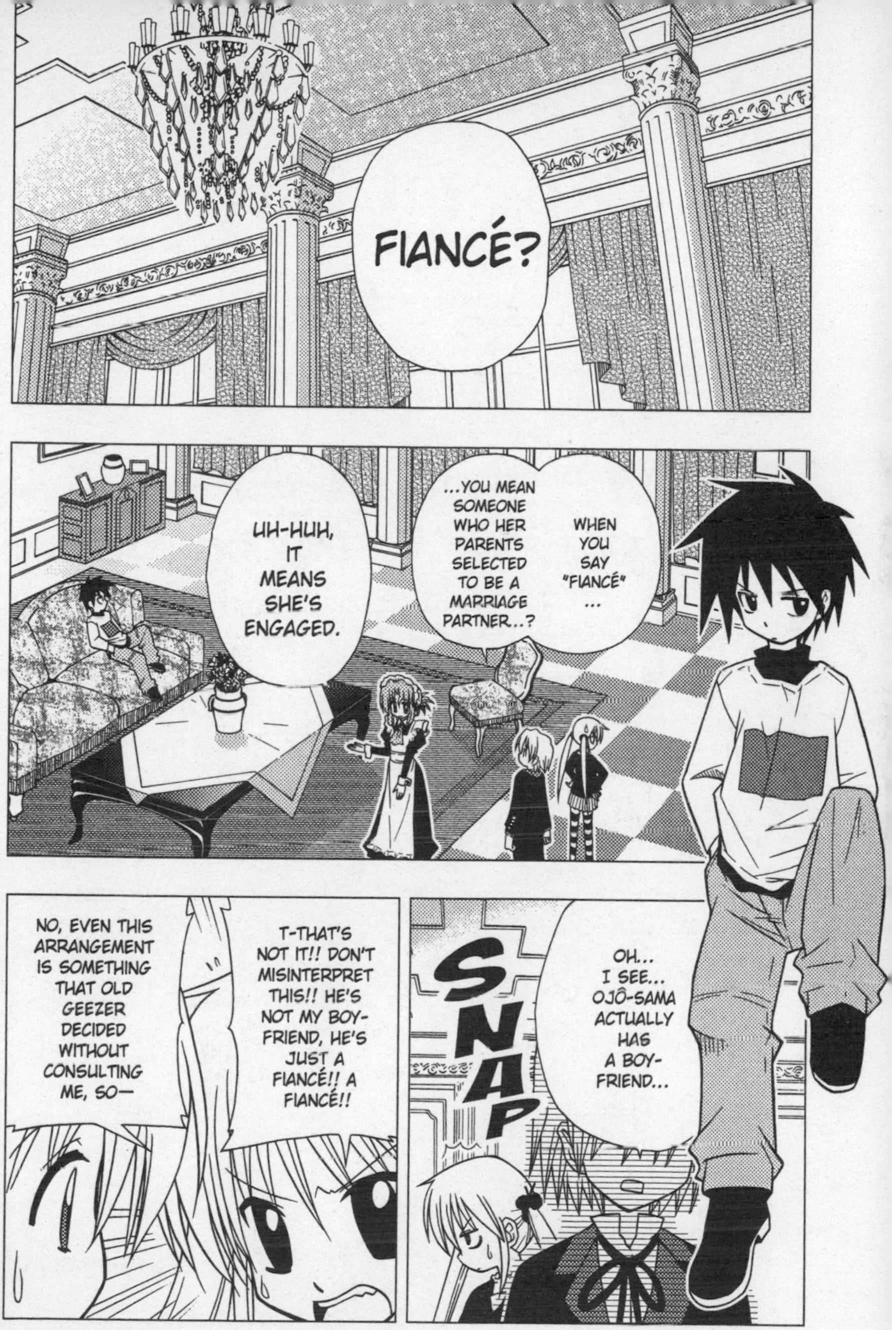
FIANCÉ?
WHEN YOU SAY "FIANCÉ"...
...YOU MEAN SOMEONE WHO HER PARENTS SELECTED TO BE A MARRIAGE PARTNER...?
UH-HUH, IT MEANS SHE'S ENGAGED.
SNAP
OH... I SEE... OJÔ-SAMA ACTUALLY HAS A BOY-FRIEND...
T-THAT'S NOT IT!! DON'T MISINTERPRET THIS!! HE'S NOT MY BOY-FRIEND, HE'S JUST A FIANCÉ!! A FIANCÉ!!
NO, EVEN THIS ARRANGEMENT IS SOMETHING THAT OLD GEEZER DECIDED WITHOUT CONSULTING ME, SO—

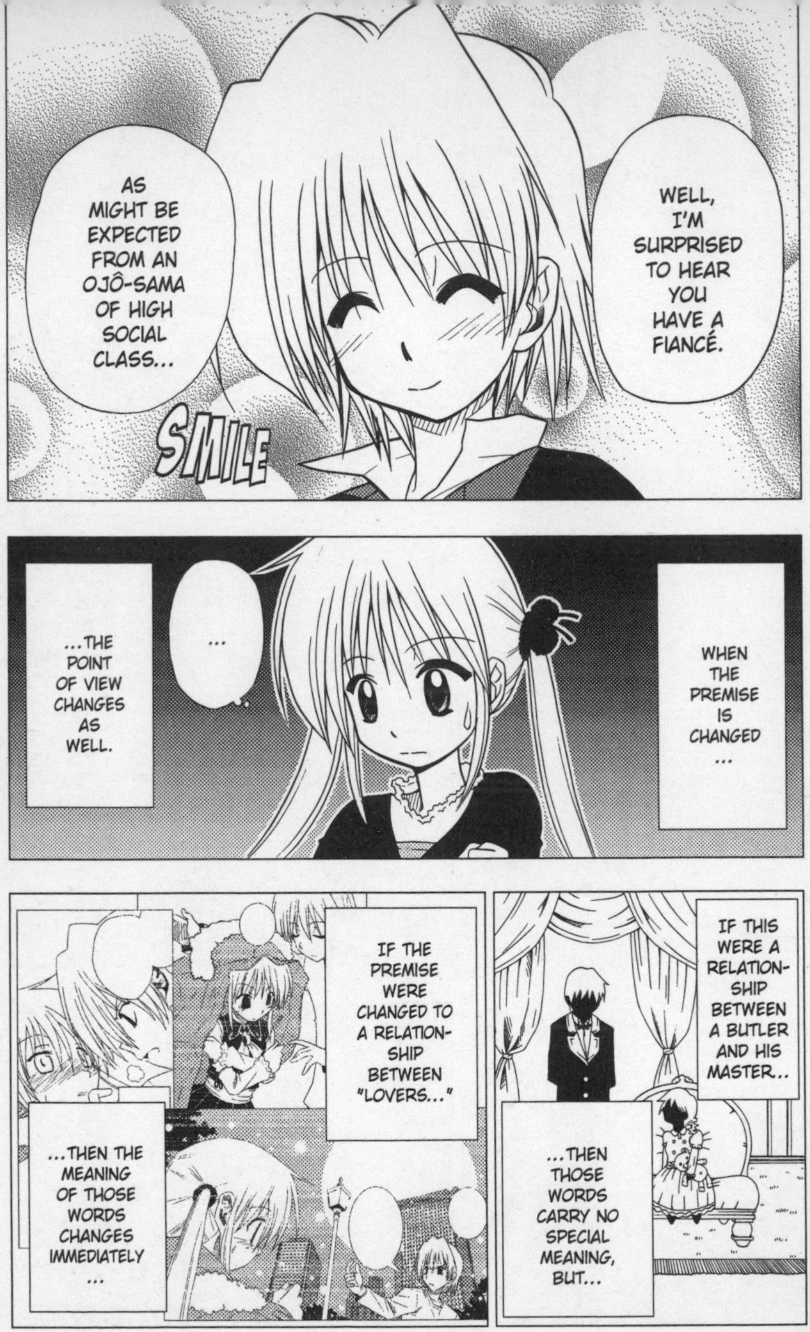
WELL, I'M SURPRISED TO HEAR YOU HAVE A FIANCÉ.
AS MIGHT BE EXPECTED FROM AN OJÔ-SAMA OF HIGH SOCIAL CLASS...
SMILE
WHEN THE PREMISE IS CHANGED...
...
...THE POINT OF VIEW CHANGES AS WELL.
IF THIS WERE A RELATION-SHIP BETWEEN A BUTLER AND HIS MASTER...
...THEN THOSE WORDS CARRY NO SPECIAL MEANING, BUT...
IF THE PREMISE WERE CHANGED TO A RELATION-SHIP BETWEEN "LOVERS..."
...THEN THE MEANING OF THOSE WORDS CHANGES IMMEDIATELY...

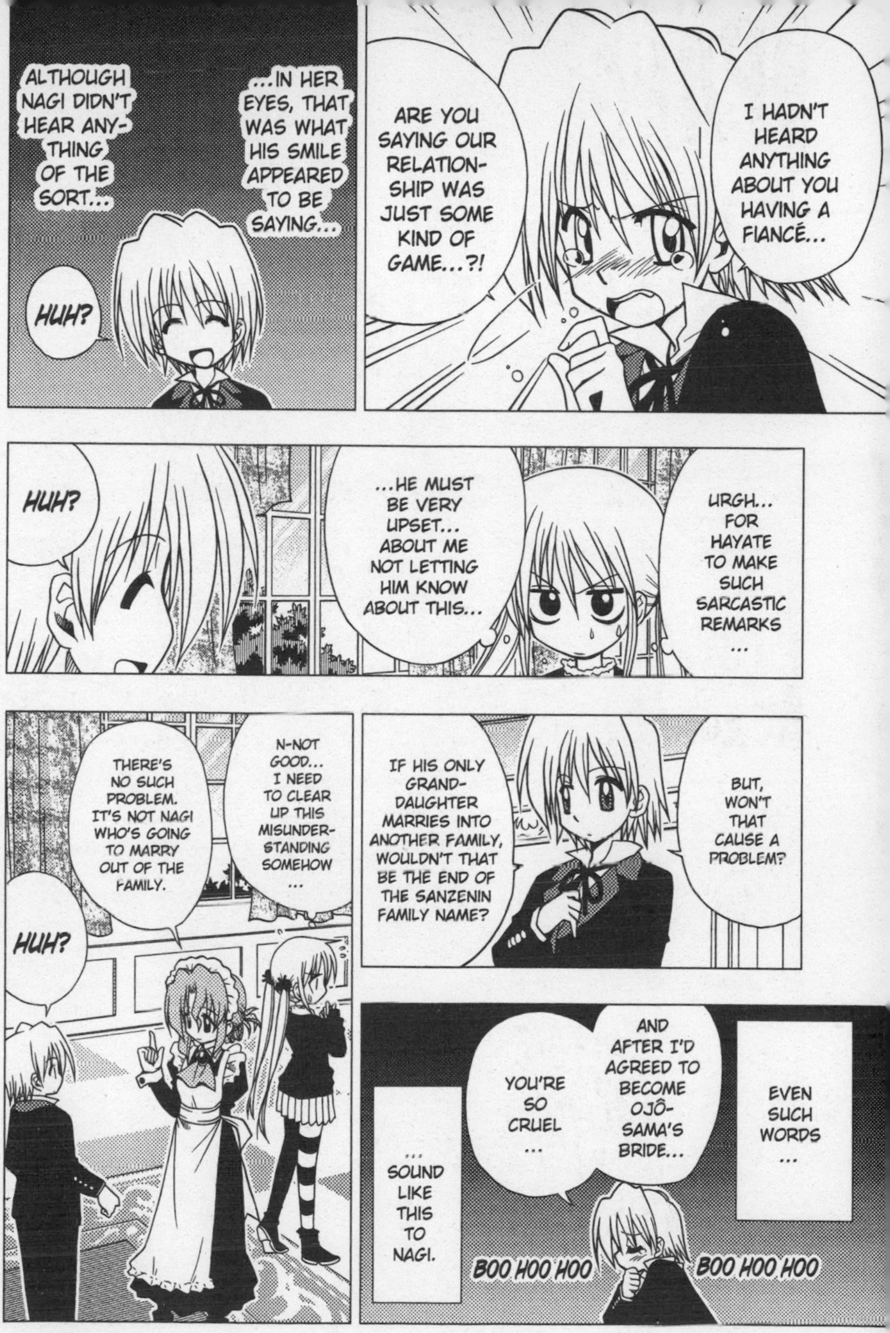
I HADN'T HEARD ANYTHING ABOUT YOU HAVING A FIANCÉ...
ARE YOU SAYING OUR RELATIONSHIP WAS JUST SOME KIND OF GAME...?!
ALTHOUGH NAGI DIDN'T HEAR ANYTHING OF THE SORT...
...IN HER EYES, THAT WAS WHAT HIS SMILE APPEARED TO BE SAYING...
HUH?
URGH... FOR HAYATE TO MAKE SUCH SARCASTIC REMARKS...
...HE MUST BE VERY UPSET... ABOUT ME NOT LETTING HIM KNOW ABOUT THIS...
HUH?
BUT, WON'T THAT CAUSE A PROBLEM?
IF HIS ONLY GRANDDAUGHTER MARRIES INTO ANOTHER FAMILY, WOULDN'T THAT BE THE END OF THE SANZENIN FAMILY NAME?
EVEN SUCH WORDS...
AND AFTER I'D AGREED TO BECOME OJÔ-SAMA'S BRIDE...
YOU'RE SO CRUEL...
...SOUND LIKE THIS TO NAGI.
BOO HOO HOO
BOO HOO HOO
N-NOT GOOD... I NEED TO CLEAR UP THIS MISUNDERSTANDING SOMEHOW...
THERE'S NO SUCH PROBLEM. IT'S NOT NAGI WHO'S GOING TO MARRY OUT OF THE FAMILY.
HUH?

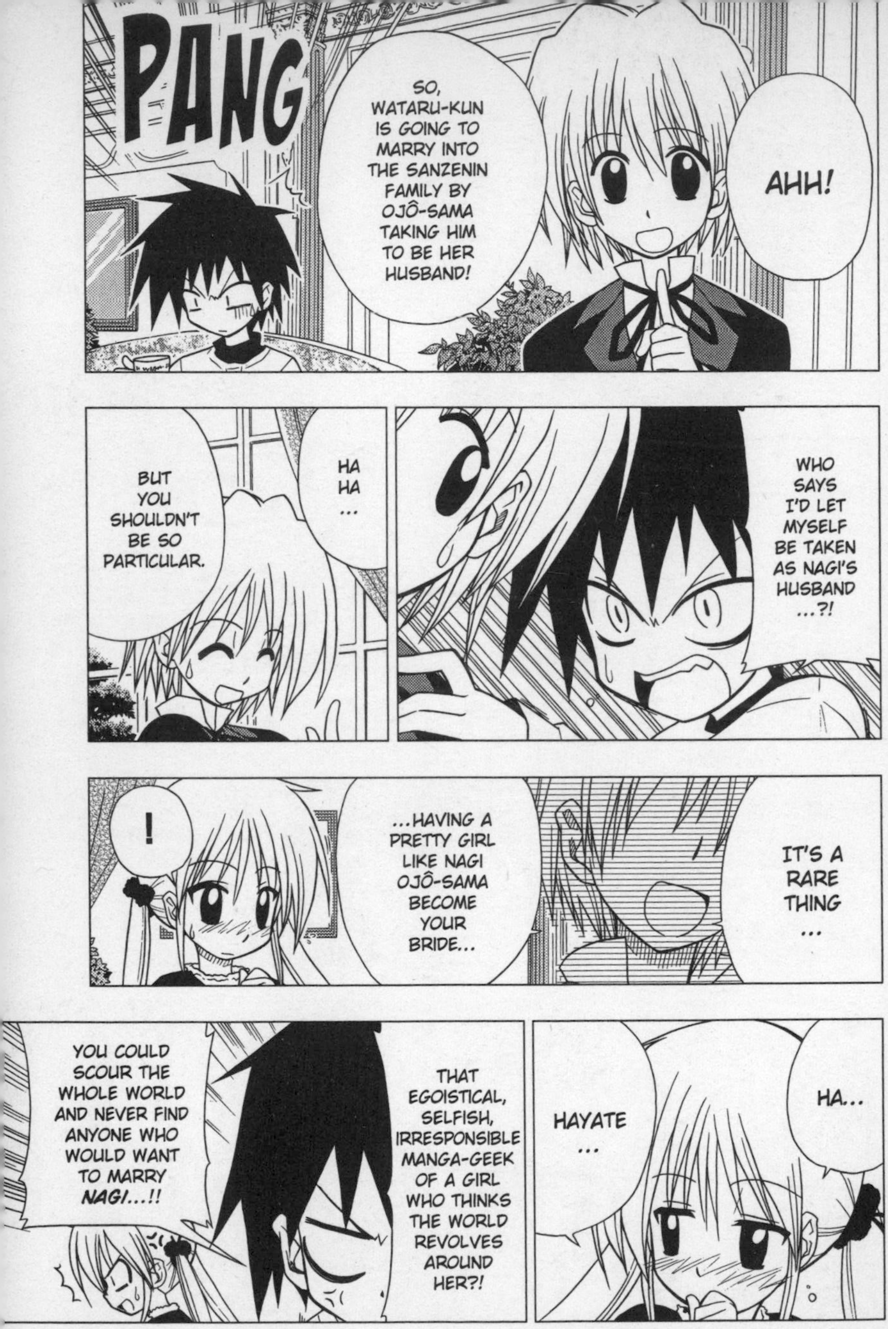
AHH!
SO, WATARU-KUN IS GOING TO MARRY INTO THE SANZENIN FAMILY BY OJÔ-SAMA TAKING HIM TO BE HER HUSBAND!
PANG
WHO SAYS I'D LET MYSELF BE TAKEN AS NAGI'S HUSBAND ...?!
HA HA ...
BUT YOU SHOULDN'T BE SO PARTICULAR.
IT'S A RARE THING ...
...HAVING A PRETTY GIRL LIKE NAGI OJÔ-SAMA BECOME YOUR BRIDE...
!
HA...
HAYATE ...
THAT EGOISTICAL, SELFISH, IRRESPONSIBLE MANGA-GEEK OF A GIRL WHO THINKS THE WORLD REVOLVES AROUND HER?!
YOU COULD SCOUR THE WHOLE WORLD AND NEVER FIND ANYONE WHO WOULD WANT TO MARRY NAGI...!!

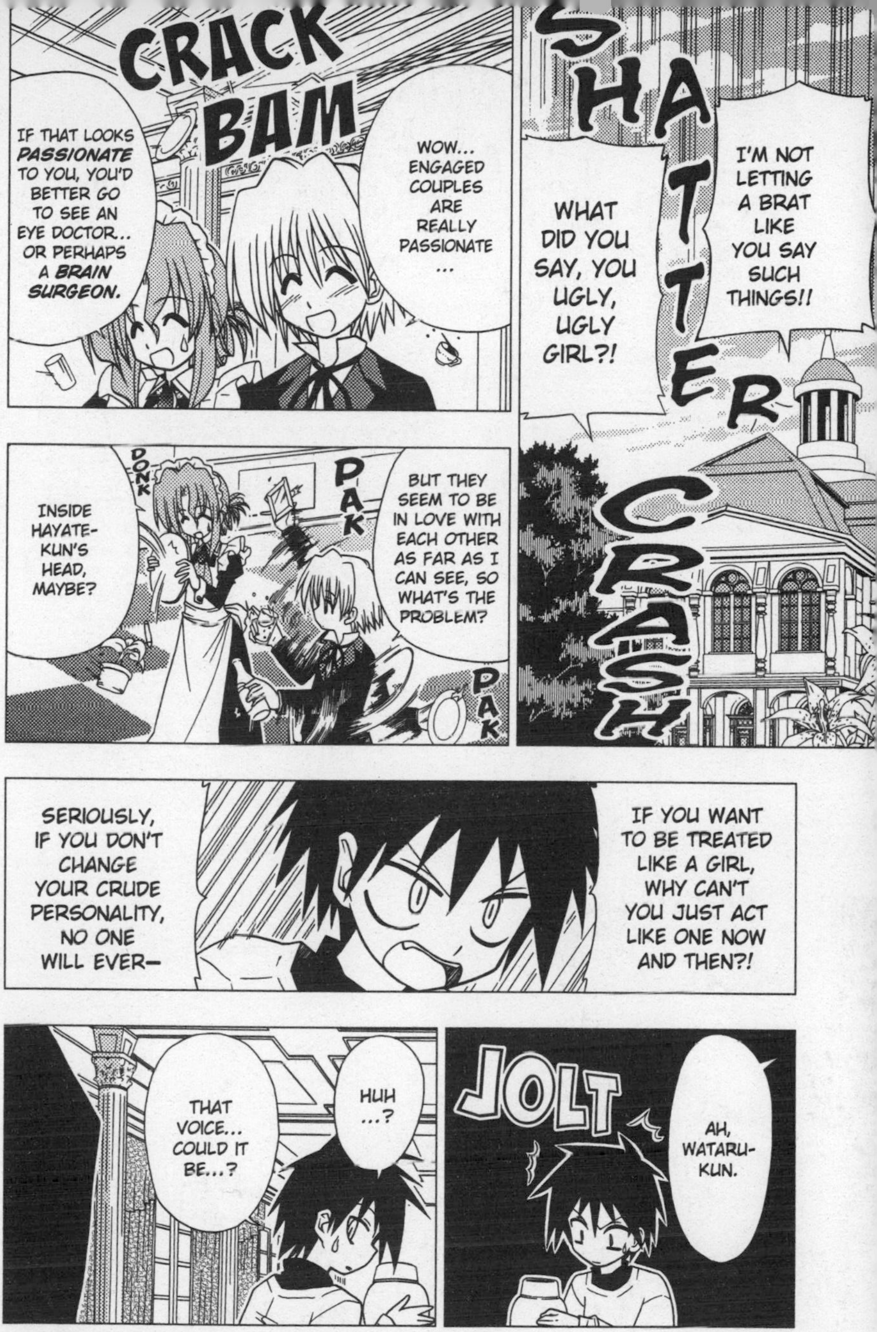
SHATTER
I'M NOT LETTING A BRAT LIKE YOU SAY SUCH THINGS!!
WHAT DID YOU SAY, YOU UGLY, UGLY GIRL?!
CRASH
CRACK
BAM
WOW... ENGAGED COUPLES ARE REALLY PASSIONATE ...
IF THAT LOOKS *PASSIONATE* TO YOU, YOU'D BETTER GO TO SEE AN EYE DOCTOR... OR PERHAPS A *BRAIN SURGEON.*
DONK
PAK
PAK
BUT THEY SEEM TO BE IN LOVE WITH EACH OTHER AS FAR AS I CAN SEE, SO WHAT'S THE PROBLEM?
INSIDE HAYATE-KUN'S HEAD, MAYBE?
IF YOU WANT TO BE TREATED LIKE A GIRL, WHY CAN'T YOU JUST ACT LIKE ONE NOW AND THEN?!
SERIOUSLY, IF YOU DON'T CHANGE YOUR CRUDE PERSONALITY, NO ONE WILL EVER—
JOLT
AH, WATARU-KUN.
HUH ...?
THAT VOICE... COULD IT BE...?

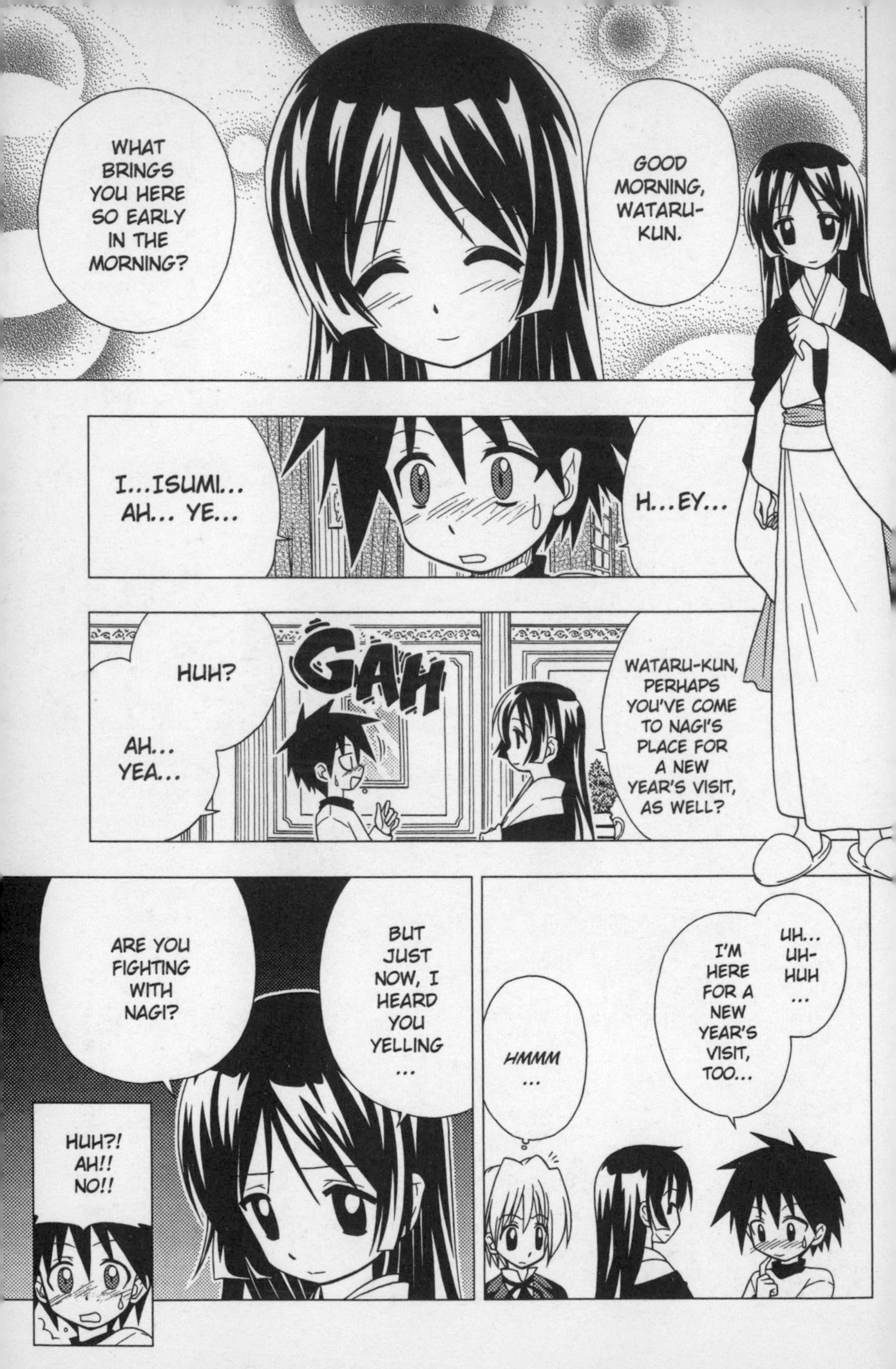
GOOD MORNING, WATARU-KUN.
WHAT BRINGS YOU HERE SO EARLY IN THE MORNING?
H...EY...
I...ISUMI... AH... YE...
WATARU-KUN, PERHAPS YOU'VE COME TO NAGI'S PLACE FOR A NEW YEAR'S VISIT, AS WELL?
GAH
HUH?
AH... YEA...
UH... UH-HUH...
I'M HERE FOR A NEW YEAR'S VISIT, TOO...
HMMM...
BUT JUST NOW, I HEARD YOU YELLING...
ARE YOU FIGHTING WITH NAGI?
HUH?! AH!! NO!!

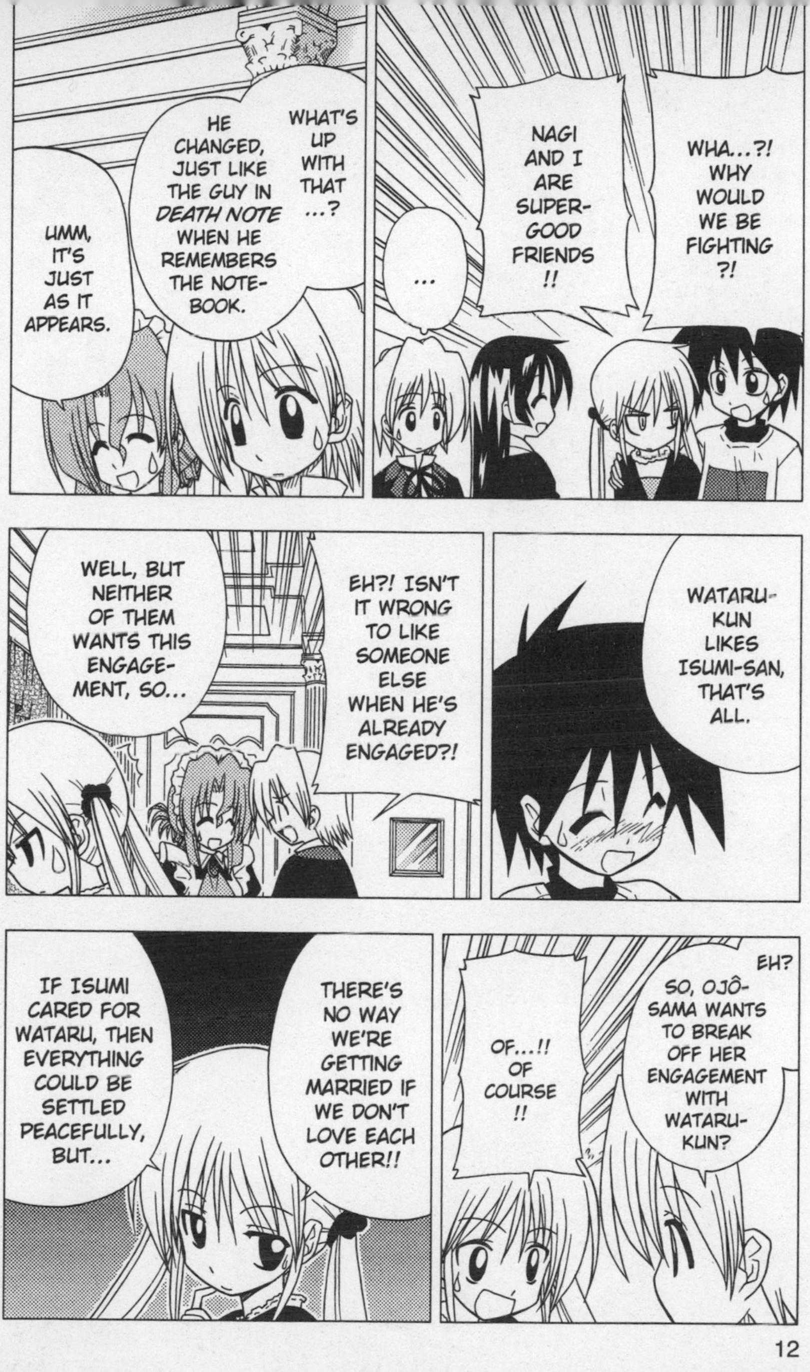
WHA...?! WHY WOULD WE BE FIGHTING?!
NAGI AND I ARE SUPER-GOOD FRIENDS!!
...
WHAT'S UP WITH THAT...?
HE CHANGED, JUST LIKE THE GUY IN *DEATH NOTE* WHEN HE REMEMBERS THE NOTE-BOOK.
UMM, IT'S JUST AS IT APPEARS.
WATARU-KUN LIKES ISUMI-SAN, THAT'S ALL.
EH?! ISN'T IT WRONG TO LIKE SOMEONE ELSE WHEN HE'S ALREADY ENGAGED?!
WELL, BUT NEITHER OF THEM WANTS THIS ENGAGE-MENT, SO...
EH?
SO, OJÔ-SAMA WANTS TO BREAK OFF HER ENGAGEMENT WITH WATARU-KUN?
OF...!! OF COURSE!!
THERE'S NO WAY WE'RE GETTING MARRIED IF WE DON'T LOVE EACH OTHER!!
IF ISUMI CARED FOR WATARU, THEN EVERYTHING COULD BE SETTLED PEACEFULLY, BUT...

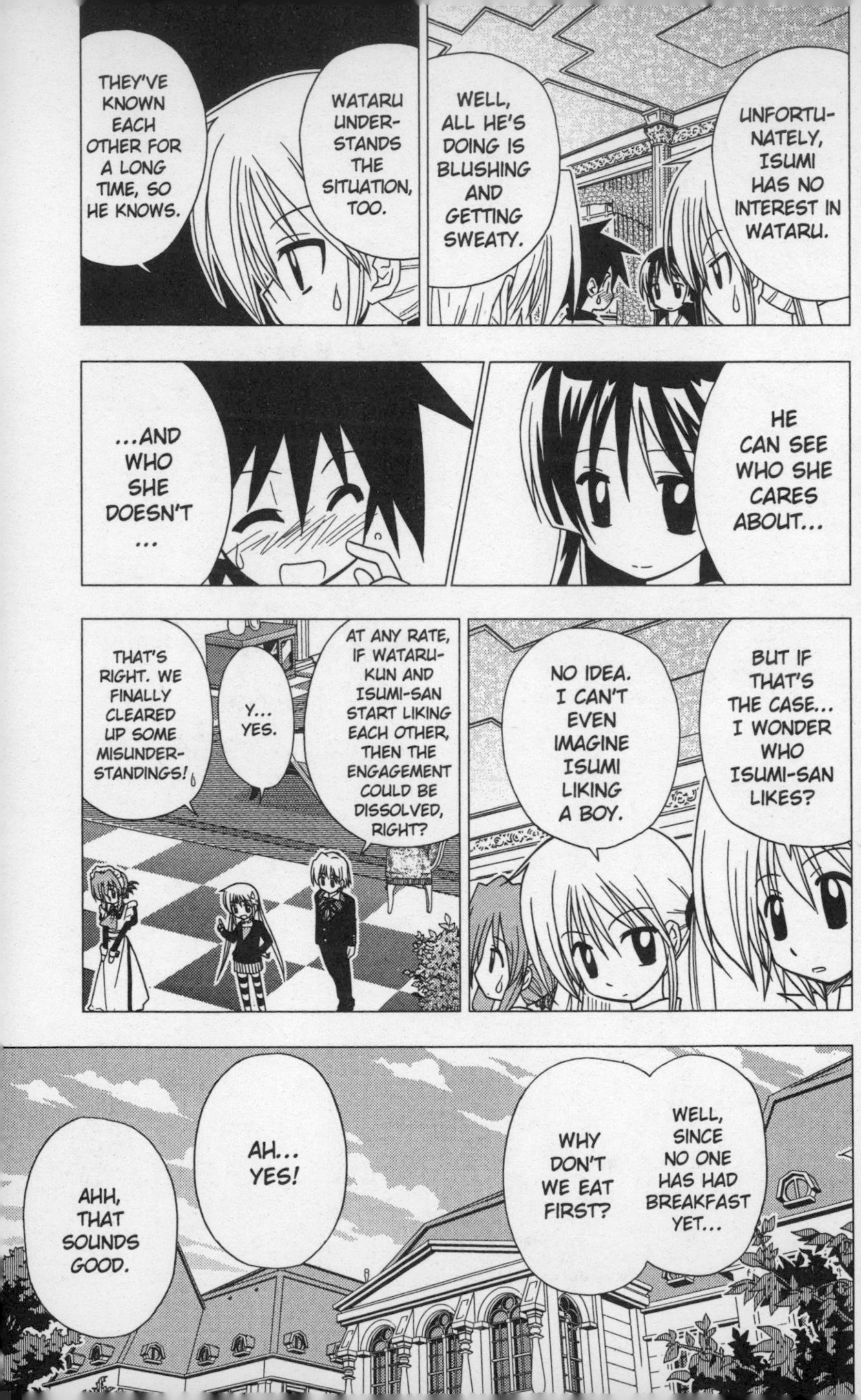
UNFORTUNATELY, ISUMI HAS NO INTEREST IN WATARU.
WELL, ALL HE'S DOING IS BLUSHING AND GETTING SWEATY.
WATARU UNDERSTANDS THE SITUATION, TOO.
THEY'VE KNOWN EACH OTHER FOR A LONG TIME, SO HE KNOWS.
HE CAN SEE WHO SHE CARES ABOUT...
...AND WHO SHE DOESN'T...
BUT IF THAT'S THE CASE... I WONDER WHO ISUMI-SAN LIKES?
NO IDEA. I CAN'T EVEN IMAGINE ISUMI LIKING A BOY.
AT ANY RATE, IF WATARU-KUN AND ISUMI-SAN START LIKING EACH OTHER, THEN THE ENGAGEMENT COULD BE DISSOLVED, RIGHT?
Y... YES.
THAT'S RIGHT. WE FINALLY CLEARED UP SOME MISUNDERSTANDINGS!
WELL, SINCE NO ONE HAS HAD BREAKFAST YET...
WHY DON'T WE EAT FIRST?
AH... YES!
AHH, THAT SOUNDS GOOD.

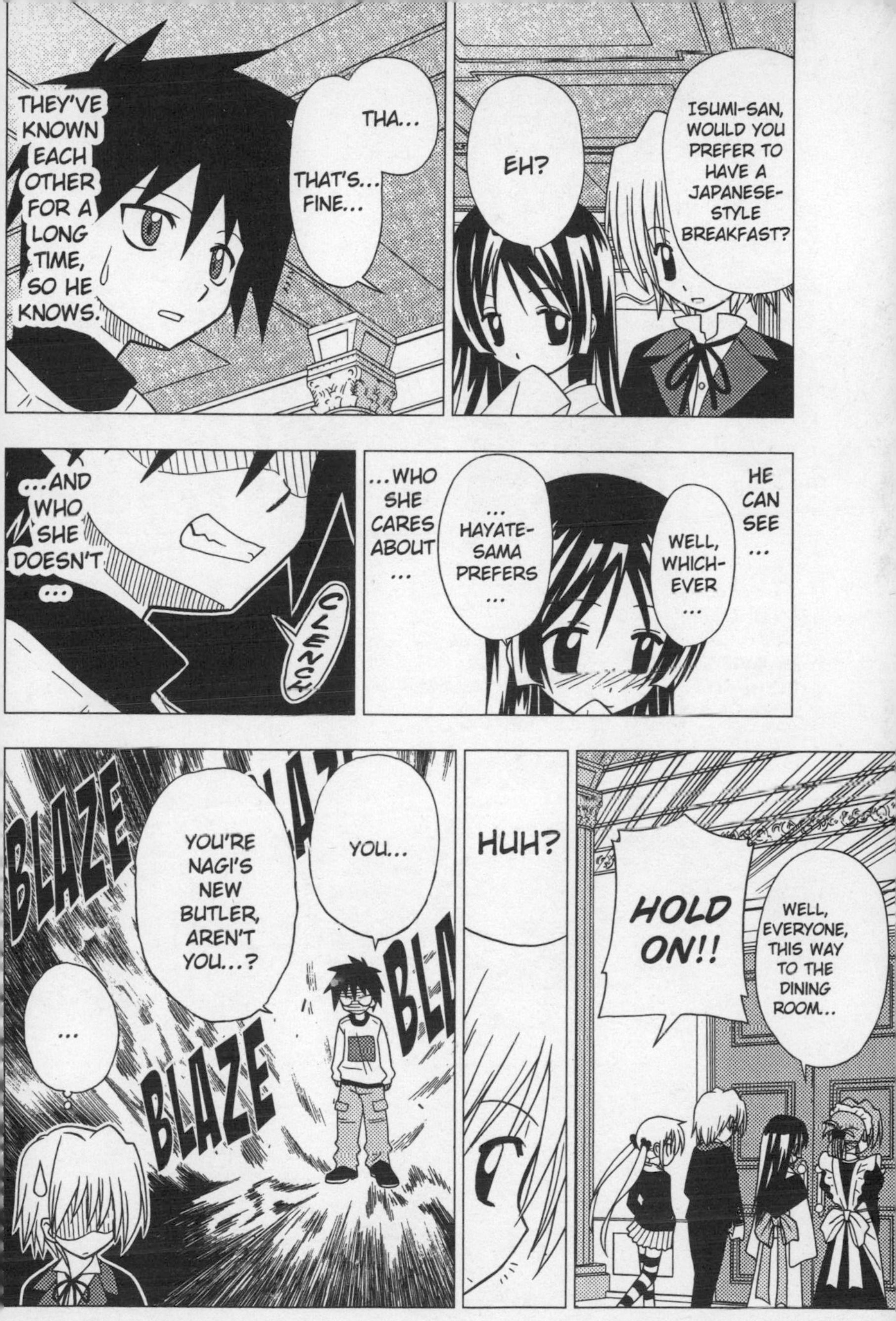
ISUMI-SAN, WOULD YOU PREFER TO HAVE A JAPANESE-STYLE BREAKFAST?
EH?
THA...
THAT'S... FINE...
THEY'VE KNOWN EACH OTHER FOR A LONG TIME, SO HE KNOWS.
HE CAN SEE...
WELL, WHICHEVER...
...HAYATE-SAMA PREFERS...
...WHO SHE CARES ABOUT...
CLENCH
...AND WHO SHE DOESN'T...
WELL, EVERYONE, THIS WAY TO THE DINING ROOM...
HOLD ON!!
HUH?
YOU...
BLAZE
YOU'RE NAGI'S NEW BUTLER, AREN'T YOU...?
BLAZE
...

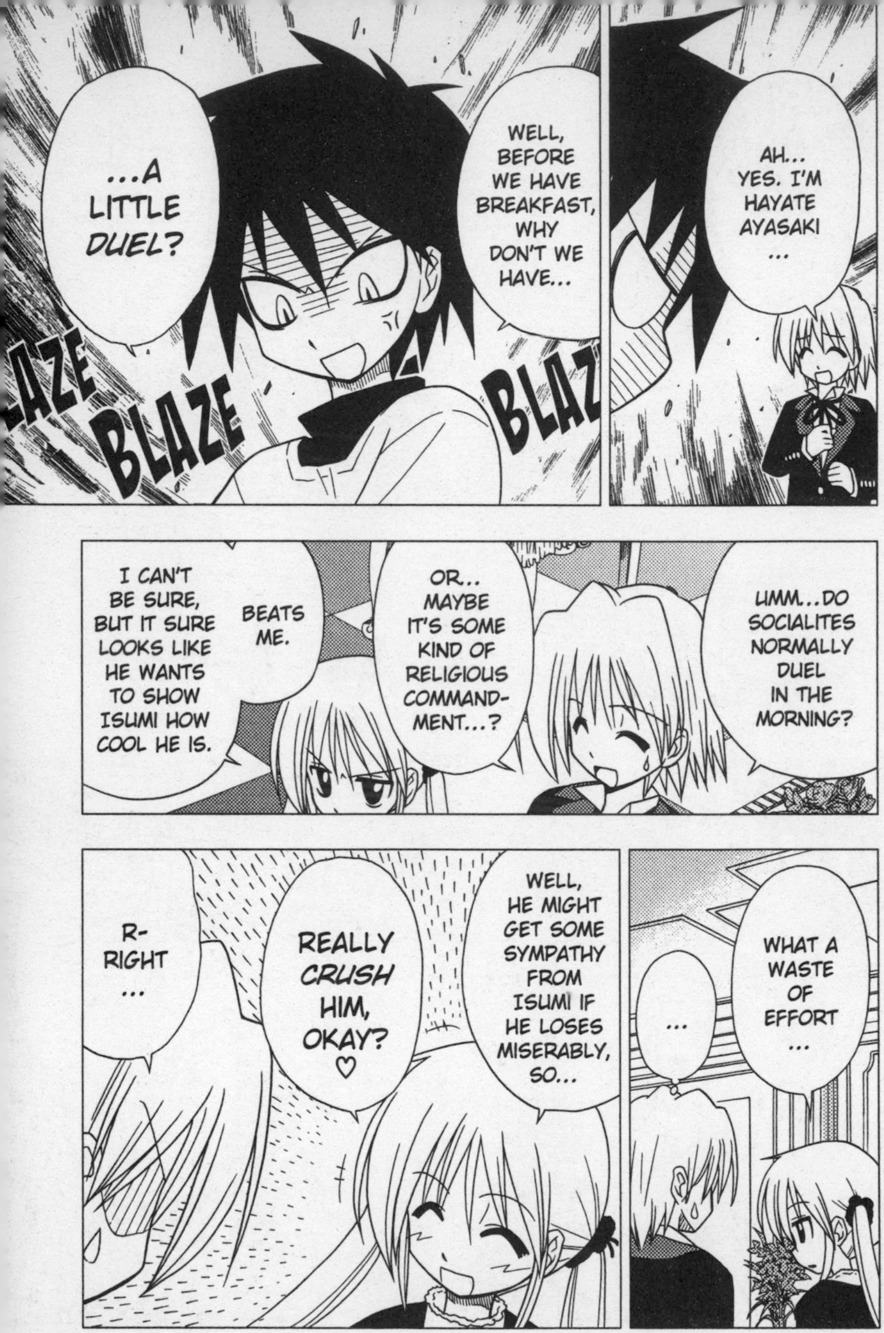
AH... YES. I'M HAYATE AYASAKI ...
WELL, BEFORE WE HAVE BREAKFAST, WHY DON'T WE HAVE...
BLAZ
...A LITTLE DUEL?
BLAZE
LAZE
UMM...DO SOCIALITES NORMALLY DUEL IN THE MORNING?
OR.. MAYBE IT'S SOME KIND OF RELIGIOUS COMMAND-MENT...?
BEATS ME.
I CAN'T BE SURE, BUT IT SURE LOOKS LIKE HE WANTS TO SHOW ISUMI HOW COOL HE IS.
WHAT A WASTE OF EFFORT ...
...
WELL, HE MIGHT GET SOME SYMPATHY FROM ISUMI IF HE LOSES MISERABLY, SO...
REALLY CRUSH HIM, OKAY? ♡
R-RIGHT ...

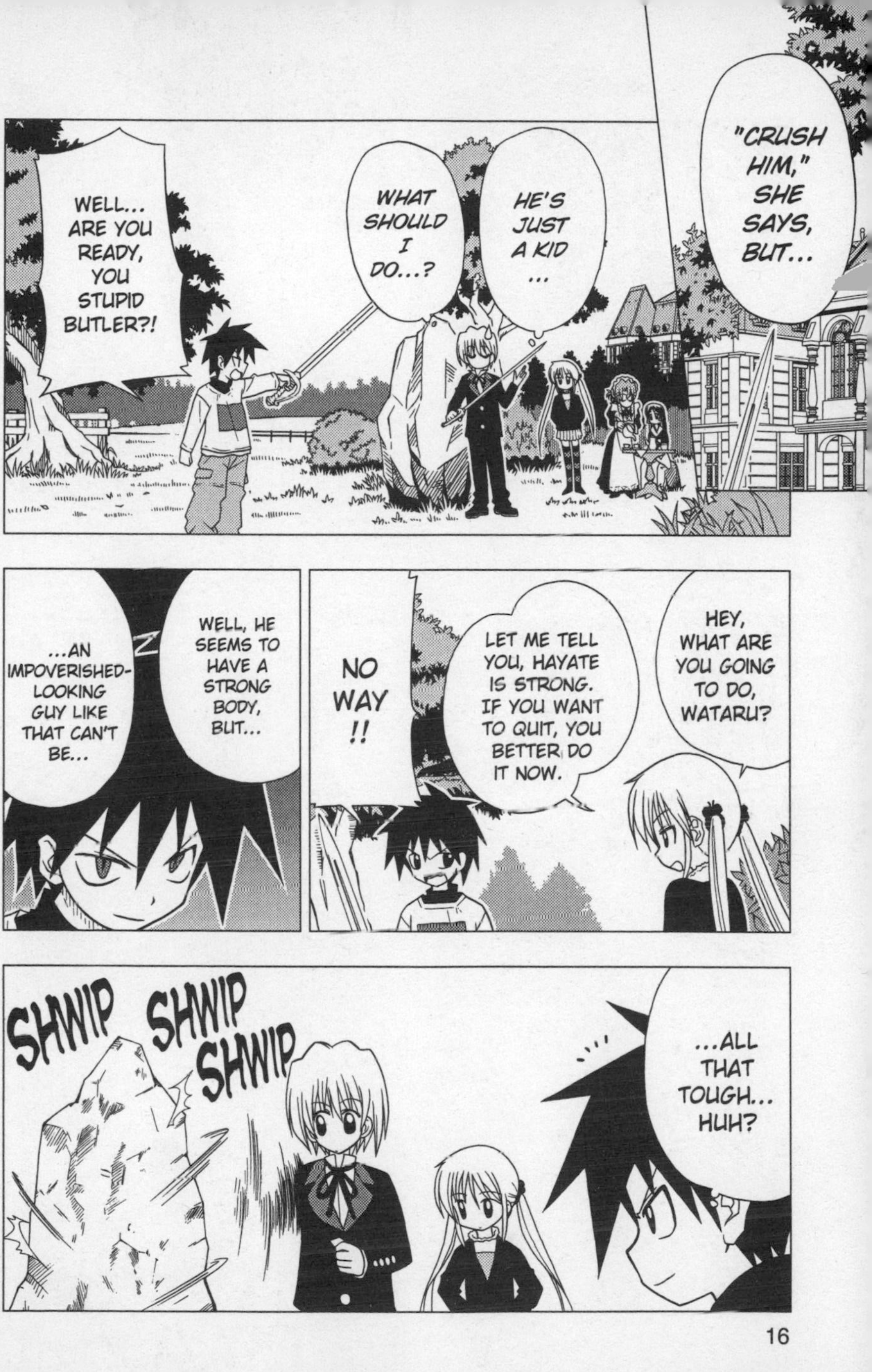
"CRUSH HIM," SHE SAYS, BUT...
HE'S JUST A KID ...
WHAT SHOULD I DO...?
WELL... ARE YOU READY, YOU STUPID BUTLER?!
HEY, WHAT ARE YOU GOING TO DO, WATARU?
LET ME TELL YOU, HAYATE IS STRONG. IF YOU WANT TO QUIT, YOU BETTER DO IT NOW.
NO WAY !!
WELL, HE SEEMS TO HAVE A STRONG BODY, BUT...
...AN IMPOVERISHED-LOOKING GUY LIKE THAT CAN'T BE...
...ALL THAT TOUGH... HUH?
SHWIP
SHWIP
SHWIP

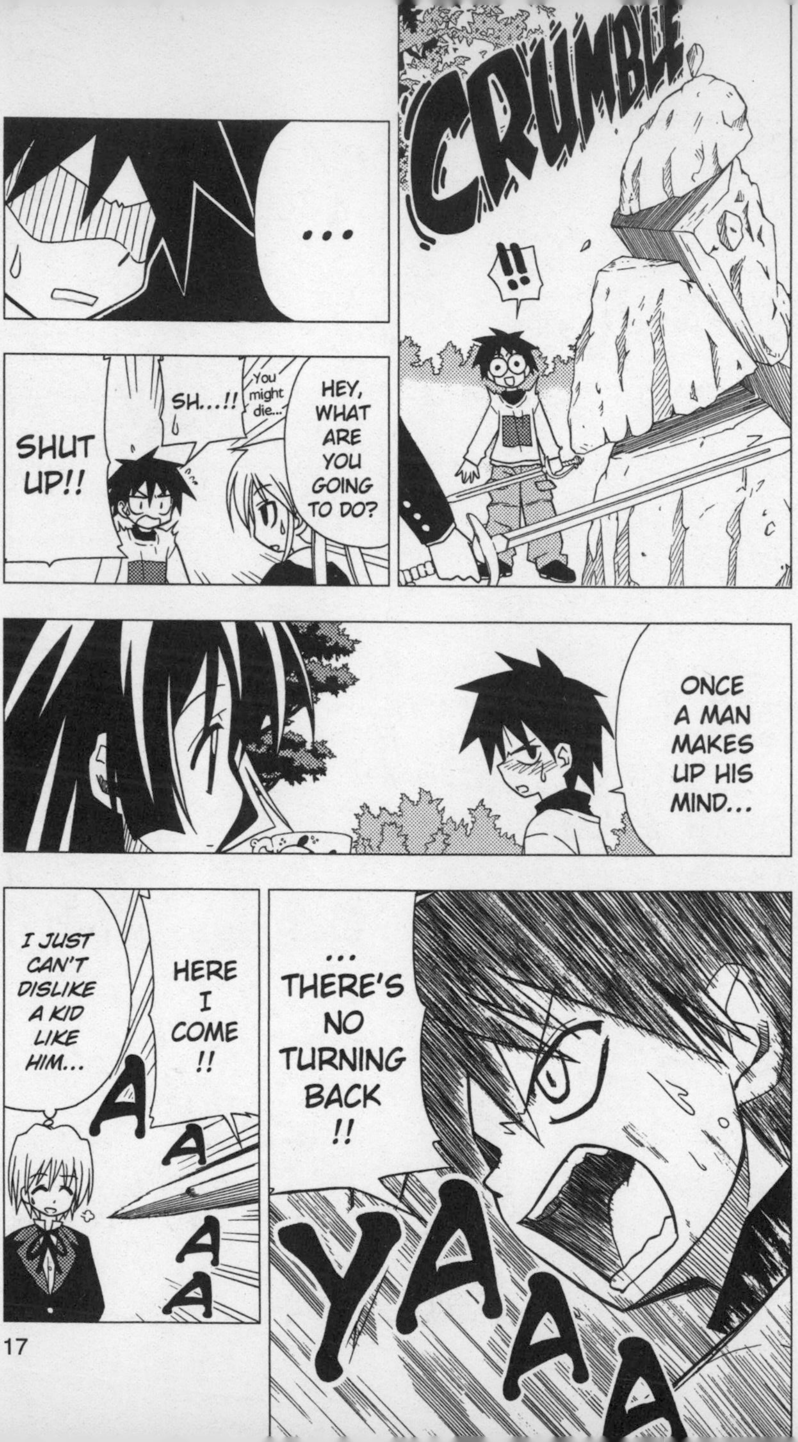
CRUMBLE
!!
...
HEY, WHAT ARE YOU GOING TO DO?
You might die...
SH...!!
SHUT UP!!
ONCE A MAN MAKES UP HIS MIND...
... THERE'S NO TURNING BACK !!
YAAAA
HERE I COME !!
I JUST CAN'T DISLIKE A KID LIKE HIM...
AAAA

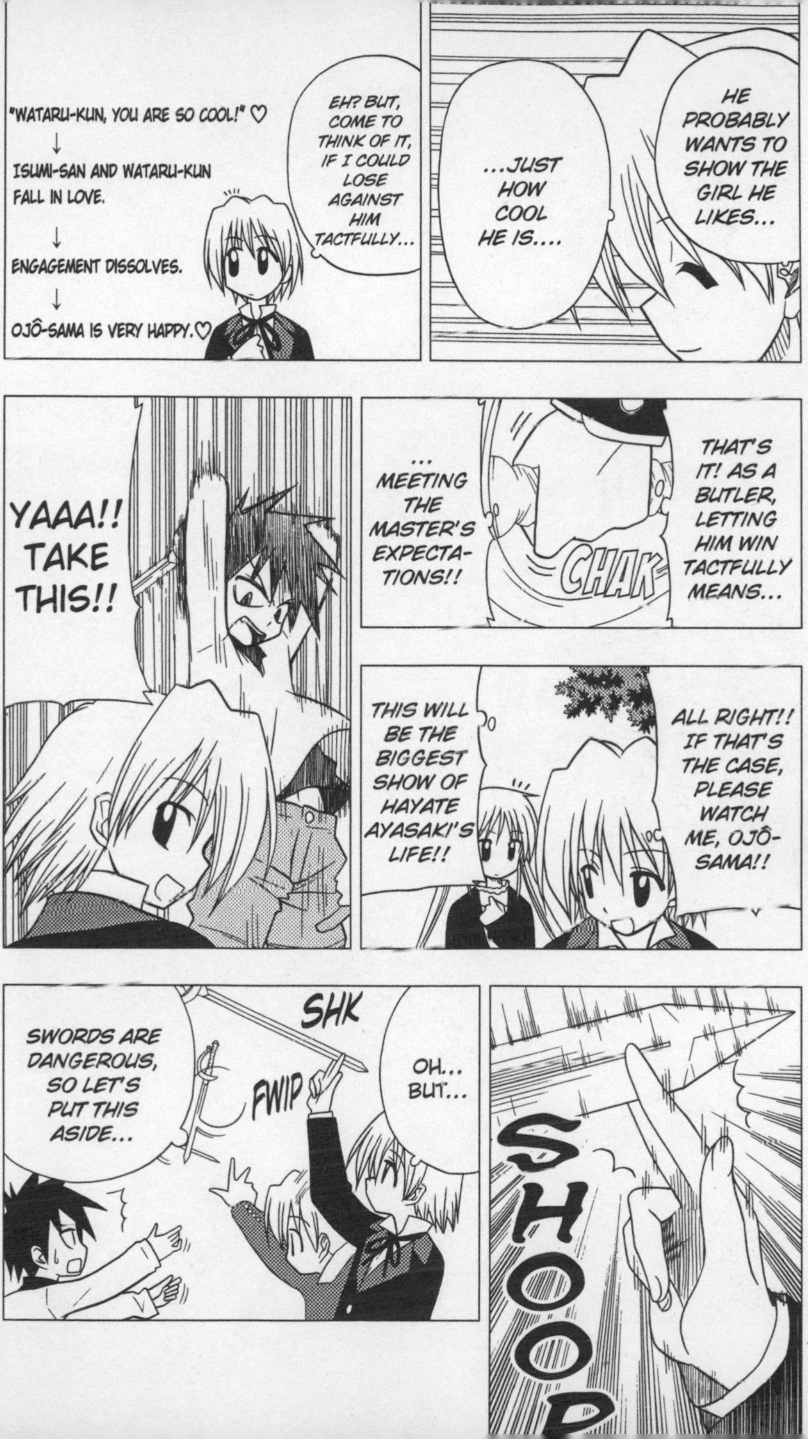
HE PROBABLY WANTS TO SHOW THE GIRL HE LIKES...
...JUST HOW COOL HE IS....
EH? BUT, COME TO THINK OF IT, IF I COULD LOSE AGAINST HIM TACTFULLY...
"WATARU-KUN, YOU ARE SO COOL!" ♡
↓
ISUMI-SAN AND WATARU-KUN FALL IN LOVE.
↓
ENGAGEMENT DISSOLVES.
↓
OJÔ-SAMA IS VERY HAPPY.♡
THAT'S IT! AS A BUTLER, LETTING HIM WIN TACTFULLY MEANS...
CHAK
...MEETING THE MASTER'S EXPECTATIONS!!
ALL RIGHT!! IF THAT'S THE CASE, PLEASE WATCH ME, OJÔ-SAMA!!
THIS WILL BE THE BIGGEST SHOW OF HAYATE AYASAKI'S LIFE!!
YAAA!! TAKE THIS!!
SHOOP
OH... BUT...
SHK
FWIP
SWORDS ARE DANGEROUS, SO LET'S PUT THIS ASIDE...

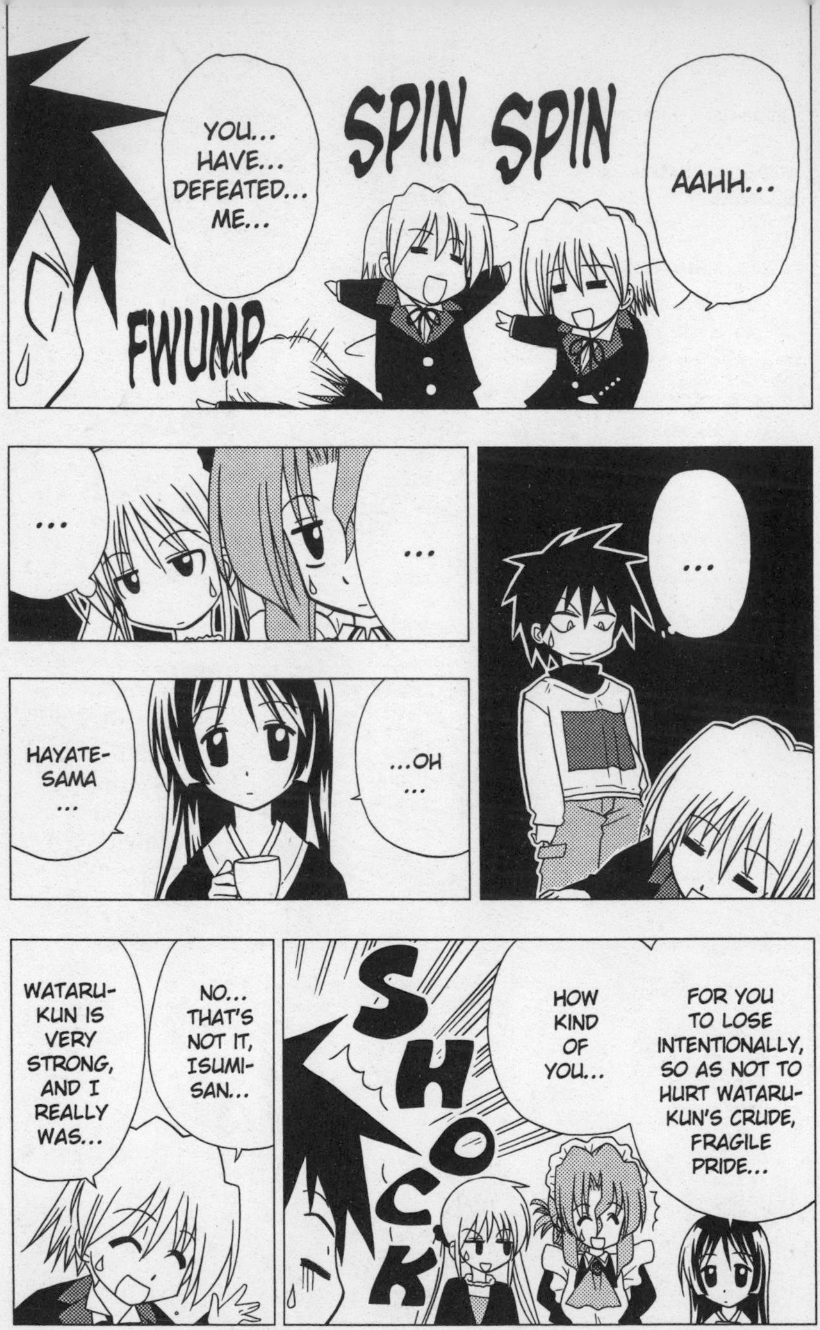
AAHH...
SPIN SPIN
YOU... HAVE... DEFEATED... ME...
FWUMP
...
...
...
...OH ...
HAYATE-SAMA ...
FOR YOU TO LOSE INTENTIONALLY, SO AS NOT TO HURT WATARU-KUN'S CRUDE, FRAGILE PRIDE...
HOW KIND OF YOU...
SHOCK
NO... THAT'S NOT IT, ISUMI-SAN...
WATARU-KUN IS VERY STRONG, AND I REALLY WAS...

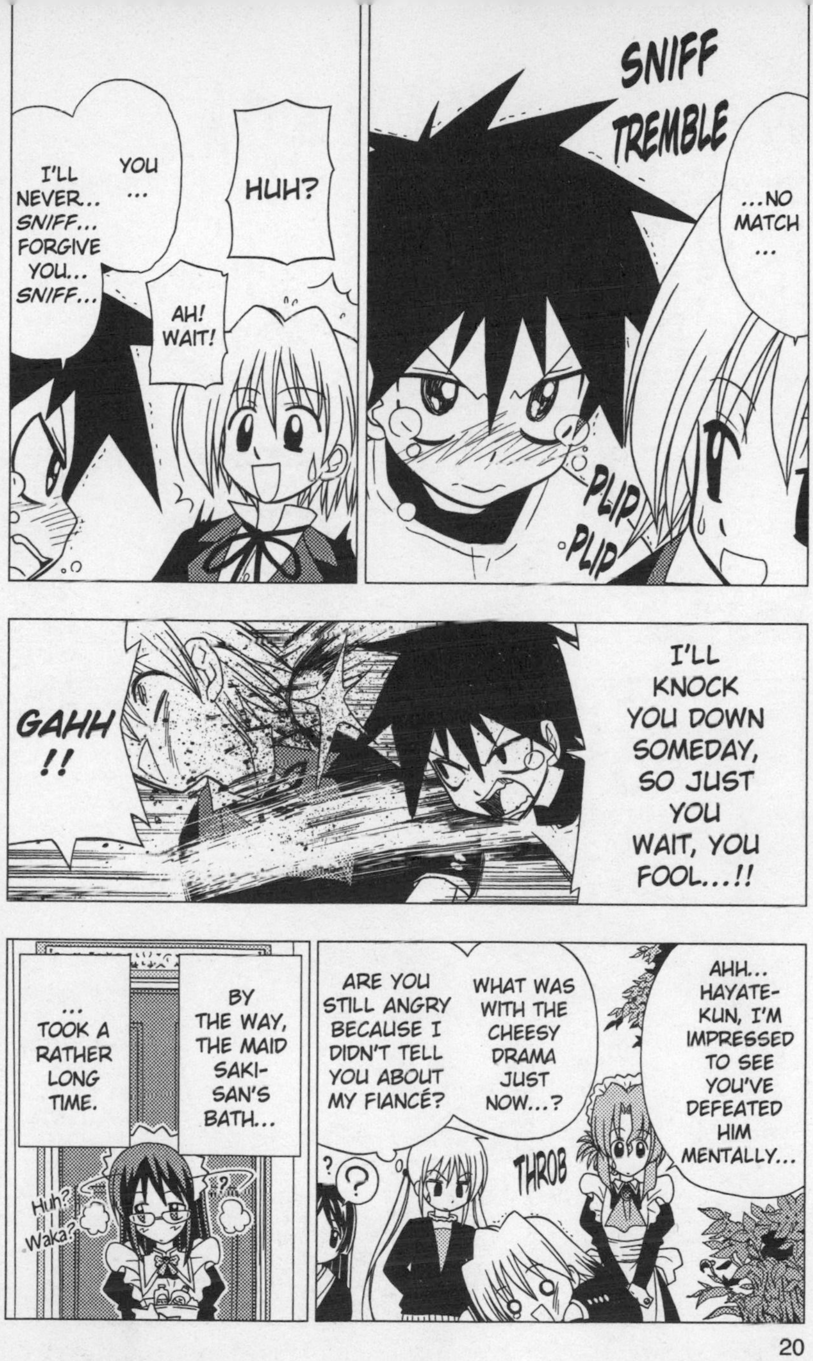
SNIFF
TREMBLE
...NO MATCH...
PLIP
PLIP
HUH?
YOU...
I'LL NEVER... SNIFF... FORGIVE YOU... SNIFF...
AH! WAIT!
I'LL KNOCK YOU DOWN SOMEDAY, SO JUST YOU WAIT, YOU FOOL...!!
GAHH!!
AHH... HAYATE-KUN, I'M IMPRESSED TO SEE YOU'VE DEFEATED HIM MENTALLY...
WHAT WAS WITH THE CHEESY DRAMA JUST NOW...?
ARE YOU STILL ANGRY BECAUSE I DIDN'T TELL YOU ABOUT MY FIANCÉ?
THROB
?
?
BY THE WAY, THE MAID SAKI-SAN'S BATH...
...TOOK A RATHER LONG TIME.
?
Huh? Waka?

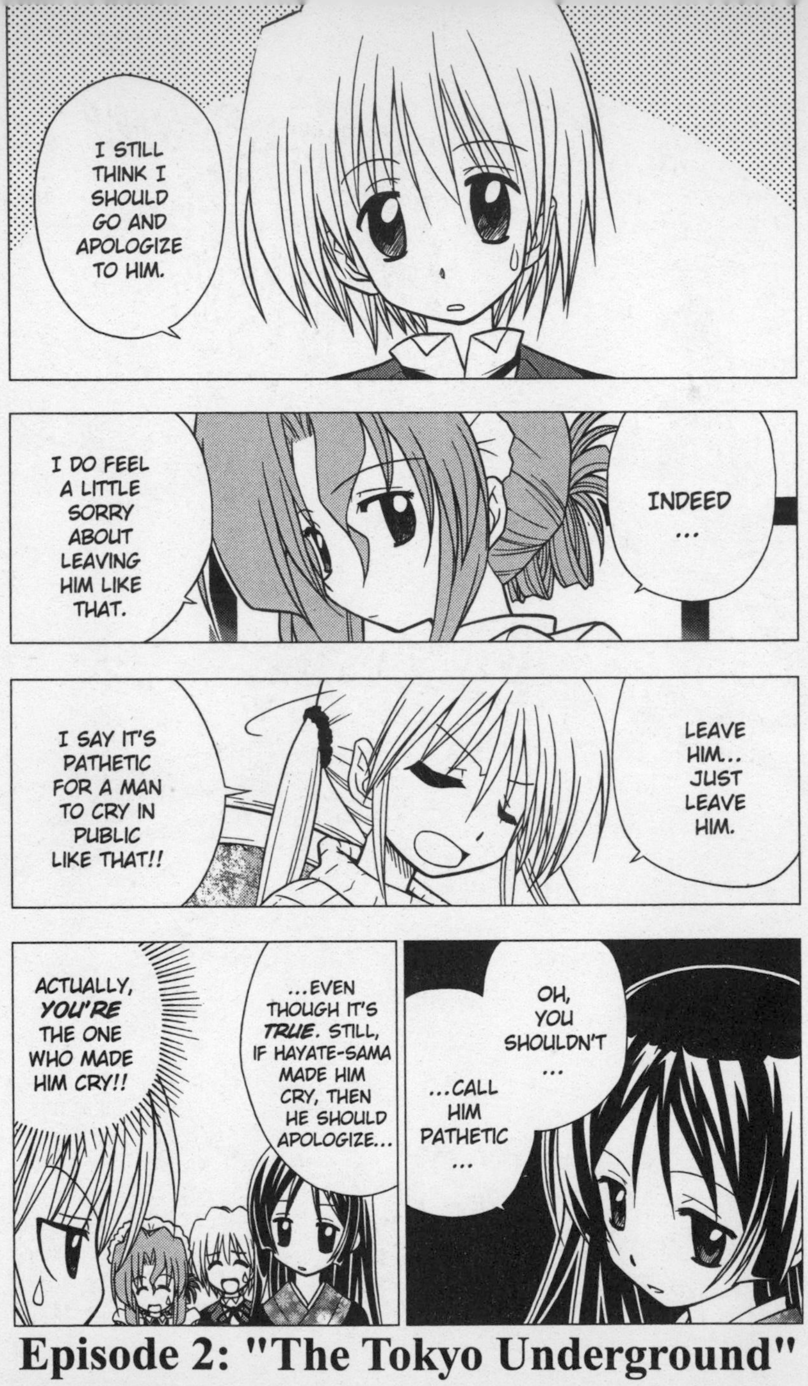
I STILL THINK I SHOULD GO AND APOLOGIZE TO HIM.
INDEED ...
I DO FEEL A LITTLE SORRY ABOUT LEAVING HIM LIKE THAT.
LEAVE HIM.. JUST LEAVE HIM.
I SAY IT'S PATHETIC FOR A MAN TO CRY IN PUBLIC LIKE THAT!!
OH, YOU SHOULDN'T ...
...CALL HIM PATHETIC ...
...EVEN THOUGH IT'S TRUE. STILL, IF HAYATE-SAMA MADE HIM CRY, THEN HE SHOULD APOLOGIZE...
ACTUALLY, YOU'RE THE ONE WHO MADE HIM CRY!!

Episode 2: "The Tokyo Underground"

Episode 2: "The Tokyo Underground"

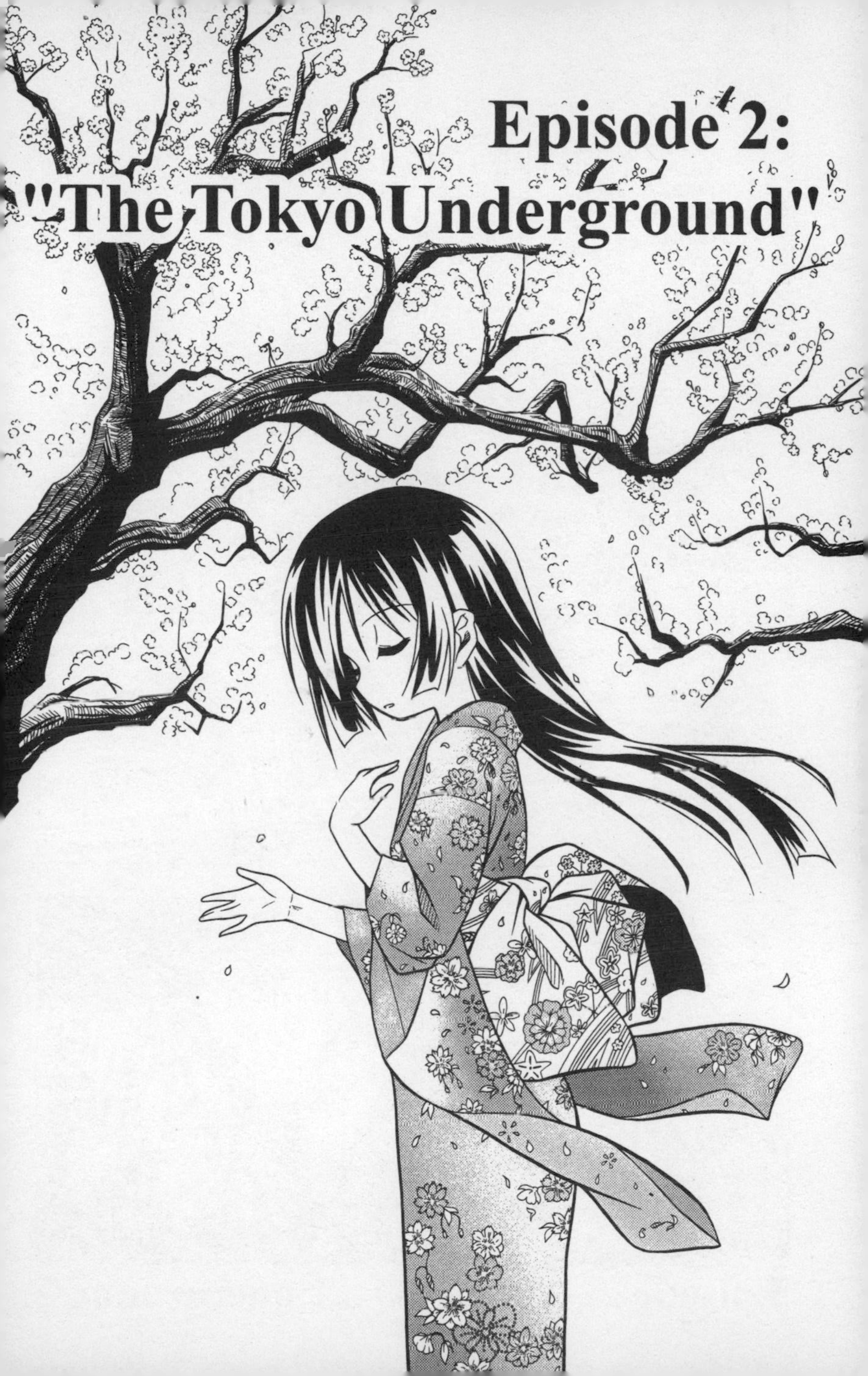

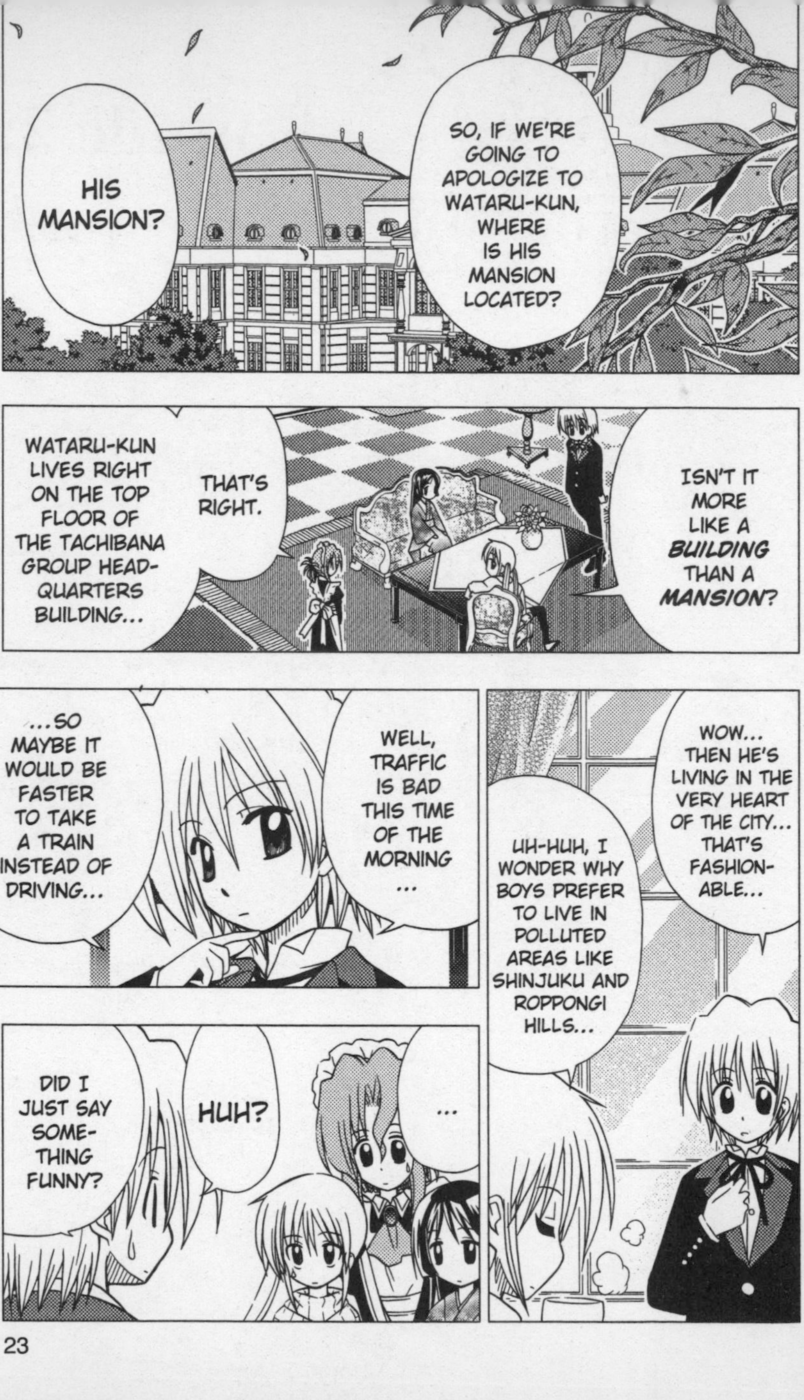
SO, IF WE'RE GOING TO APOLOGIZE TO WATARU-KUN, WHERE IS HIS MANSION LOCATED?
HIS MANSION?
ISN'T IT MORE LIKE A *BUILDING* THAN A *MANSION*?
THAT'S RIGHT.
WATARU-KUN LIVES RIGHT ON THE TOP FLOOR OF THE TACHIBANA GROUP HEAD-QUARTERS BUILDING...
WOW... THEN HE'S LIVING IN THE VERY HEART OF THE CITY... THAT'S FASHION-ABLE...
UH-HUH, I WONDER WHY BOYS PREFER TO LIVE IN POLLUTED AREAS LIKE SHINJUKU AND ROPPONGI HILLS...
WELL, TRAFFIC IS BAD THIS TIME OF THE MORNING ...
...SO MAYBE IT WOULD BE FASTER TO TAKE A TRAIN INSTEAD OF DRIVING...
...
HUH?
DID I JUST SAY SOME-THING FUNNY?

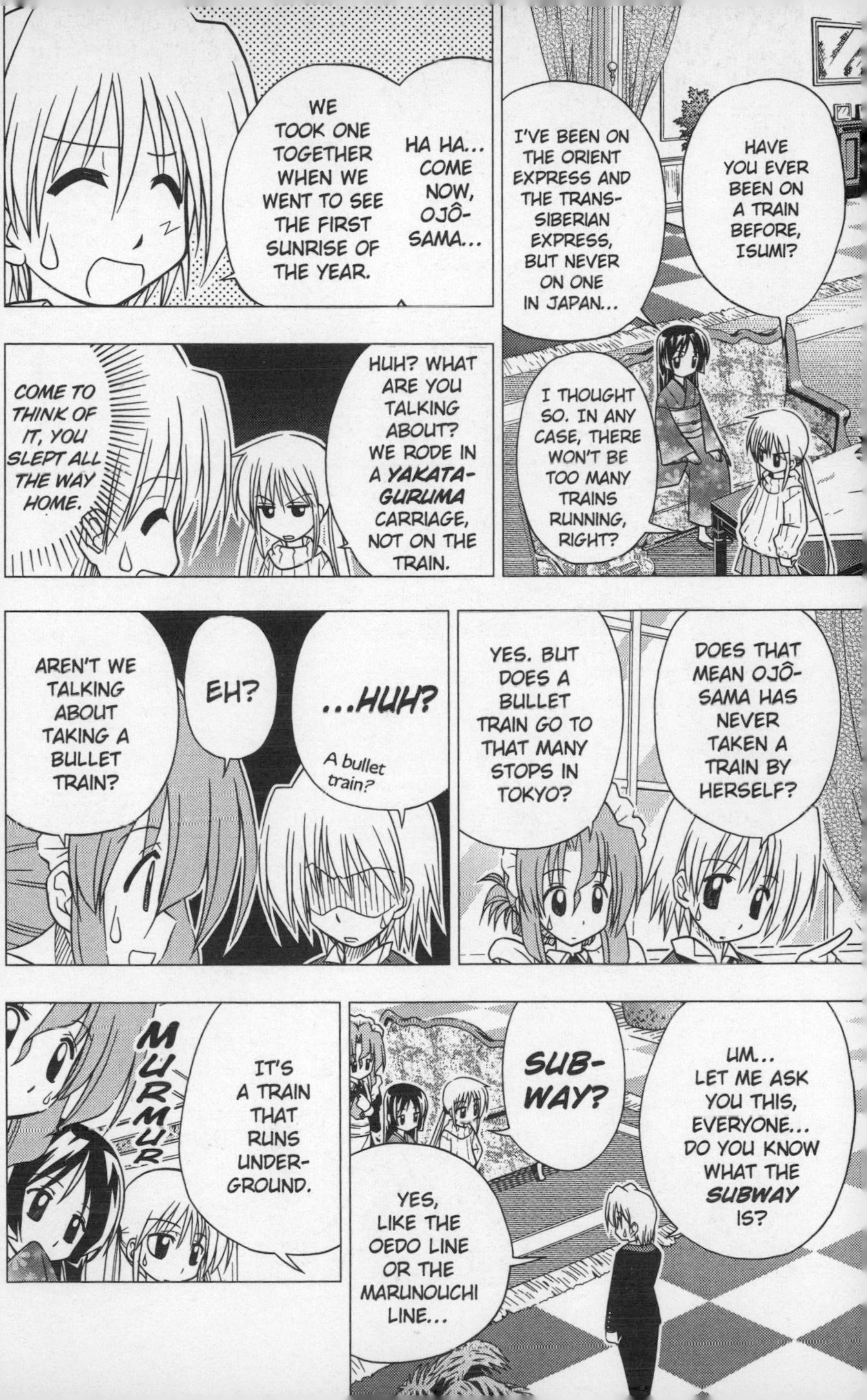
HAVE YOU EVER BEEN ON A TRAIN BEFORE, ISUMI?
I'VE BEEN ON THE ORIENT EXPRESS AND THE TRANS-SIBERIAN EXPRESS, BUT NEVER ON ONE IN JAPAN...
I THOUGHT SO. IN ANY CASE, THERE WON'T BE TOO MANY TRAINS RUNNING, RIGHT?
HA HA... COME NOW, OJÔ-SAMA...
WE TOOK ONE TOGETHER WHEN WE WENT TO SEE THE FIRST SUNRISE OF THE YEAR.
HUH? WHAT ARE YOU TALKING ABOUT? WE RODE IN A *YAKATA-GURUMA* CARRIAGE, NOT ON THE TRAIN.
COME TO THINK OF IT, YOU SLEPT ALL THE WAY HOME.
DOES THAT MEAN OJÔ-SAMA HAS NEVER TAKEN A TRAIN BY HERSELF?
YES. BUT DOES A BULLET TRAIN GO TO THAT MANY STOPS IN TOKYO?
...HUH?
A bullet train?
EH?
AREN'T WE TALKING ABOUT TAKING A BULLET TRAIN?
UM... LET ME ASK YOU THIS, EVERYONE... DO YOU KNOW WHAT THE *SUBWAY* IS?
SUB-WAY?
YES, LIKE THE OEDO LINE OR THE MARUNOUCHI LINE...
IT'S A TRAIN THAT RUNS UNDER-GROUND.
MURMUR

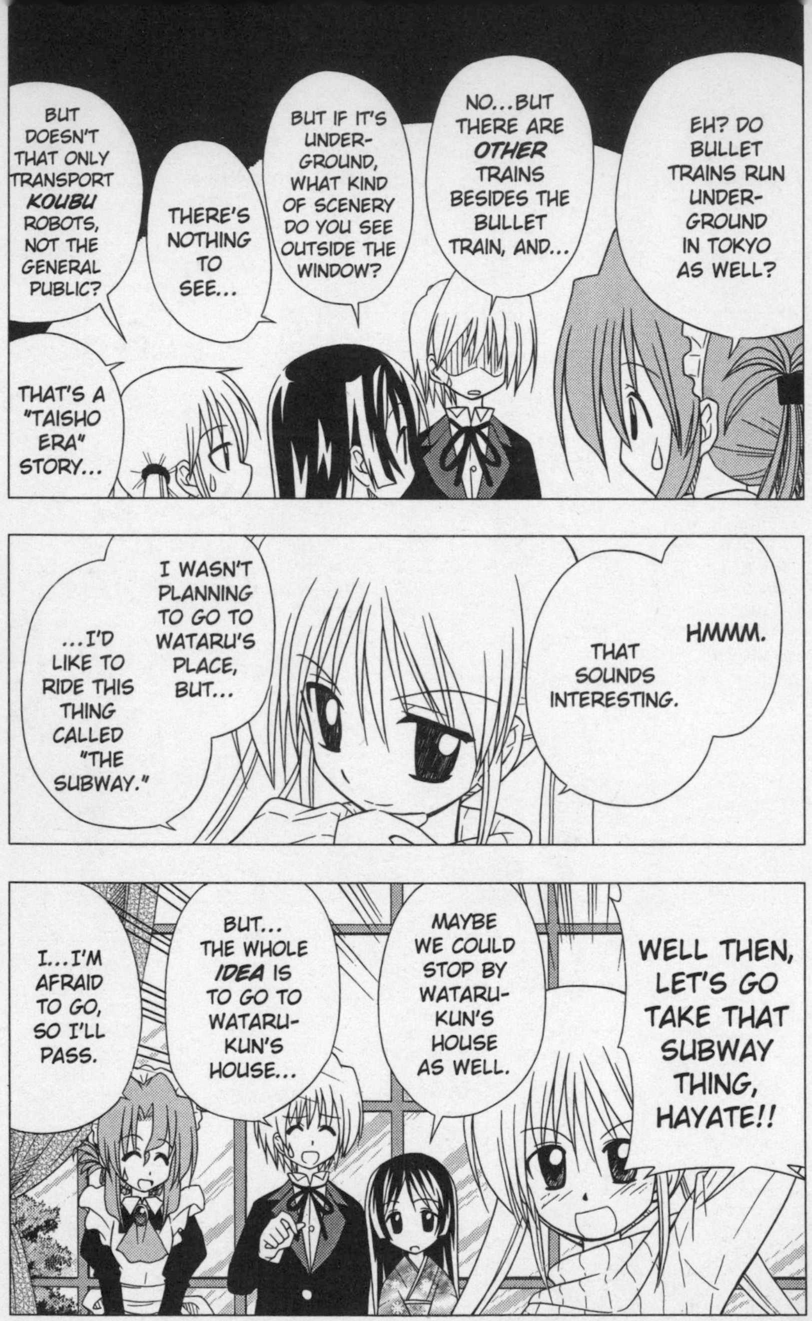
EH? DO BULLET TRAINS RUN UNDER-GROUND IN TOKYO AS WELL?
NO...BUT THERE ARE *OTHER* TRAINS BESIDES THE BULLET TRAIN, AND...
BUT IF IT'S UNDER-GROUND, WHAT KIND OF SCENERY DO YOU SEE OUTSIDE THE WINDOW?
THERE'S NOTHING TO SEE...
BUT DOESN'T THAT ONLY TRANSPORT *KOUBU* ROBOTS, NOT THE GENERAL PUBLIC?
THAT'S A "TAISHO ERA" STORY...
HMMM.
THAT SOUNDS INTERESTING.
I WASN'T PLANNING TO GO TO WATARU'S PLACE, BUT...
...I'D LIKE TO RIDE THIS THING CALLED "THE SUBWAY."
WELL THEN, LET'S GO TAKE THAT SUBWAY THING, HAYATE!!
MAYBE WE COULD STOP BY WATARU-KUN'S HOUSE AS WELL.
BUT... THE WHOLE *IDEA* IS TO GO TO WATARU-KUN'S HOUSE...
I...I'M AFRAID TO GO, SO I'LL PASS.

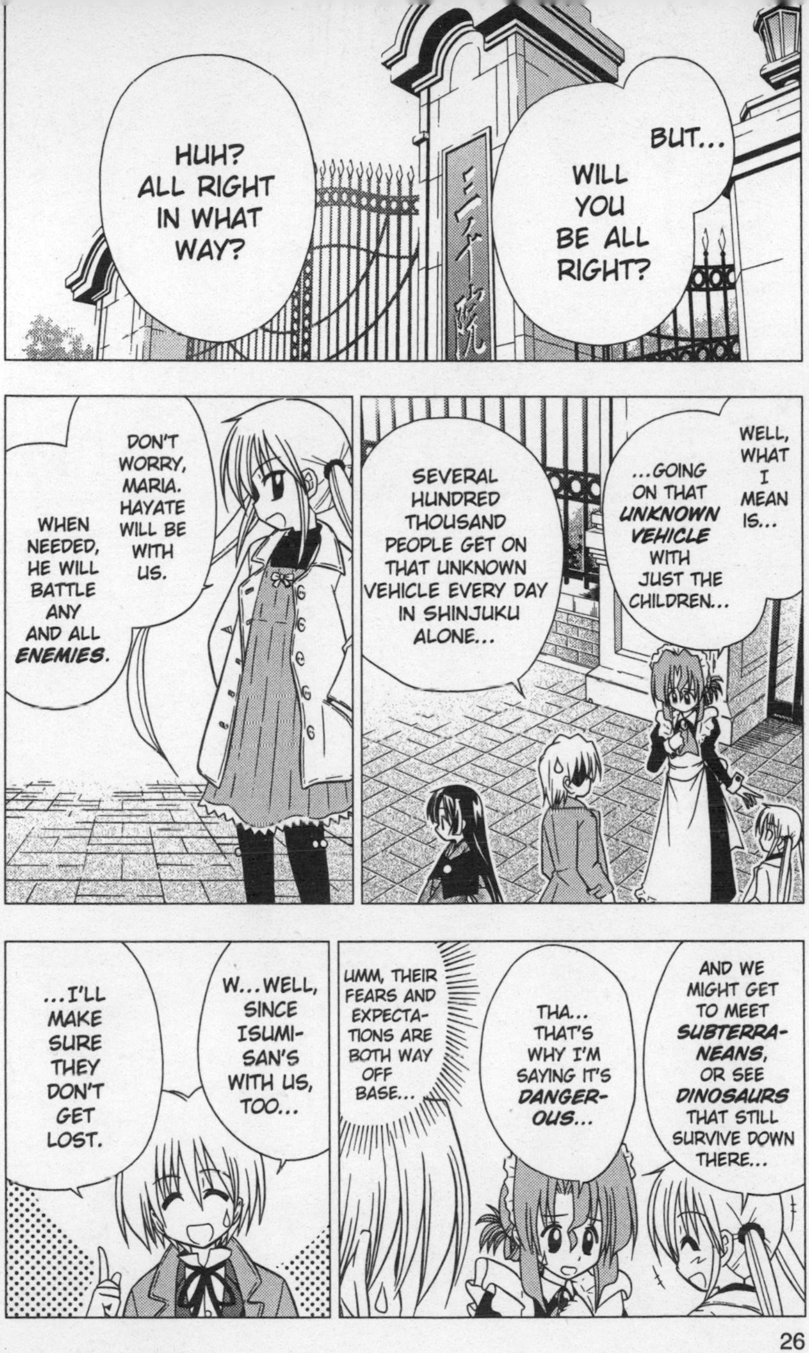
BUT... WILL YOU BE ALL RIGHT?
HUH? ALL RIGHT IN WHAT WAY?
WELL, WHAT I MEAN IS...
...GOING ON THAT UNKNOWN VEHICLE WITH JUST THE CHILDREN...
SEVERAL HUNDRED THOUSAND PEOPLE GET ON THAT UNKNOWN VEHICLE EVERY DAY IN SHINJUKU ALONE...
DON'T WORRY, MARIA. HAYATE WILL BE WITH US.
WHEN NEEDED, HE WILL BATTLE ANY AND ALL ENEMIES.
AND WE MIGHT GET TO MEET SUBTERRANEANS, OR SEE DINOSAURS THAT STILL SURVIVE DOWN THERE...
THA... THAT'S WHY I'M SAYING IT'S DANGEROUS...
UMM, THEIR FEARS AND EXPECTATIONS ARE BOTH WAY OFF BASE...
W...WELL, SINCE ISUMI-SAN'S WITH US, TOO...
...I'LL MAKE SURE THEY DON'T GET LOST.

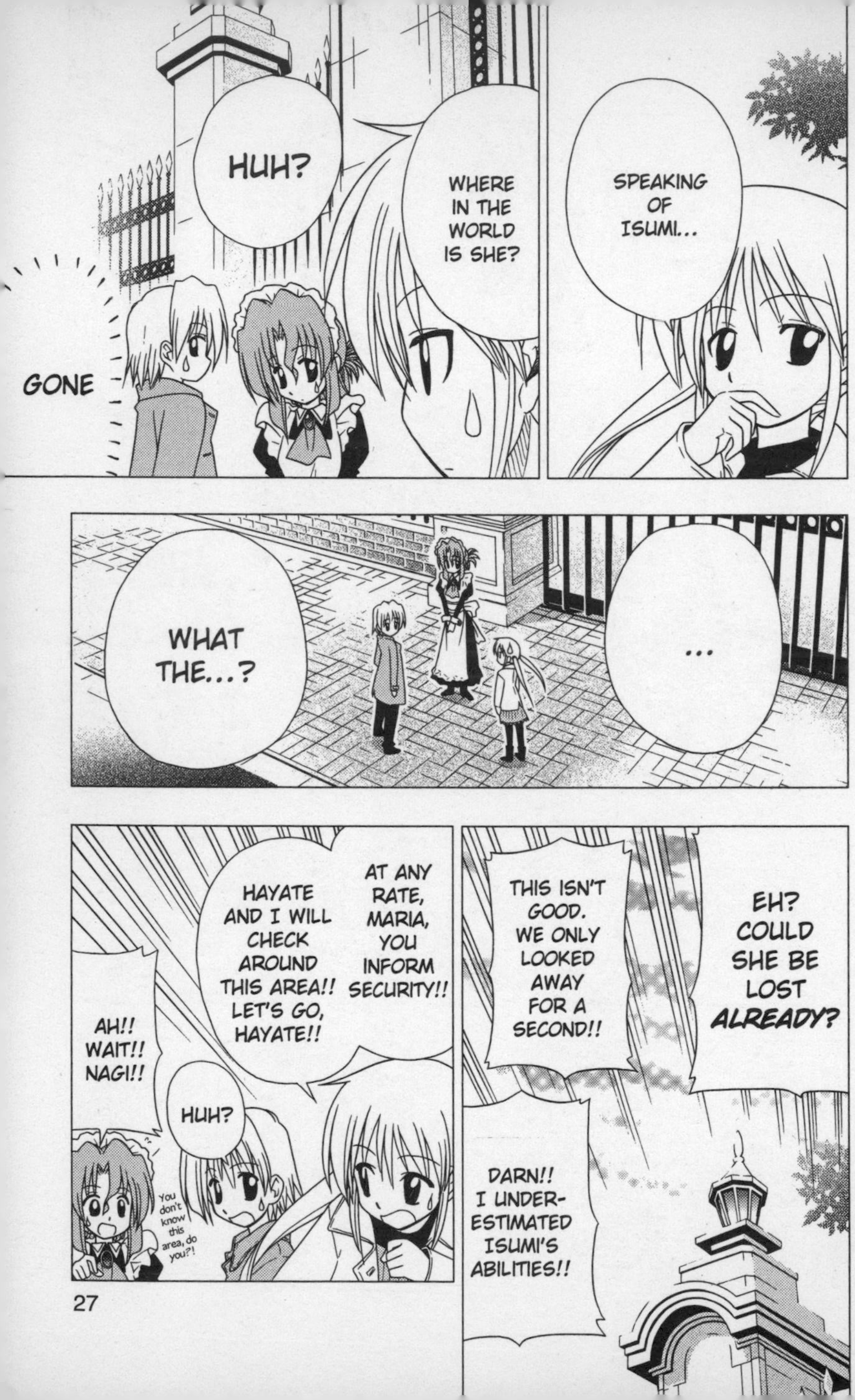
SPEAKING OF ISUMI...
WHERE IN THE WORLD IS SHE?
HUH?
GONE
...
WHAT THE...?
EH? COULD SHE BE LOST *ALREADY?*
THIS ISN'T GOOD. WE ONLY LOOKED AWAY FOR A SECOND!!
DARN!! I UNDER-ESTIMATED ISUMI'S ABILITIES!!
AT ANY RATE, MARIA, YOU INFORM SECURITY!!
HAYATE AND I WILL CHECK AROUND THIS AREA!! LET'S GO, HAYATE!!
HUH?
AH!! WAIT!! NAGI!!
You don't know this area, do you?!

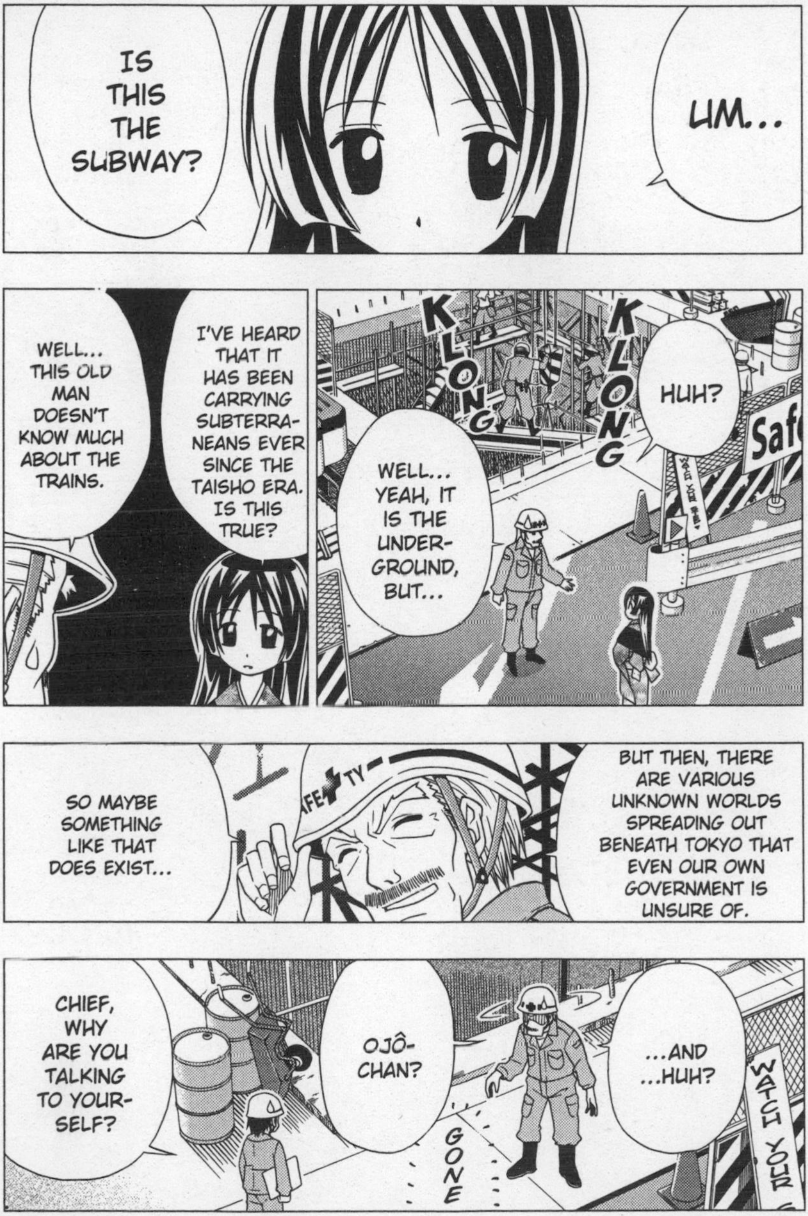
UM...
IS THIS THE SUBWAY?
KLONG
KLONG
HUH?
WELL... YEAH, IT IS THE UNDERGROUND, BUT...
I'VE HEARD THAT IT HAS BEEN CARRYING SUBTERRA-NEANS EVER SINCE THE TAISHO ERA. IS THIS TRUE?
WELL... THIS OLD MAN DOESN'T KNOW MUCH ABOUT THE TRAINS.
BUT THEN, THERE ARE VARIOUS UNKNOWN WORLDS SPREADING OUT BENEATH TOKYO THAT EVEN OUR OWN GOVERNMENT IS UNSURE OF.
SO MAYBE SOMETHING LIKE THAT DOES EXIST...
...AND ...HUH?
WATCH YOUR
OJÔ-CHAN?
GONE
CHIEF, WHY ARE YOU TALKING TO YOUR-SELF?

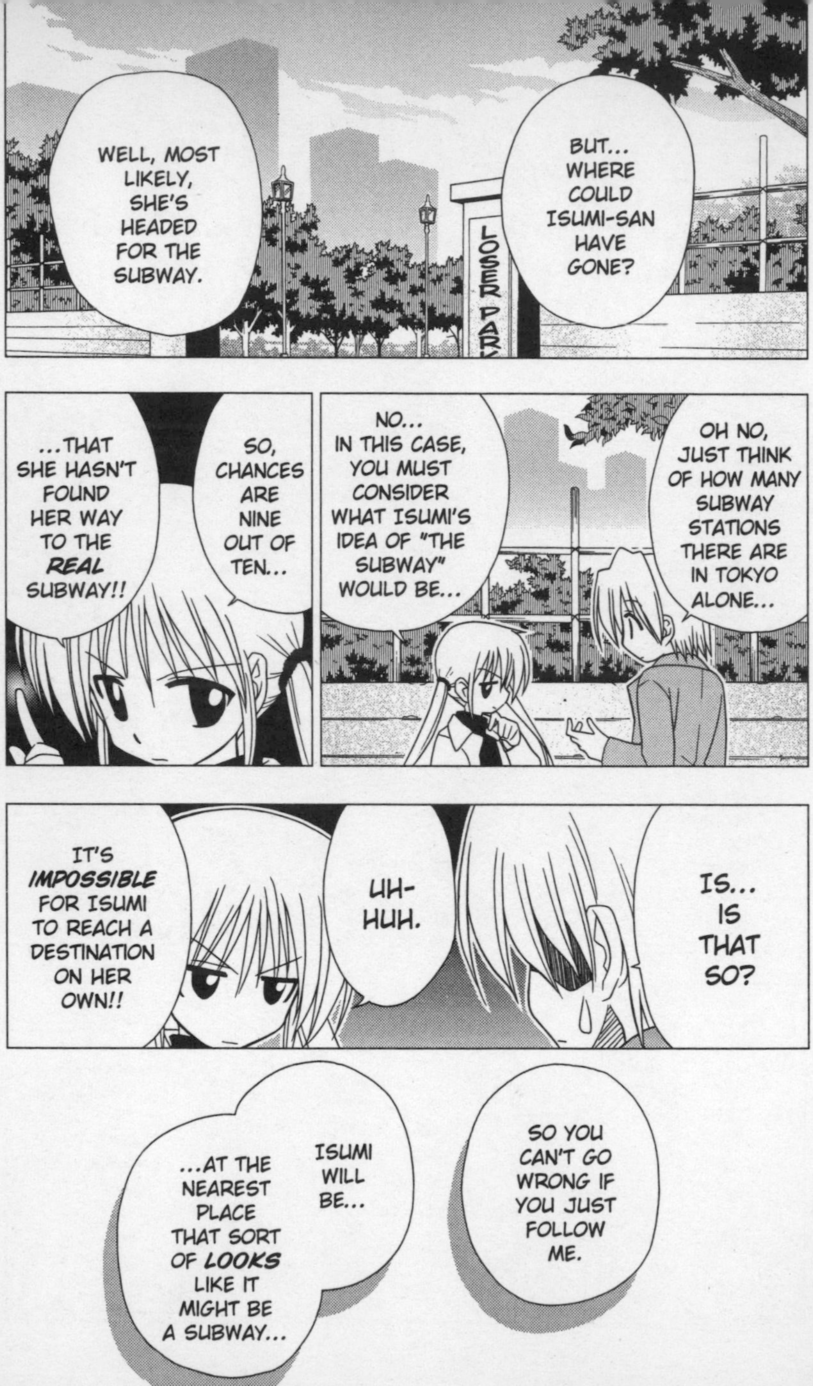
BUT... WHERE COULD ISUMI-SAN HAVE GONE?
LOSER PARK
WELL, MOST LIKELY, SHE'S HEADED FOR THE SUBWAY.
OH NO, JUST THINK OF HOW MANY SUBWAY STATIONS THERE ARE IN TOKYO ALONE...
NO... IN THIS CASE, YOU MUST CONSIDER WHAT ISUMI'S IDEA OF "THE SUBWAY" WOULD BE...
SO, CHANCES ARE NINE OUT OF TEN...
...THAT SHE HASN'T FOUND HER WAY TO THE *REAL* SUBWAY!!
IS... IS THAT SO?
UH-HUH.
IT'S *IMPOSSIBLE* FOR ISUMI TO REACH A DESTINATION ON HER OWN!!
SO YOU CAN'T GO WRONG IF YOU JUST FOLLOW ME.
ISUMI WILL BE...
...AT THE NEAREST PLACE THAT SORT OF *LOOKS* LIKE IT MIGHT BE A SUBWAY...

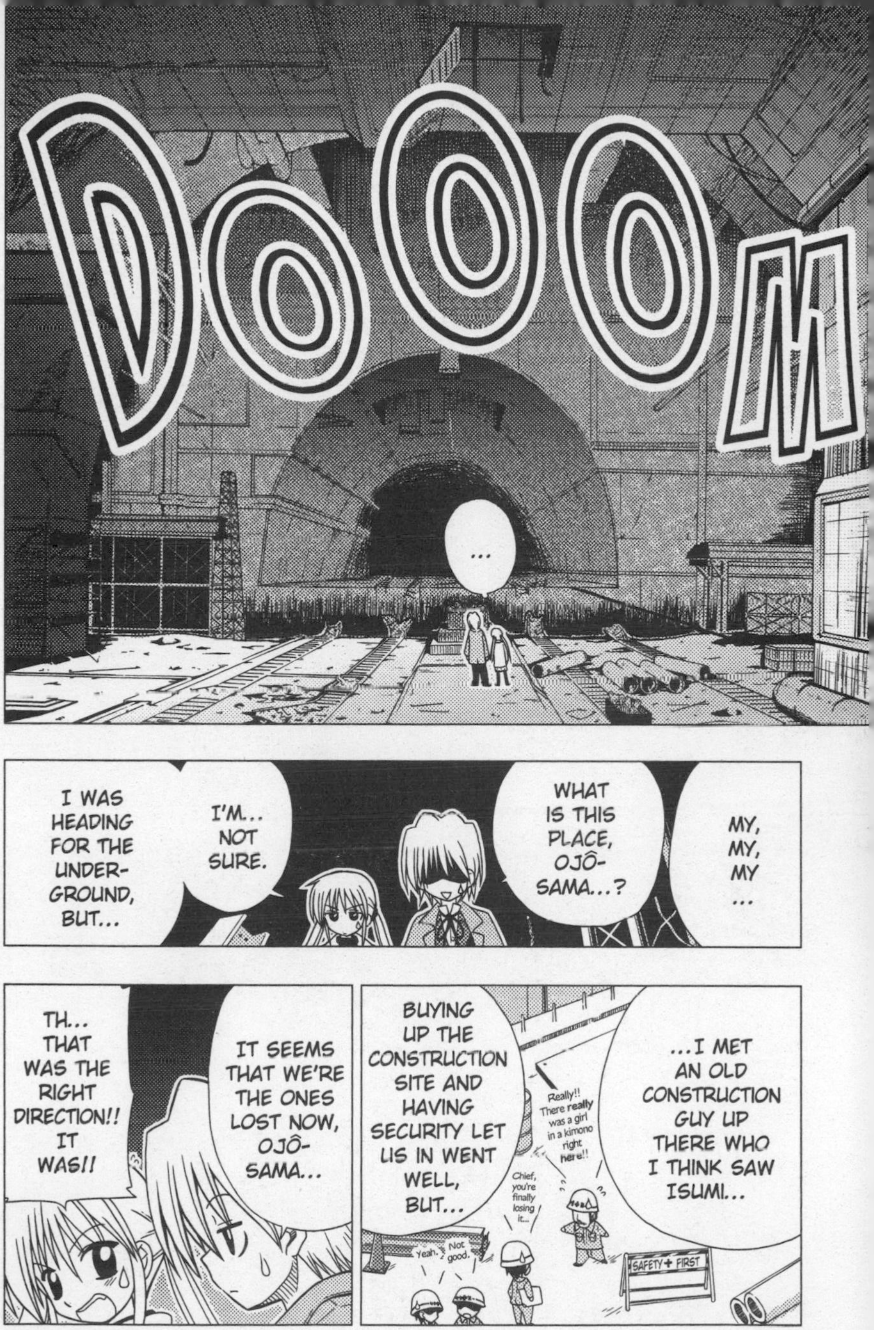
DOOOM
...
MY, MY, MY...
WHAT IS THIS PLACE, OJÔ-SAMA...?
I'M... NOT SURE.
I WAS HEADING FOR THE UNDERGROUND, BUT...
...I MET AN OLD CONSTRUCTION GUY UP THERE WHO I THINK SAW ISUMI...
Really!! There really was a girl in a kimono right here!!
Chief, you're finally losing it...
SAFETY FIRST
BUYING UP THE CONSTRUCTION SITE AND HAVING SECURITY LET US IN WENT WELL, BUT...
Not good.
Yeah.
IT SEEMS THAT WE'RE THE ONES LOST NOW, OJÔ-SAMA...
TH... THAT WAS THE RIGHT DIRECTION!! IT WAS!!

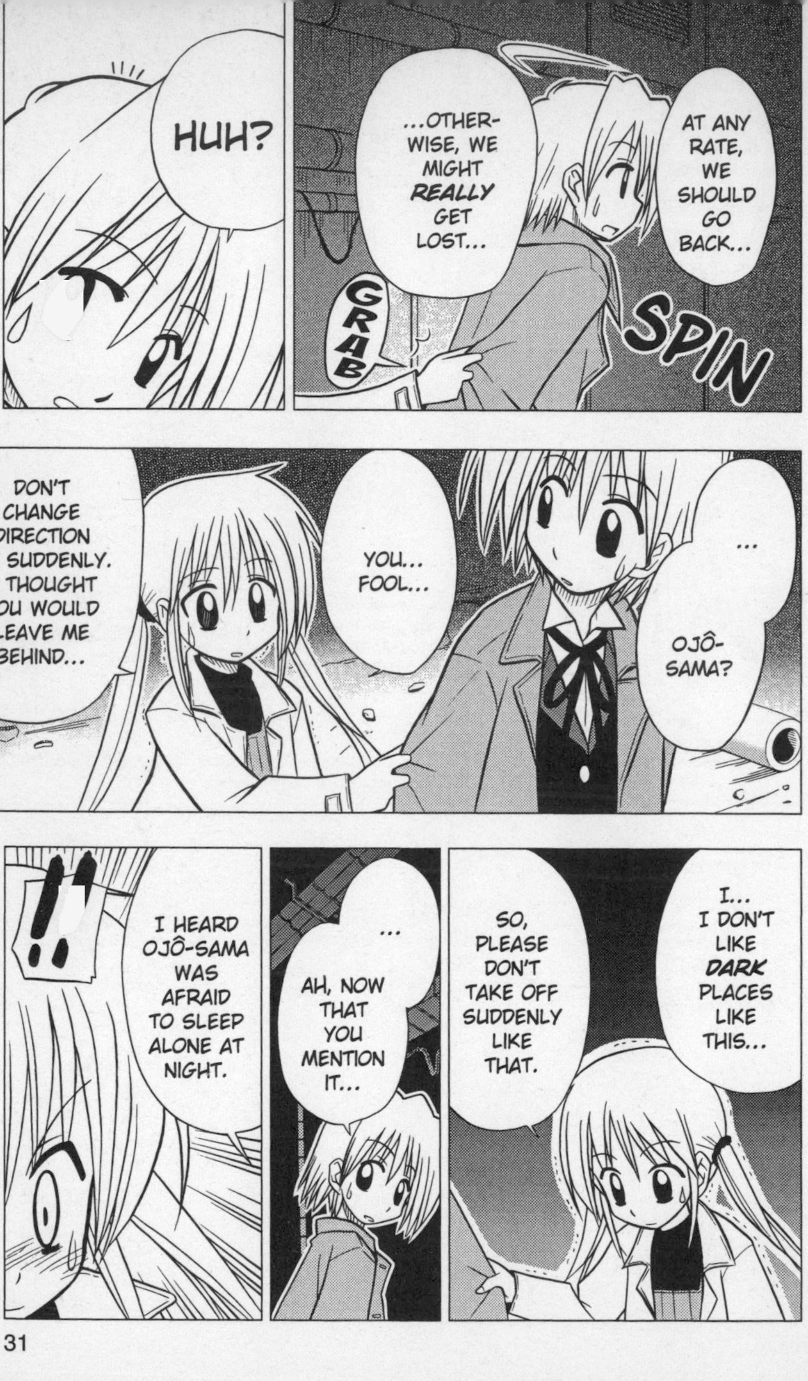
AT ANY RATE, WE SHOULD GO BACK...
...OTHER-WISE, WE MIGHT *REALLY* GET LOST...
SPIN
GRAB
HUH?
...
OJÔ-SAMA?
YOU... FOOL...
DON'T CHANGE DIRECTION SO SUDDENLY. I THOUGHT YOU WOULD LEAVE ME BEHIND...
I... I DON'T LIKE *DARK* PLACES LIKE THIS...
SO, PLEASE DON'T TAKE OFF SUDDENLY LIKE THAT.
...
AH, NOW THAT YOU MENTION IT...
I HEARD OJÔ-SAMA WAS AFRAID TO SLEEP ALONE AT NIGHT.
!!

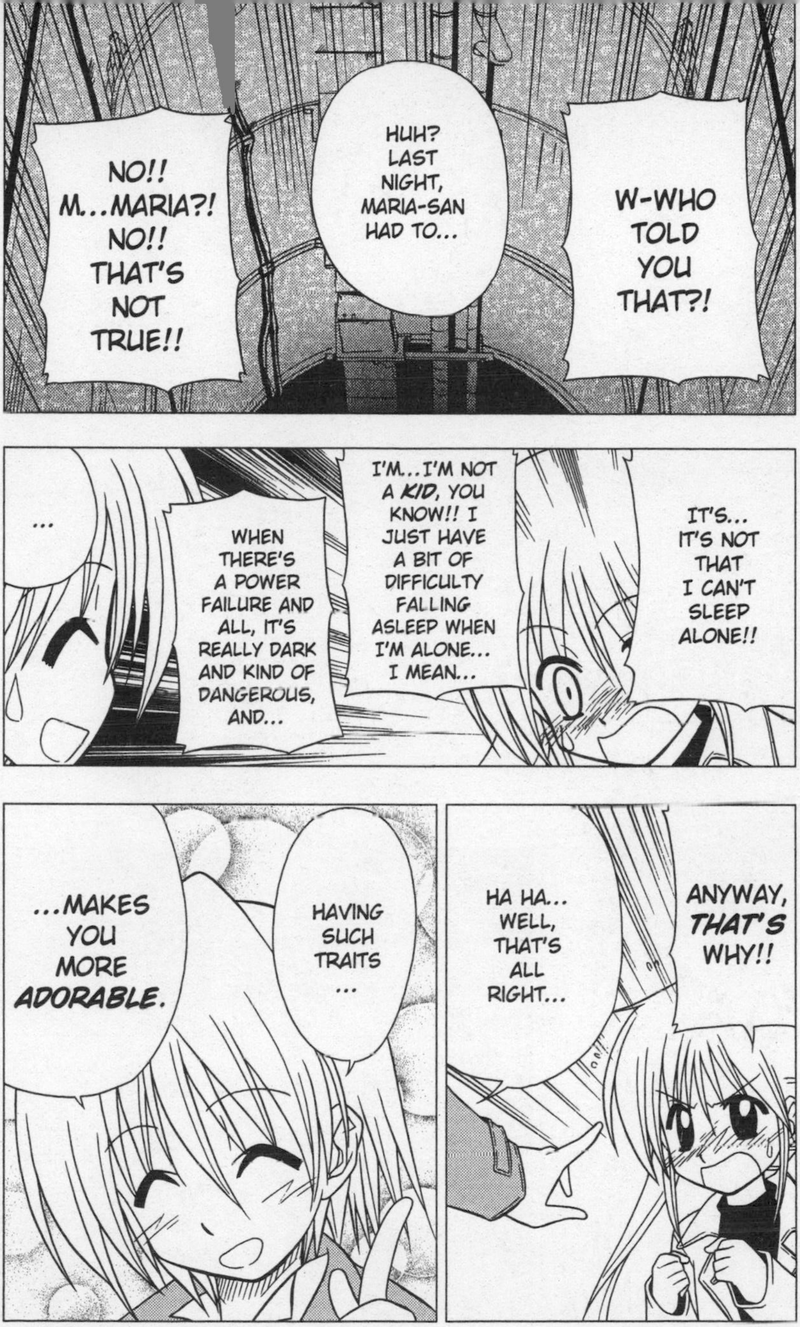
HUH? LAST NIGHT, MARIA-SAN HAD TO...
W-WHO TOLD YOU THAT?!
NO!! M...MARIA?! NO!! THAT'S NOT TRUE!!
IT'S... IT'S NOT THAT I CAN'T SLEEP ALONE!!
I'M...I'M NOT A KID, YOU KNOW!! I JUST HAVE A BIT OF DIFFICULTY FALLING ASLEEP WHEN I'M ALONE... I MEAN...
WHEN THERE'S A POWER FAILURE AND ALL, IT'S REALLY DARK AND KIND OF DANGEROUS, AND...
...
ANYWAY, THAT'S WHY!!
HA HA... WELL, THAT'S ALL RIGHT...
HAVING SUCH TRAITS...
...MAKES YOU MORE ADORABLE.

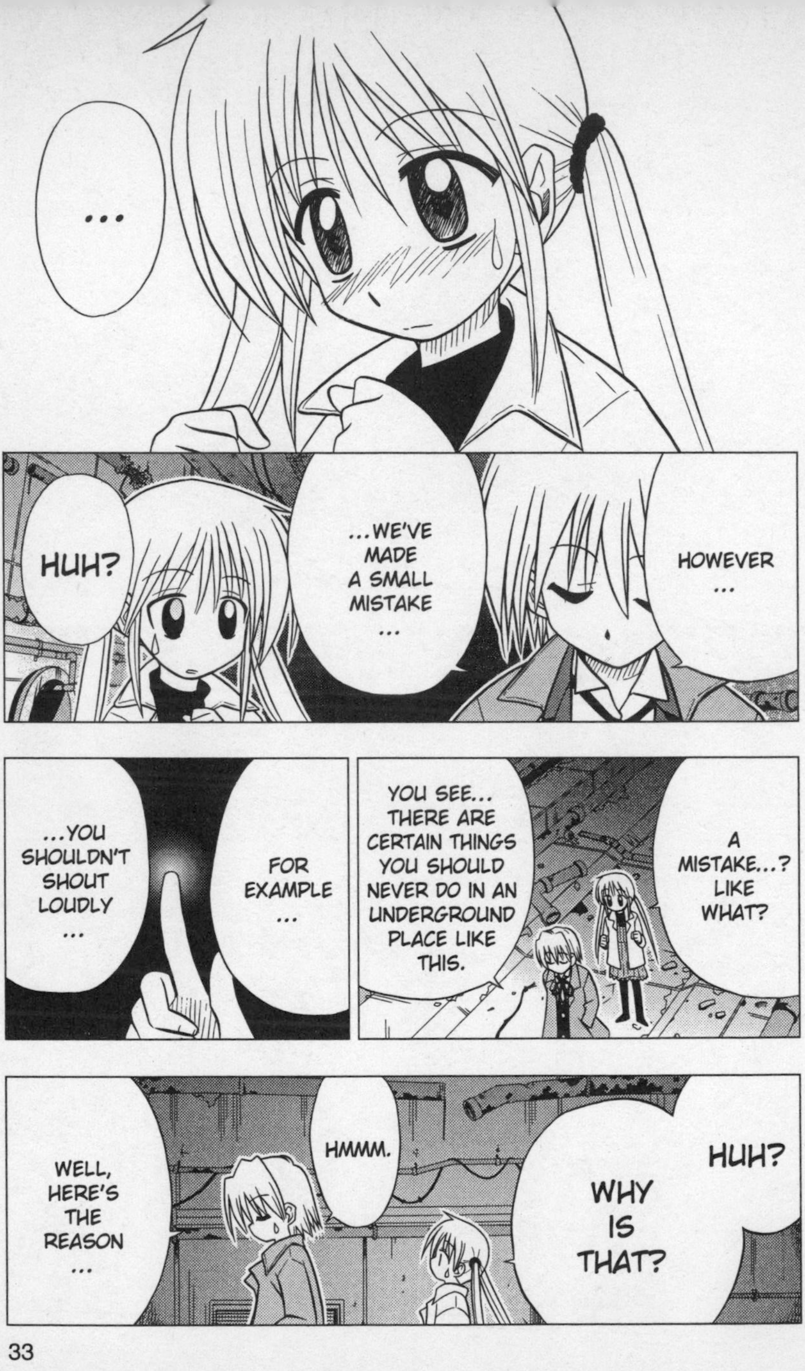
...
HOWEVER ...
...WE'VE MADE A SMALL MISTAKE ...
HUH?
A MISTAKE...? LIKE WHAT?
YOU SEE... THERE ARE CERTAIN THINGS YOU SHOULD NEVER DO IN AN UNDERGROUND PLACE LIKE THIS.
FOR EXAMPLE ...
...YOU SHOULDN'T SHOUT LOUDLY ...
HUH?
WHY IS THAT?
HMMM.
WELL, HERE'S THE REASON ...

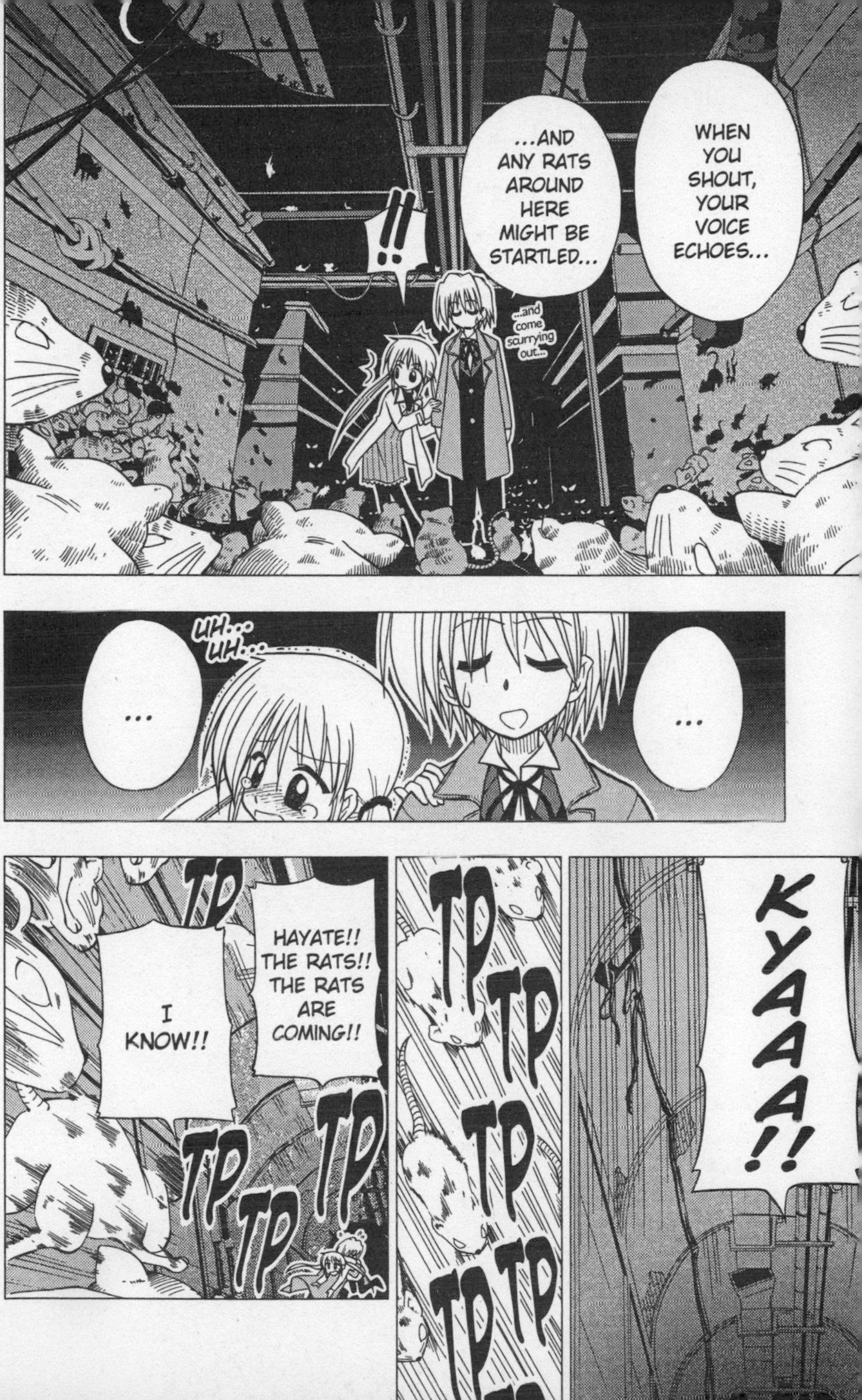
WHEN YOU SHOUT, YOUR VOICE ECHOES...
...AND ANY RATS AROUND HERE MIGHT BE STARTLED...
...and come scurrying out...
!!
...
...
UH... UH...
KYAAAA!!
TP TP TP TP TP TP
HAYATE!! THE RATS!! THE RATS ARE COMING!!
I KNOW!!
TP TP TP TP

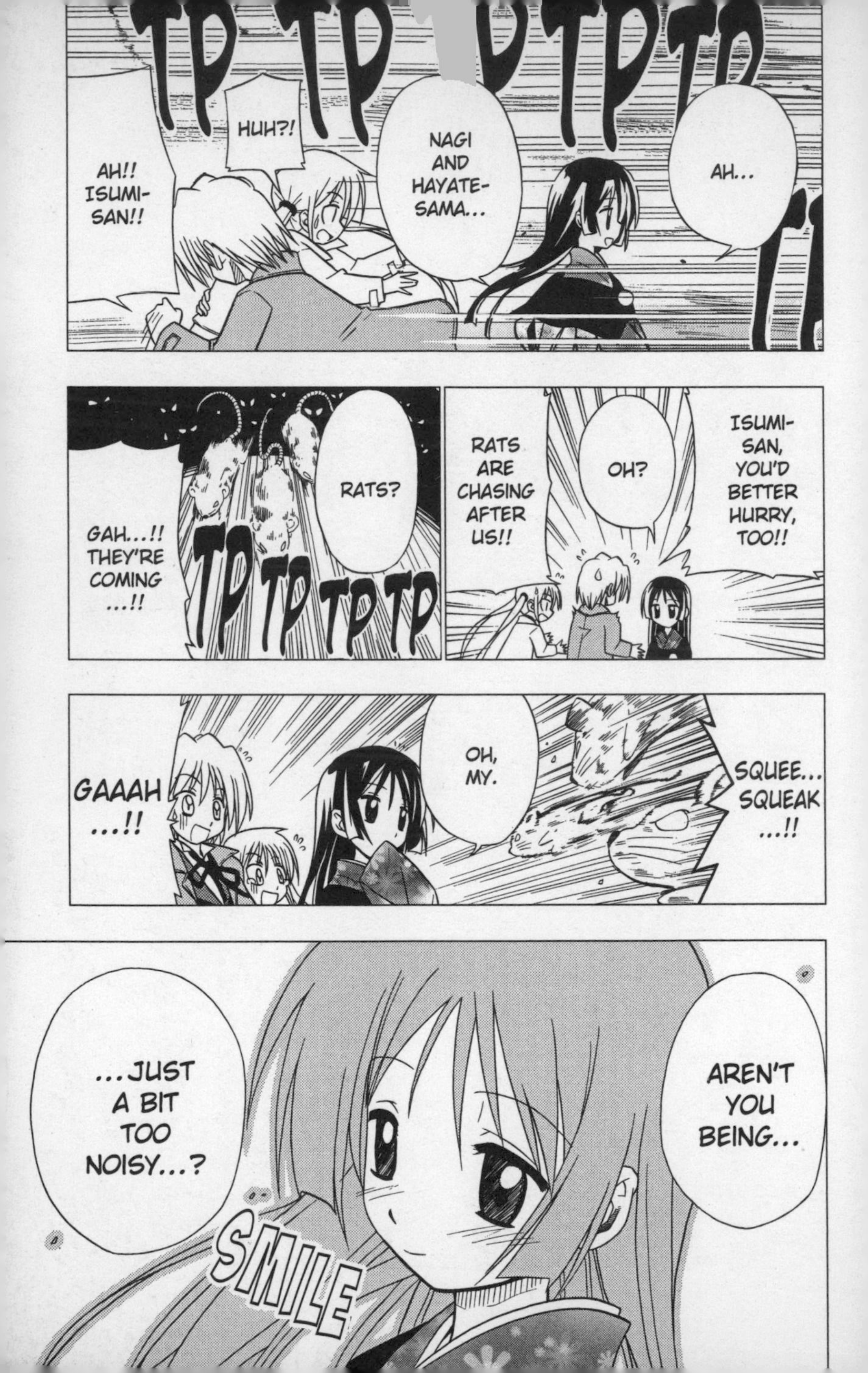
TP TP TP TP TP
AH...
NAGI AND HAYATE-SAMA...
HUH?!
AH!! ISUMI-SAN!!
ISUMI-SAN, YOU'D BETTER HURRY, TOO!!
OH?
RATS ARE CHASING AFTER US!!
RATS?
GAH...!! THEY'RE COMING...!!
TP TP TP TP
SQUEE... SQUEAK...!!
OH, MY.
GAAAH...!!
AREN'T YOU BEING...
...JUST A BIT TOO NOISY...?
SMILE

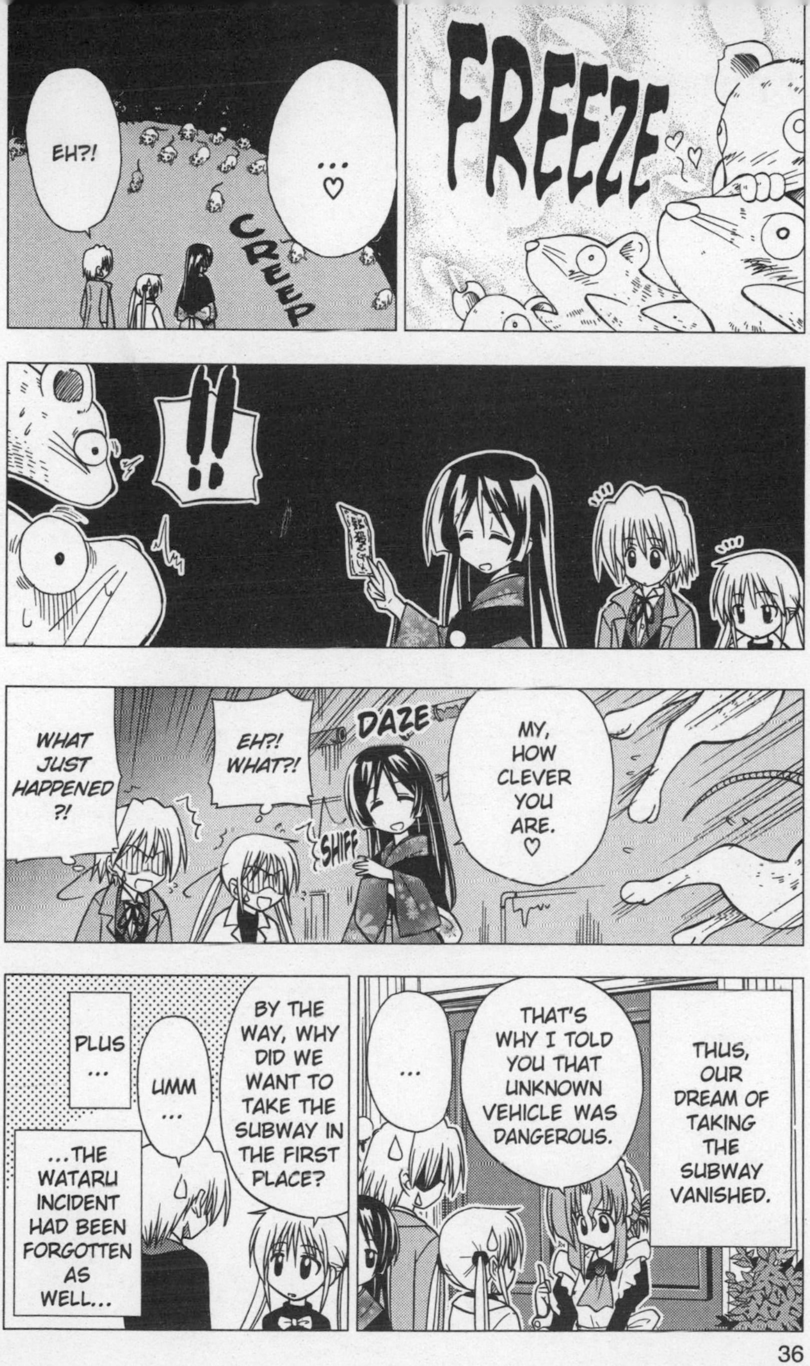
FREEZE
...♡
CREEP
EH?!
!!
MY, HOW CLEVER YOU ARE. ♡
DAZE
EH?! WHAT?!
SHIFF
WHAT JUST HAPPENED?!
THUS, OUR DREAM OF TAKING THE SUBWAY VANISHED.
THAT'S WHY I TOLD YOU THAT UNKNOWN VEHICLE WAS DANGEROUS.
...
BY THE WAY, WHY DID WE WANT TO TAKE THE SUBWAY IN THE FIRST PLACE?
UMM...
PLUS...
...THE WATARU INCIDENT HAD BEEN FORGOTTEN AS WELL...

Episode 3: "The Kingdom of Ambition"

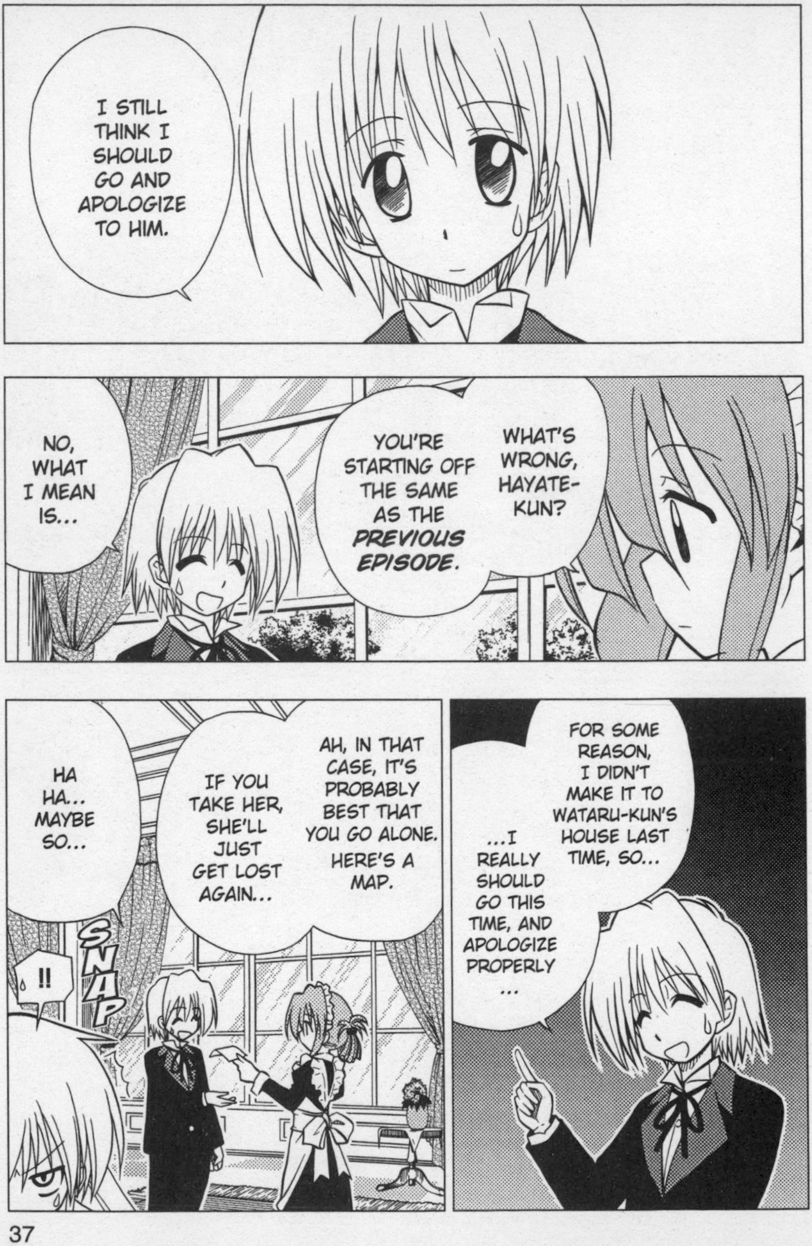
I STILL THINK I SHOULD GO AND APOLOGIZE TO HIM.
WHAT'S WRONG, HAYATE-KUN?
YOU'RE STARTING OFF THE SAME AS THE *PREVIOUS EPISODE*.
NO, WHAT I MEAN IS...
FOR SOME REASON, I DIDN'T MAKE IT TO WATARU-KUN'S HOUSE LAST TIME, SO...
...I REALLY SHOULD GO THIS TIME, AND APOLOGIZE PROPERLY ...
AH, IN THAT CASE, IT'S PROBABLY BEST THAT YOU GO ALONE.
HERE'S A MAP.
IF YOU TAKE HER, SHE'LL JUST GET LOST AGAIN...
HA HA... MAYBE SO...
SNAP
!!

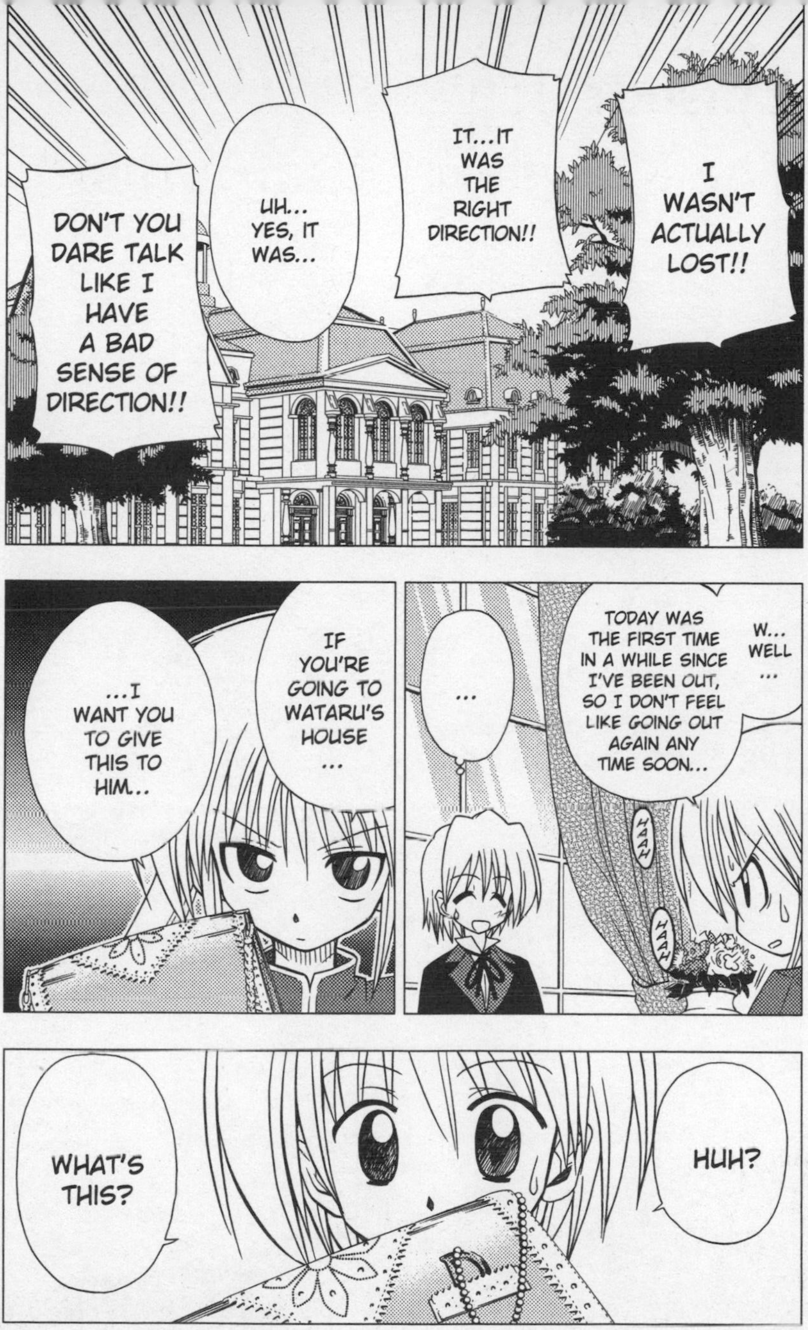
I WASN'T ACTUALLY LOST!!
IT...IT WAS THE RIGHT DIRECTION!!
UH... YES, IT WAS...
DON'T YOU DARE TALK LIKE I HAVE A BAD SENSE OF DIRECTION!!
W... WELL ...
TODAY WAS THE FIRST TIME IN A WHILE SINCE I'VE BEEN OUT, SO I DON'T FEEL LIKE GOING OUT AGAIN ANY TIME SOON...
HAAH
HAAH
...
IF YOU'RE GOING TO WATARU'S HOUSE ...
...I WANT YOU TO GIVE THIS TO HIM..
HUH?
WHAT'S THIS?

Episode 3: "The Kingdom of Ambition"

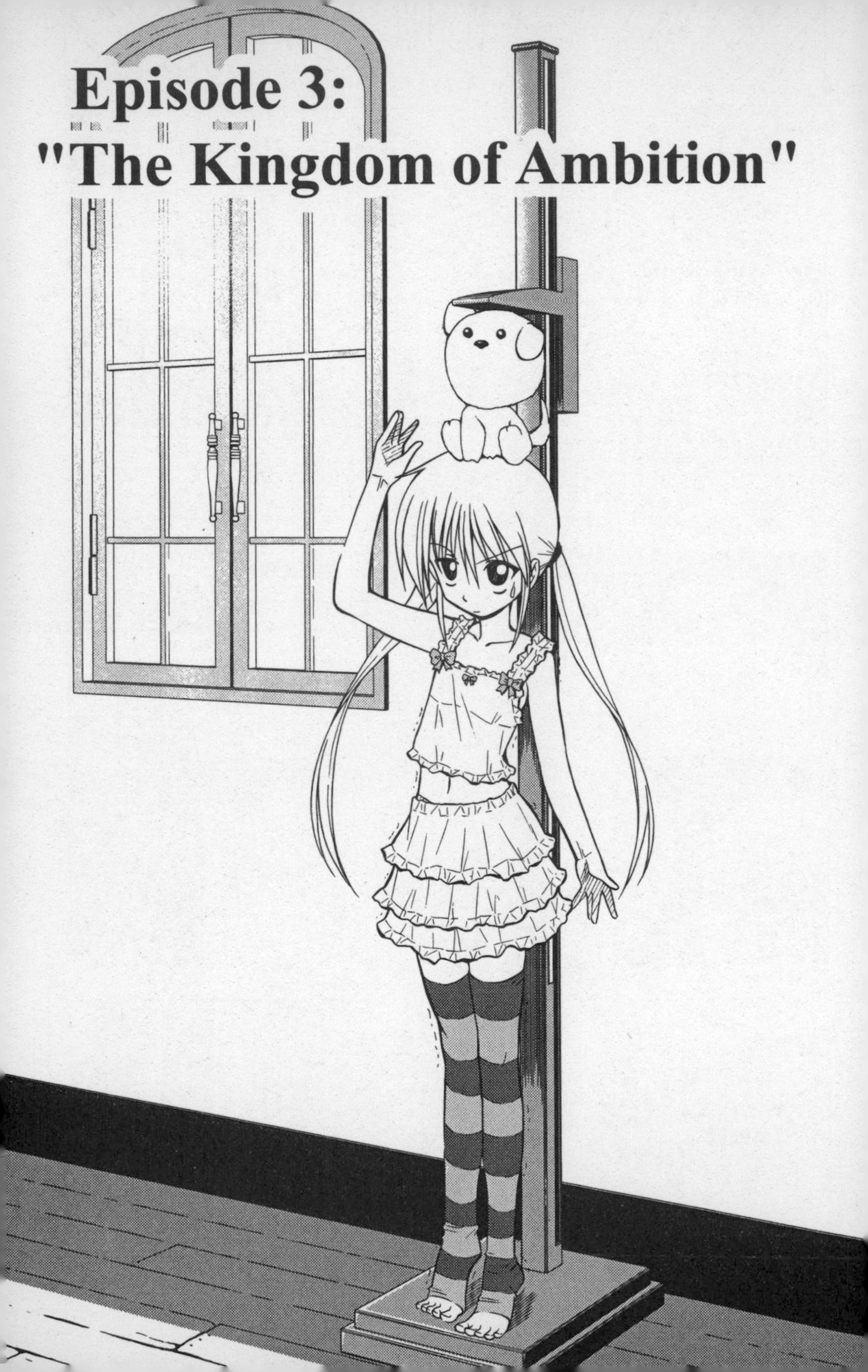

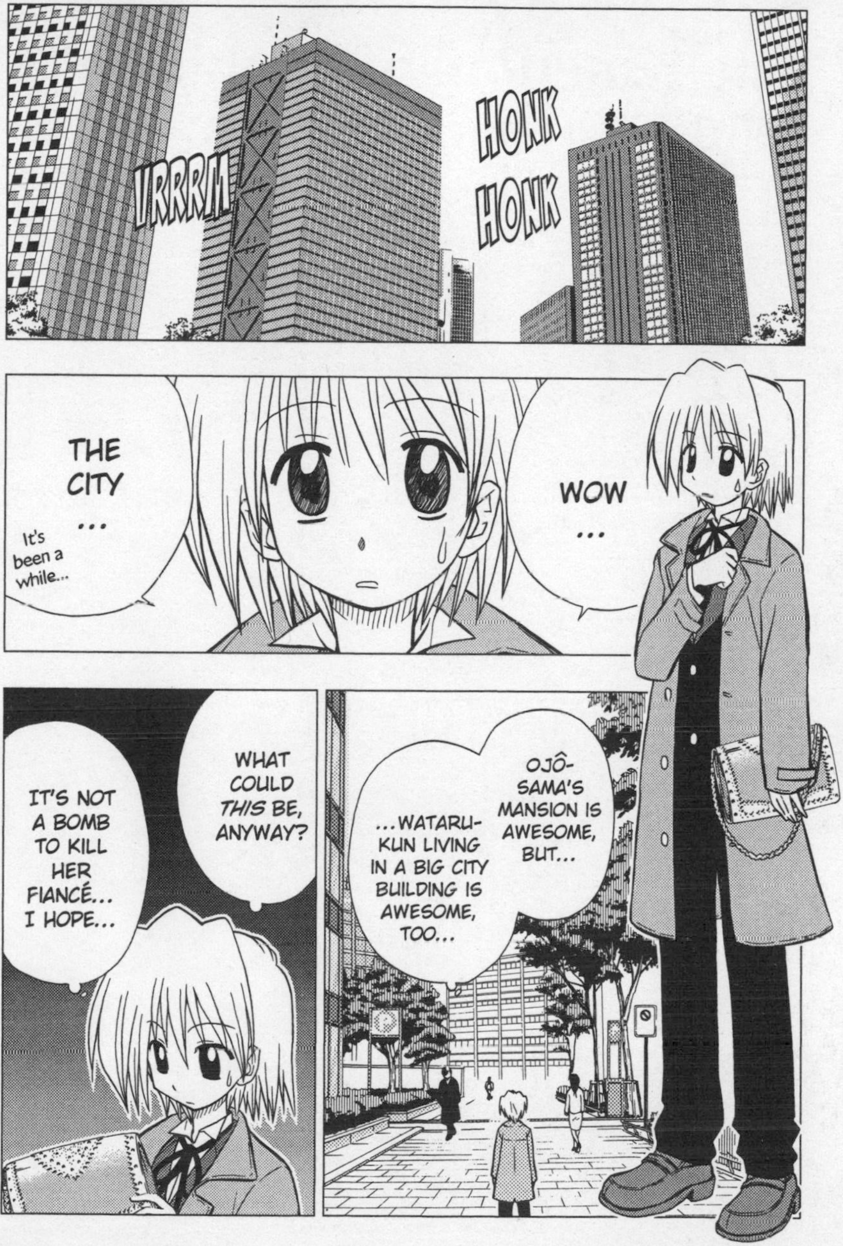
HONK HONK
VRRRM
WOW ...
THE CITY ...
It's been a while...
OJÔ-SAMA'S MANSION IS AWESOME, BUT...
...WATARU-KUN LIVING IN A BIG CITY BUILDING IS AWESOME, TOO...
WHAT COULD *THIS* BE, ANYWAY?
IT'S NOT A BOMB TO KILL HER FIANCÉ... I HOPE...

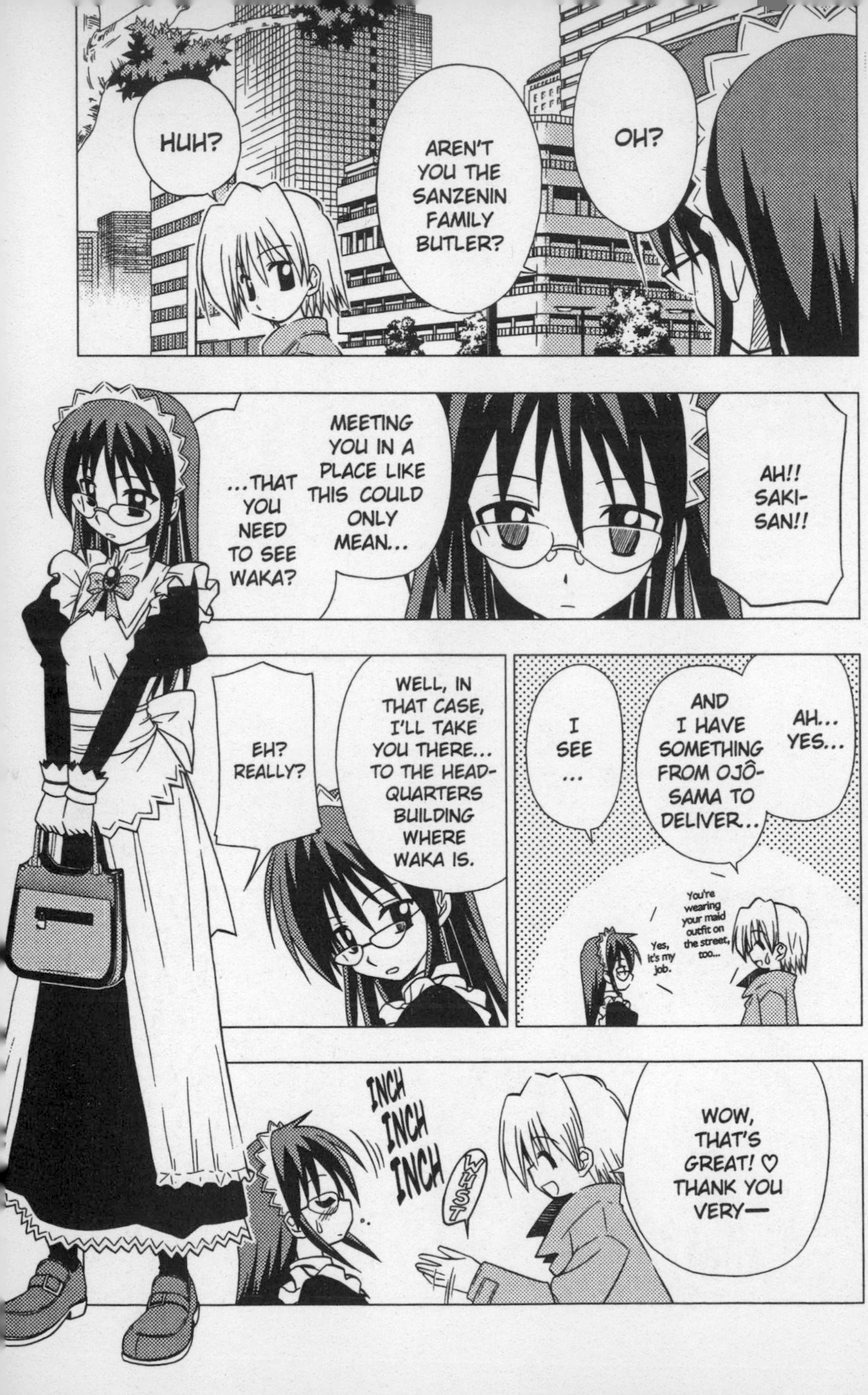
OH?
AREN'T YOU THE SANZENIN FAMILY BUTLER?
HUH?
AH!! SAKI-SAN!!
MEETING YOU IN A PLACE LIKE THIS COULD ONLY MEAN...
...THAT YOU NEED TO SEE WAKA?
AH... YES...
AND I HAVE SOMETHING FROM OJÔ-SAMA TO DELIVER...
I SEE ...
You're wearing your maid outfit on the street, too...
Yes, it's my job.
WELL, IN THAT CASE, I'LL TAKE YOU THERE... TO THE HEAD-QUARTERS BUILDING WHERE WAKA IS.
EH? REALLY?
WOW, THAT'S GREAT! ♡ THANK YOU VERY—
WHST
INCH INCH INCH

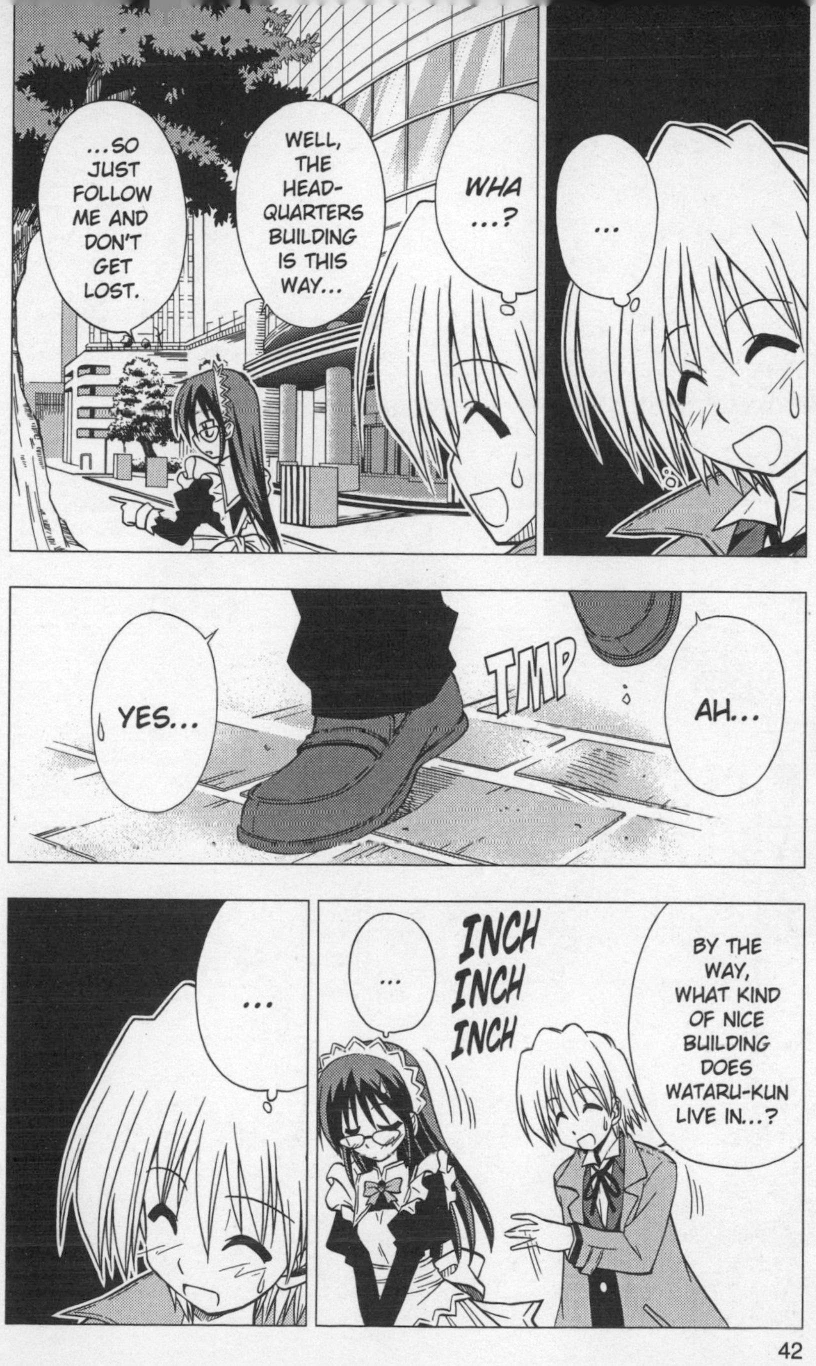
...
WHA ...?
WELL, THE HEAD-QUARTERS BUILDING IS THIS WAY...
...SO JUST FOLLOW ME AND DON'T GET LOST.
AH...
TMP
YES...
BY THE WAY, WHAT KIND OF NICE BUILDING DOES WATARU-KUN LIVE IN...?
INCH INCH INCH
...
...

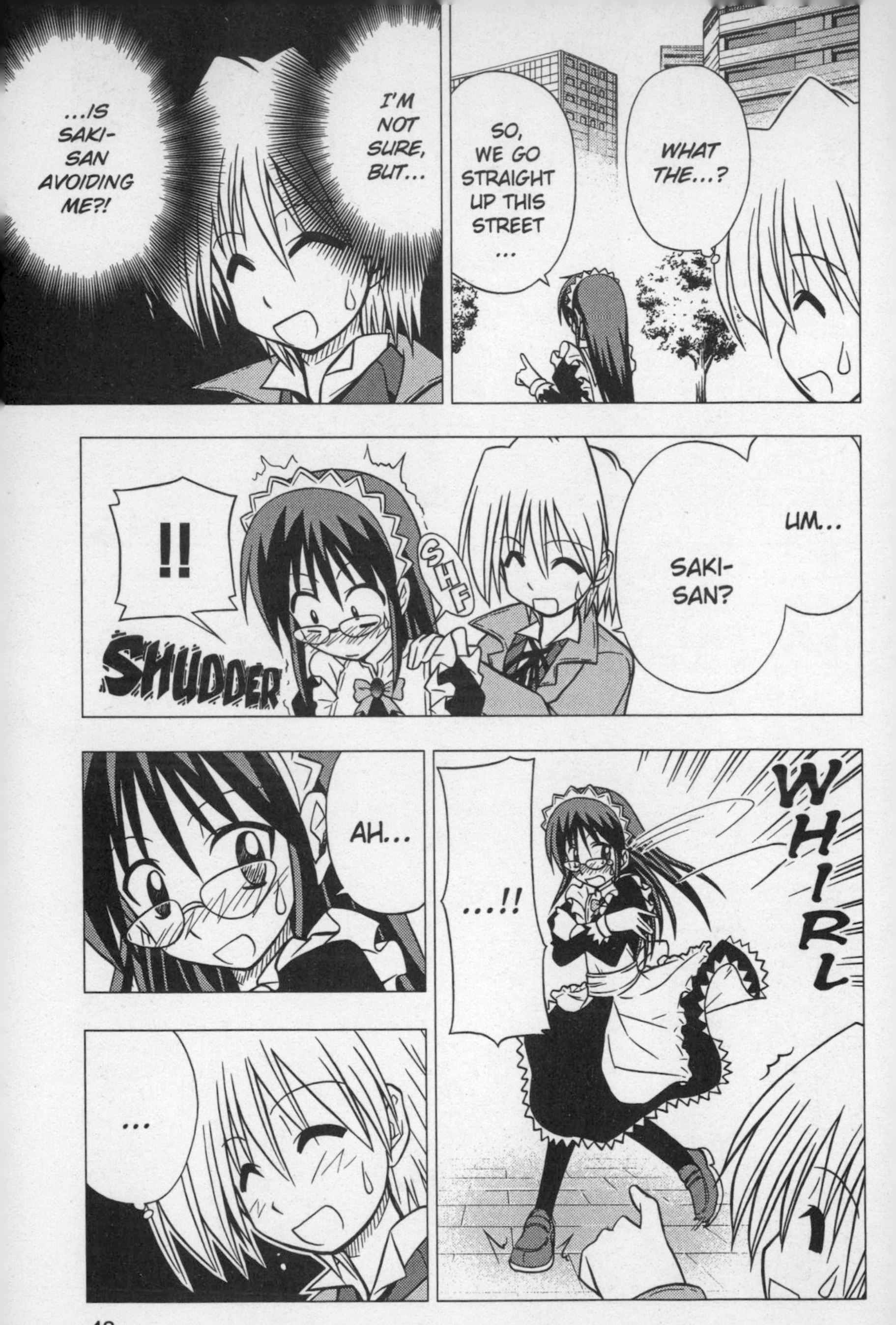
WHAT THE...?
SO, WE GO STRAIGHT UP THIS STREET ...
I'M NOT SURE, BUT...
...IS SAKI-SAN AVOIDING ME?!
UM... SAKI-SAN?
SHF
!!
SHUDDER
WHIRL
...!!
AH...
...

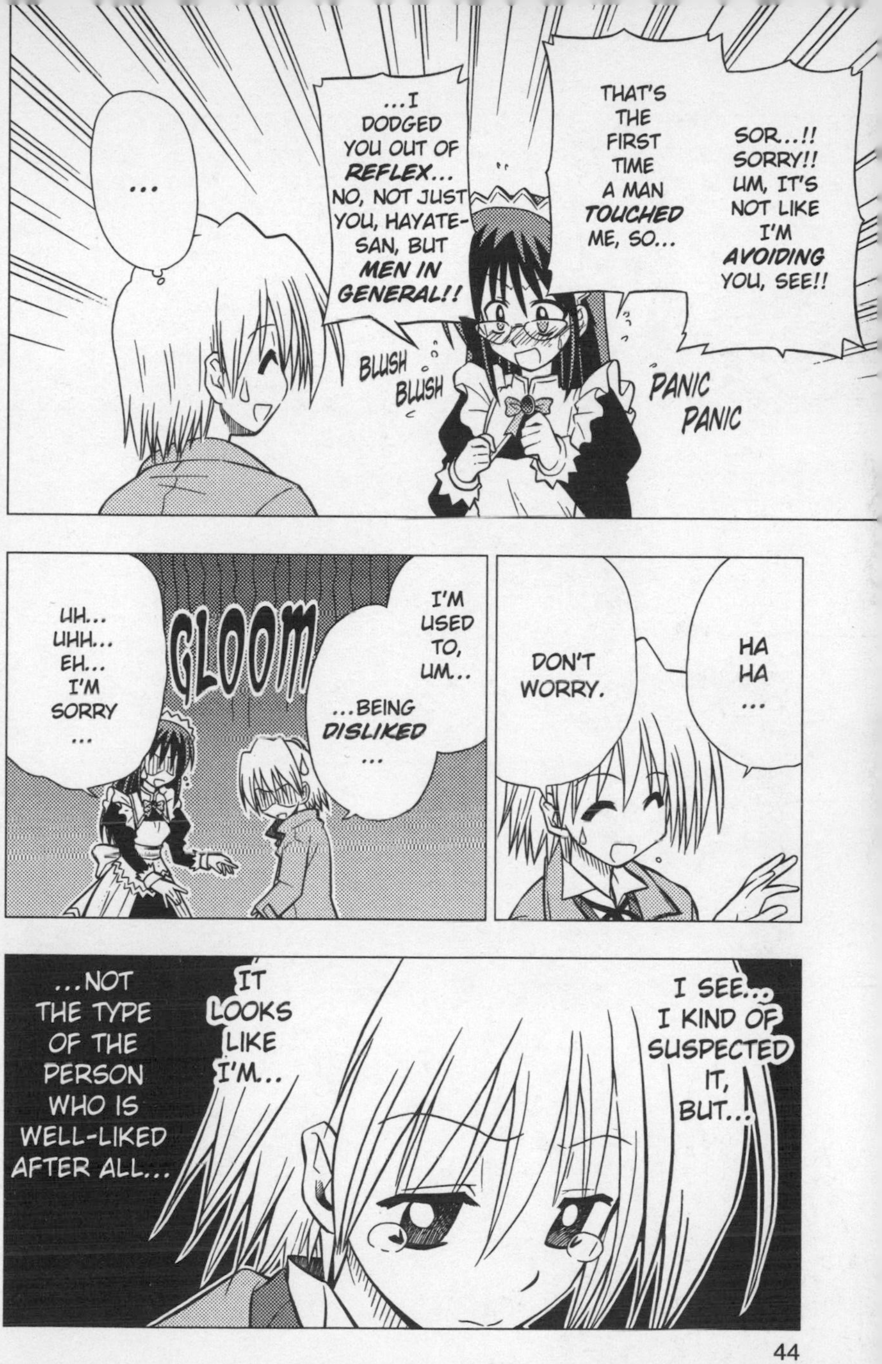
SOR...!! SORRY!! UM, IT'S NOT LIKE I'M AVOIDING YOU, SEE!!
THAT'S THE FIRST TIME A MAN TOUCHED ME, SO...
...I DODGED YOU OUT OF REFLEX... NO, NOT JUST YOU, HAYATE-SAN, BUT MEN IN GENERAL!!
PANIC PANIC
BLUSH BLUSH
...
HA HA ...
DON'T WORRY.
I'M USED TO, UM...
...BEING DISLIKED ...
GLOOM
UH... UHH... EH... I'M SORRY ...
I SEE... I KIND OF SUSPECTED IT, BUT...
IT LOOKS LIKE I'M...
...NOT THE TYPE OF THE PERSON WHO IS WELL-LIKED AFTER ALL...

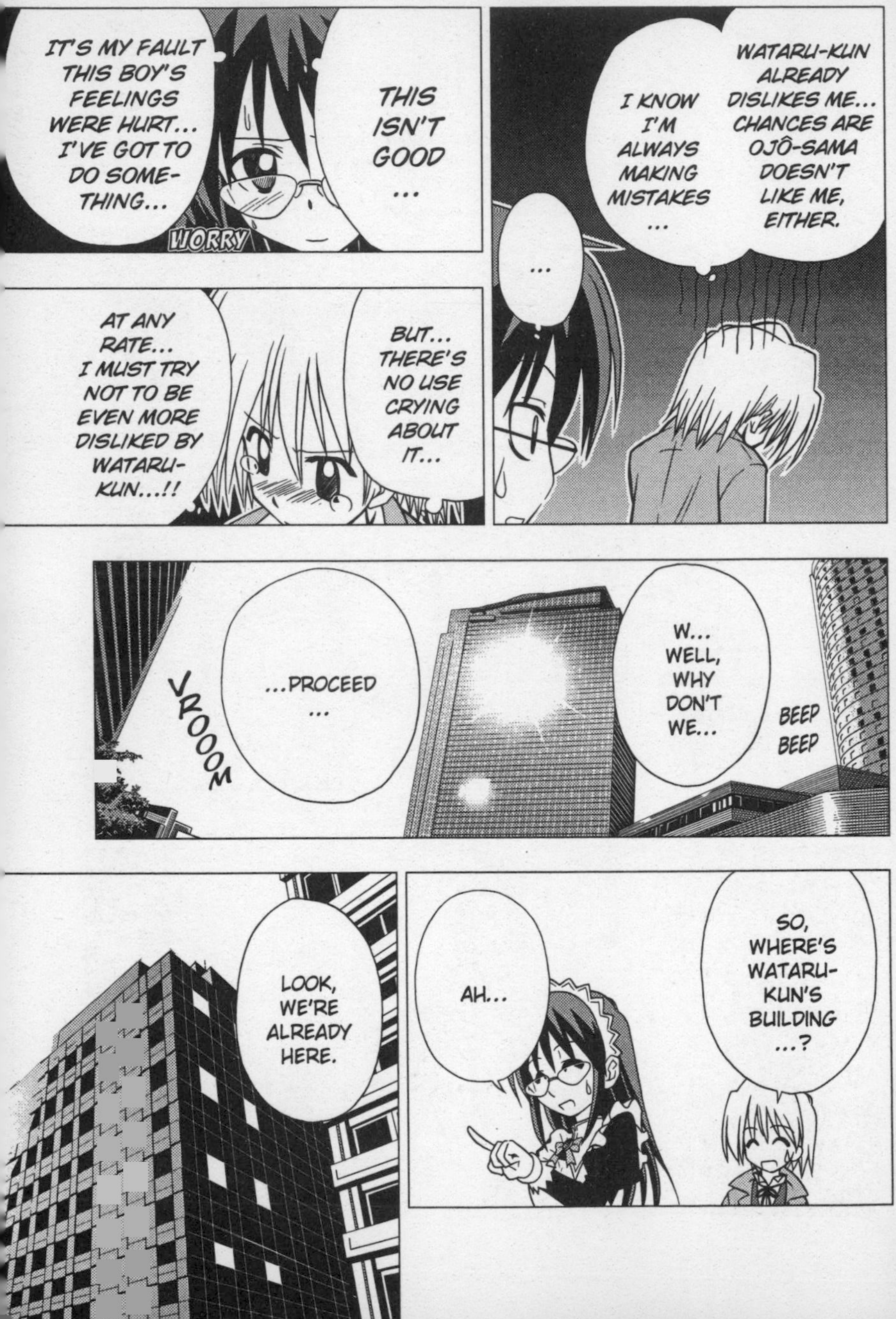
WATARU-KUN ALREADY DISLIKES ME... CHANCES ARE OJÔ-SAMA DOESN'T LIKE ME, EITHER.
I KNOW I'M ALWAYS MAKING MISTAKES...
...
THIS ISN'T GOOD...
IT'S MY FAULT THIS BOY'S FEELINGS WERE HURT... I'VE GOT TO DO SOME-THING...
WORRY
BUT... THERE'S NO USE CRYING ABOUT IT...
AT ANY RATE... I MUST TRY NOT TO BE EVEN MORE DISLIKED BY WATARU-KUN...!!
BEEP BEEP
W... WELL, WHY DON'T WE...
...PROCEED...
VROOOOM
SO, WHERE'S WATARU-KUN'S BUILDING...?
AH...
LOOK, WE'RE ALREADY HERE.

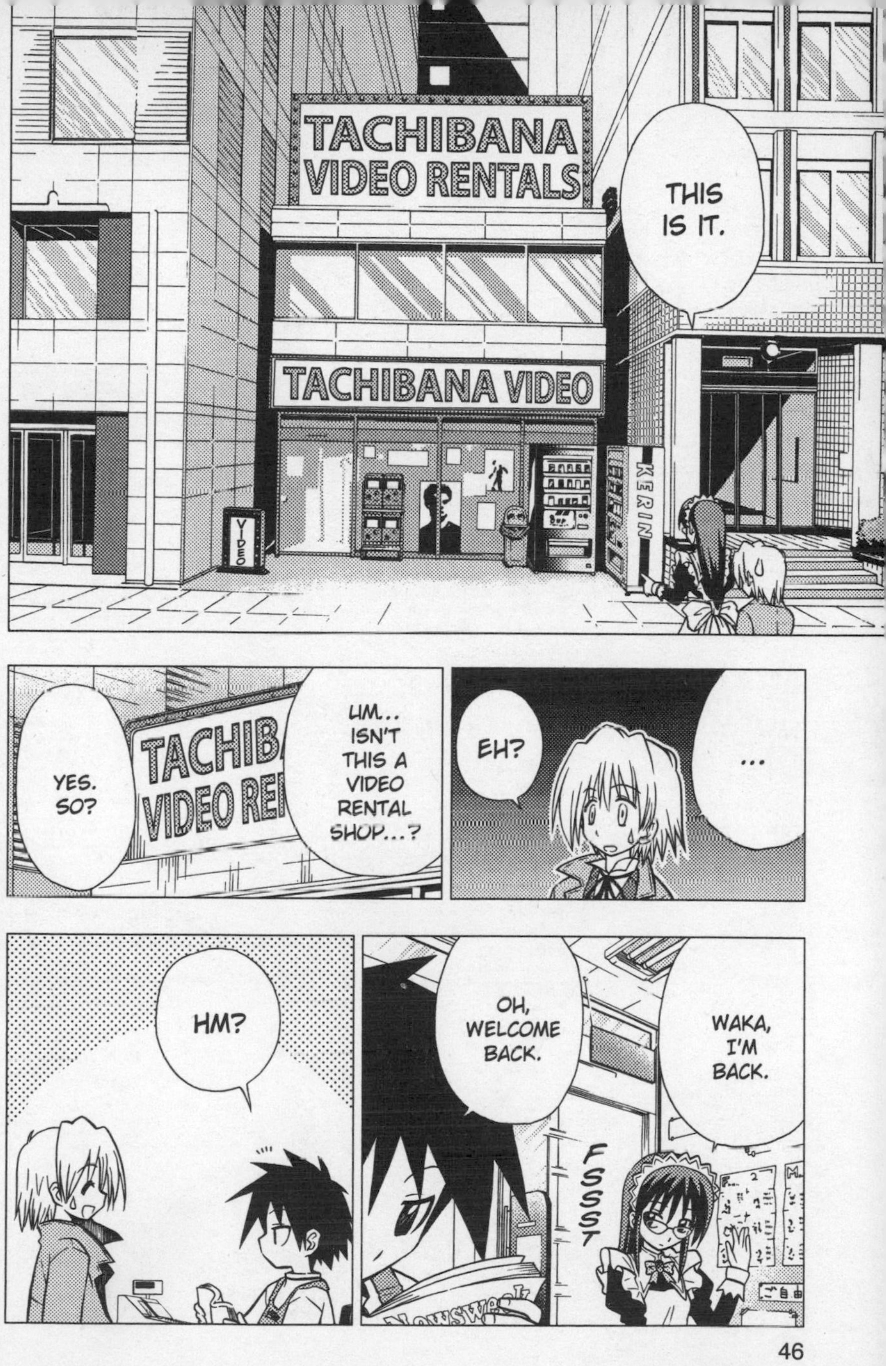
THIS IS IT.
TACHIBANA VIDEO RENTALS
TACHIBANA VIDEO
KERIN
VIDEO
...
EH?
UM... ISN'T THIS A VIDEO RENTAL SHOP...?
YES. SO?
WAKA, I'M BACK.
OH, WELCOME BACK.
FSSST
HM?

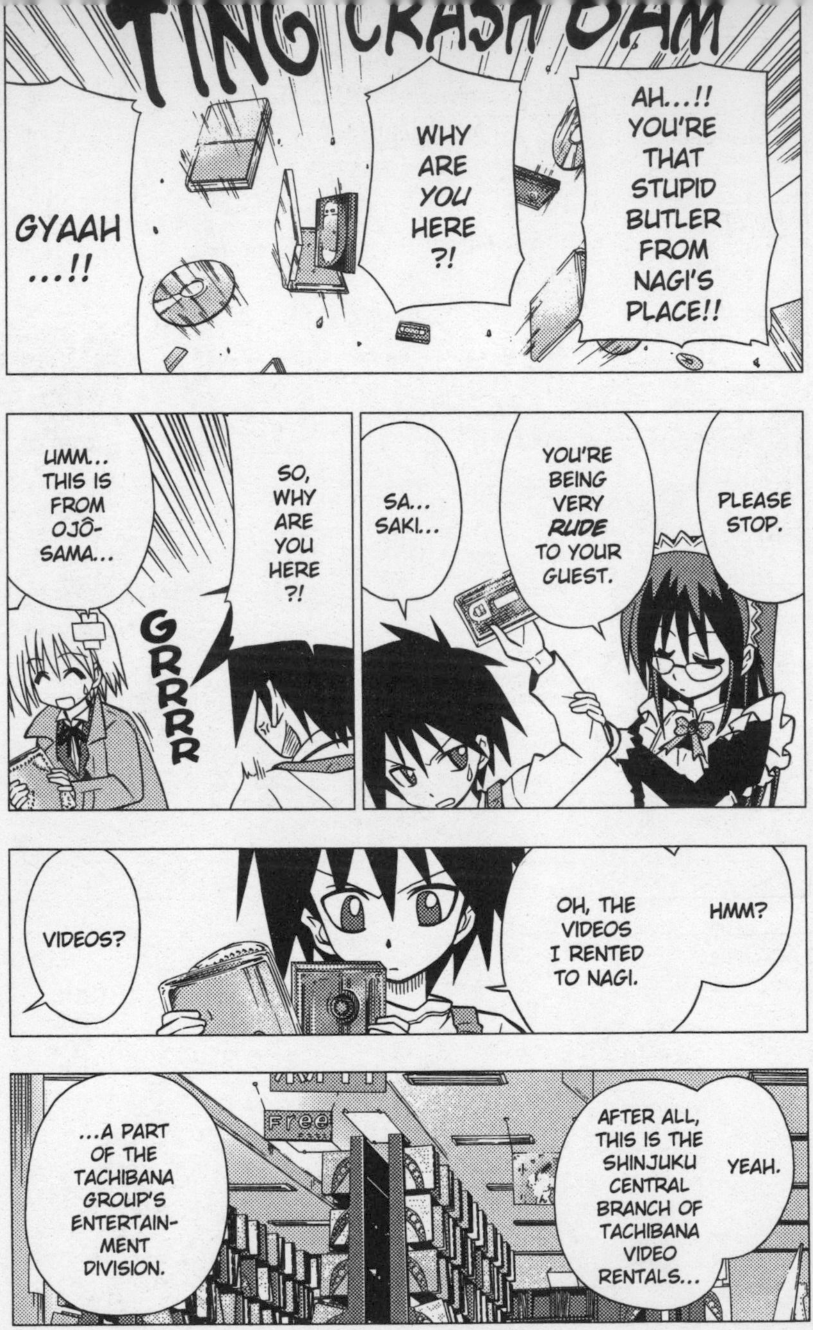
TING CRASH BAM
AH...!! YOU'RE THAT STUPID BUTLER FROM NAGI'S PLACE!!
WHY ARE *YOU* HERE?!
GYAAH...!!
PLEASE STOP.
YOU'RE BEING VERY *RUDE* TO YOUR GUEST.
SA... SAKI...
SO, WHY ARE YOU HERE?!
GRRRR
UMM... THIS IS FROM OJÔ-SAMA...
HMM?
OH, THE VIDEOS I RENTED TO NAGI.
VIDEOS?
YEAH.
AFTER ALL, THIS IS THE SHINJUKU CENTRAL BRANCH OF TACHIBANA VIDEO RENTALS...
...A PART OF THE TACHIBANA GROUP'S ENTERTAIN-MENT DIVISION.
Free

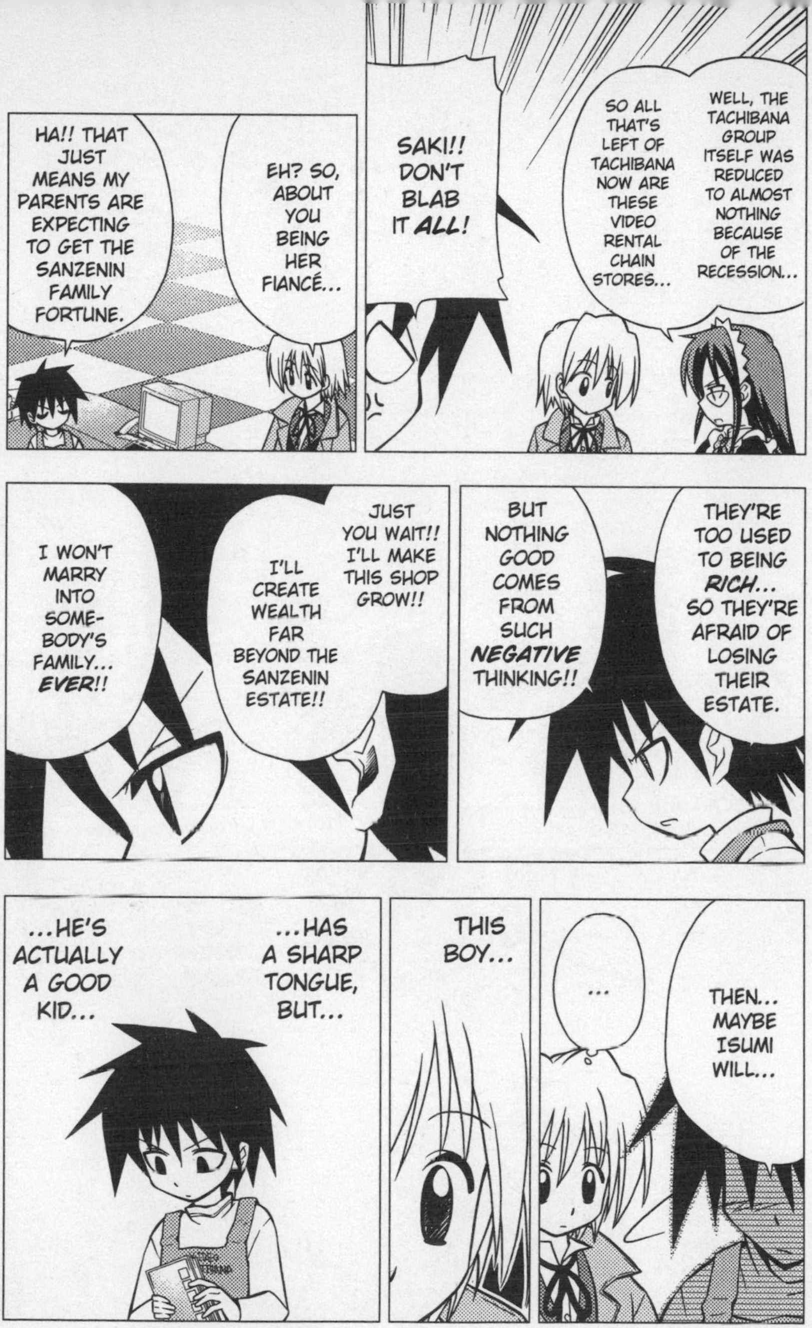
WELL, THE TACHIBANA GROUP ITSELF WAS REDUCED TO ALMOST NOTHING BECAUSE OF THE RECESSION...
SO ALL THAT'S LEFT OF TACHIBANA NOW ARE THESE VIDEO RENTAL CHAIN STORES...
SAKI!! DON'T BLAB IT ALL!
EH? SO, ABOUT YOU BEING HER FIANCÉ...
HA!! THAT JUST MEANS MY PARENTS ARE EXPECTING TO GET THE SANZENIN FAMILY FORTUNE.
THEY'RE TOO USED TO BEING RICH... SO THEY'RE AFRAID OF LOSING THEIR ESTATE.
BUT NOTHING GOOD COMES FROM SUCH NEGATIVE THINKING!!
JUST YOU WAIT!! I'LL MAKE THIS SHOP GROW!!
I'LL CREATE WEALTH FAR BEYOND THE SANZENIN ESTATE!!
I WON'T MARRY INTO SOME-BODY'S FAMILY... EVER!!
THEN... MAYBE ISUMI WILL...
...
THIS BOY...
...HAS A SHARP TONGUE, BUT...
...HE'S ACTUALLY A GOOD KID...

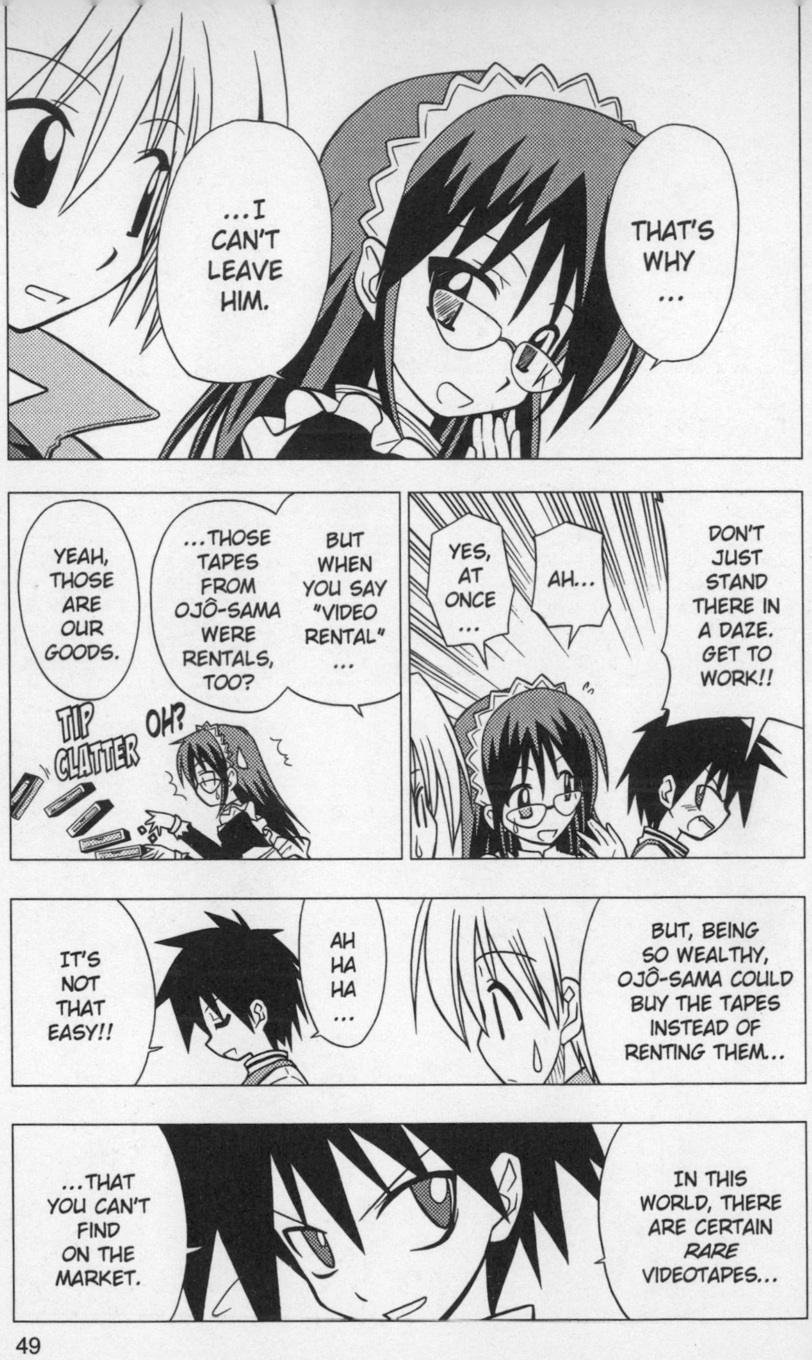
THAT'S WHY ...
...I CAN'T LEAVE HIM.
DON'T JUST STAND THERE IN A DAZE. GET TO WORK!!
AH...
YES, AT ONCE ...
BUT WHEN YOU SAY "VIDEO RENTAL" ...
...THOSE TAPES FROM OJÔ-SAMA WERE RENTALS, TOO?
YEAH, THOSE ARE OUR GOODS.
OH?
TIP CLATTER
BUT, BEING SO WEALTHY, OJÔ-SAMA COULD BUY THE TAPES INSTEAD OF RENTING THEM...
AH HA HA ...
IT'S NOT THAT EASY!!
IN THIS WORLD, THERE ARE CERTAIN *RARE* VIDEOTAPES...
...THAT YOU CAN'T FIND ON THE MARKET.

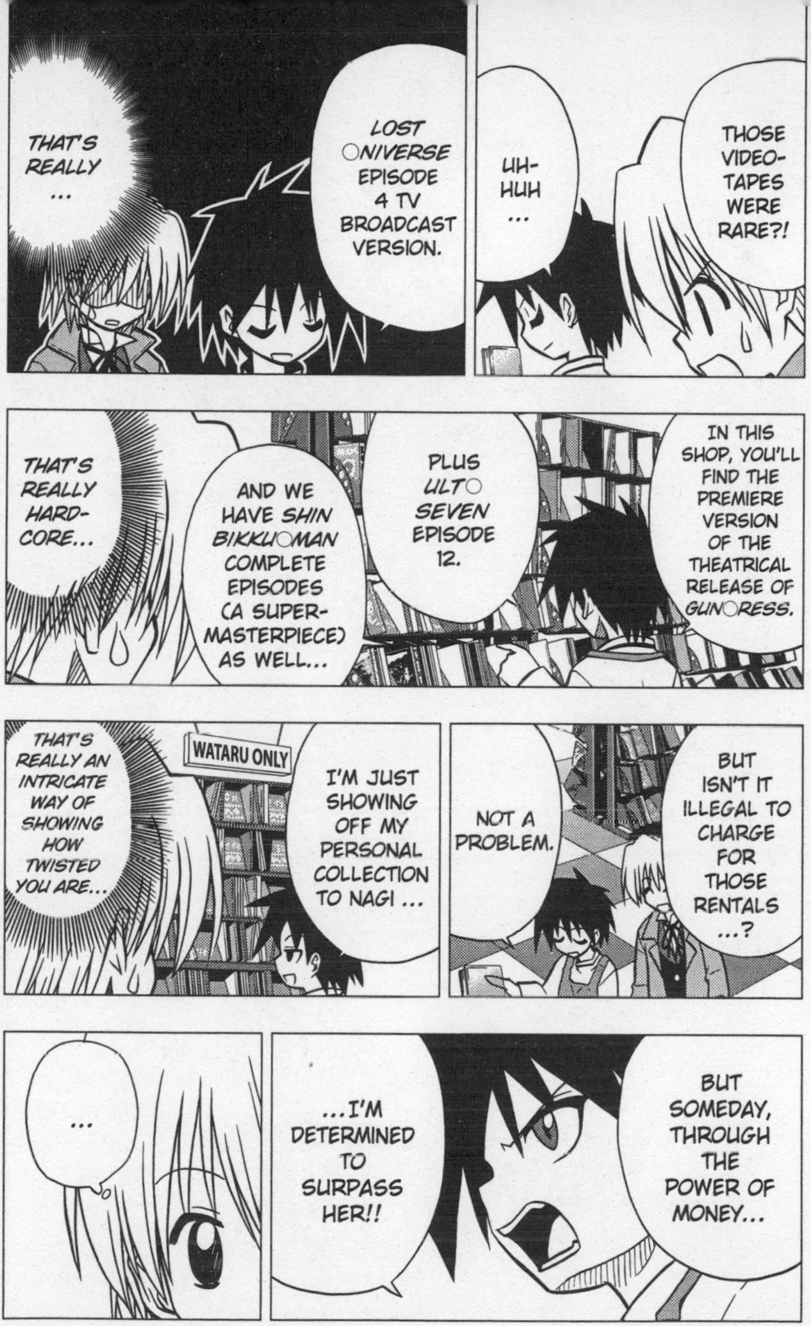
THOSE VIDEO-TAPES WERE RARE?!
UH-HUH ...
LOST ◯NIVERSE EPISODE 4 TV BROADCAST VERSION.
THAT'S REALLY ...
IN THIS SHOP, YOU'LL FIND THE PREMIERE VERSION OF THE THEATRICAL RELEASE OF GUN◯RESS.
PLUS ULT◯ SEVEN EPISODE 12.
AND WE HAVE SHIN BIKKU◯MAN COMPLETE EPISODES (A SUPER-MASTERPIECE) AS WELL...
THAT'S REALLY HARD-CORE...
BUT ISN'T IT ILLEGAL TO CHARGE FOR THOSE RENTALS ...?
NOT A PROBLEM.
I'M JUST SHOWING OFF MY PERSONAL COLLECTION TO NAGI ...
WATARU ONLY
THAT'S REALLY AN INTRICATE WAY OF SHOWING HOW TWISTED YOU ARE...
BUT SOMEDAY, THROUGH THE POWER OF MONEY...
...I'M DETERMINED TO SURPASS HER!!
...

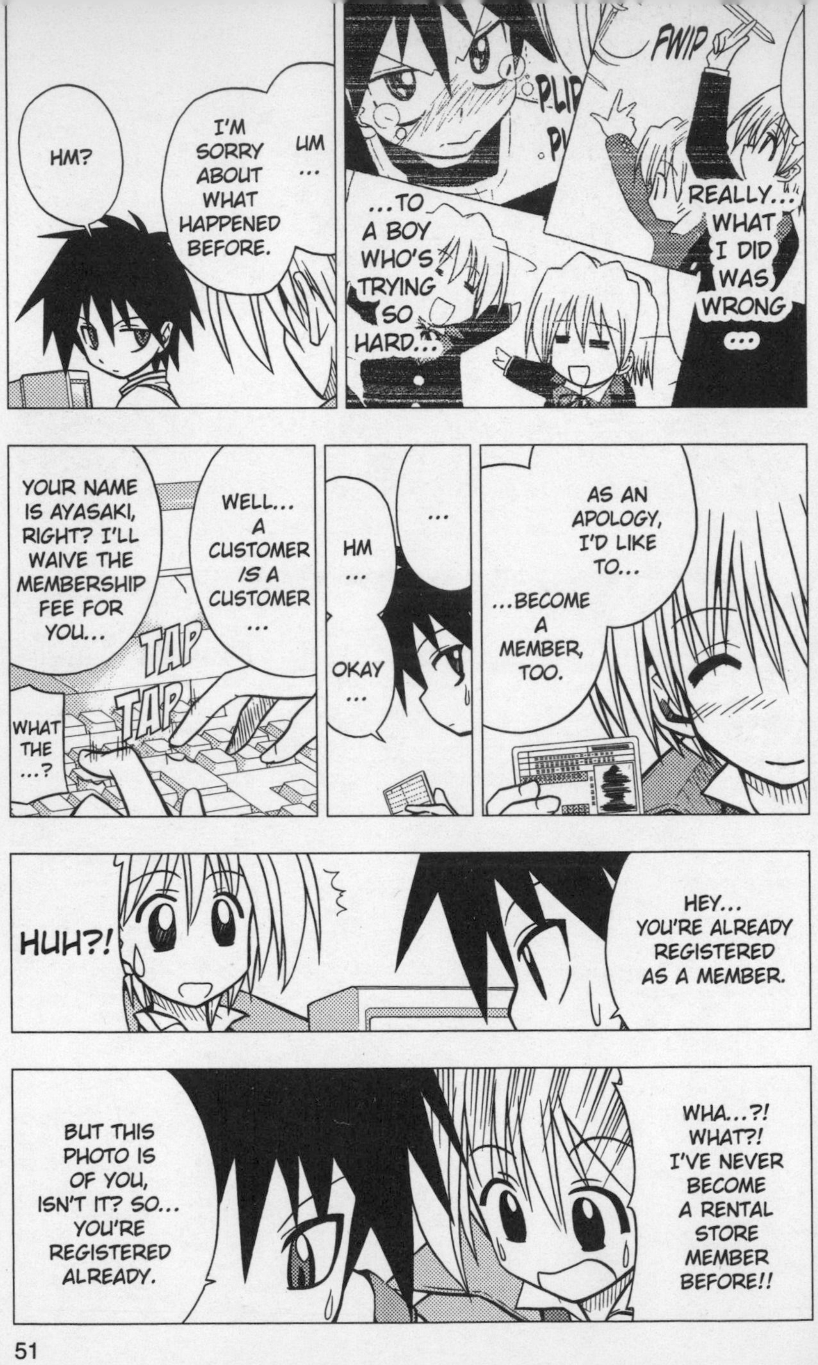
FWIP
PLIP
REALLY... WHAT I DID WAS WRONG...
...TO A BOY WHO'S TRYING SO HARD...
UM...
I'M SORRY ABOUT WHAT HAPPENED BEFORE.
HM?
AS AN APOLOGY, I'D LIKE TO...
...BECOME A MEMBER, TOO.
...
HM... OKAY...
WELL... A CUSTOMER *IS* A CUSTOMER...
YOUR NAME IS AYASAKI, RIGHT? I'LL WAIVE THE MEMBERSHIP FEE FOR YOU...
TAP
TAP
WHAT THE ...?
HEY... YOU'RE ALREADY REGISTERED AS A MEMBER.
HUH?!
WHA...?! WHAT?! I'VE NEVER BECOME A RENTAL STORE MEMBER BEFORE!!
BUT THIS PHOTO IS OF YOU, ISN'T IT? SO... YOU'RE REGISTERED ALREADY.

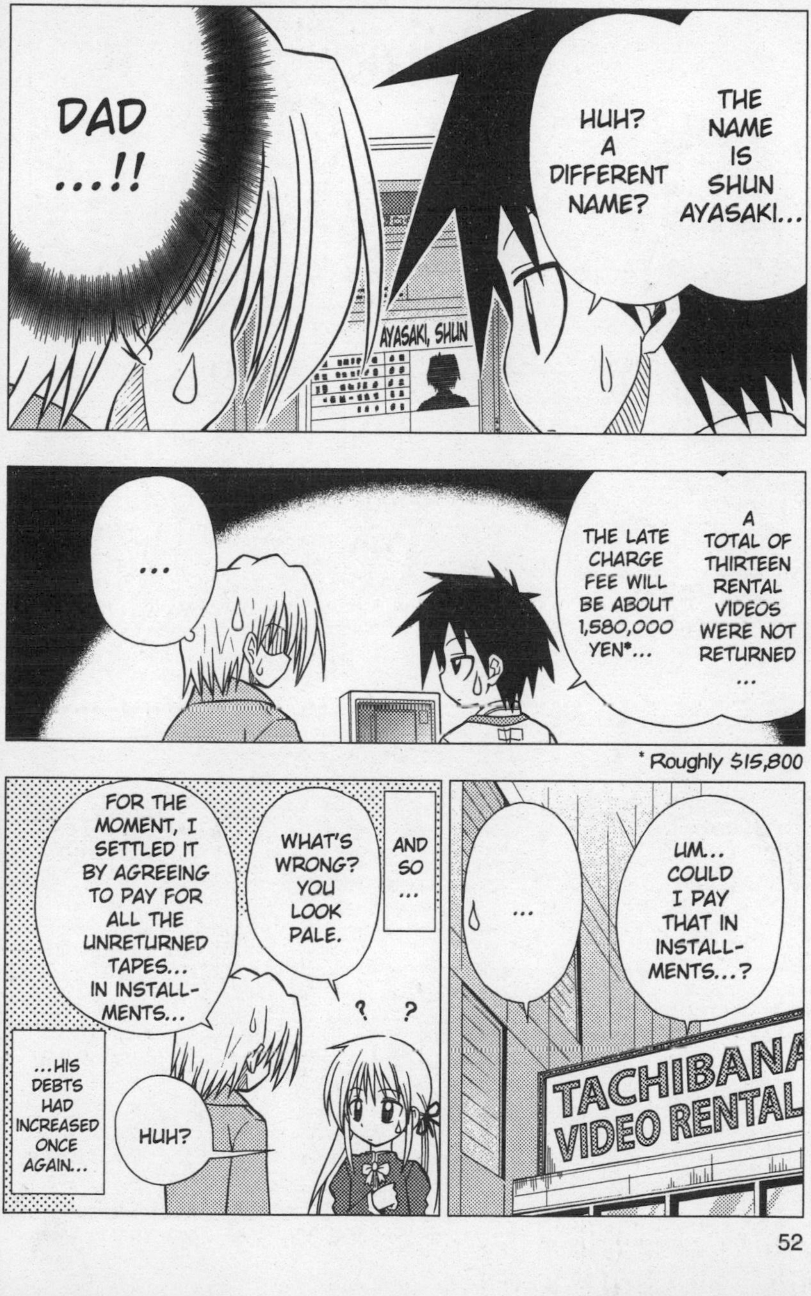
THE NAME IS SHUN AYASAKI...
HUH? A DIFFERENT NAME?
AYASAKI, SHUN
DAD ...!!
A TOTAL OF THIRTEEN RENTAL VIDEOS WERE NOT RETURNED ...
THE LATE CHARGE FEE WILL BE ABOUT 1,580,000 YEN*...
...
UM... COULD I PAY THAT IN INSTALL-MENTS...?
...
TACHIBANA VIDEO RENTAL
AND SO ...
WHAT'S WRONG? YOU LOOK PALE.
FOR THE MOMENT, I SETTLED IT BY AGREEING TO PAY FOR ALL THE UNRETURNED TAPES... IN INSTALL-MENTS...
? ?
HUH?
...HIS DEBTS HAD INCREASED ONCE AGAIN...

* Roughly $15,800

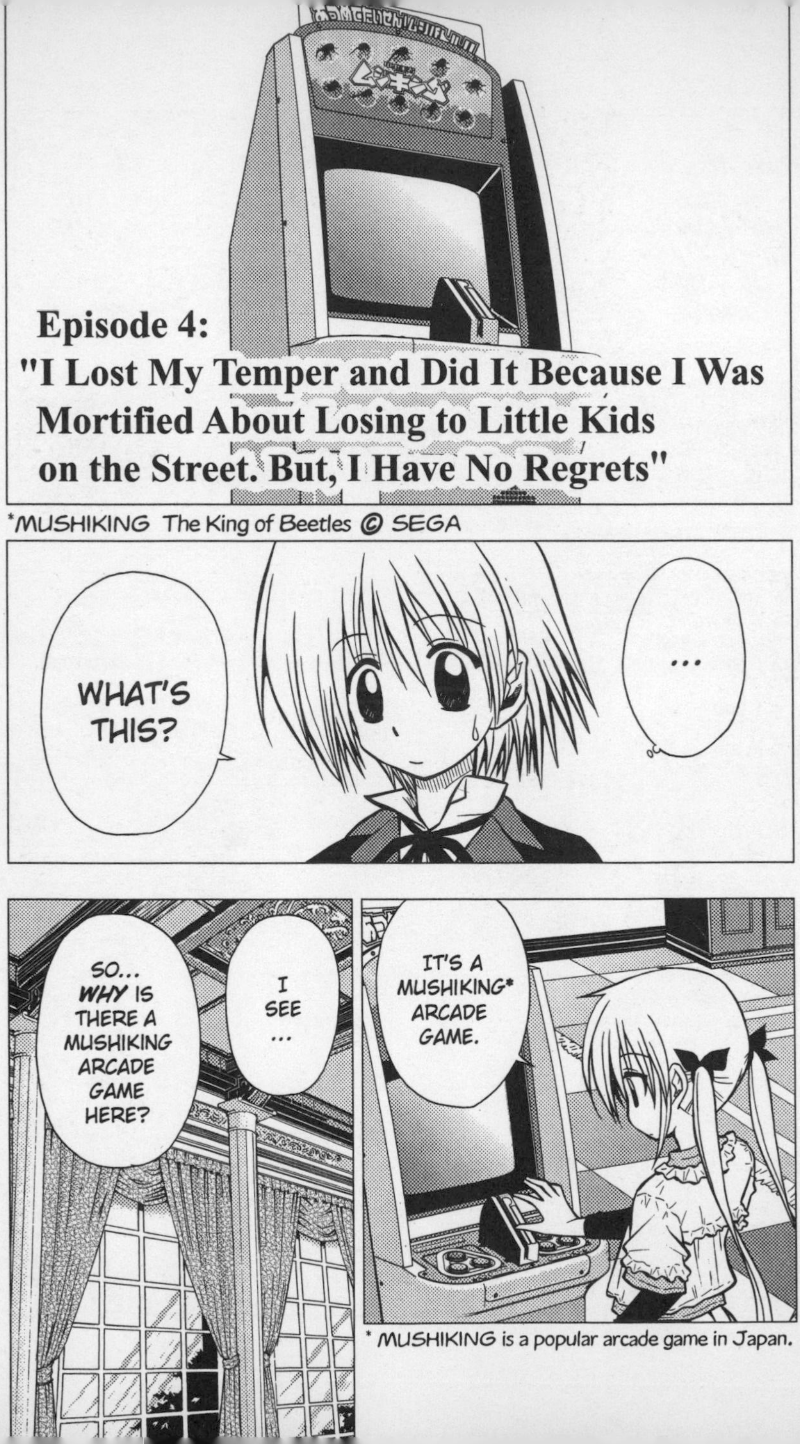
Episode 4:
"I Lost My Temper and Did It Because I Was Mortified About Losing to Little Kids on the Street. But, I Have No Regrets"
...
WHAT'S THIS?
IT'S A MUSHIKING* ARCADE GAME.
I SEE ...
SO... *WHY* IS THERE A MUSHIKING ARCADE GAME HERE?

*MUSHIKING The King of Beetles © SEGA

* MUSHIKING is a popular arcade game in Japan.

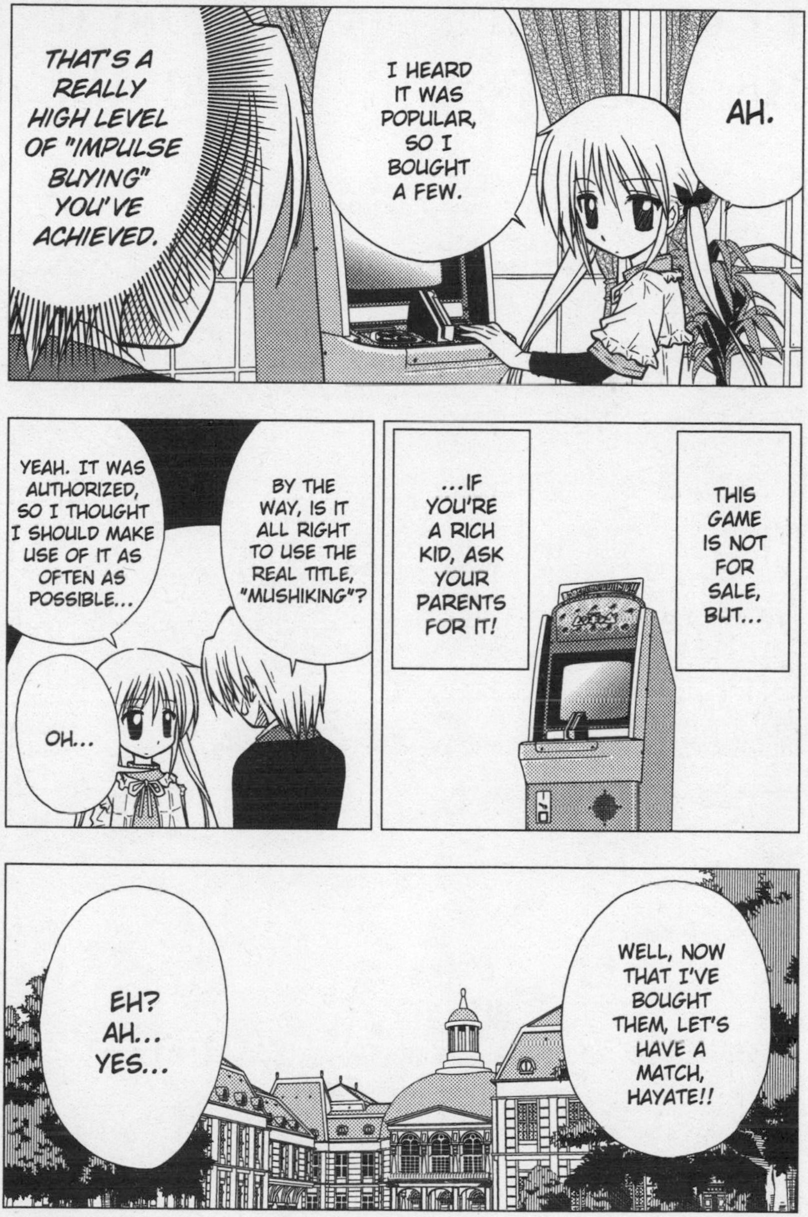
AH.
I HEARD IT WAS POPULAR, SO I BOUGHT A FEW.
THAT'S A REALLY HIGH LEVEL OF "IMPULSE BUYING" YOU'VE ACHIEVED.
THIS GAME IS NOT FOR SALE, BUT...
...IF YOU'RE A RICH KID, ASK YOUR PARENTS FOR IT!
BY THE WAY, IS IT ALL RIGHT TO USE THE REAL TITLE, "MUSHIKING"?
YEAH. IT WAS AUTHORIZED, SO I THOUGHT I SHOULD MAKE USE OF IT AS OFTEN AS POSSIBLE...
OH...
WELL, NOW THAT I'VE BOUGHT THEM, LET'S HAVE A MATCH, HAYATE!!
EH? AH... YES...

Episode 4:
"I Lost My Temper and Did It Because I Was Mortified About

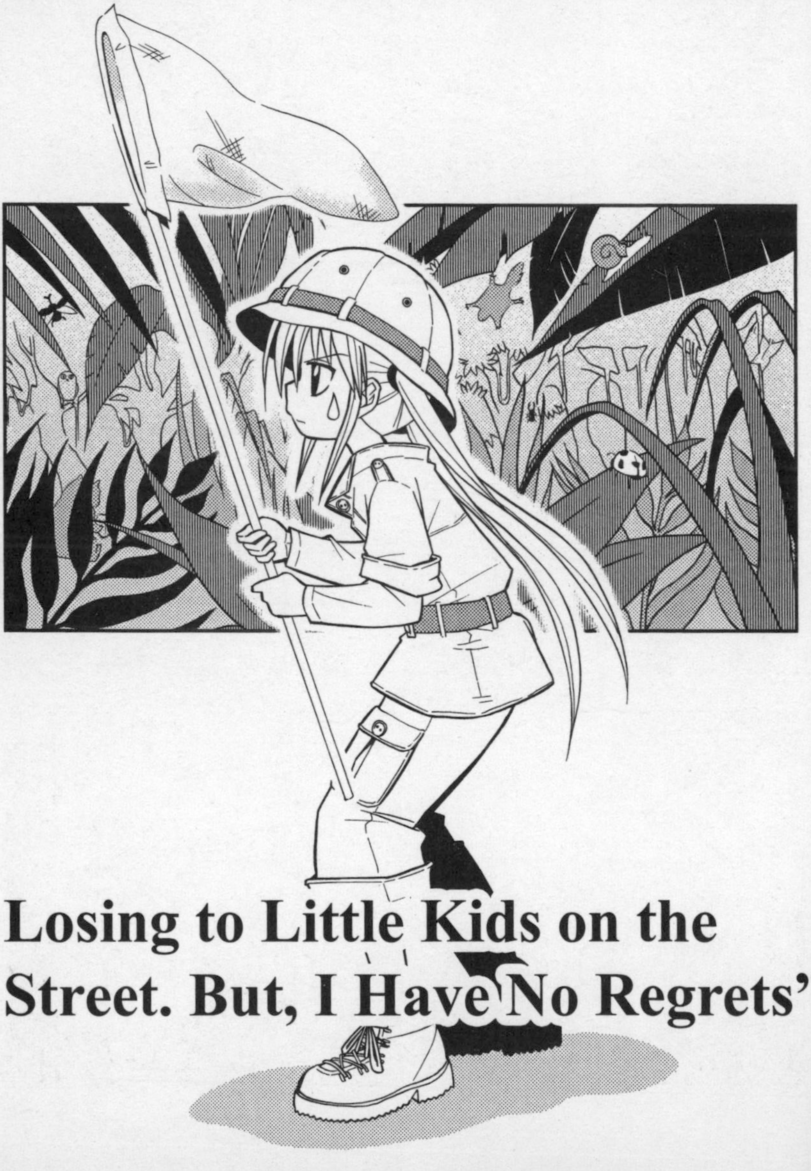

Losing to Little Kids on the Street. But, I Have No Regrets"

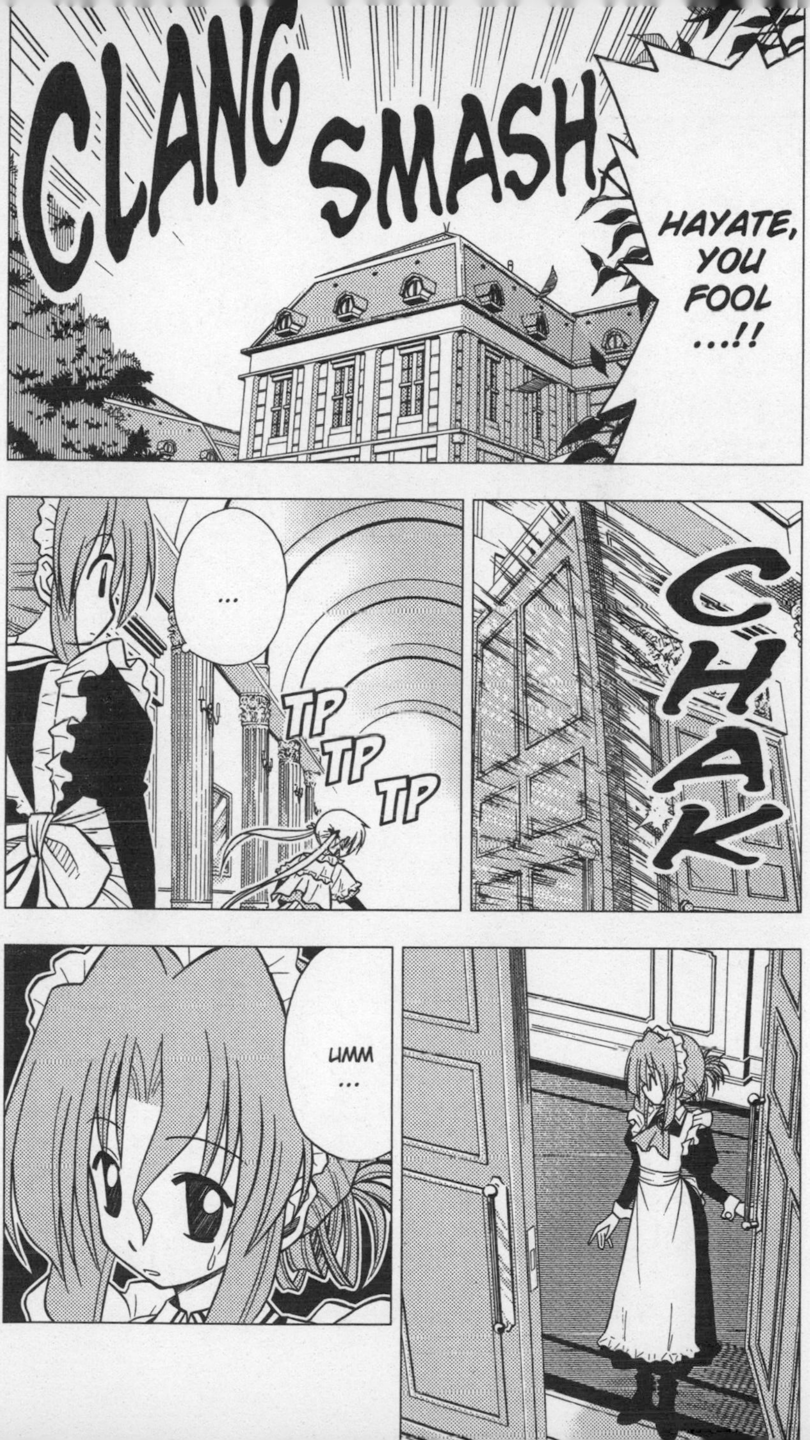
CLANG
SMASH
HAYATE, YOU FOOL ...!!
CHAK
...
TP TP TP
UMM ...

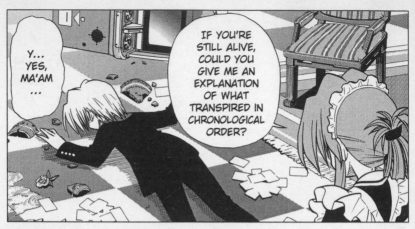

IF YOU'RE STILL ALIVE, COULD YOU GIVE ME AN EXPLANATION OF WHAT TRANSPIRED IN CHRONOLOGICAL ORDER?
Y... YES, MA'AM ...
BECAUSE OF THAT INCIDENT WITH WATARU-KUN...
...I THOUGHT I BETTER NOT GO EASY ON HER.
IF I LOST ON PURPOSE, THEN I MIGHT MAKE HER ANGRY AGAIN...
...AND SHE MIGHT EVEN CRY, LIKE WATARU-KUN...
SO, I THOUGHT I SHOULD PLAY FOR *KEEPS*...
SKITTER
SKITTER
FOR KEEPS ...
FOR KEEPS ...
FOR KEEPS ...

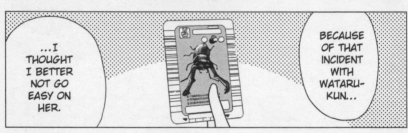

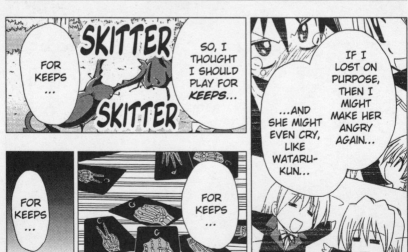

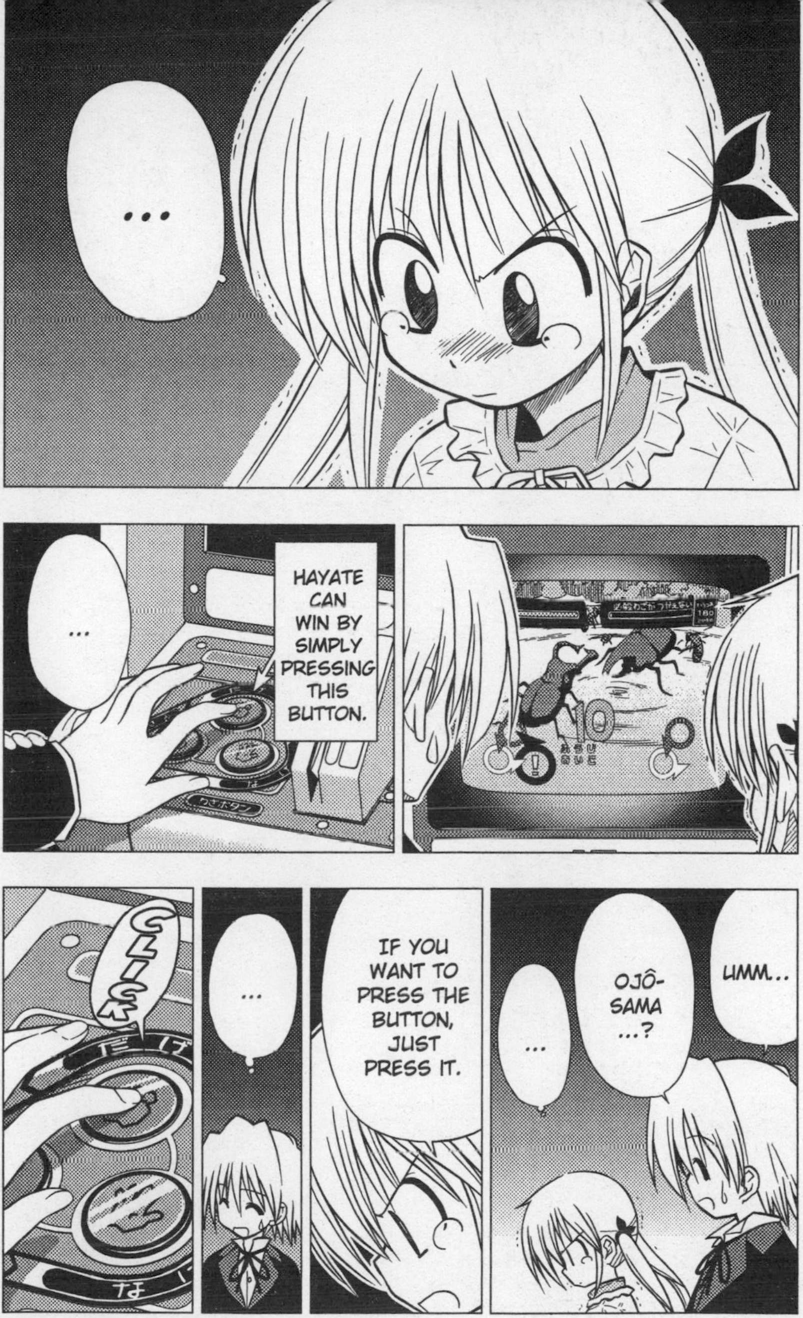
...
HAYATE CAN WIN BY SIMPLY PRESSING THIS BUTTON.
...
UMM...
OJÔ-SAMA ...?
...
IF YOU WANT TO PRESS THE BUTTON, JUST PRESS IT.
...
CLICK

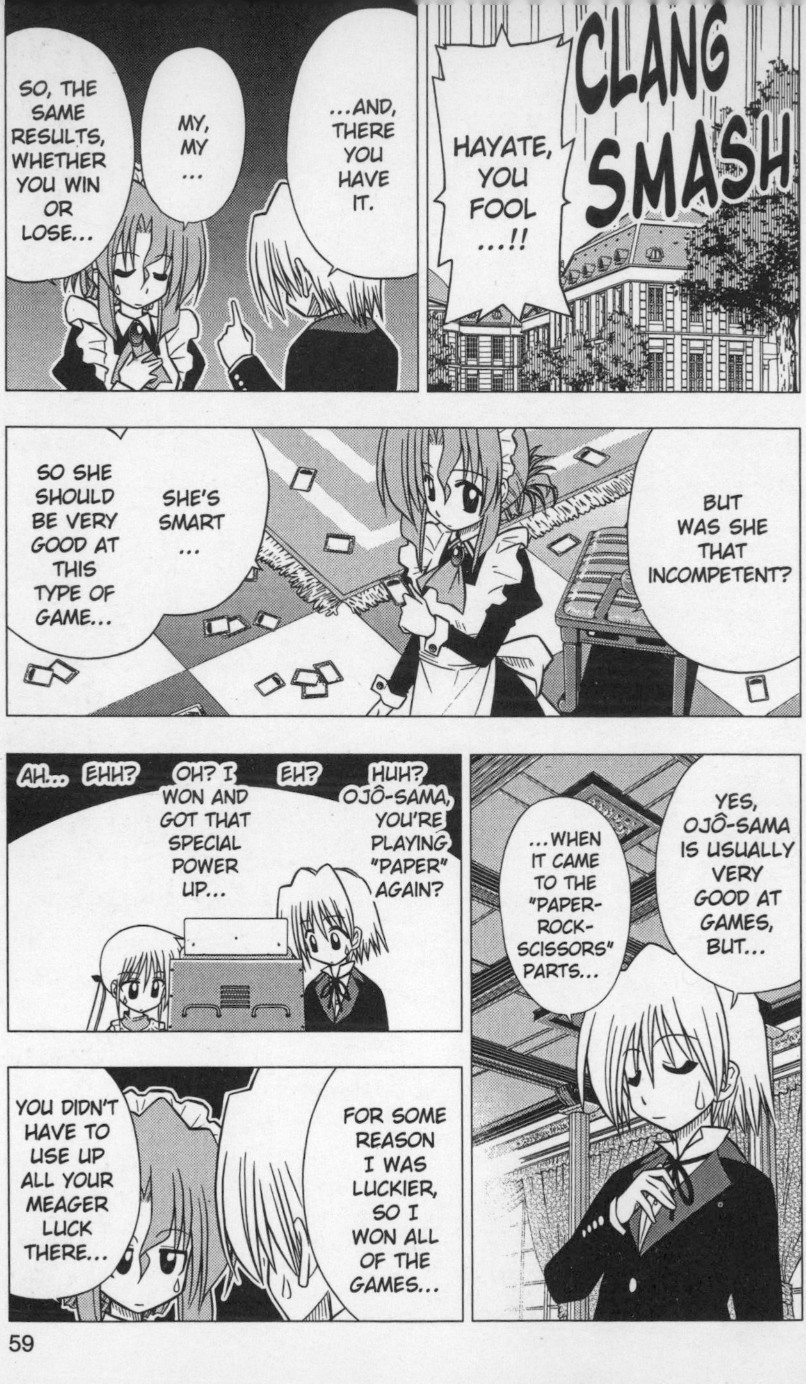
CLANG SMASH
HAYATE, YOU FOOL ...!!
...AND, THERE YOU HAVE IT.
MY, MY ...
SO, THE SAME RESULTS, WHETHER YOU WIN OR LOSE...
BUT WAS SHE THAT INCOMPETENT?
SHE'S SMART ...
SO SHE SHOULD BE VERY GOOD AT THIS TYPE OF GAME...
YES, OJÔ-SAMA IS USUALLY VERY GOOD AT GAMES, BUT...
...WHEN IT CAME TO THE "PAPER-ROCK-SCISSORS" PARTS...
HUH? OJÔ-SAMA, YOU'RE PLAYING "PAPER" AGAIN?
EH?
OH? I WON AND GOT THAT SPECIAL POWER UP...
AH... EHH?
FOR SOME REASON I WAS LUCKIER, SO I WON ALL OF THE GAMES...
YOU DIDN'T HAVE TO USE UP ALL YOUR MEAGER LUCK THERE...

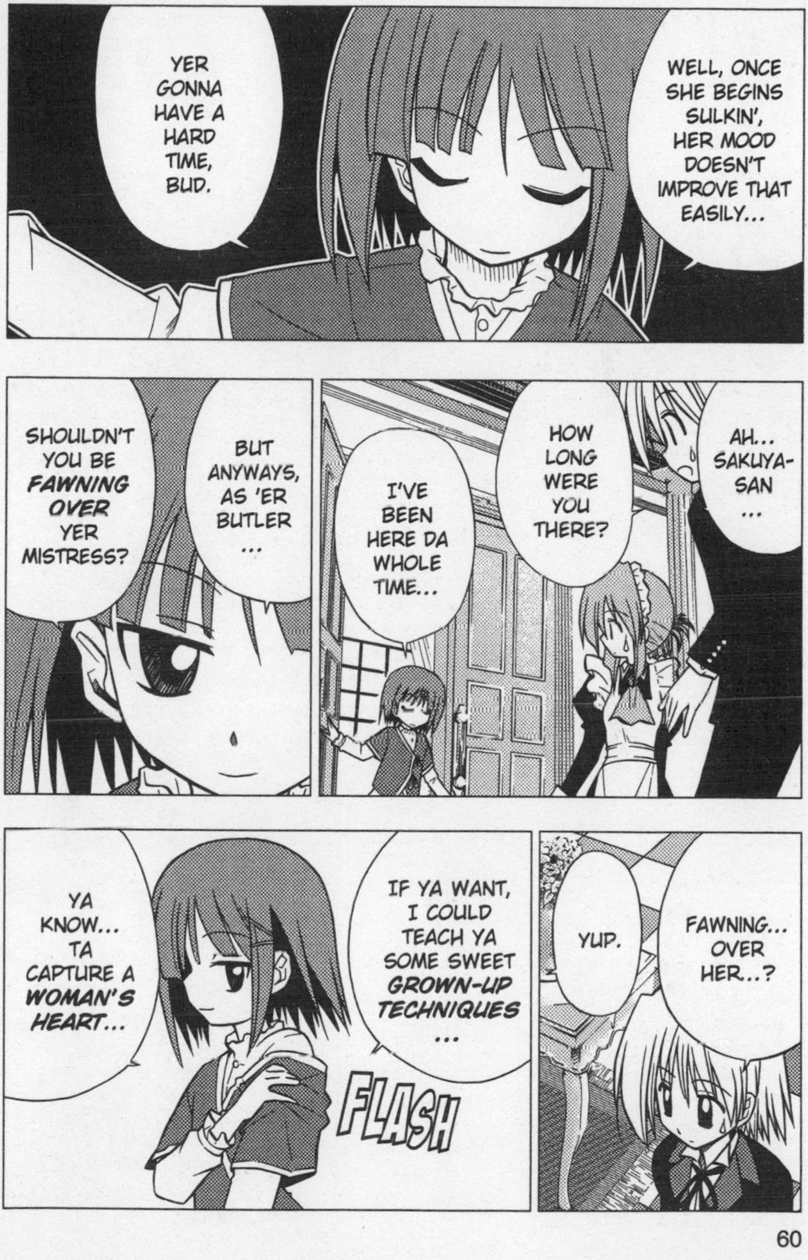
WELL, ONCE SHE BEGINS SULKIN', HER MOOD DOESN'T IMPROVE THAT EASILY...
YER GONNA HAVE A HARD TIME, BUD.
AH... SAKUYA-SAN...
HOW LONG WERE YOU THERE?
I'VE BEEN HERE DA WHOLE TIME...
BUT ANYWAYS, AS 'ER BUTLER...
SHOULDN'T YOU BE FAWNING OVER YER MISTRESS?
FAWNING... OVER HER...?
YUP.
IF YA WANT, I COULD TEACH YA SOME SWEET GROWN-UP TECHNIQUES...
YA KNOW... TA CAPTURE A WOMAN'S HEART...
FLASH

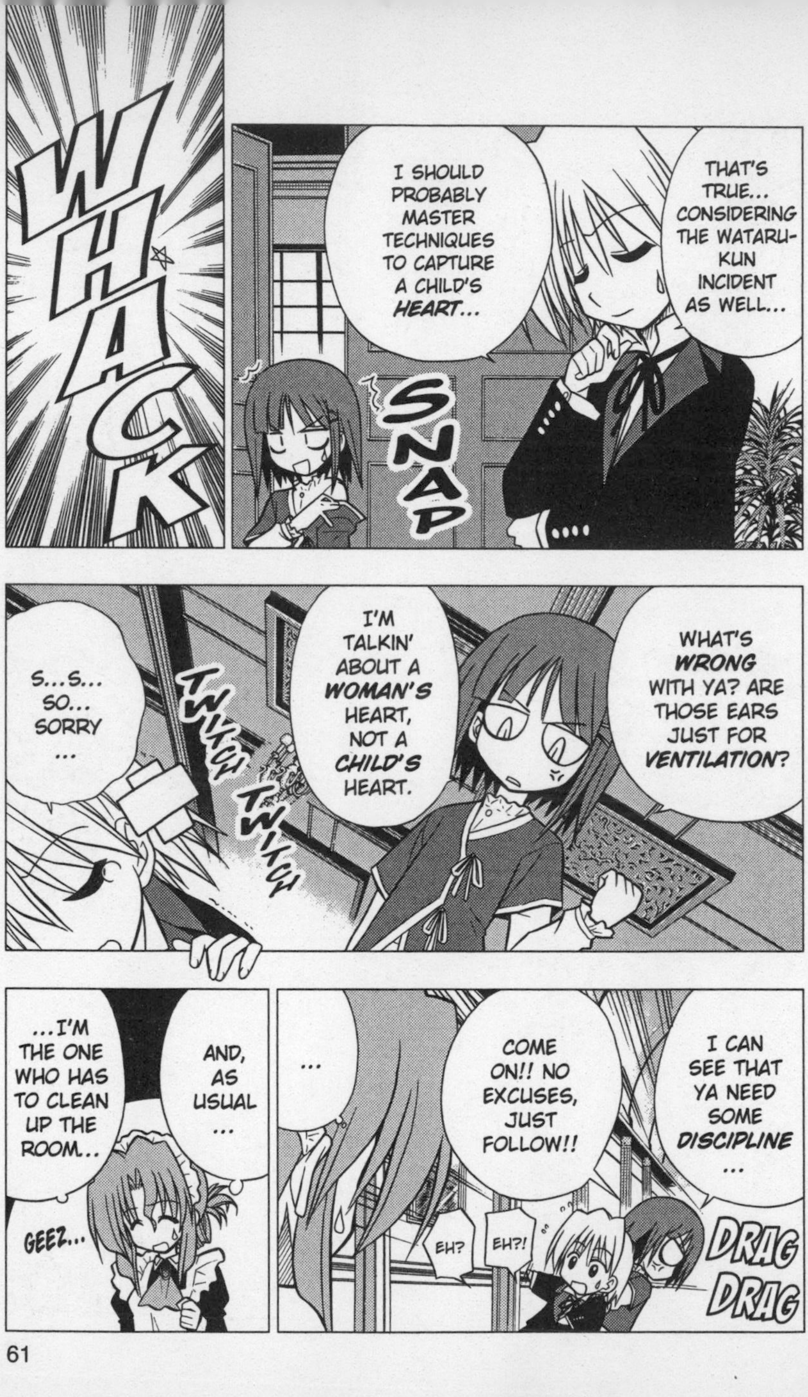
THAT'S TRUE... CONSIDERING THE WATARU-KUN INCIDENT AS WELL...
I SHOULD PROBABLY MASTER TECHNIQUES TO CAPTURE A CHILD'S HEART...
SNAP
WHACK
WHAT'S WRONG WITH YA? ARE THOSE EARS JUST FOR VENTILATION?
I'M TALKIN' ABOUT A WOMAN'S HEART, NOT A CHILD'S HEART.
TWITCH TWITCH
S...S... SO... SORRY ...
I CAN SEE THAT YA NEED SOME DISCIPLINE ...
DRAG DRAG
COME ON!! NO EXCUSES, JUST FOLLOW!!
...
EH?!
EH?
AND, AS USUAL ...
...I'M THE ONE WHO HAS TO CLEAN UP THE ROOM...
GEEZ...

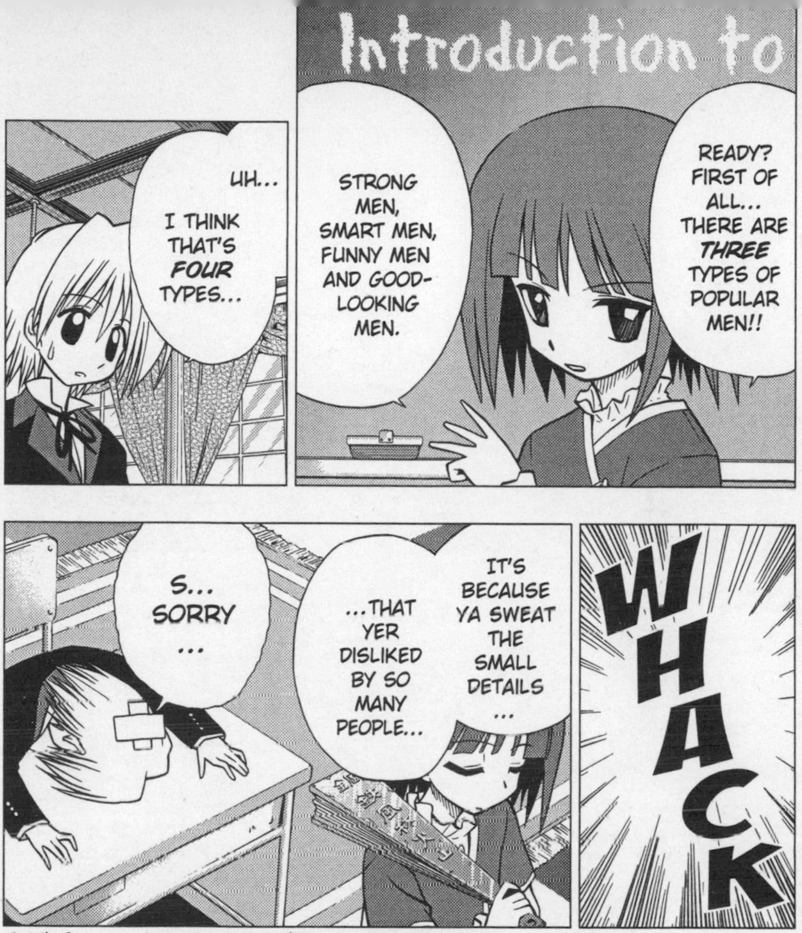
Introduction to
READY? FIRST OF ALL... THERE ARE THREE TYPES OF POPULAR MEN!!
STRONG MEN, SMART MEN, FUNNY MEN AND GOOD-LOOKING MEN.
UH...
I THINK THAT'S FOUR TYPES...
WHACK
IT'S BECAUSE YA SWEAT THE SMALL DETAILS...
...THAT YER DISLIKED BY SO MANY PEOPLE...
S... SORRY...

Saki's fan text: Iron Steel Wind Forest Fire Mountain

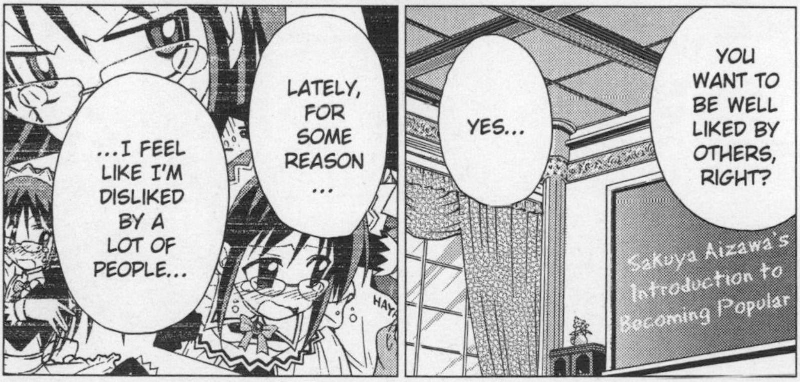
YOU WANT TO BE WELL LIKED BY OTHERS, RIGHT?
YES...
Sakuya Aizawa's Introduction to Becoming Popular
LATELY, FOR SOME REASON...
...I FEEL LIKE I'M DISLIKED BY A LOT OF PEOPLE...

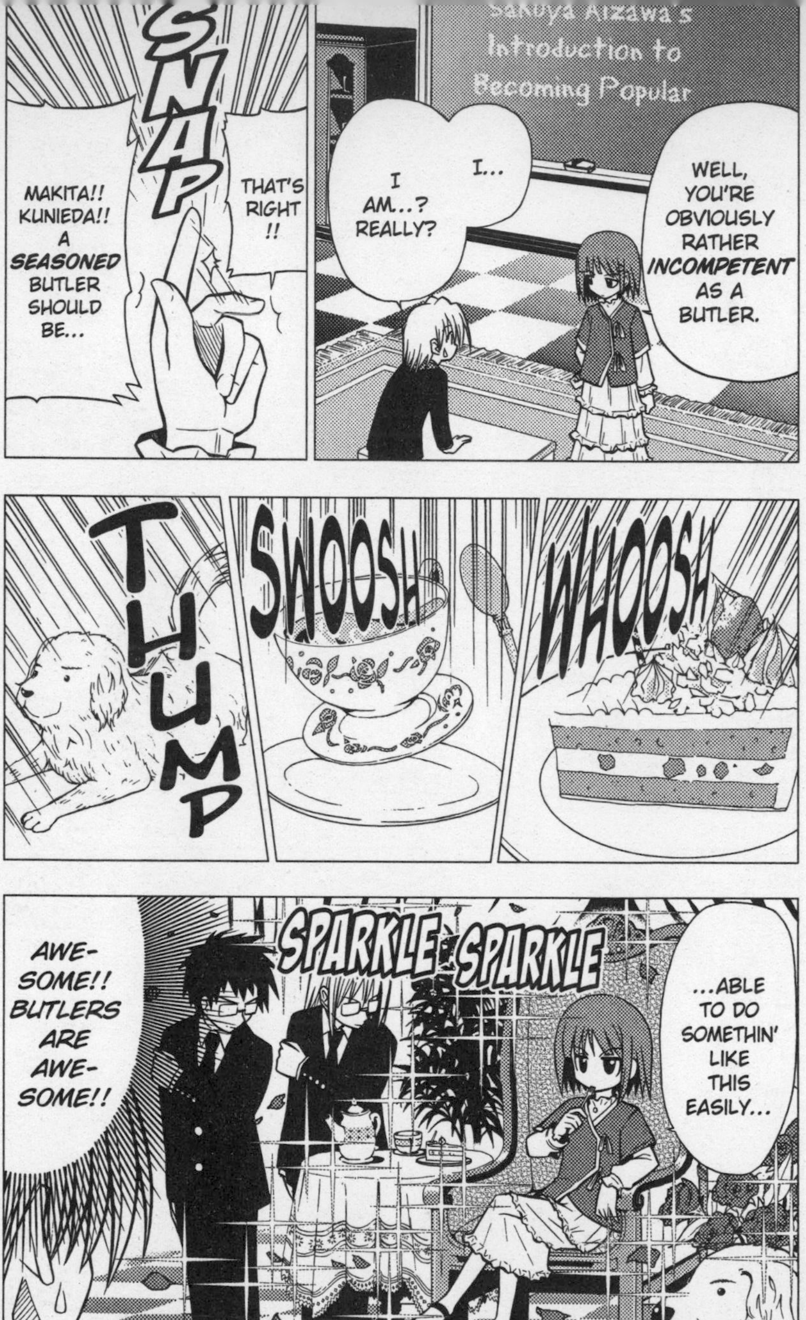
Sakuya Aizawa's Introduction to Becoming Popular
WELL, YOU'RE OBVIOUSLY RATHER INCOMPETENT AS A BUTLER.
I...
I AM...? REALLY?
THAT'S RIGHT!!
SNAP
MAKITA!! KUNIEDA!! A SEASONED BUTLER SHOULD BE...
WHOOSH
SWOOSH
THUMP
...ABLE TO DO SOMETHIN' LIKE THIS EASILY...
SPARKLE SPARKLE
AWESOME!! BUTLERS ARE AWESOME!!

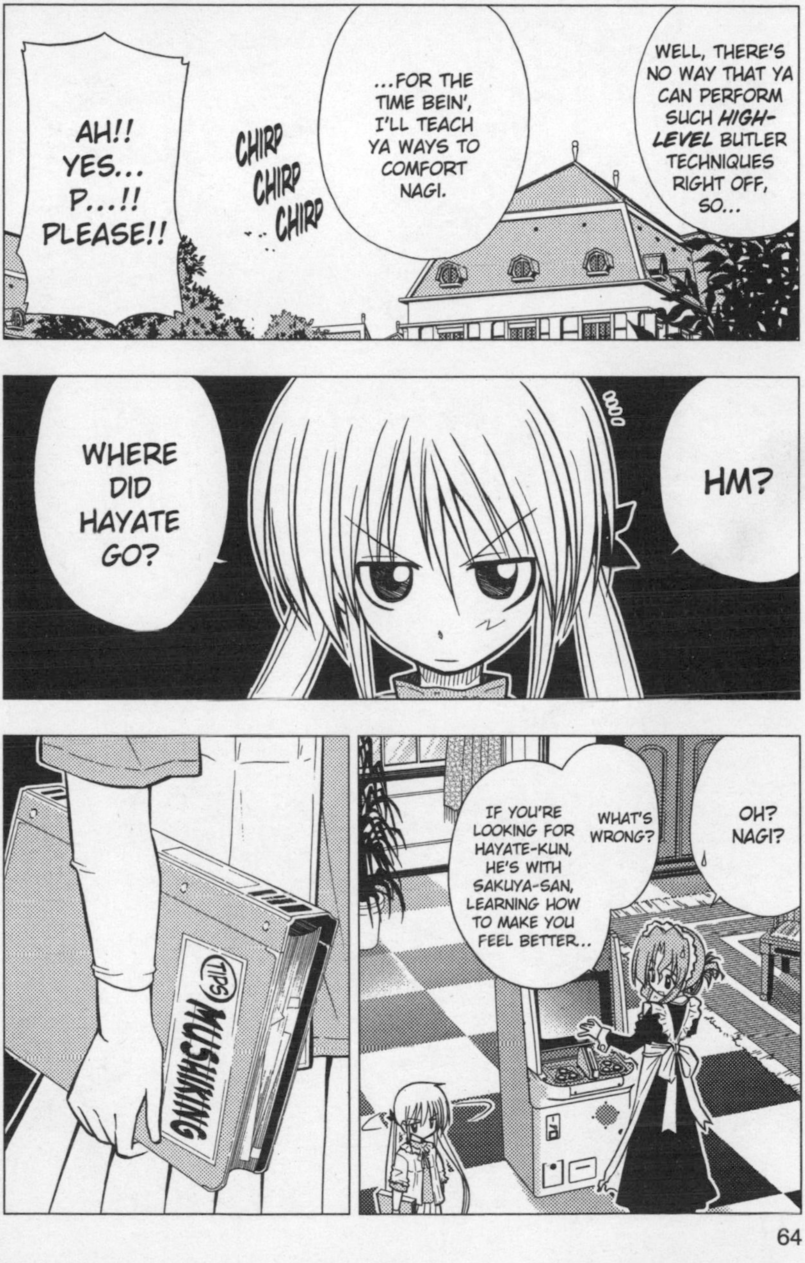

WELL, THERE'S NO WAY THAT YA CAN PERFORM SUCH HIGH-LEVEL BUTLER TECHNIQUES RIGHT OFF, SO...
...FOR THE TIME BEIN', I'LL TEACH YA WAYS TO COMFORT NAGI.
CHIRP CHIRP CHIRP
AH!! YES... P...!! PLEASE!!
HM?
WHERE DID HAYATE GO?
OH? NAGI?
WHAT'S WRONG?
IF YOU'RE LOOKING FOR HAYATE-KUN, HE'S WITH SAKUYA-SAN, LEARNING HOW TO MAKE YOU FEEL BETTER...
TIPS
MUSHIKING

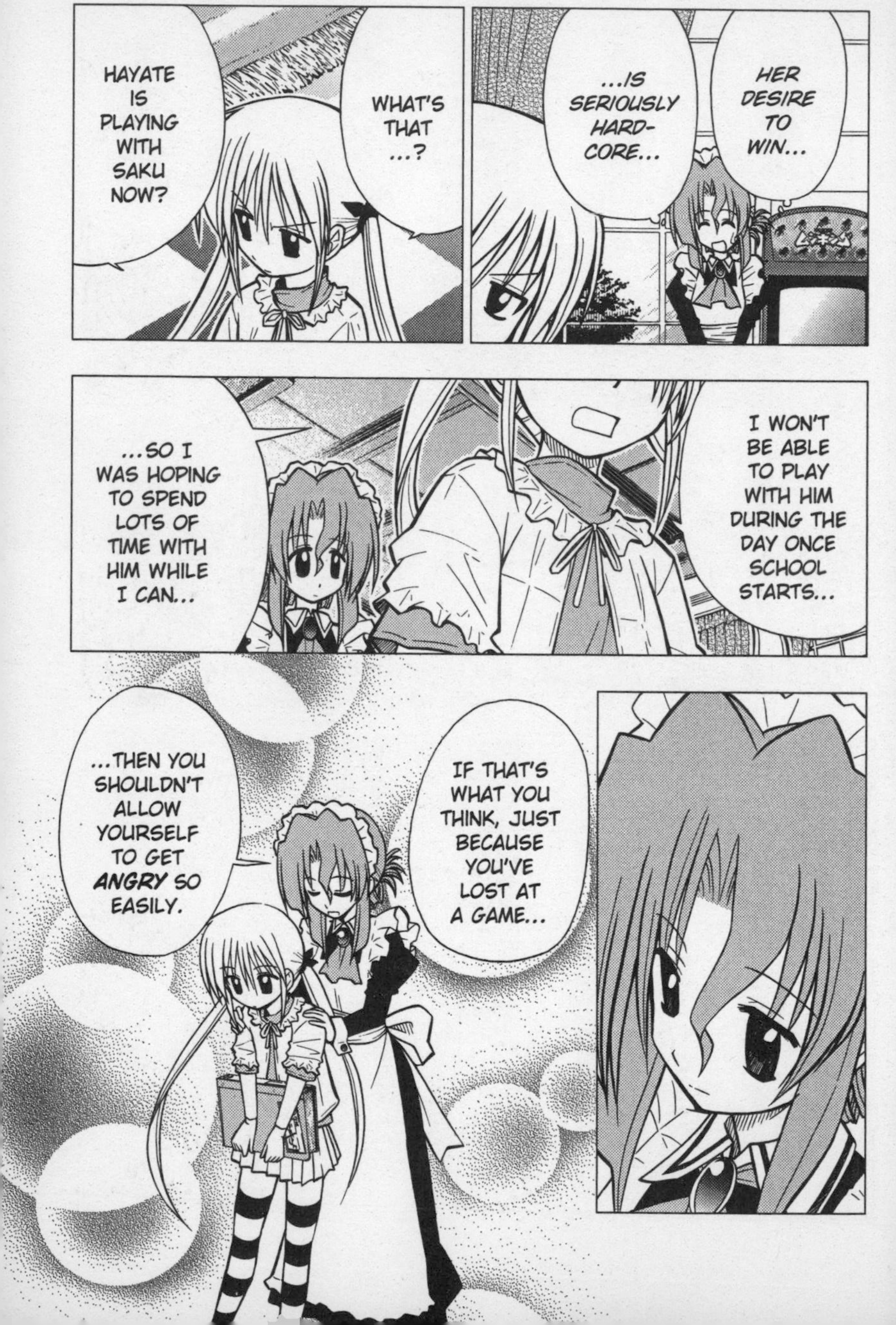
HER DESIRE TO WIN...
...IS SERIOUSLY HARD-CORE...
WHAT'S THAT ...?
HAYATE IS PLAYING WITH SAKU NOW?
I WON'T BE ABLE TO PLAY WITH HIM DURING THE DAY ONCE SCHOOL STARTS...
...SO I WAS HOPING TO SPEND LOTS OF TIME WITH HIM WHILE I CAN...
IF THAT'S WHAT YOU THINK, JUST BECAUSE YOU'VE LOST AT A GAME...
...THEN YOU SHOULDN'T ALLOW YOURSELF TO GET ANGRY SO EASILY.

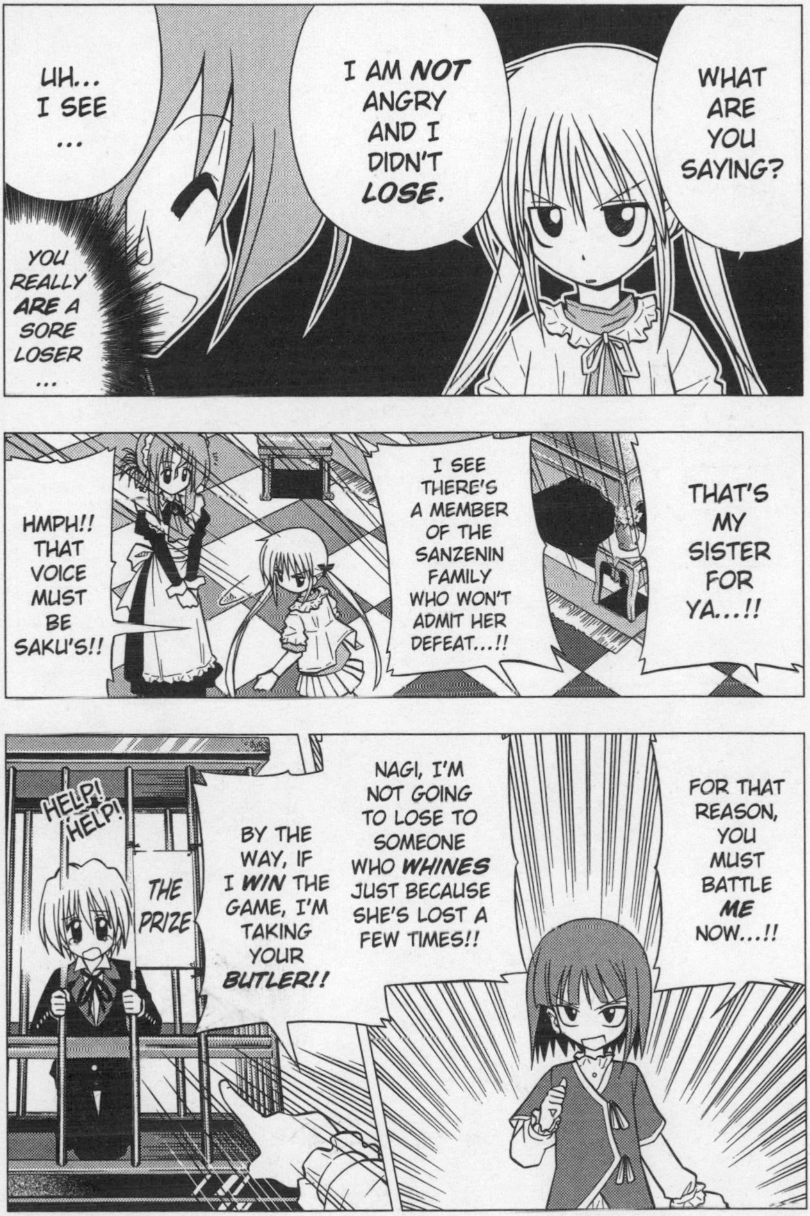
WHAT ARE YOU SAYING?
I AM NOT ANGRY AND I DIDN'T LOSE.
UH... I SEE ...
YOU REALLY ARE A SORE LOSER ...
THAT'S MY SISTER FOR YA...!!
I SEE THERE'S A MEMBER OF THE SANZENIN FAMILY WHO WON'T ADMIT HER DEFEAT...!!
HMPH!! THAT VOICE MUST BE SAKU'S!!
FOR THAT REASON, YOU MUST BATTLE ME NOW...!!
NAGI, I'M NOT GOING TO LOSE TO SOMEONE WHO WHINES JUST BECAUSE SHE'S LOST A FEW TIMES!!
BY THE WAY, IF I WIN THE GAME, I'M TAKING YOUR BUTLER!!
THE PRIZE
HELP! HELP!

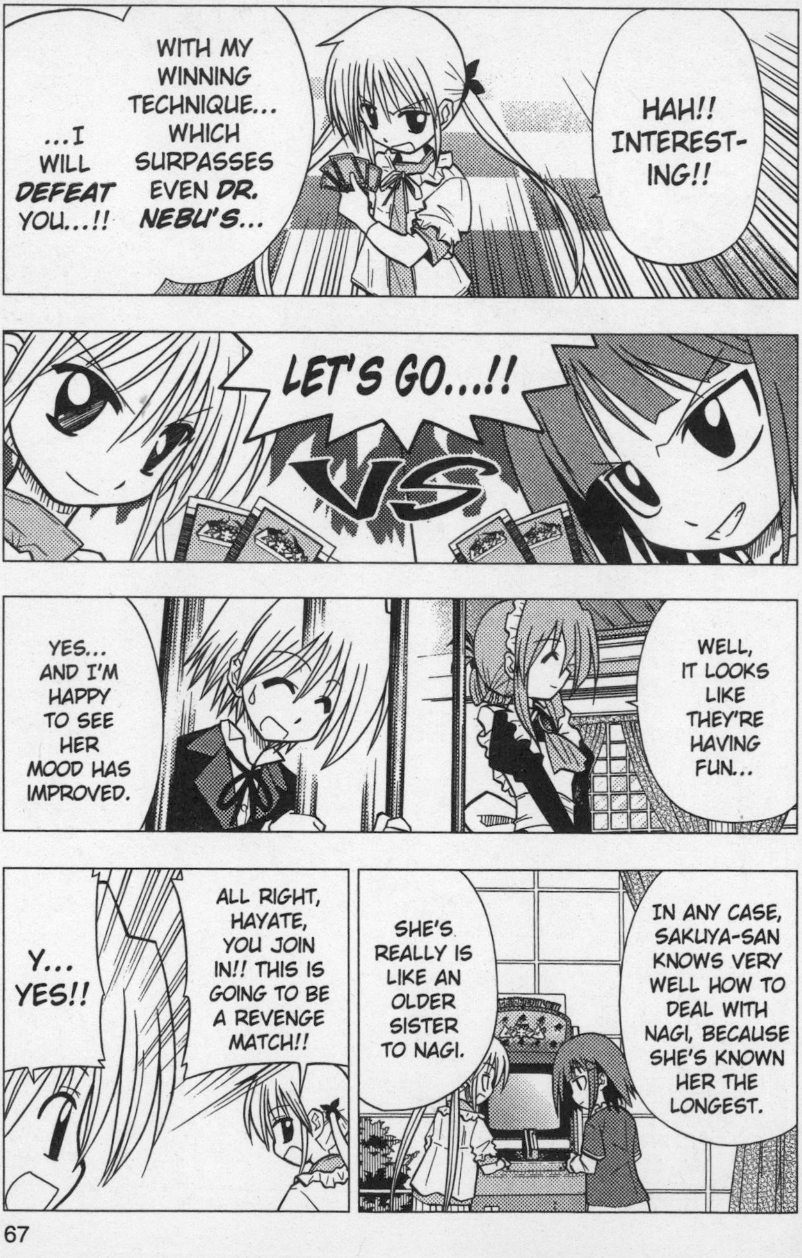
HAH!! INTEREST-ING!!
WITH MY WINNING TECHNIQUE... WHICH SURPASSES EVEN DR. NEBU'S...
...I WILL DEFEAT YOU...!!
LET'S GO...!!
VS
WELL, IT LOOKS LIKE THEY'RE HAVING FUN...
YES... AND I'M HAPPY TO SEE HER MOOD HAS IMPROVED.
IN ANY CASE, SAKUYA-SAN KNOWS VERY WELL HOW TO DEAL WITH NAGI, BECAUSE SHE'S KNOWN HER THE LONGEST.
SHE'S REALLY IS LIKE AN OLDER SISTER TO NAGI.
ALL RIGHT, HAYATE, YOU JOIN IN!! THIS IS GOING TO BE A REVENGE MATCH!!
Y... YES!!

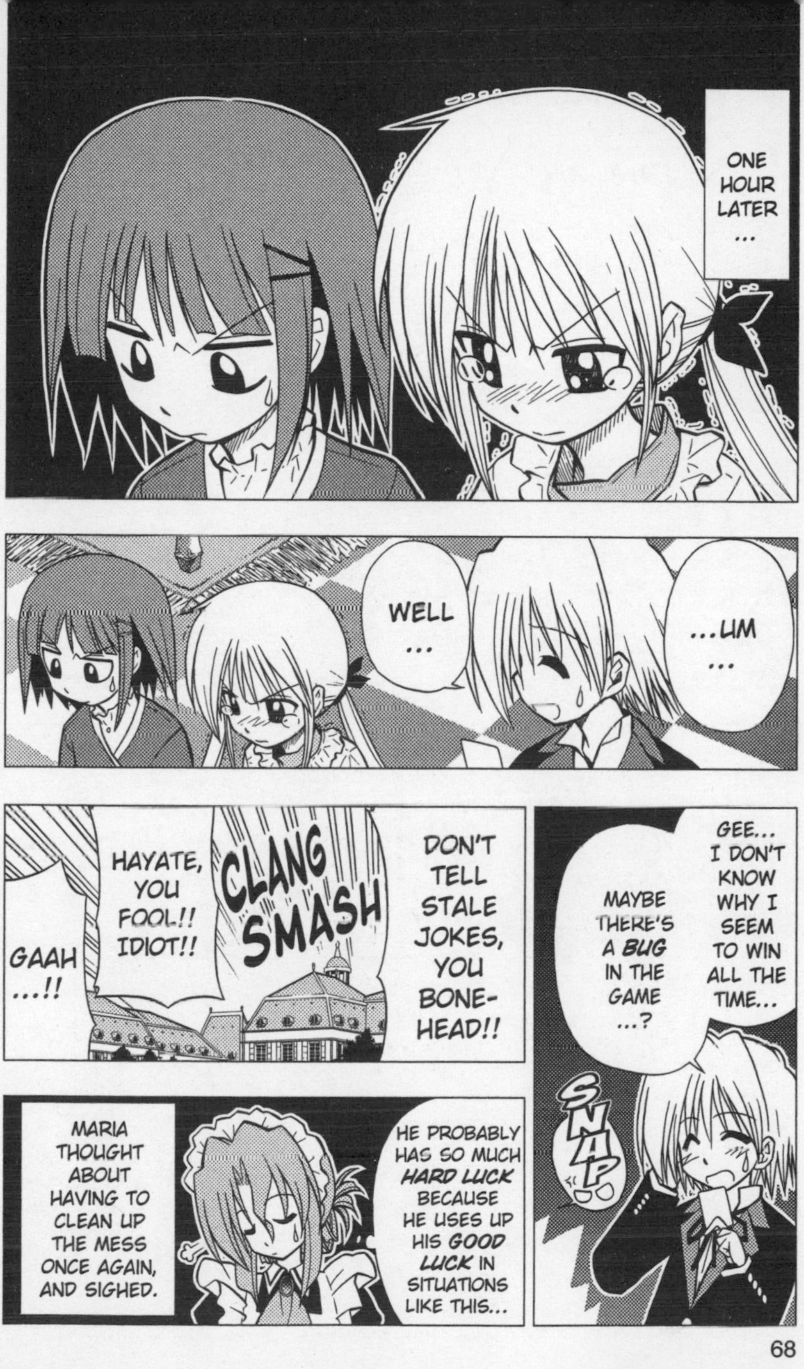
ONE HOUR LATER ...
...UM ...
WELL ...
GEE... I DON'T KNOW WHY I SEEM TO WIN ALL THE TIME...
MAYBE THERE'S A *BUG* IN THE GAME ...?
SNAP
DON'T TELL STALE JOKES, YOU BONE-HEAD!!
CLANG SMASH
HAYATE, YOU FOOL!! IDIOT!!
GAAH ...!!
HE PROBABLY HAS SO MUCH *HARD LUCK* BECAUSE HE USES UP HIS *GOOD LUCK* IN SITUATIONS LIKE THIS...
MARIA THOUGHT ABOUT HAVING TO CLEAN UP THE MESS ONCE AGAIN, AND SIGHED.

Episode 5:
"A Nuisance,
Even for Peter Pan"

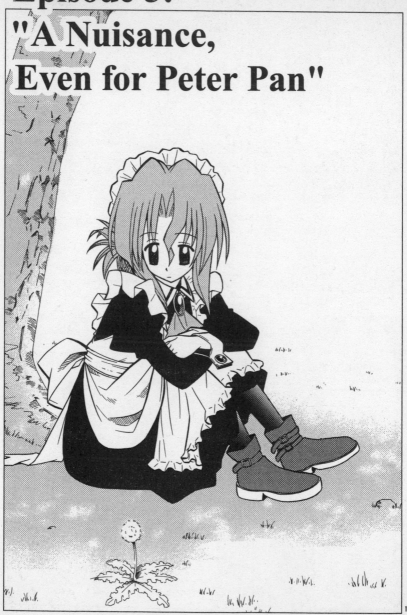

1

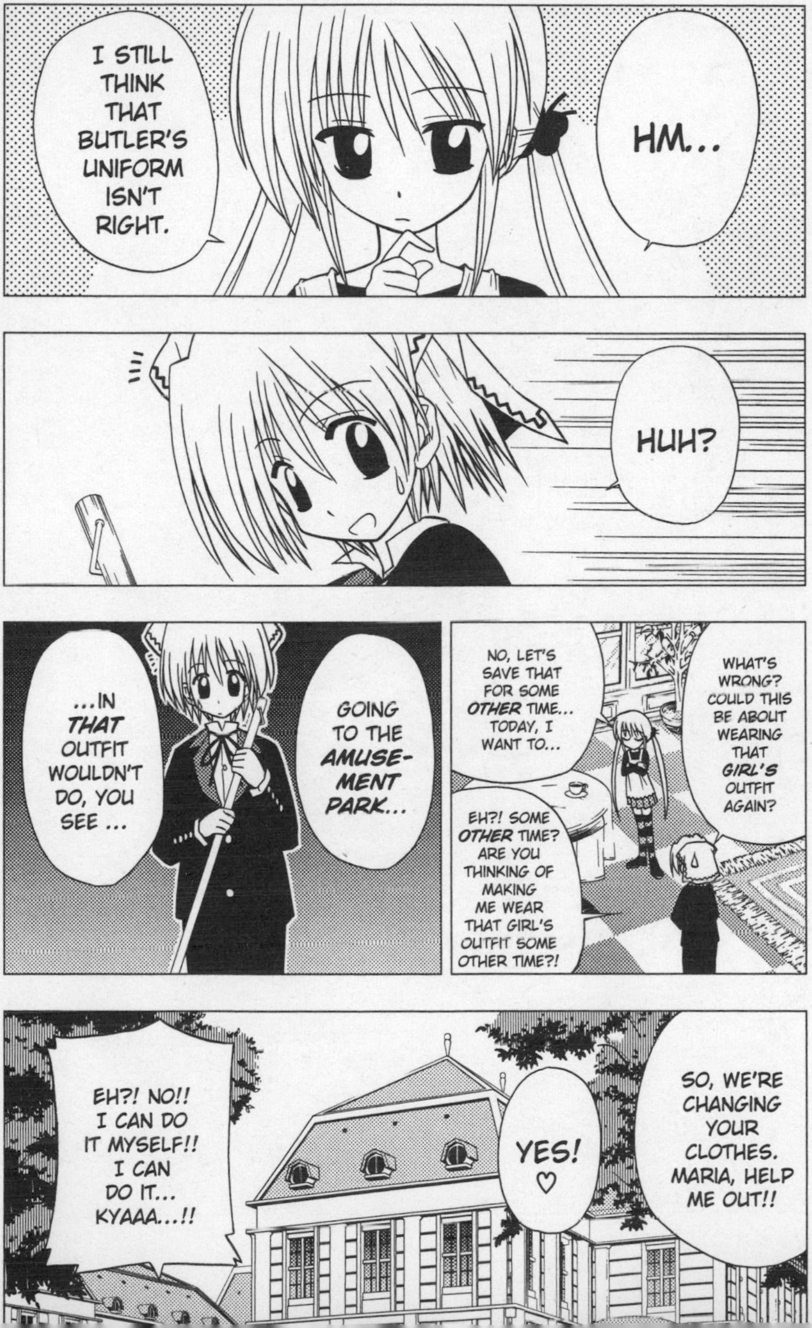
HM...
I STILL THINK THAT BUTLER'S UNIFORM ISN'T RIGHT.
HUH?
WHAT'S WRONG? COULD THIS BE ABOUT WEARING THAT GIRL'S OUTFIT AGAIN?
NO, LET'S SAVE THAT FOR SOME OTHER TIME... TODAY, I WANT TO...
EH?! SOME OTHER TIME? ARE YOU THINKING OF MAKING ME WEAR THAT GIRL'S OUTFIT SOME OTHER TIME?!
GOING TO THE AMUSEMENT PARK...
...IN THAT OUTFIT WOULDN'T DO, YOU SEE ...
SO, WE'RE CHANGING YOUR CLOTHES. MARIA, HELP ME OUT!!
YES! ♡
EH?! NO!! I CAN DO IT MYSELF!! I CAN DO IT... KYAAA...!!

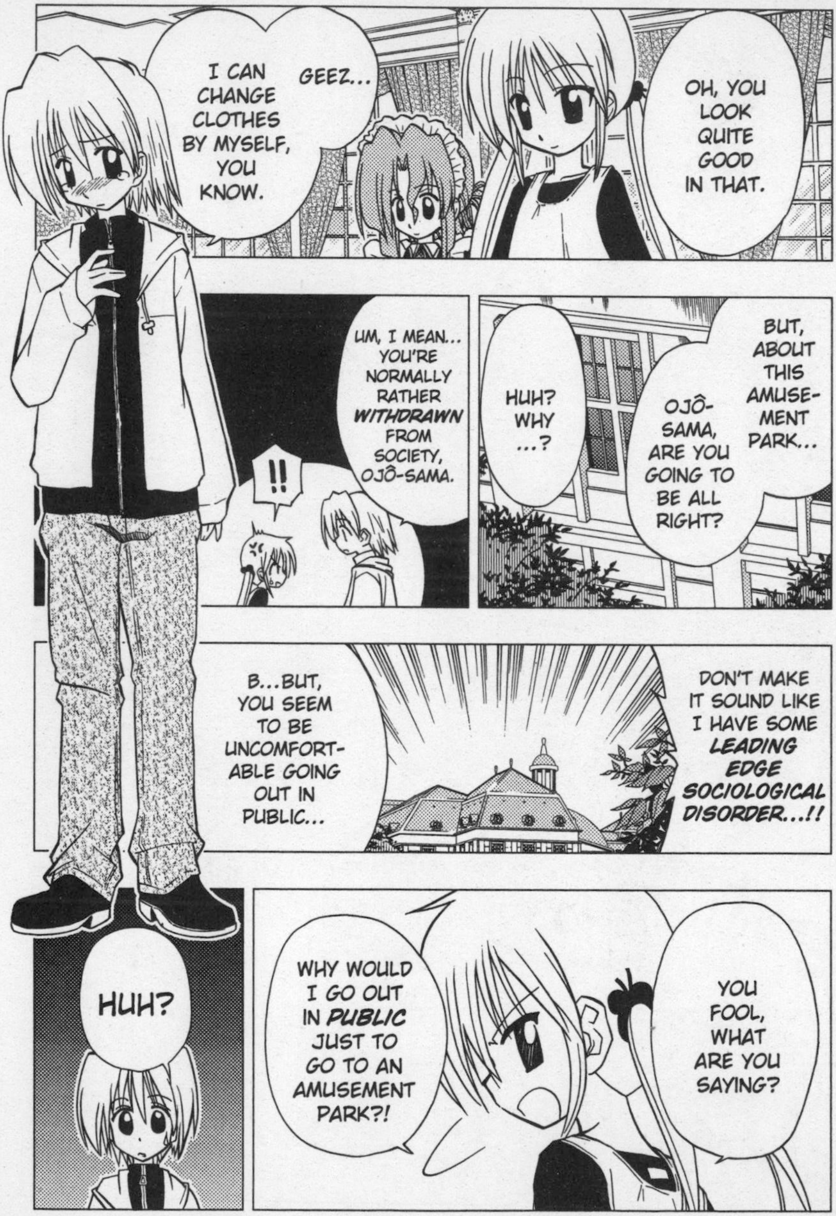
OH, YOU LOOK QUITE GOOD IN THAT.
GEEZ...
I CAN CHANGE CLOTHES BY MYSELF, YOU KNOW.
BUT, ABOUT THIS AMUSEMENT PARK...
OJÔ-SAMA, ARE YOU GOING TO BE ALL RIGHT?
HUH? WHY ...?
UM, I MEAN... YOU'RE NORMALLY RATHER *WITHDRAWN* FROM SOCIETY, OJÔ-SAMA.
!!
DON'T MAKE IT SOUND LIKE I HAVE SOME *LEADING EDGE SOCIOLOGICAL DISORDER...!!*
B...BUT, YOU SEEM TO BE UNCOMFORTABLE GOING OUT IN PUBLIC...
YOU FOOL, WHAT ARE YOU SAYING?
WHY WOULD I GO OUT IN *PUBLIC* JUST TO GO TO AN AMUSEMENT PARK?!
HUH?

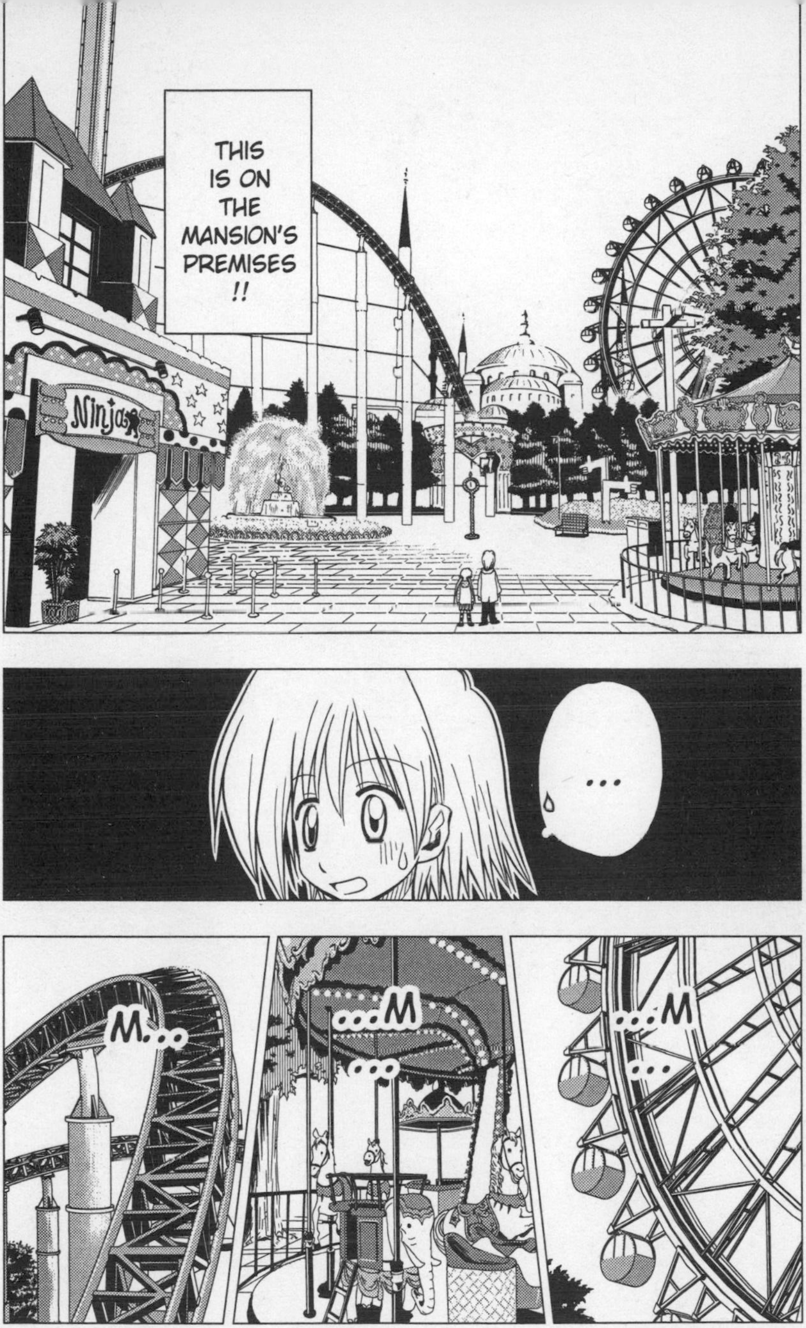
THIS IS ON THE MANSION'S PREMISES !!
Ninja
...
...M
...
...M
...
M...

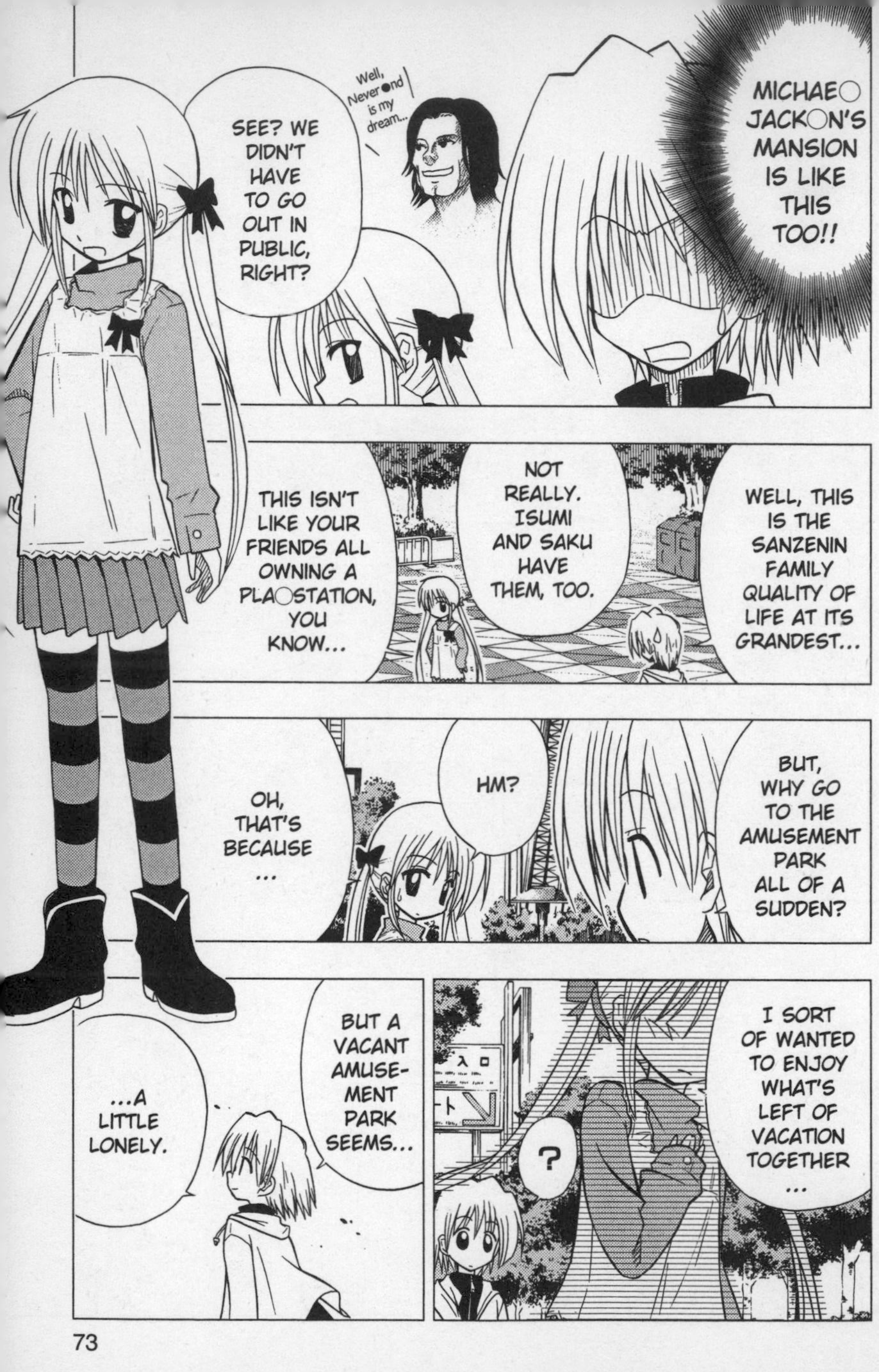
MICHAE○ JACK○N'S MANSION IS LIKE THIS TOO!!
Well, Never●nd is my dream...
SEE? WE DIDN'T HAVE TO GO OUT IN PUBLIC, RIGHT?
WELL, THIS IS THE SANZENIN FAMILY QUALITY OF LIFE AT ITS GRANDEST...
NOT REALLY. ISUMI AND SAKU HAVE THEM, TOO.
THIS ISN'T LIKE YOUR FRIENDS ALL OWNING A PLA○STATION, YOU KNOW...
BUT, WHY GO TO THE AMUSEMENT PARK ALL OF A SUDDEN?
HM?
OH, THAT'S BECAUSE ...
I SORT OF WANTED TO ENJOY WHAT'S LEFT OF VACATION TOGETHER ...
?
BUT A VACANT AMUSEMENT PARK SEEMS...
...A LITTLE LONELY.

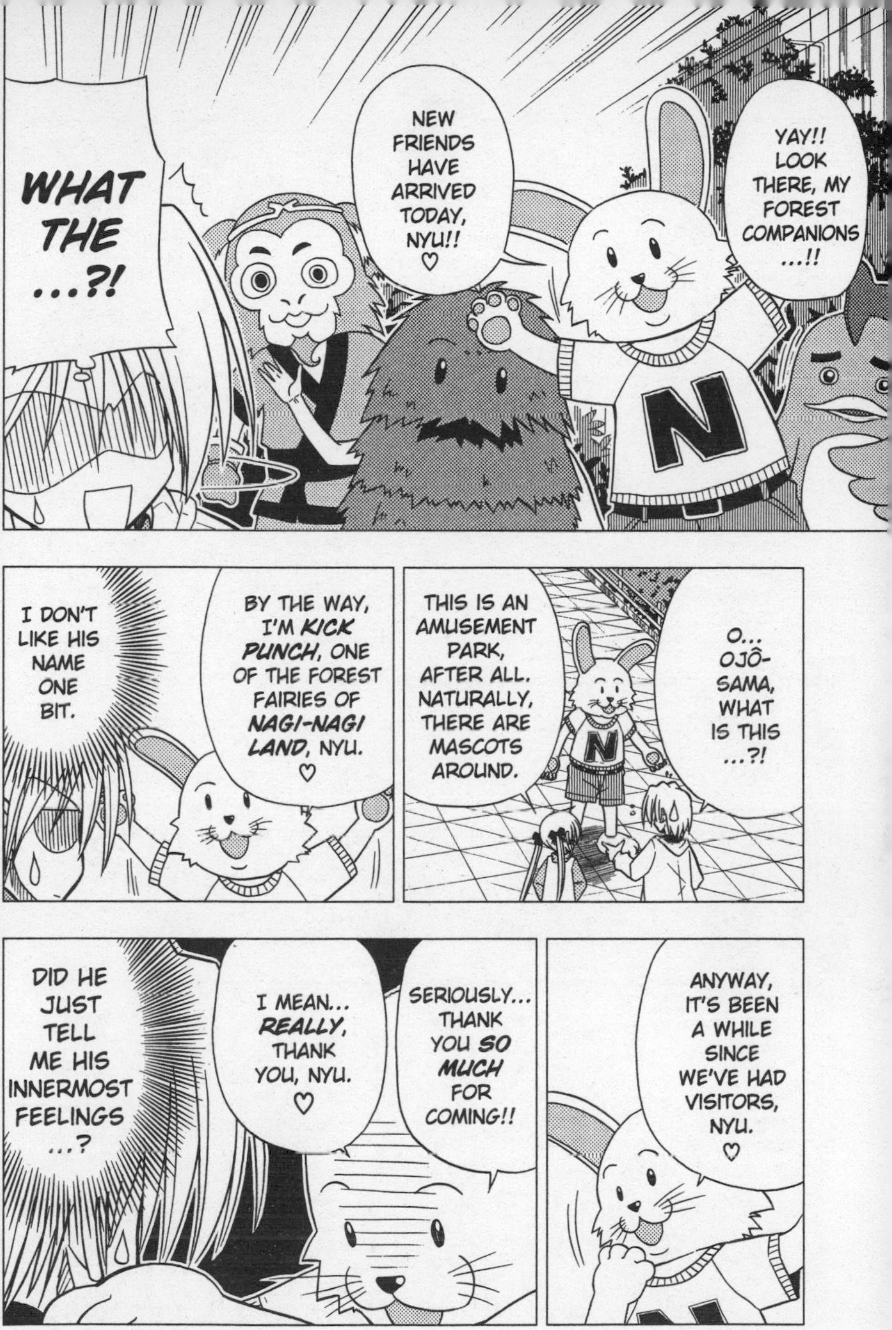
YAY!! LOOK THERE, MY FOREST COMPANIONS ...!!
NEW FRIENDS HAVE ARRIVED TODAY, NYU!! ♡
WHAT THE ...?!
O... OJÔ-SAMA, WHAT IS THIS ...?!
THIS IS AN AMUSEMENT PARK, AFTER ALL. NATURALLY, THERE ARE MASCOTS AROUND.
BY THE WAY, I'M KICK PUNCH, ONE OF THE FOREST FAIRIES OF NAGI-NAGI LAND, NYU. ♡
I DON'T LIKE HIS NAME ONE BIT.
ANYWAY, IT'S BEEN A WHILE SINCE WE'VE HAD VISITORS, NYU. ♡
SERIOUSLY... THANK YOU SO MUCH FOR COMING!!
I MEAN... REALLY, THANK YOU, NYU. ♡
DID HE JUST TELL ME HIS INNERMOST FEELINGS ...?

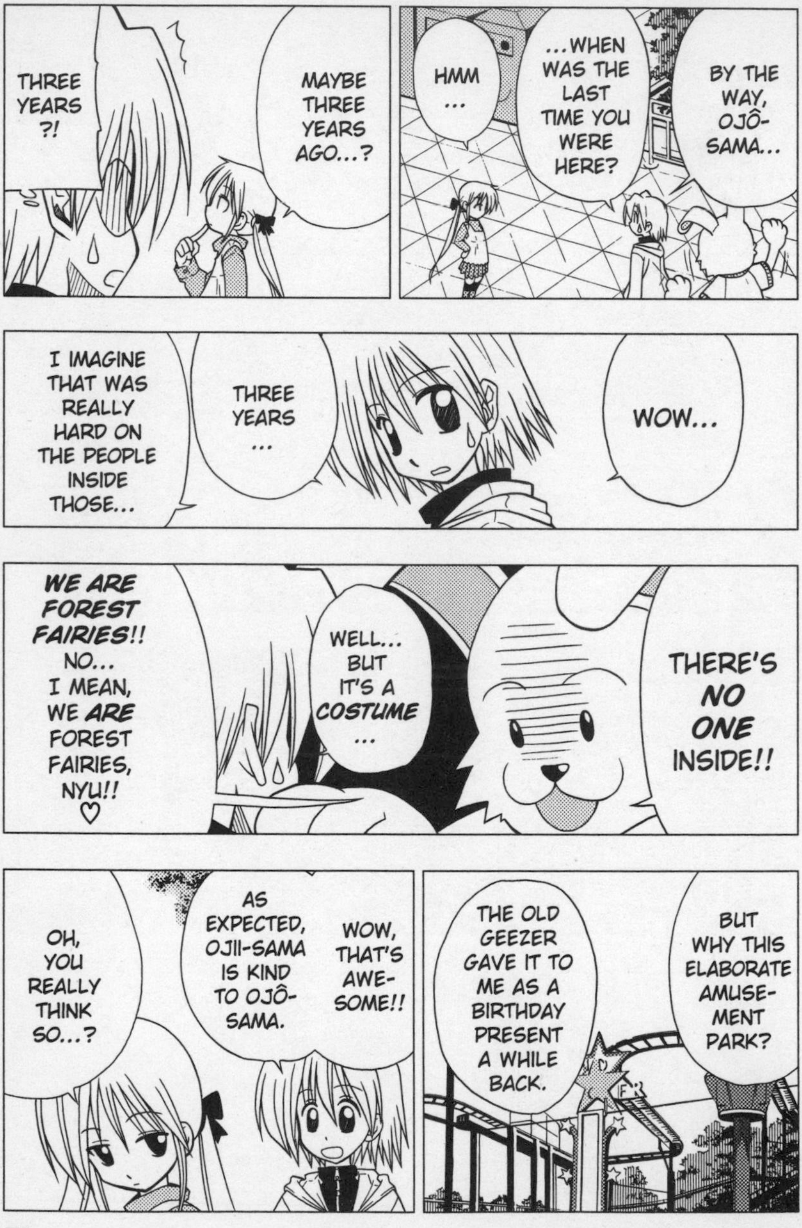
BY THE WAY, OJÔ-SAMA...
...WHEN WAS THE LAST TIME YOU WERE HERE?
HMM ...
MAYBE THREE YEARS AGO...?
THREE YEARS ?!
WOW...
THREE YEARS ...
I IMAGINE THAT WAS REALLY HARD ON THE PEOPLE INSIDE THOSE...
THERE'S NO ONE INSIDE!!
WELL... BUT IT'S A COSTUME ...
WE ARE FOREST FAIRIES!! NO... I MEAN, WE ARE FOREST FAIRIES, NYU!! ♡
BUT WHY THIS ELABORATE AMUSEMENT PARK?
THE OLD GEEZER GAVE IT TO ME AS A BIRTHDAY PRESENT A WHILE BACK.
WOW, THAT'S AWESOME!!
AS EXPECTED, OJII-SAMA IS KIND TO OJÔ-SAMA.
OH, YOU REALLY THINK SO...?

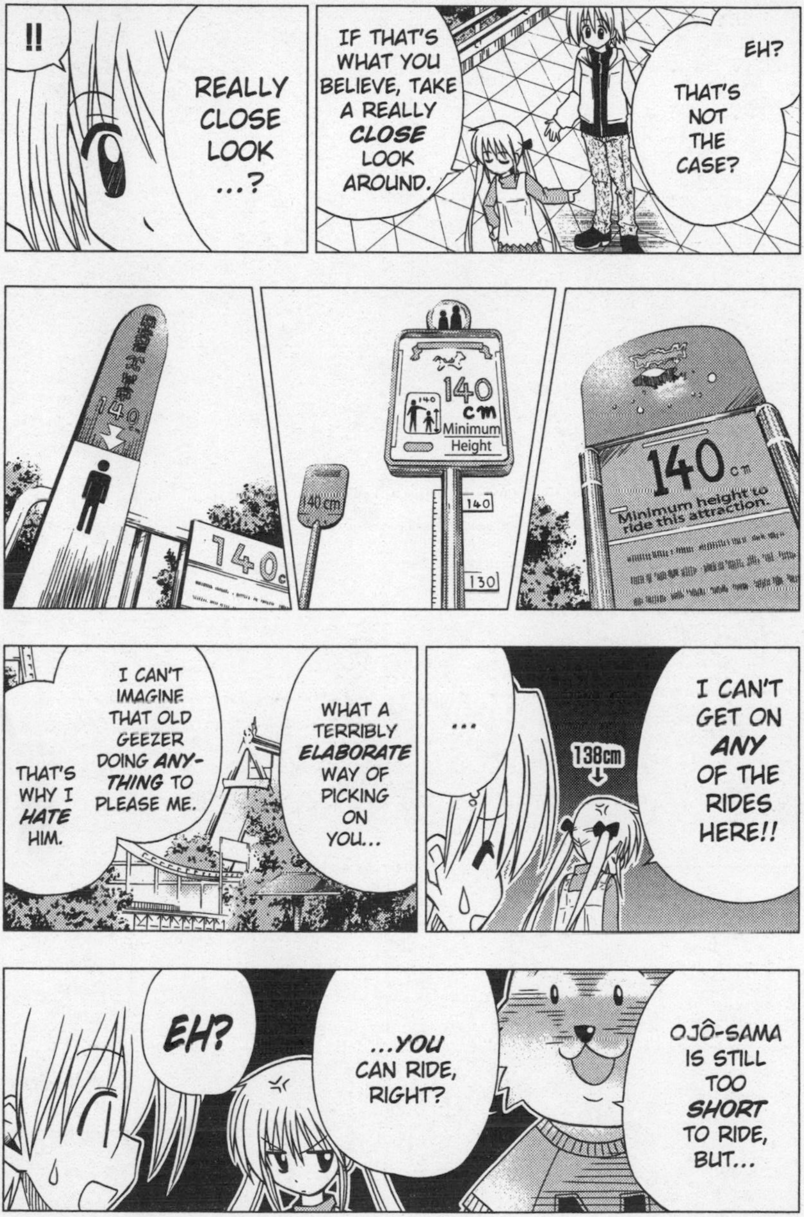
EH?
THAT'S NOT THE CASE?
IF THAT'S WHAT YOU BELIEVE, TAKE A REALLY CLOSE LOOK AROUND.
REALLY CLOSE LOOK ...?
!!
140 cm
Minimum height to ride this attraction.
140 cm Minimum Height
140
130
140 cm
140
140
I CAN'T GET ON ANY OF THE RIDES HERE!!
138cm
...
WHAT A TERRIBLY ELABORATE WAY OF PICKING ON YOU...
I CAN'T IMAGINE THAT OLD GEEZER DOING ANYTHING TO PLEASE ME.
THAT'S WHY I HATE HIM.
OJÔ-SAMA IS STILL TOO SHORT TO RIDE, BUT...
...YOU CAN RIDE, RIGHT?
EH?

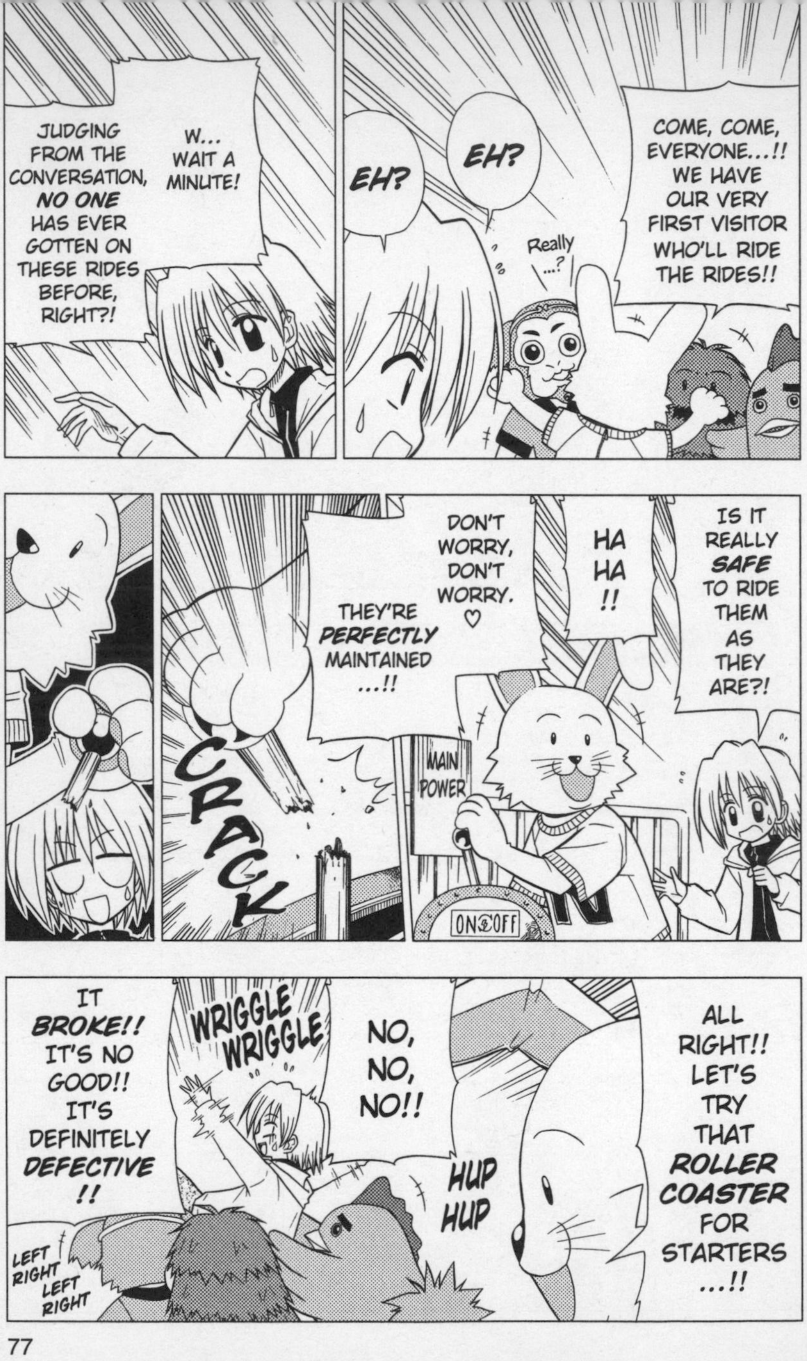
COME, COME, EVERYONE...!! WE HAVE OUR VERY FIRST VISITOR WHO'LL RIDE THE RIDES!!
EH?
EH?
Really ...?
W... WAIT A MINUTE!
JUDGING FROM THE CONVERSATION, NO ONE HAS EVER GOTTEN ON THESE RIDES BEFORE, RIGHT?!
IS IT REALLY SAFE TO RIDE THEM AS THEY ARE?!
HA HA!!
DON'T WORRY, DON'T WORRY. ♡
THEY'RE PERFECTLY MAINTAINED ...!!
MAIN POWER
ON OFF
CRACK
ALL RIGHT!! LET'S TRY THAT ROLLER COASTER FOR STARTERS ...!!
HUP HUP
NO, NO, NO!!
WRIGGLE WRIGGLE
IT BROKE!! IT'S NO GOOD!! IT'S DEFINITELY DEFECTIVE !!
LEFT RIGHT LEFT RIGHT

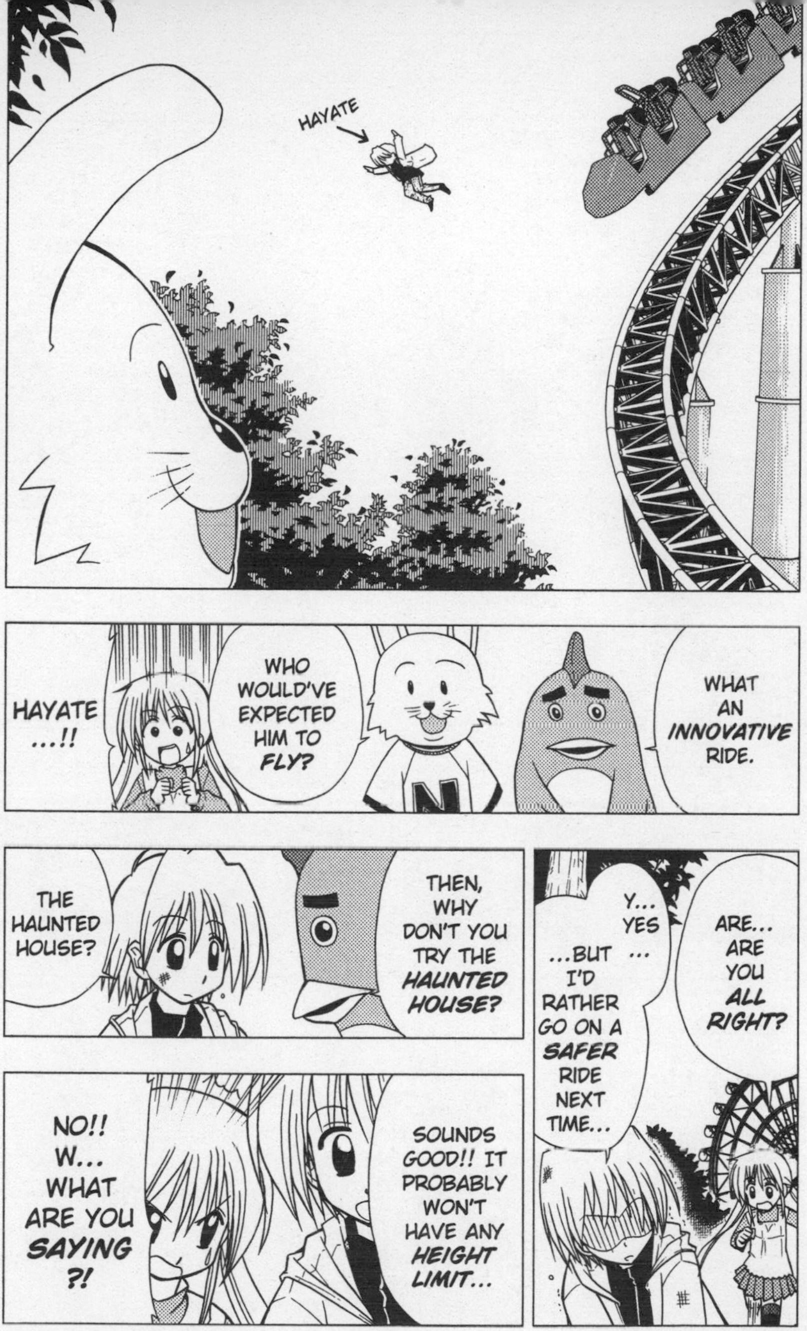
HAYATE
WHAT AN INNOVATIVE RIDE.
WHO WOULD'VE EXPECTED HIM TO FLY?
HAYATE ...!!
ARE... ARE YOU ALL RIGHT?
Y... YES ...
...BUT I'D RATHER GO ON A SAFER RIDE NEXT TIME...
THEN, WHY DON'T YOU TRY THE HAUNTED HOUSE?
THE HAUNTED HOUSE?
SOUNDS GOOD!! IT PROBABLY WON'T HAVE ANY HEIGHT LIMIT...
NO!! W... WHAT ARE YOU SAYING ?!

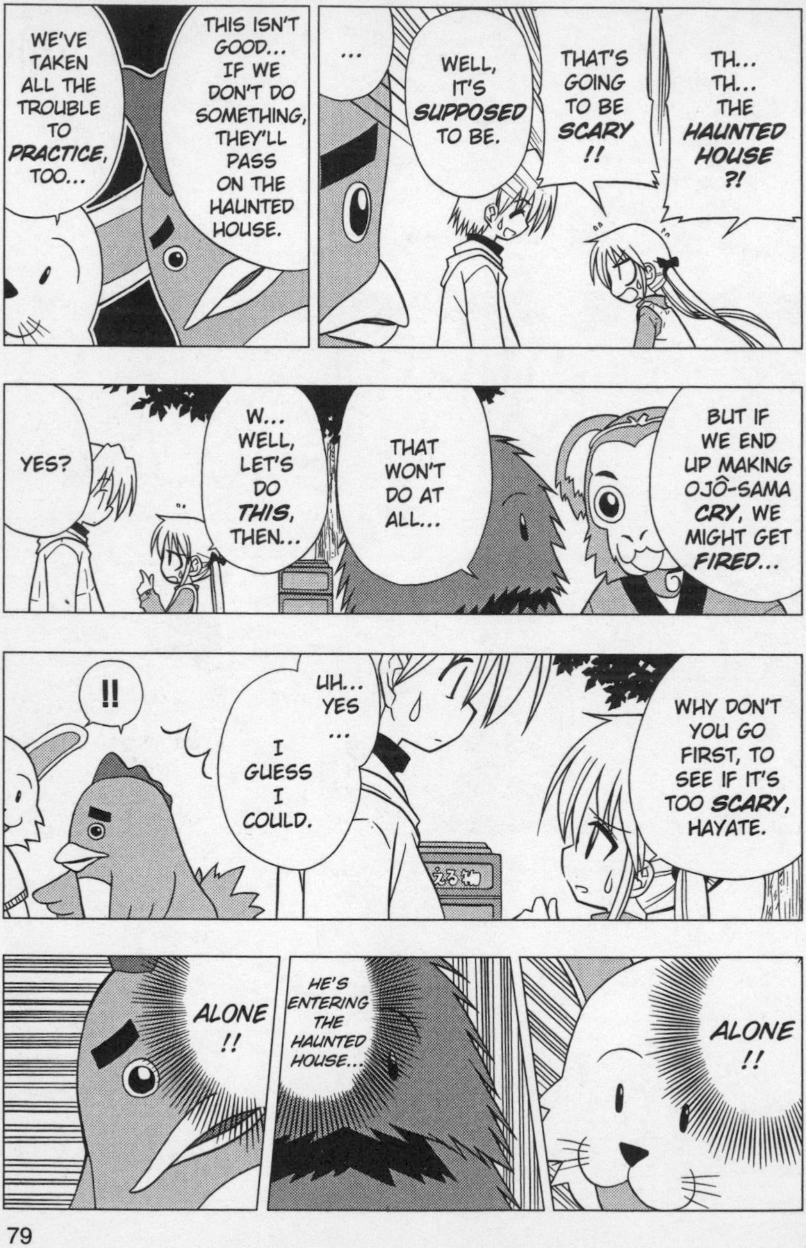
TH... TH... THE HAUNTED HOUSE ?!
THAT'S GOING TO BE SCARY !!
WELL, IT'S SUPPOSED TO BE.
...
THIS ISN'T GOOD... IF WE DON'T DO SOMETHING, THEY'LL PASS ON THE HAUNTED HOUSE.
WE'VE TAKEN ALL THE TROUBLE TO PRACTICE, TOO...
BUT IF WE END UP MAKING OJÔ-SAMA CRY, WE MIGHT GET FIRED...
THAT WON'T DO AT ALL...
W... WELL, LET'S DO THIS, THEN...
YES?
WHY DON'T YOU GO FIRST, TO SEE IF IT'S TOO SCARY, HAYATE.
UH... YES ... I GUESS I COULD.
!!
ALONE !!
HE'S ENTERING THE HAUNTED HOUSE...
ALONE !!

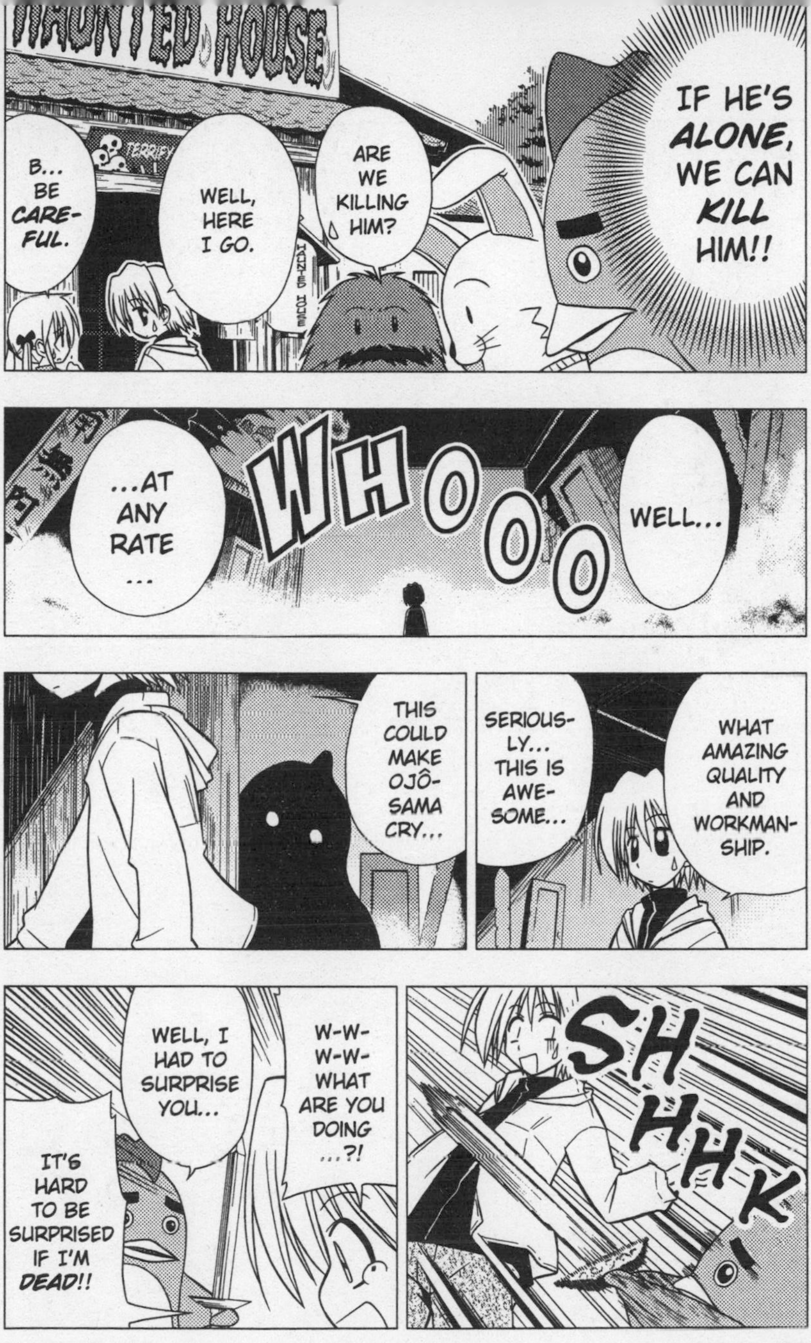
HAUNTED HOUSE
IF HE'S ALONE, WE CAN KILL HIM!!
ARE WE KILLING HIM?
HAUNTED HOUSE
WELL, HERE I GO.
B... BE CAREFUL.
WELL...
WHOOOO
...AT ANY RATE ...
WHAT AMAZING QUALITY AND WORKMANSHIP.
SERIOUSLY... THIS IS AWESOME...
THIS COULD MAKE OJÔ-SAMA CRY...
SHHHK
W-W-W-W-WHAT ARE YOU DOING ...?!
WELL, I HAD TO SURPRISE YOU...
IT'S HARD TO BE SURPRISED IF I'M DEAD!!

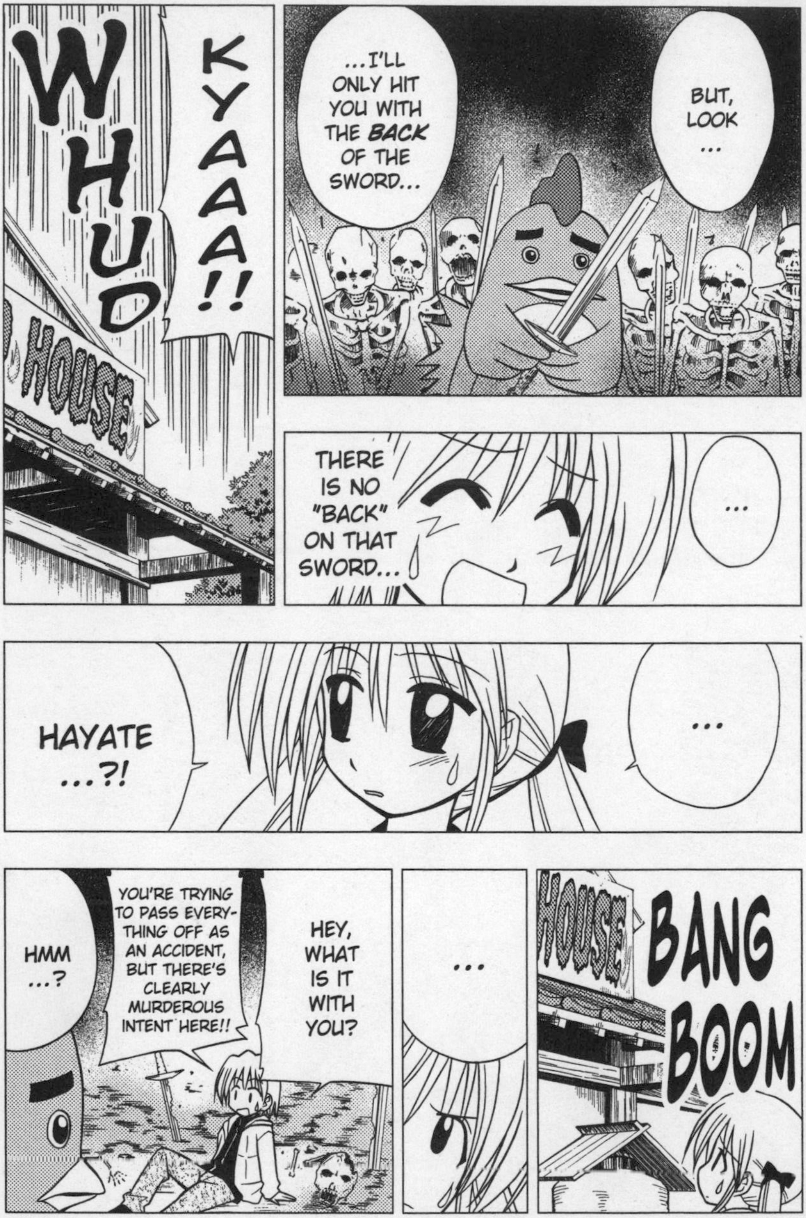

BUT, LOOK ...
...I'LL ONLY HIT YOU WITH THE *BACK* OF THE SWORD...
...
THERE IS NO "BACK" ON THAT SWORD...
KYAAA!!
WHUD
HOUSE
...
HAYATE ...?!
BANG BOOM
HOUSE
...
HEY, WHAT IS IT WITH YOU?
YOU'RE TRYING TO PASS EVERY-THING OFF AS AN ACCIDENT, BUT THERE'S CLEARLY MURDEROUS INTENT HERE!!
HMM ...?

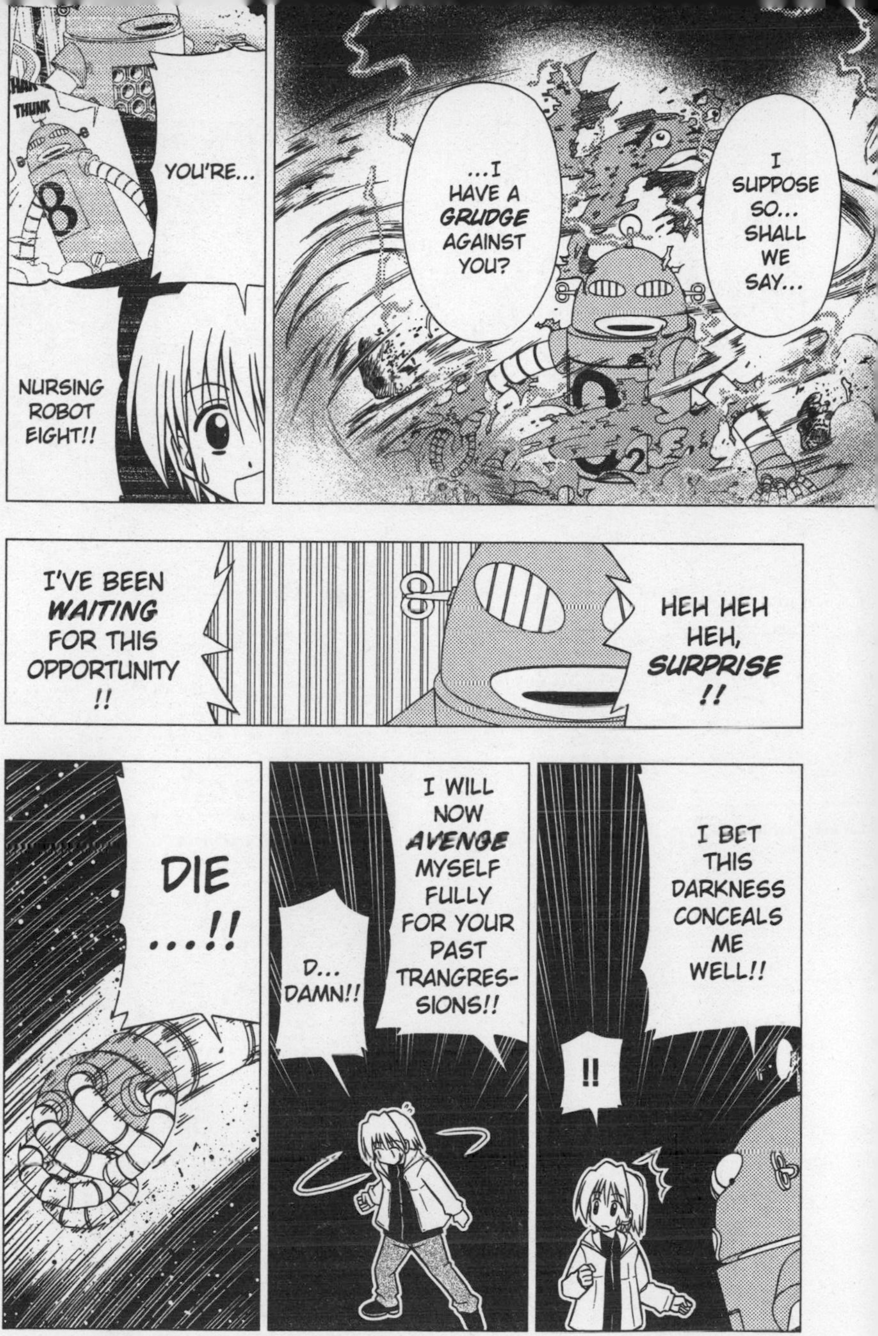
I SUPPOSE SO... SHALL WE SAY...
...I HAVE A GRUDGE AGAINST YOU?
THUNK
YOU'RE...
NURSING ROBOT EIGHT!!
HEH HEH HEH, SURPRISE!!
I'VE BEEN WAITING FOR THIS OPPORTUNITY!!
I BET THIS DARKNESS CONCEALS ME WELL!!
!!
I WILL NOW AVENGE MYSELF FULLY FOR YOUR PAST TRANGRES-SIONS!!
D... DAMN!!
DIE...!!

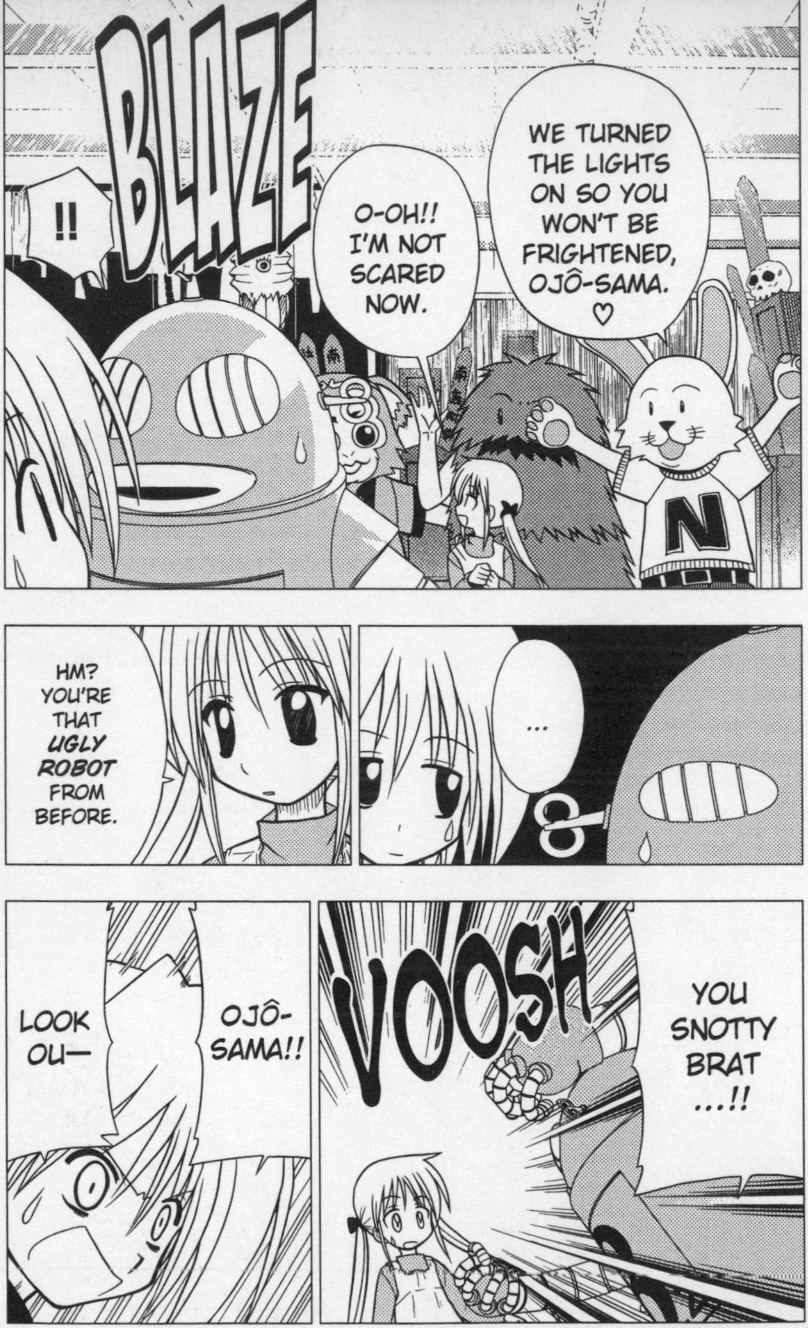
WE TURNED THE LIGHTS ON SO YOU WON'T BE FRIGHTENED, OJÔ-SAMA. ♡
O-OH!! I'M NOT SCARED NOW.
BLAZE
!!
...
HM? YOU'RE THAT *UGLY ROBOT* FROM BEFORE.
YOU SNOTTY BRAT ...!!
VOOSH
OJÔ-SAMA!!
LOOK OU—

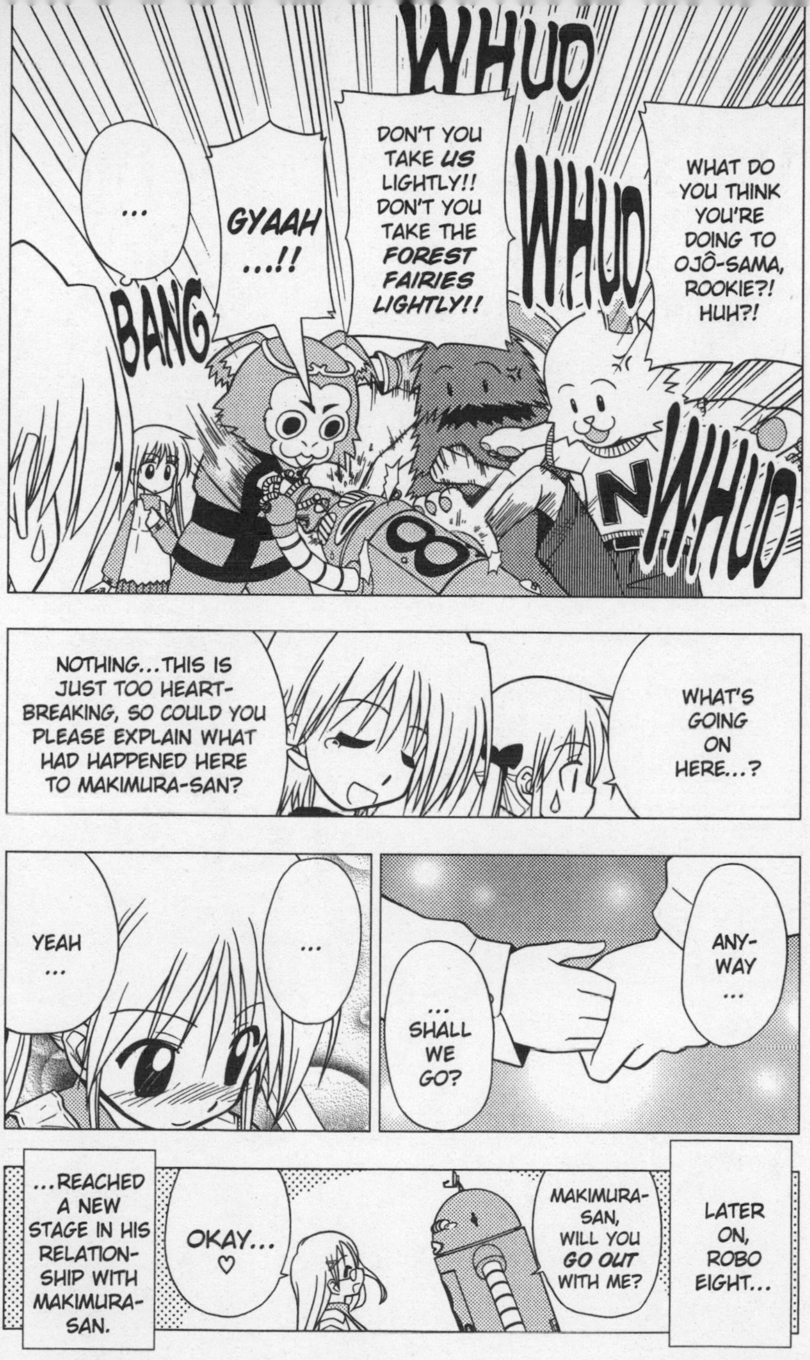
WHAT DO YOU THINK YOU'RE DOING TO OJÔ-SAMA, ROOKIE?! HUH?!
WHUD
WHUD
WHUD
DON'T YOU TAKE *US* LIGHTLY!! DON'T YOU TAKE THE *FOREST FAIRIES LIGHTLY!!*
GYAAH ...!!
...
BANG
WHAT'S GOING ON HERE...?
NOTHING...THIS IS JUST TOO HEART-BREAKING, SO COULD YOU PLEASE EXPLAIN WHAT HAD HAPPENED HERE TO MAKIMURA-SAN?
ANY-WAY ...
... SHALL WE GO?
...
YEAH ...
LATER ON, ROBO EIGHT...
MAKIMURA-SAN, WILL YOU *GO OUT* WITH ME?
OKAY... ♡
...REACHED A NEW STAGE IN HIS RELATION-SHIP WITH MAKIMURA-SAN.

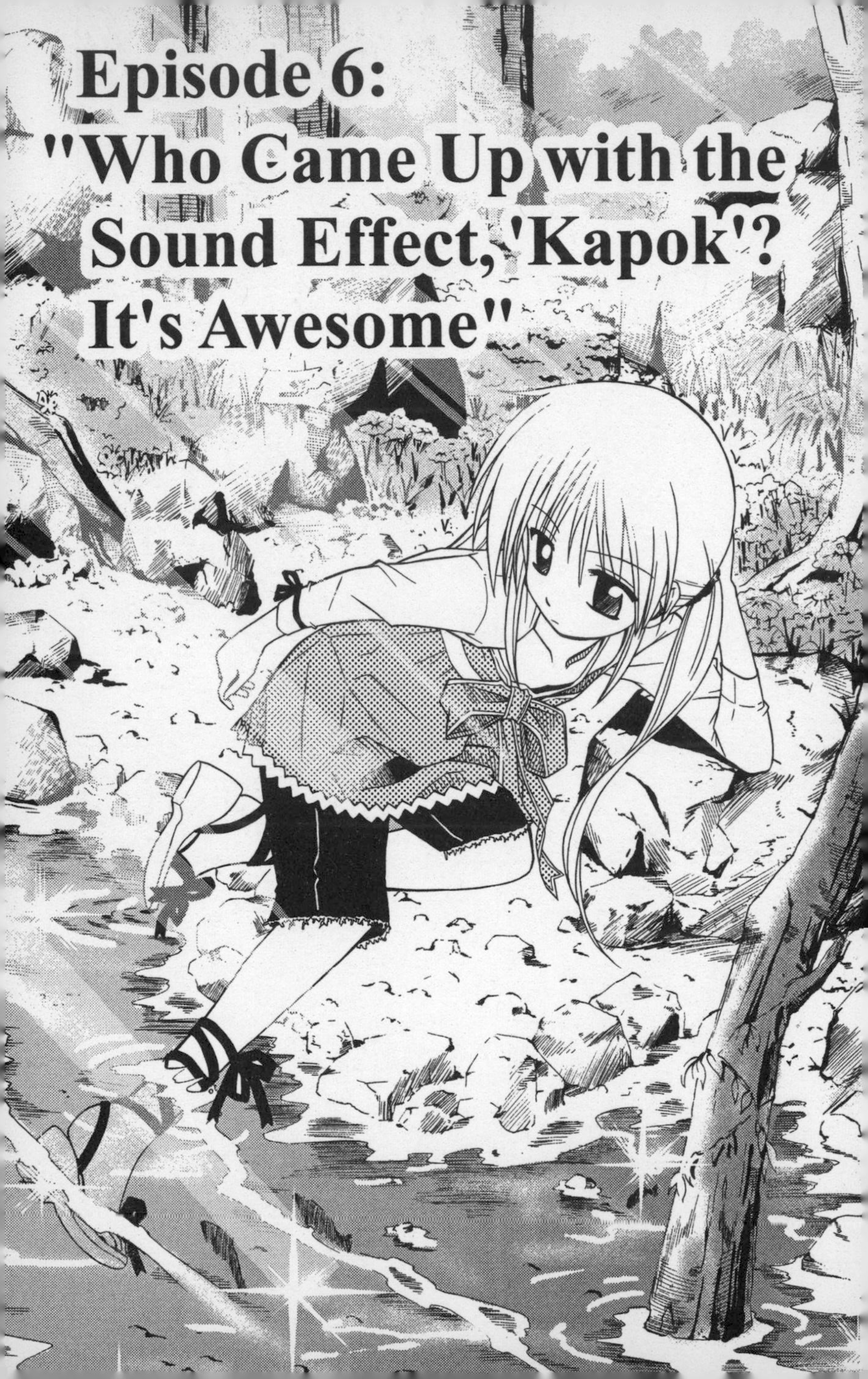
Episode 6:
"Who Came Up with the Sound Effect, 'Kapok'? It's Awesome"

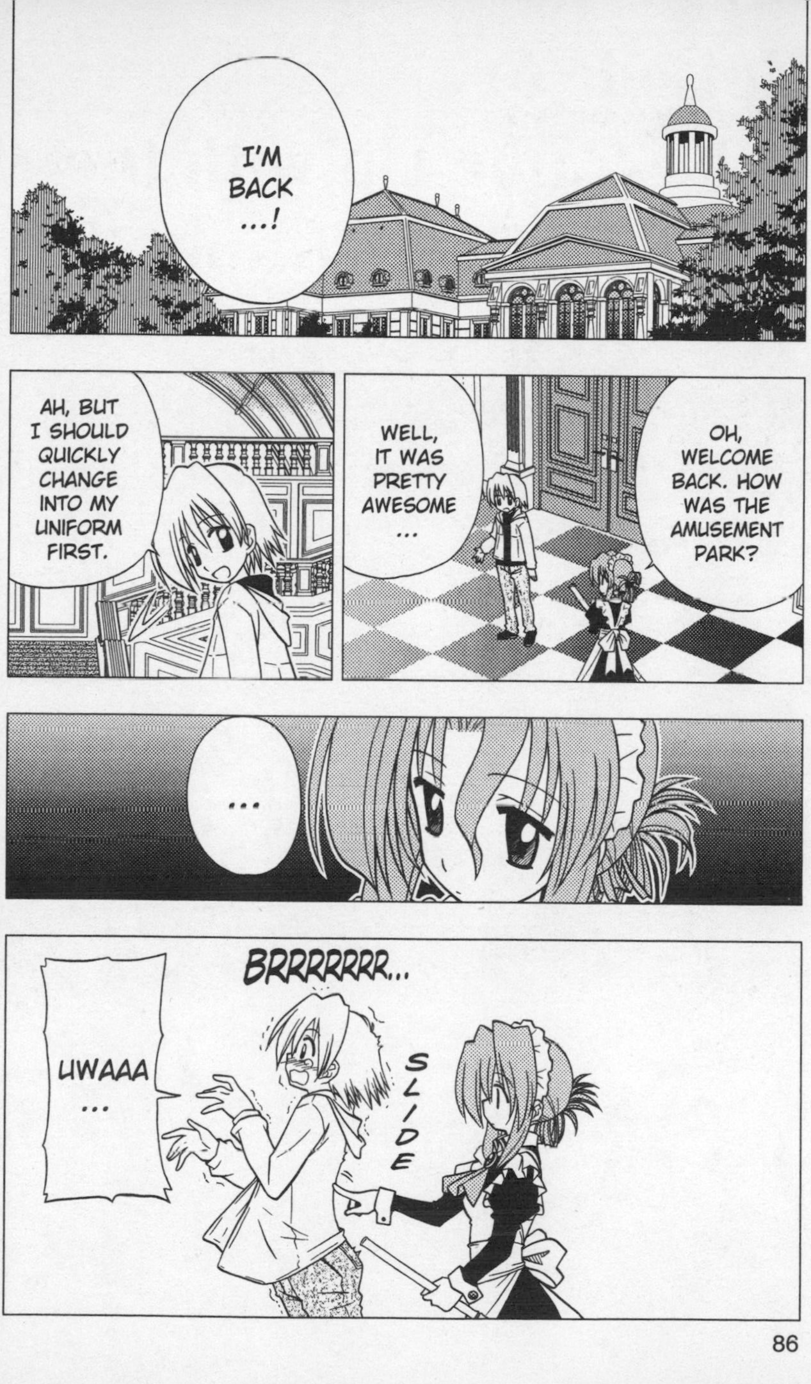
I'M BACK ...!
OH, WELCOME BACK. HOW WAS THE AMUSEMENT PARK?
WELL, IT WAS PRETTY AWESOME ...
AH, BUT I SHOULD QUICKLY CHANGE INTO MY UNIFORM FIRST.
...
BRRRRRRR...
SLIDE
UWAAA ...

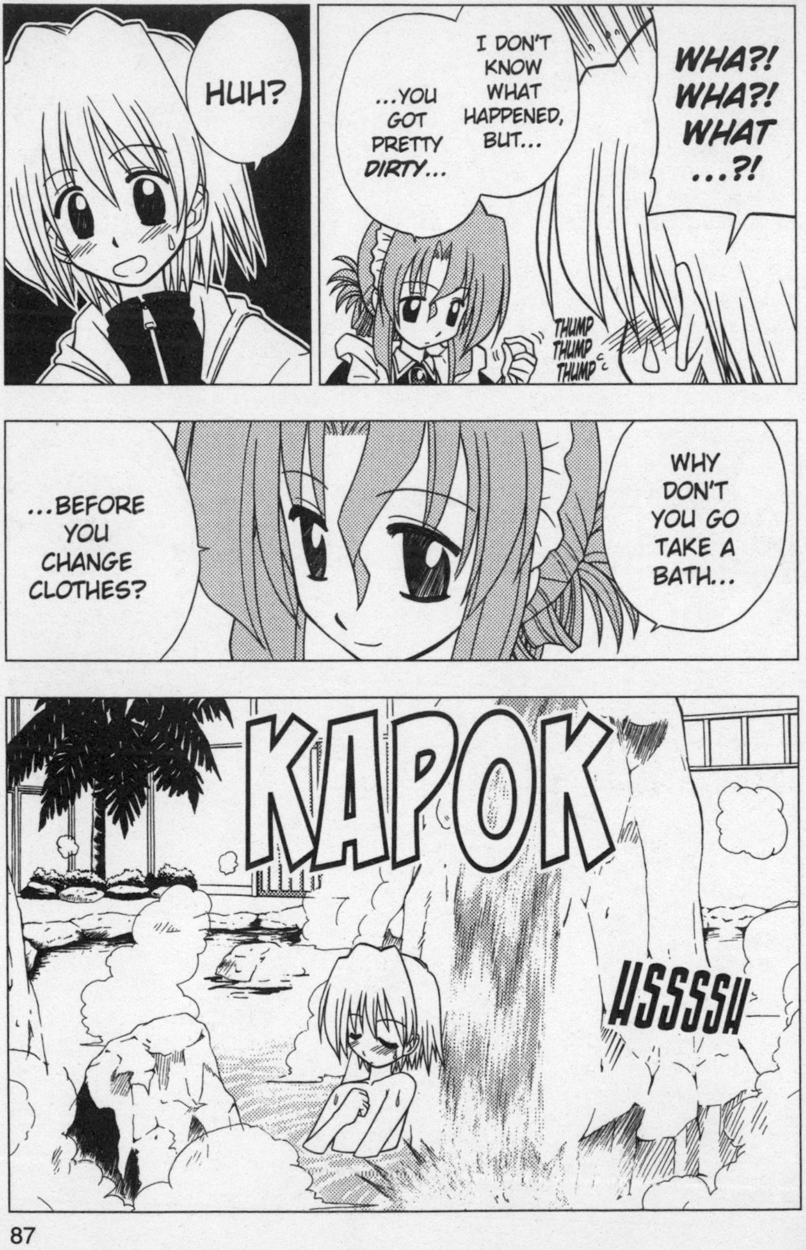
WHA?! WHA?! WHAT ...?!
I DON'T KNOW WHAT HAPPENED, BUT...
...YOU GOT PRETTY *DIRTY*...
THUMP THUMP THUMP
HUH?
WHY DON'T YOU GO TAKE A BATH...
...BEFORE YOU CHANGE CLOTHES?
KAPOK
HSSSSH

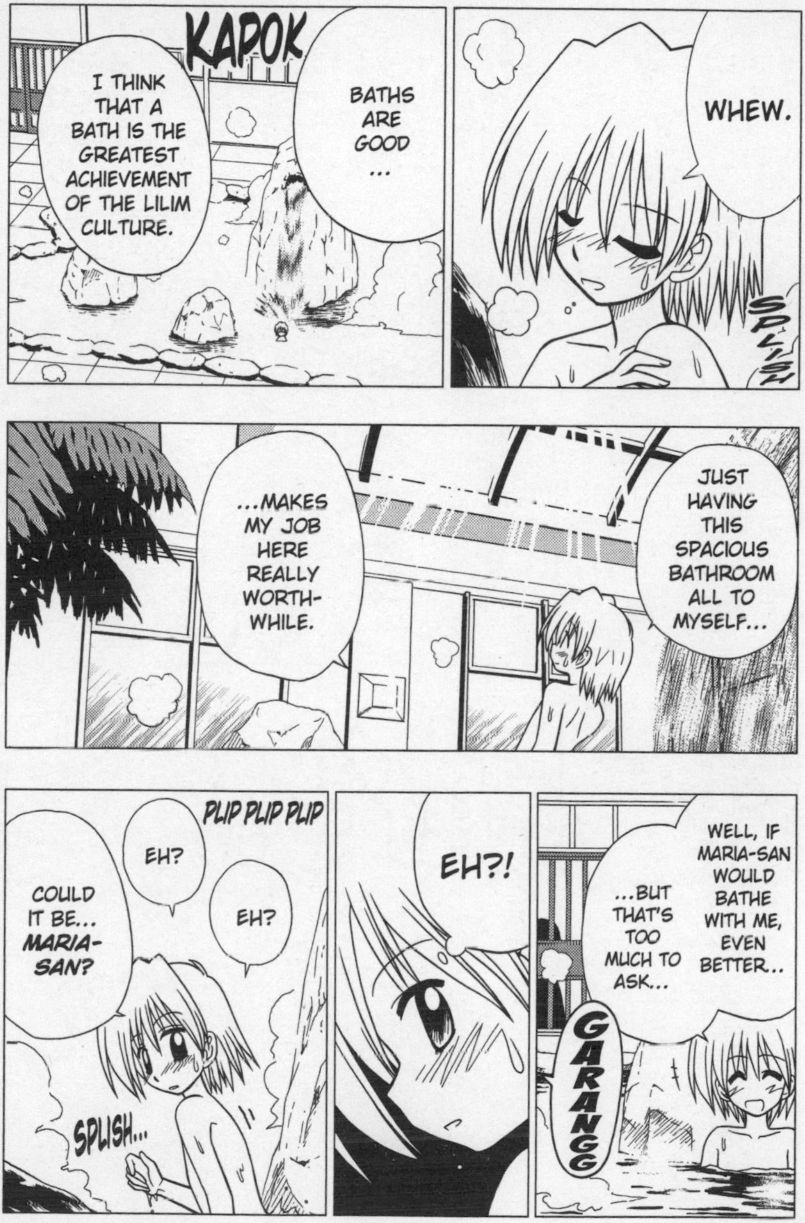
WHEW.
SPLISH
KAPOK
BATHS ARE GOOD ...
I THINK THAT A BATH IS THE GREATEST ACHIEVEMENT OF THE LILIM CULTURE.
JUST HAVING THIS SPACIOUS BATHROOM ALL TO MYSELF...
...MAKES MY JOB HERE REALLY WORTH-WHILE.
WELL, IF MARIA-SAN WOULD BATHE WITH ME, EVEN BETTER...
...BUT THAT'S TOO MUCH TO ASK...
GARANGG
EH?!
PLIP PLIP PLIP
EH?
EH?
COULD IT BE... MARIA-SAN?
SPLISH...

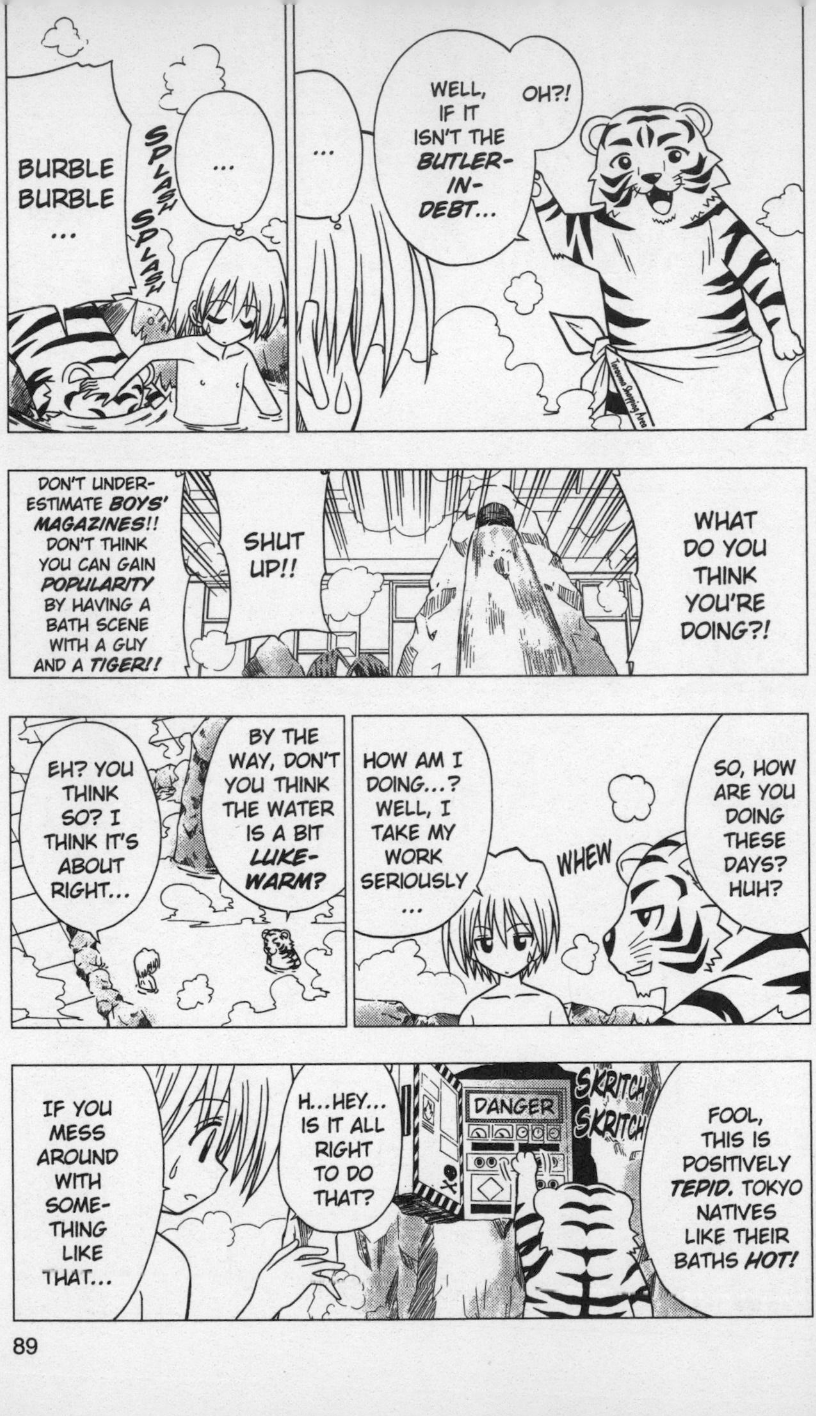

OH?!
WELL, IF IT ISN'T THE BUTLER-IN-DEBT...
...
...
SPLASH SPLASH
BURBLE BURBLE ...
WHAT DO YOU THINK YOU'RE DOING?!
SHUT UP!!
DON'T UNDER-ESTIMATE BOYS' MAGAZINES!! DON'T THINK YOU CAN GAIN POPULARITY BY HAVING A BATH SCENE WITH A GUY AND A TIGER!!
SO, HOW ARE YOU DOING THESE DAYS? HUH?
WHEW
HOW AM I DOING...? WELL, I TAKE MY WORK SERIOUSLY ...
BY THE WAY, DON'T YOU THINK THE WATER IS A BIT LUKE-WARM?
EH? YOU THINK SO? I THINK IT'S ABOUT RIGHT...
FOOL, THIS IS POSITIVELY TEPID. TOKYO NATIVES LIKE THEIR BATHS HOT!
SKRITCH SKRITCH
DANGER
H...HEY... IS IT ALL RIGHT TO DO THAT?
IF YOU MESS AROUND WITH SOME-THING LIKE THAT...

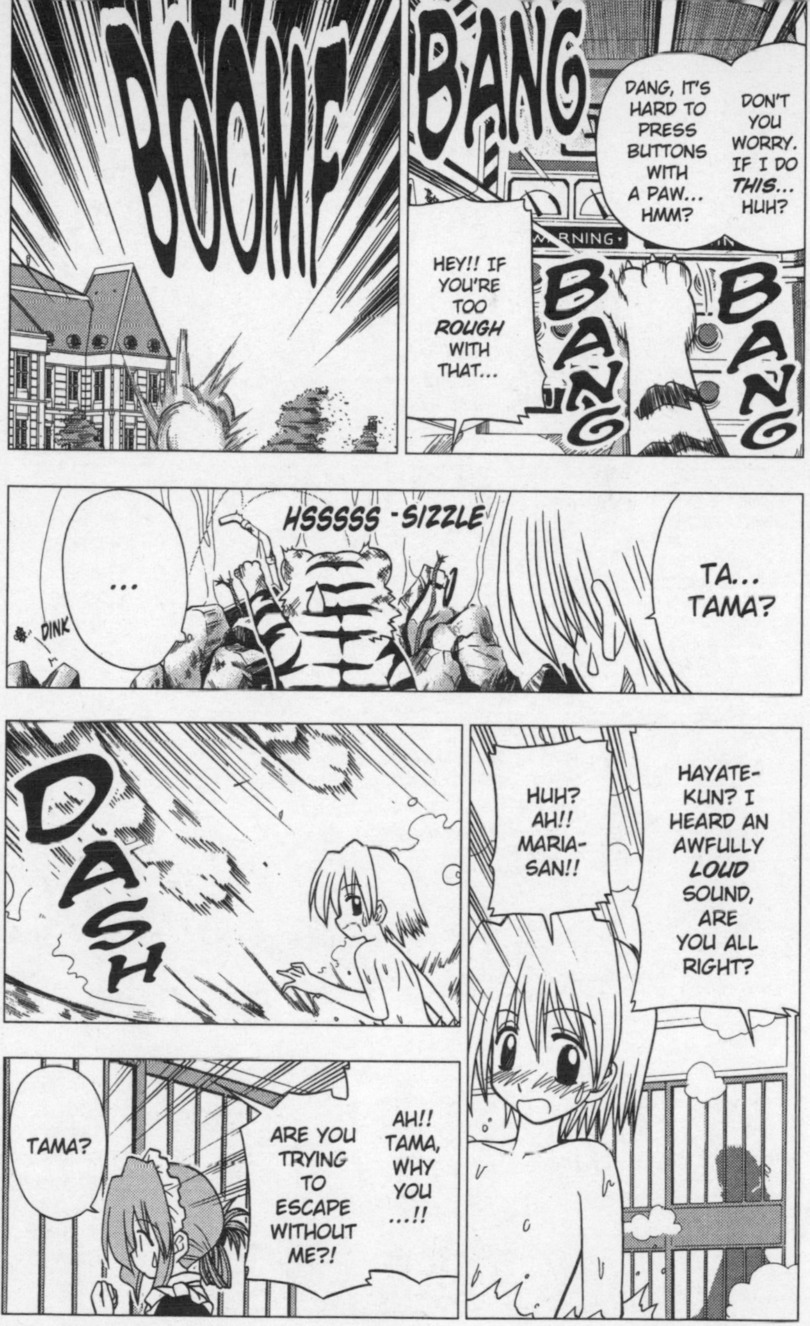
BANG
DON'T YOU WORRY. IF I DO THIS... HUH?
DANG, IT'S HARD TO PRESS BUTTONS WITH A PAW... HMM?
WARNING
HEY!! IF YOU'RE TOO ROUGH WITH THAT...
BANG
BANG
BOOMF
TA... TAMA?
HSSSSS -SIZZLE
...
DINK
HAYATE-KUN? I HEARD AN AWFULLY LOUD SOUND, ARE YOU ALL RIGHT?
HUH? AH!! MARIA-SAN!!
DASH
AH!! TAMA, WHY YOU ...!!
ARE YOU TRYING TO ESCAPE WITHOUT ME?!
TAMA?

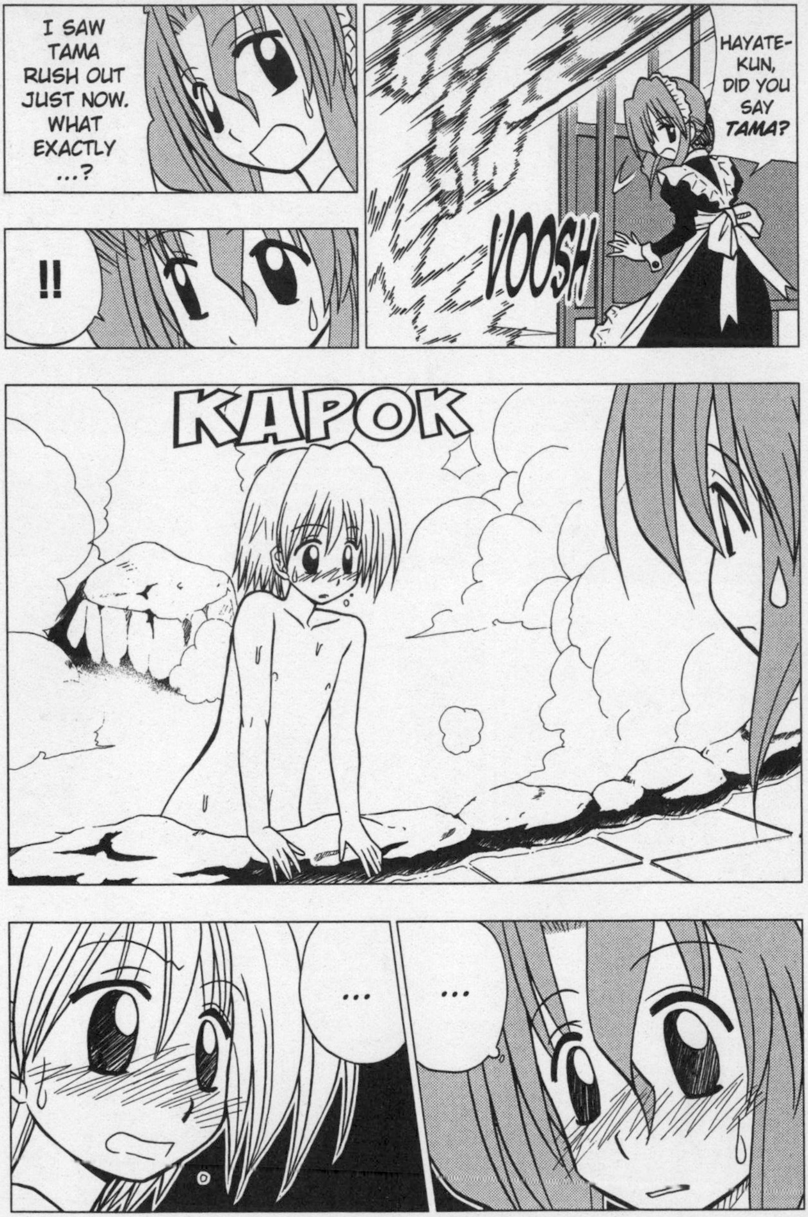
HAYATE-KUN, DID YOU SAY *TAMA?*
VOOSH
I SAW TAMA RUSH OUT JUST NOW. WHAT EXACTLY ...?
!!
KAPOK
...
...

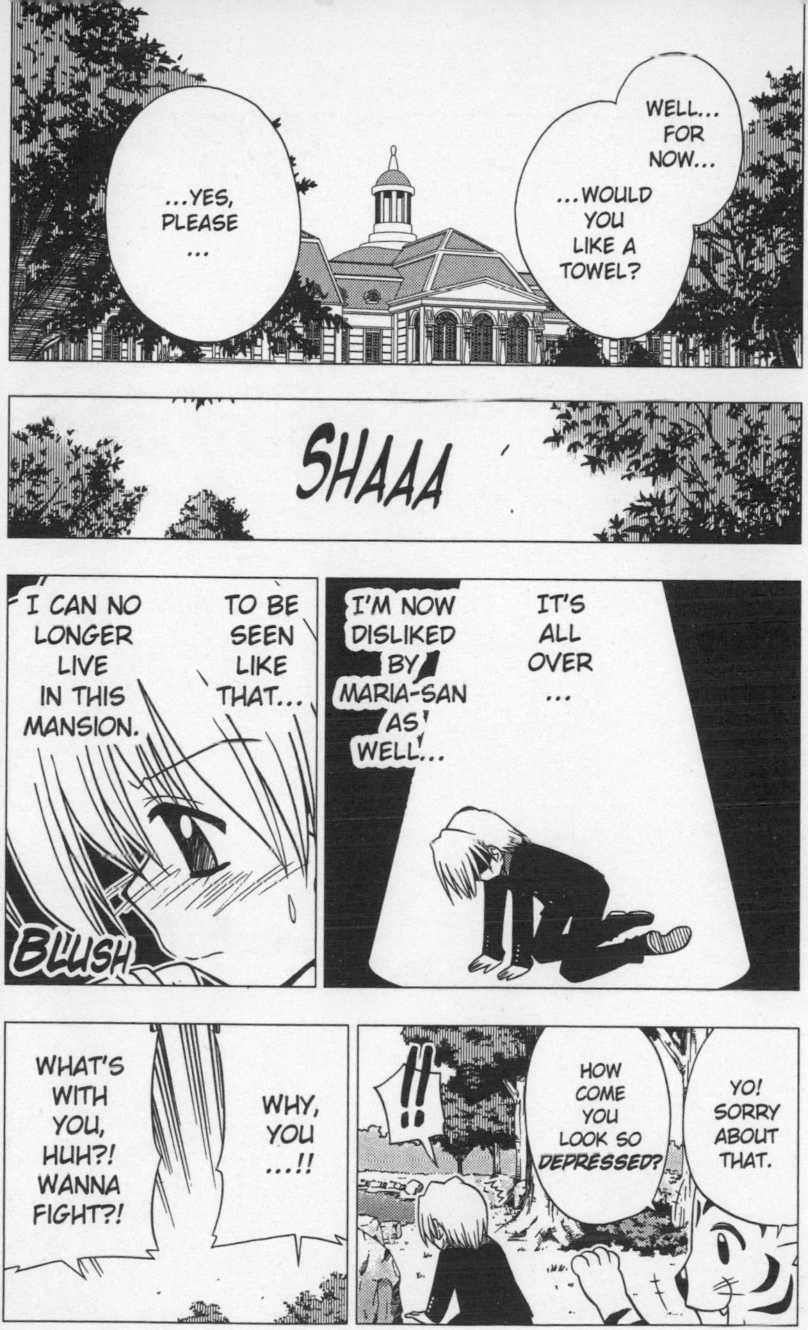
WELL... FOR NOW...
...WOULD YOU LIKE A TOWEL?
...YES, PLEASE ...
SHAAA
IT'S ALL OVER ...
I'M NOW DISLIKED BY MARIA-SAN AS WELL...
TO BE SEEN LIKE THAT...
I CAN NO LONGER LIVE IN THIS MANSION.
BLUSH
YO! SORRY ABOUT THAT.
HOW COME YOU LOOK SO DEPRESSED?
!!
WHY, YOU ...!!
WHAT'S WITH YOU, HUH?! WANNA FIGHT?!

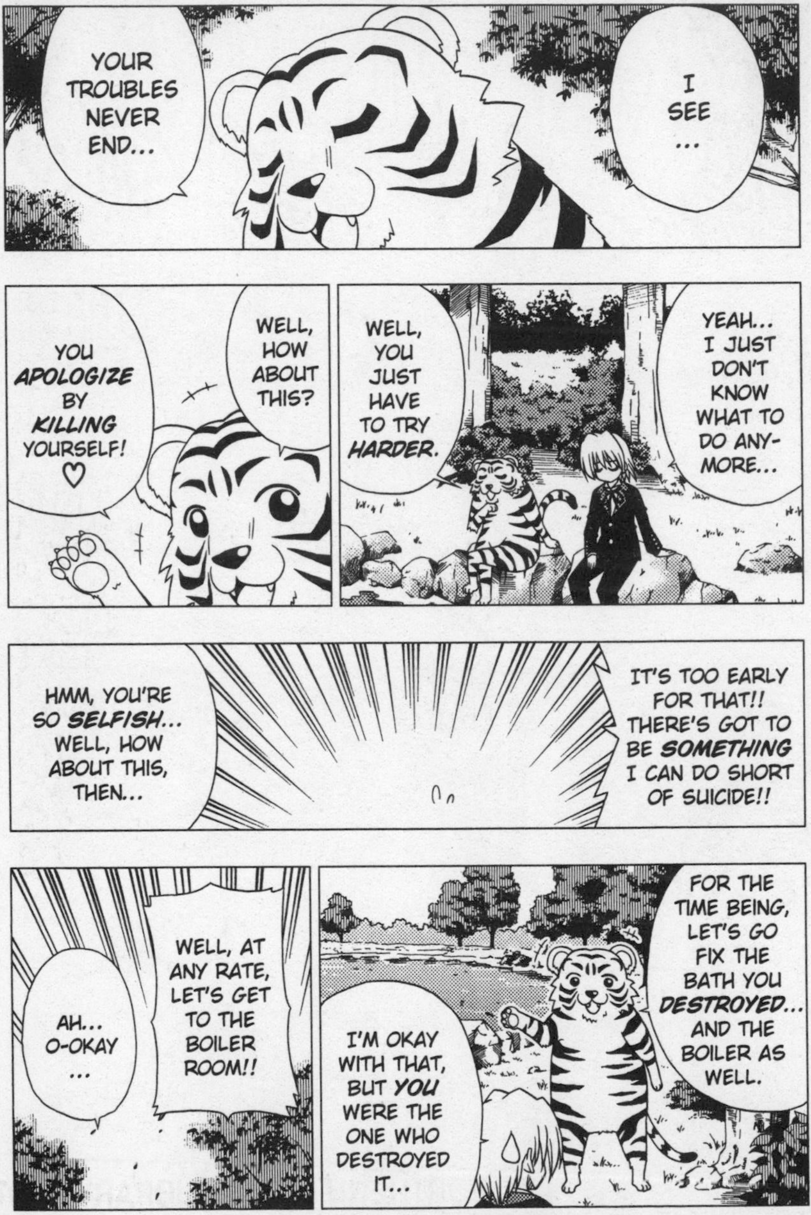
I SEE ...
YOUR TROUBLES NEVER END...
YEAH... I JUST DON'T KNOW WHAT TO DO ANY-MORE...
WELL, YOU JUST HAVE TO TRY *HARDER*.
WELL, HOW ABOUT THIS?
YOU *APOLOGIZE* BY *KILLING* YOURSELF! ♡
IT'S TOO EARLY FOR THAT!! THERE'S GOT TO BE *SOMETHING* I CAN DO SHORT OF SUICIDE!!
HMM, YOU'RE SO *SELFISH*... WELL, HOW ABOUT THIS, THEN...
FOR THE TIME BEING, LET'S GO FIX THE BATH YOU *DESTROYED*... AND THE BOILER AS WELL.
I'M OKAY WITH THAT, BUT *YOU* WERE THE ONE WHO DESTROYED IT...
WELL, AT ANY RATE, LET'S GET TO THE BOILER ROOM!!
AH... O-OKAY ...

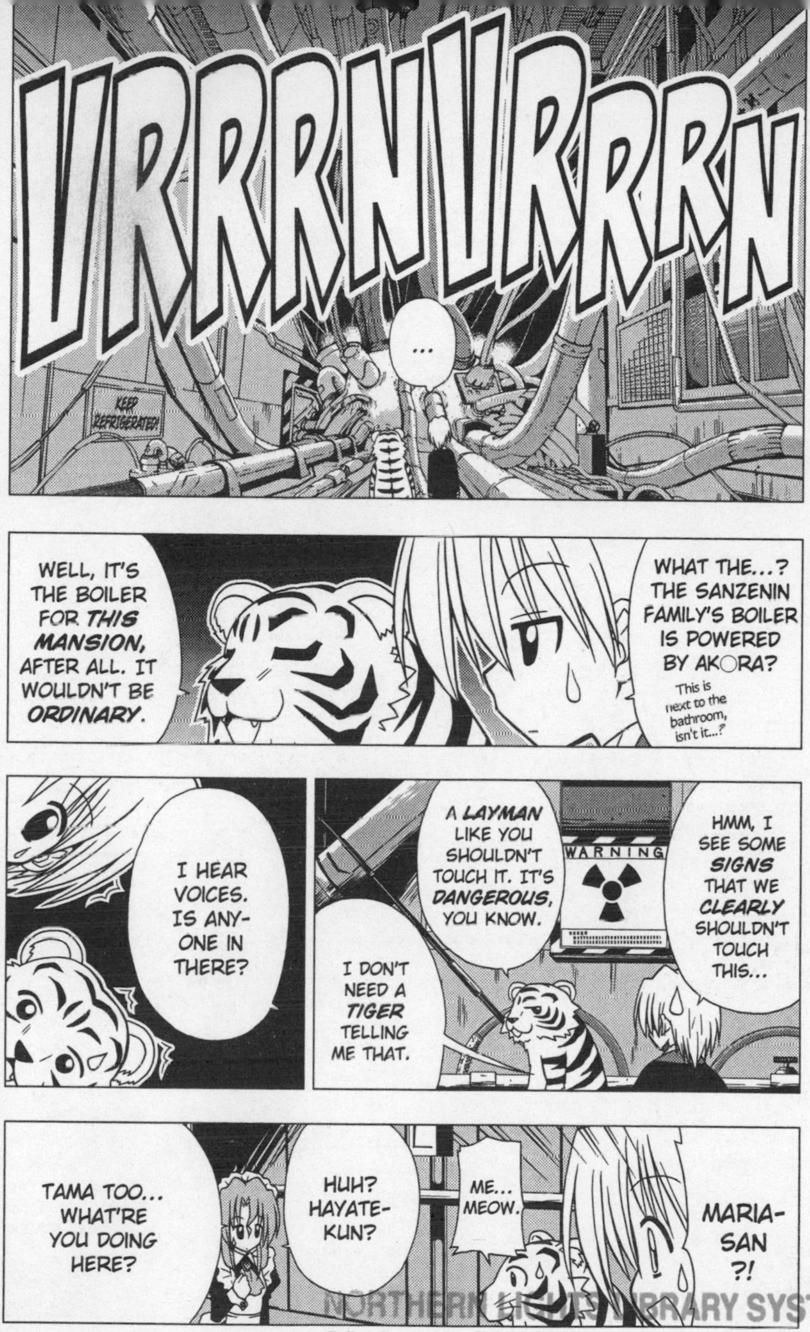
URRRNURRRN
...
KEEP REFRIGERATED!
WHAT THE...? THE SANZENIN FAMILY'S BOILER IS POWERED BY AK○RA?
This is next to the bathroom, isn't it...?
WELL, IT'S THE BOILER FOR *THIS MANSION,* AFTER ALL. IT WOULDN'T BE *ORDINARY*.
HMM, I SEE SOME *SIGNS* THAT WE *CLEARLY* SHOULDN'T TOUCH THIS...
WARNING
A *LAYMAN* LIKE YOU SHOULDN'T TOUCH IT. IT'S *DANGEROUS,* YOU KNOW.
I DON'T NEED A *TIGER* TELLING ME THAT.
I HEAR VOICES. IS ANY-ONE IN THERE?
MARIA-SAN?!
ME... MEOW.
HUH? HAYATE-KUN?
TAMA TOO... WHAT'RE YOU DOING HERE?

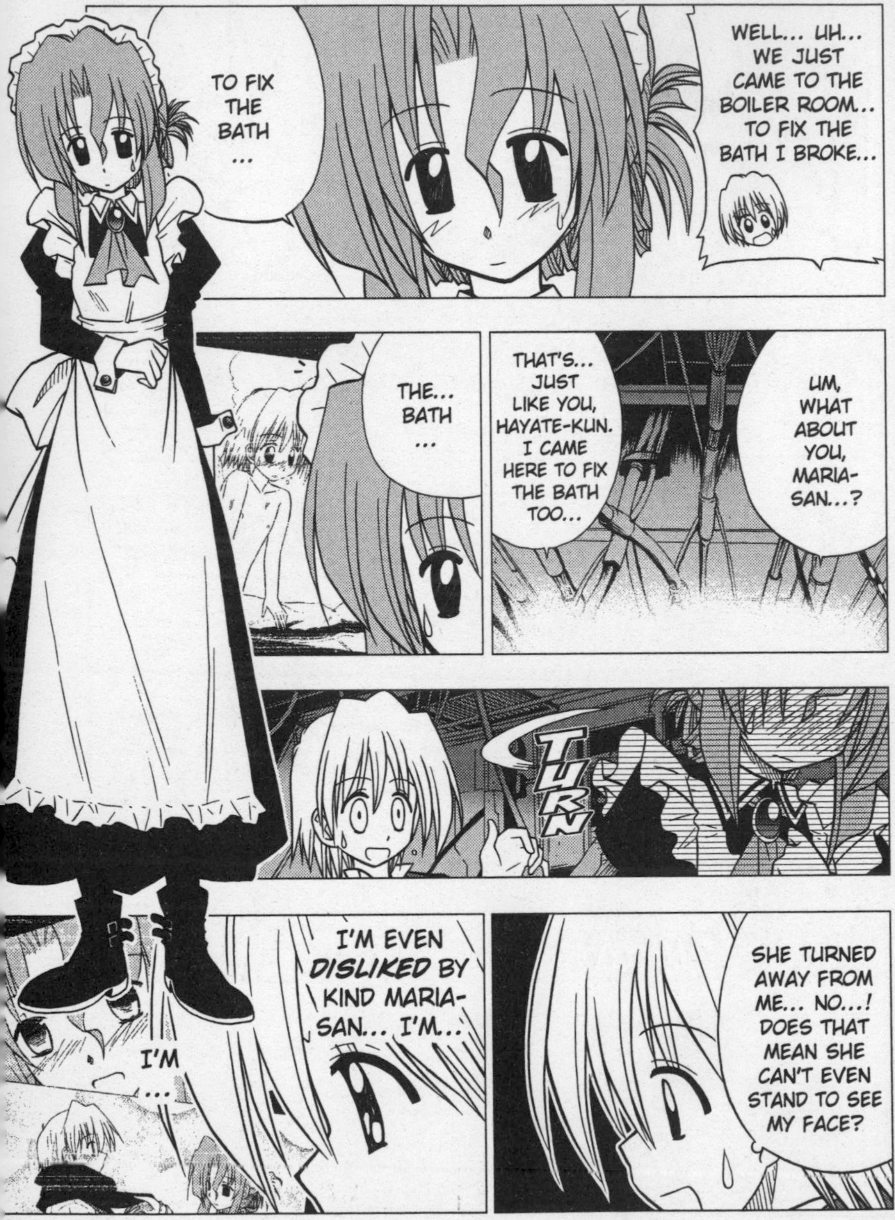
WELL... UH... WE JUST CAME TO THE BOILER ROOM... TO FIX THE BATH I BROKE...
TO FIX THE BATH ...
UM, WHAT ABOUT YOU, MARIA-SAN...?
THAT'S... JUST LIKE YOU, HAYATE-KUN. I CAME HERE TO FIX THE BATH TOO...
THE... BATH ...
TURN
SHE TURNED AWAY FROM ME... NO...! DOES THAT MEAN SHE CAN'T EVEN STAND TO SEE MY FACE?
I'M EVEN *DISLIKED* BY KIND MARIA-SAN... I'M...
I'M ...

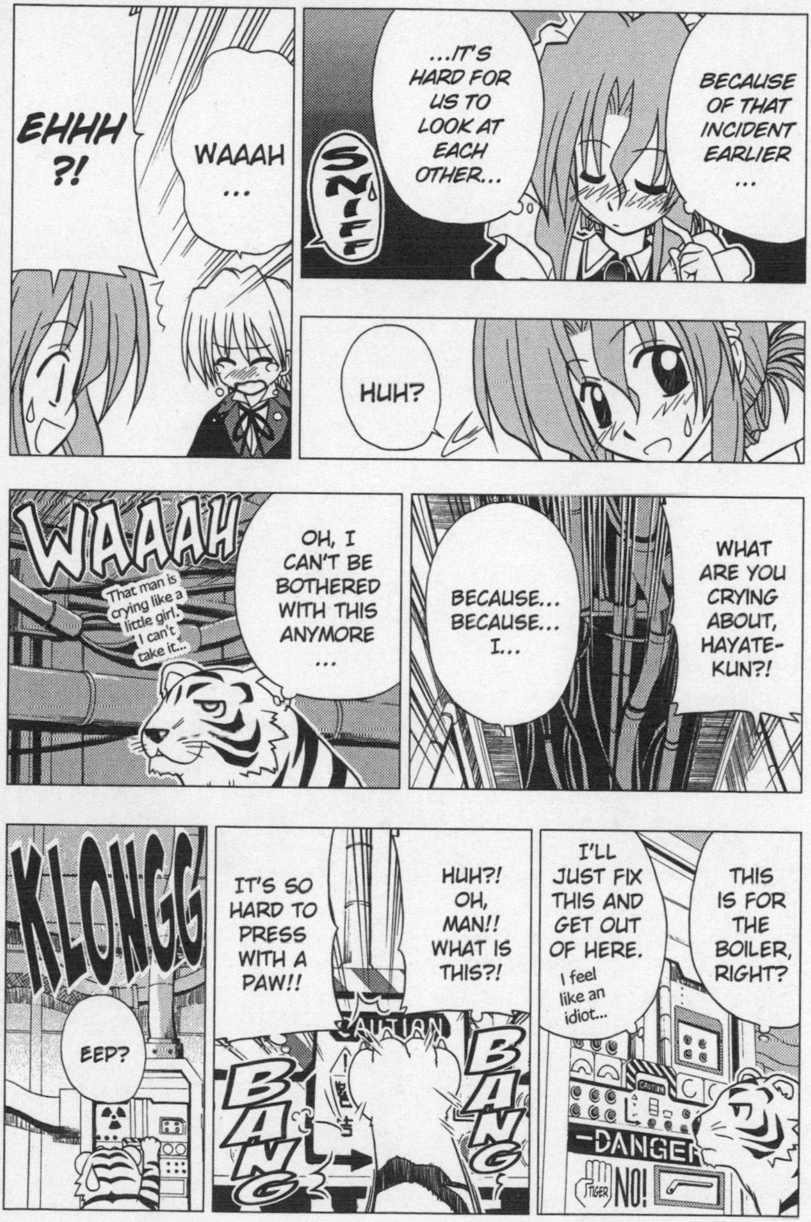
BECAUSE OF THAT INCIDENT EARLIER...
...IT'S HARD FOR US TO LOOK AT EACH OTHER...
SNIFF
HUH?
WAAAH...
EHHH?!
WHAT ARE YOU CRYING ABOUT, HAYATE-KUN?!
BECAUSE... BECAUSE... I...
OH, I CAN'T BE BOTHERED WITH THIS ANYMORE...
WAAAH
That man is crying like a little girl. I can't take it...
THIS IS FOR THE BOILER, RIGHT?
I'LL JUST FIX THIS AND GET OUT OF HERE.
I feel like an idiot...
DANGER
TIGER
NO!
HUH?! OH, MAN!! WHAT IS THIS?!
IT'S SO HARD TO PRESS WITH A PAW!!
BANG
BANG
KLONGG
EEP?

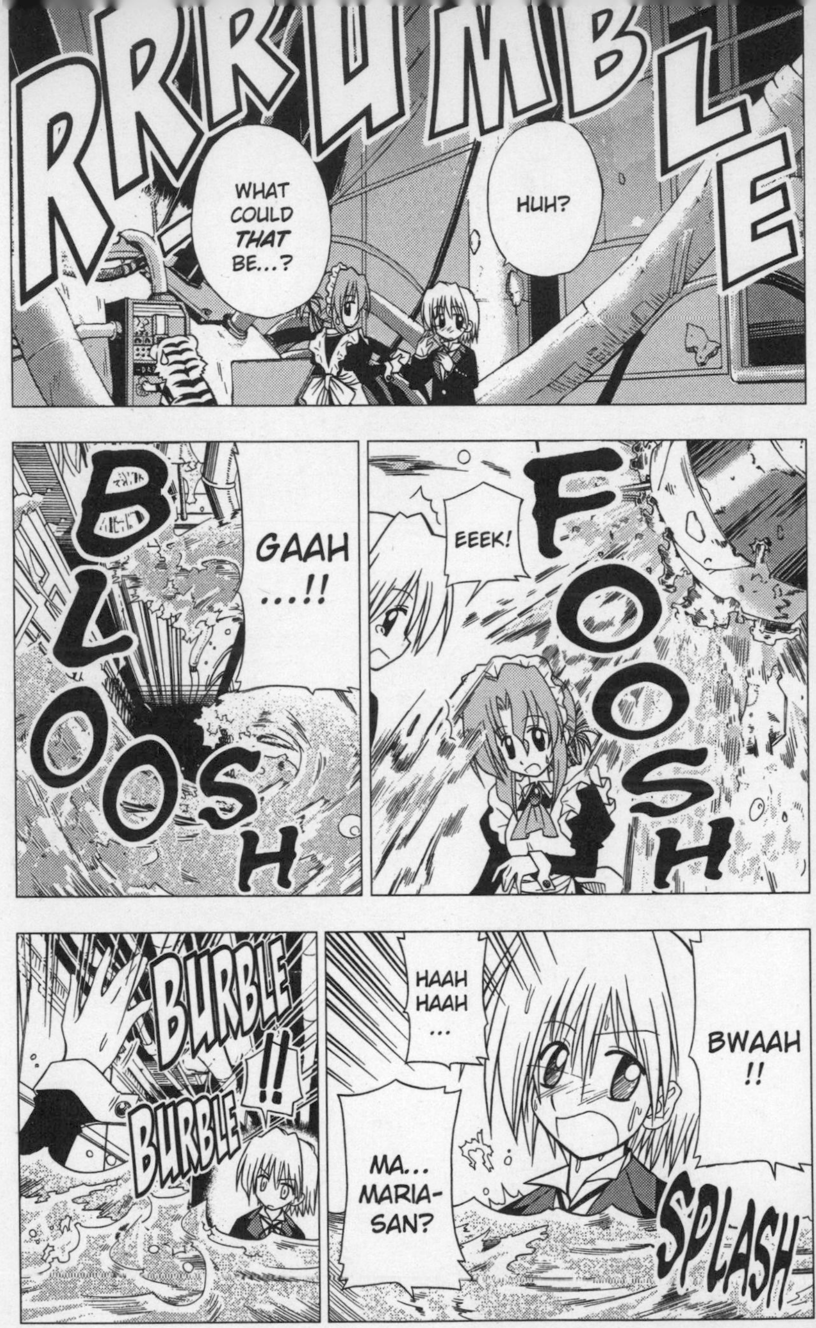
RRRUMBLE
HUH?
WHAT COULD THAT BE...?
EEEK!
FOOSH
BLOOSH
GAAH ...!!
BWAAH !!
HAAH HAAH ...
MA... MARIA-SAN?
SPLASH
BURBLE BURBLE !!

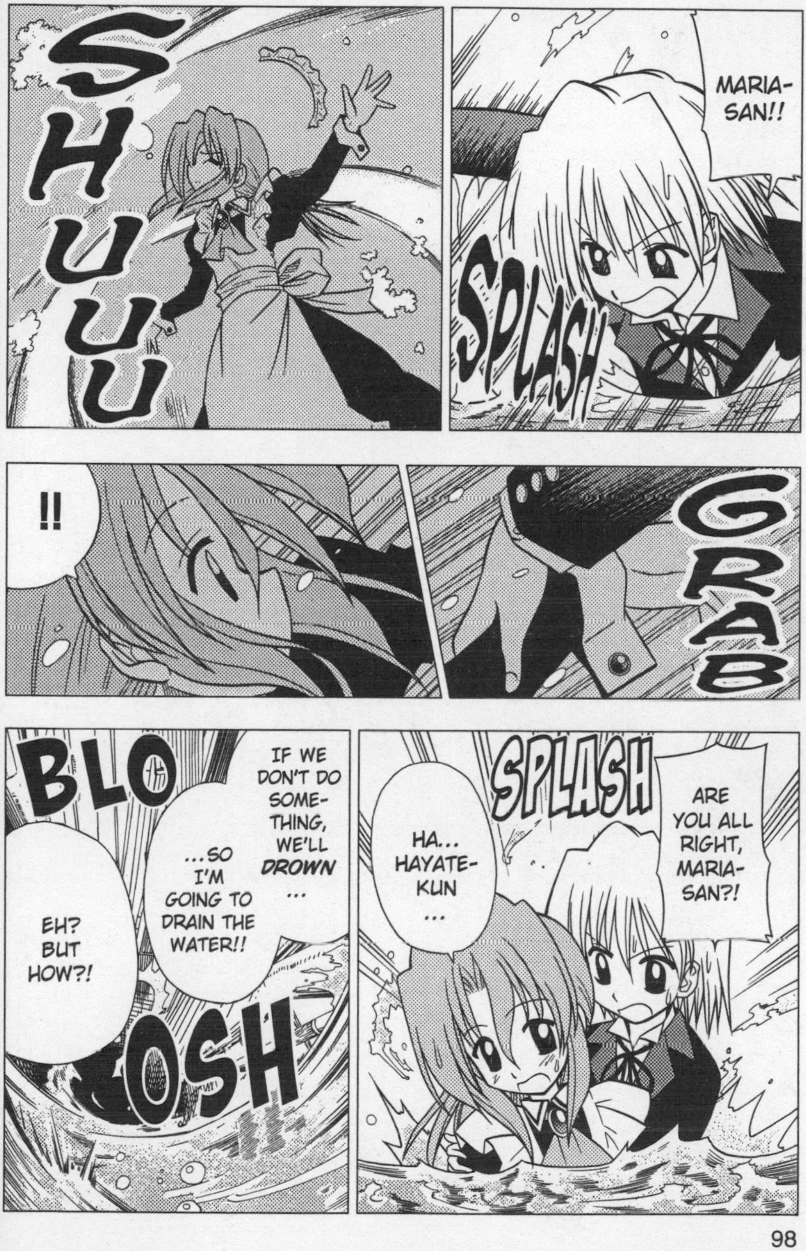
MARIA-SAN!!
SPLASH
SHUUU
GRAB
!!
SPLASH
ARE YOU ALL RIGHT, MARIA-SAN?!
HA... HAYATE-KUN ...
IF WE DON'T DO SOMETHING, WE'LL DROWN ...
...SO I'M GOING TO DRAIN THE WATER!!
EH? BUT HOW?!
BLO
OSH

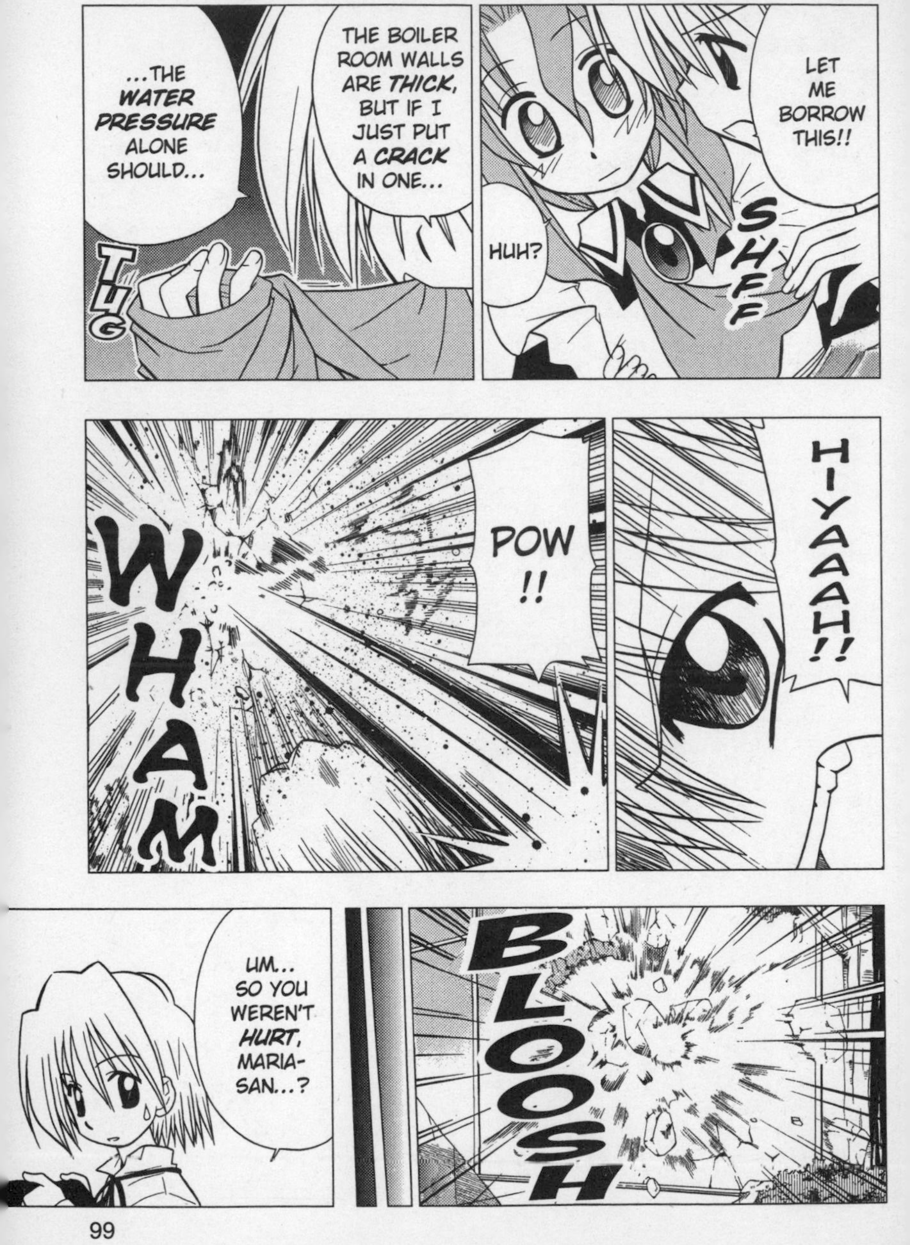
LET ME BORROW THIS!!
SHFF
HUH?
THE BOILER ROOM WALLS ARE THICK, BUT IF I JUST PUT A CRACK IN ONE...
...THE WATER PRESSURE ALONE SHOULD...
TUG
HIYAAAH!!
POW !!
WHAM
BLOOOSH
UM... SO YOU WEREN'T HURT, MARIA-SAN...?

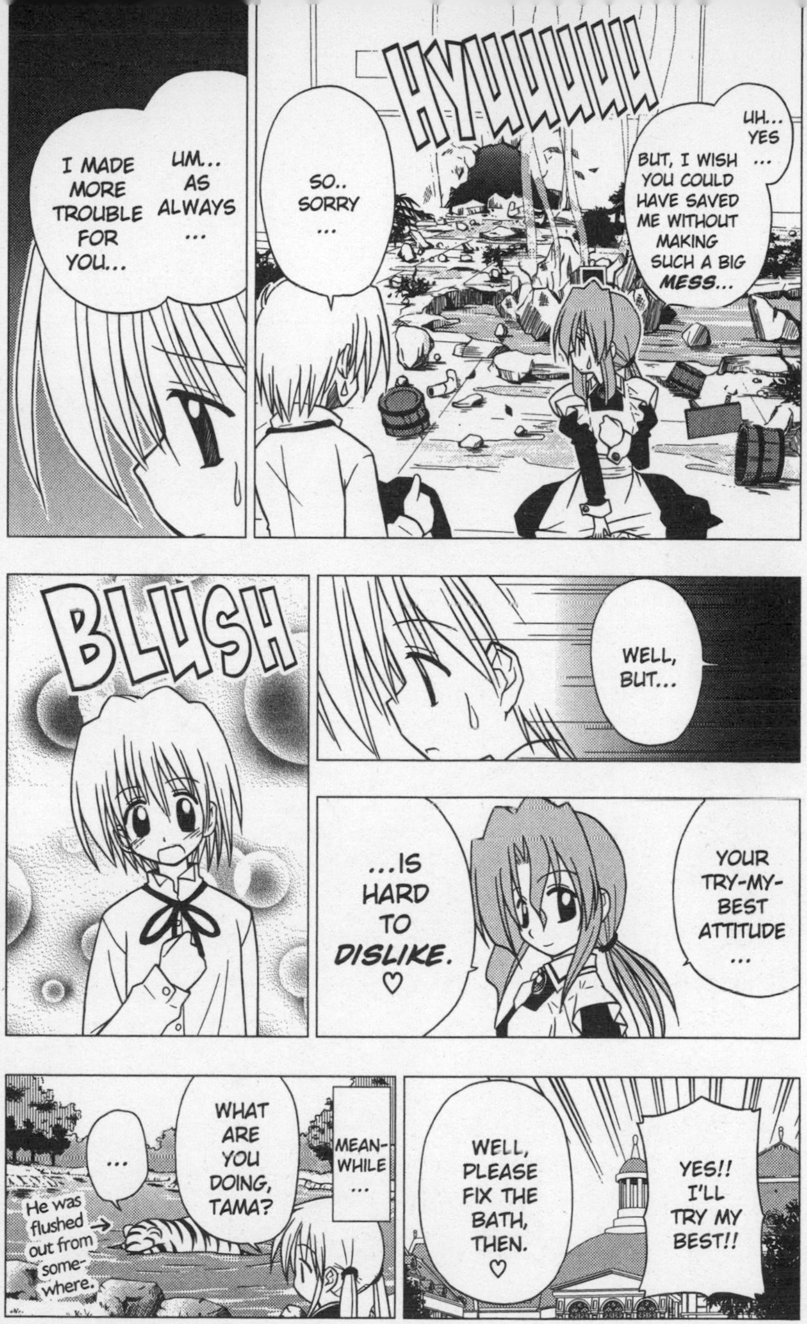
HYUUUUUUU
UH... YES...
BUT, I WISH YOU COULD HAVE SAVED ME WITHOUT MAKING SUCH A BIG MESS...
SO.. SORRY...
UM... AS ALWAYS...
I MADE MORE TROUBLE FOR YOU...
WELL, BUT...
YOUR TRY-MY-BEST ATTITUDE...
...IS HARD TO DISLIKE. ♡
BLUSH
YES!! I'LL TRY MY BEST!!
WELL, PLEASE FIX THE BATH, THEN. ♡
MEAN-WHILE...
WHAT ARE YOU DOING, TAMA?
...
He was flushed out from some-where.

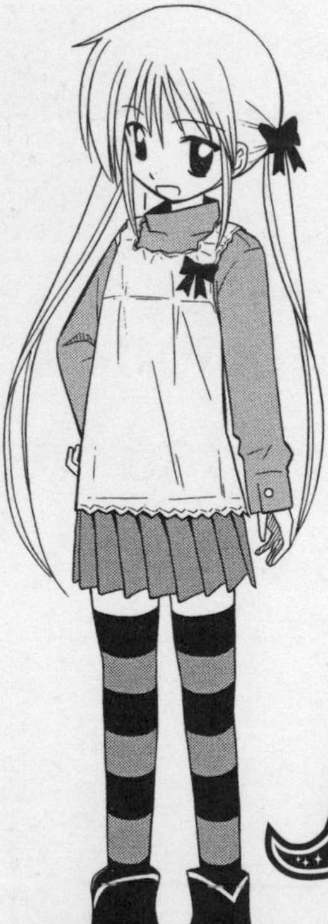

ハヤテのごとく!
Hayate the combat butler

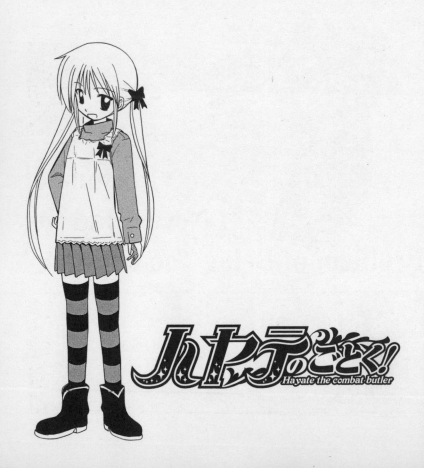

Episode 7: "I Never Had the Problem of Being Too Popular"

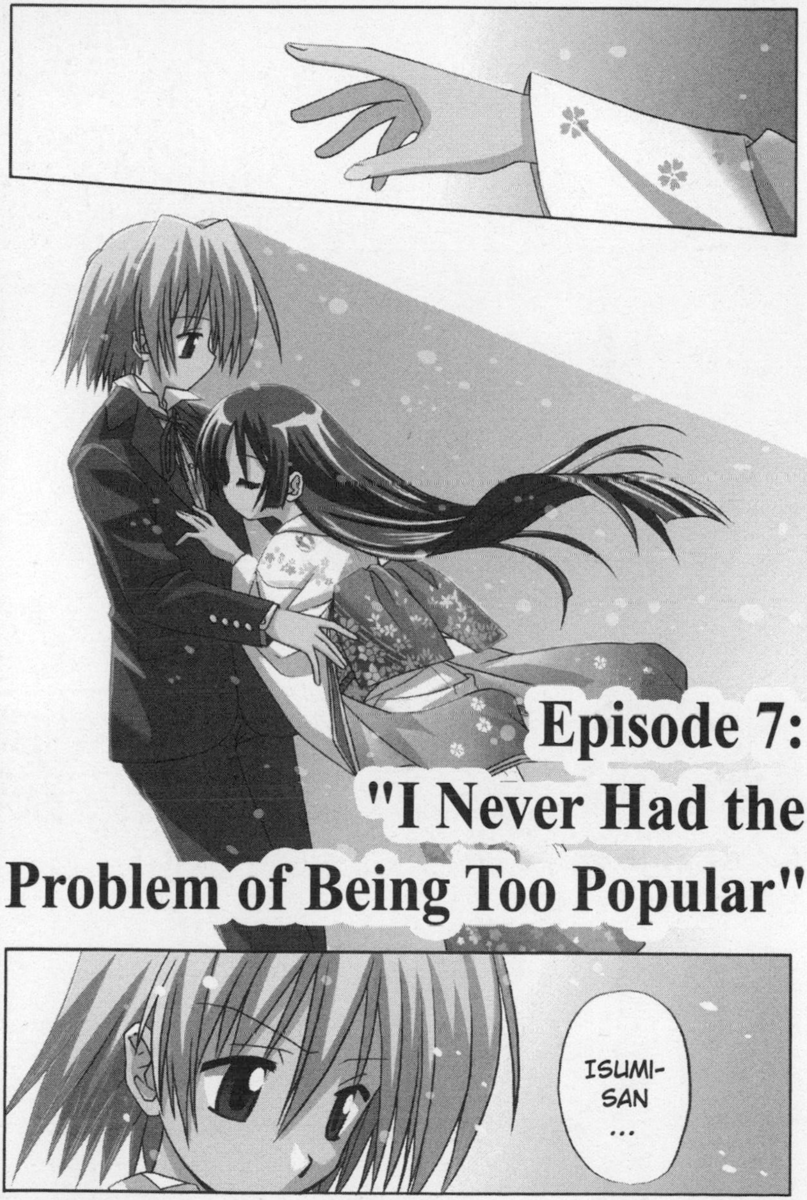
ISUMI-SAN
...

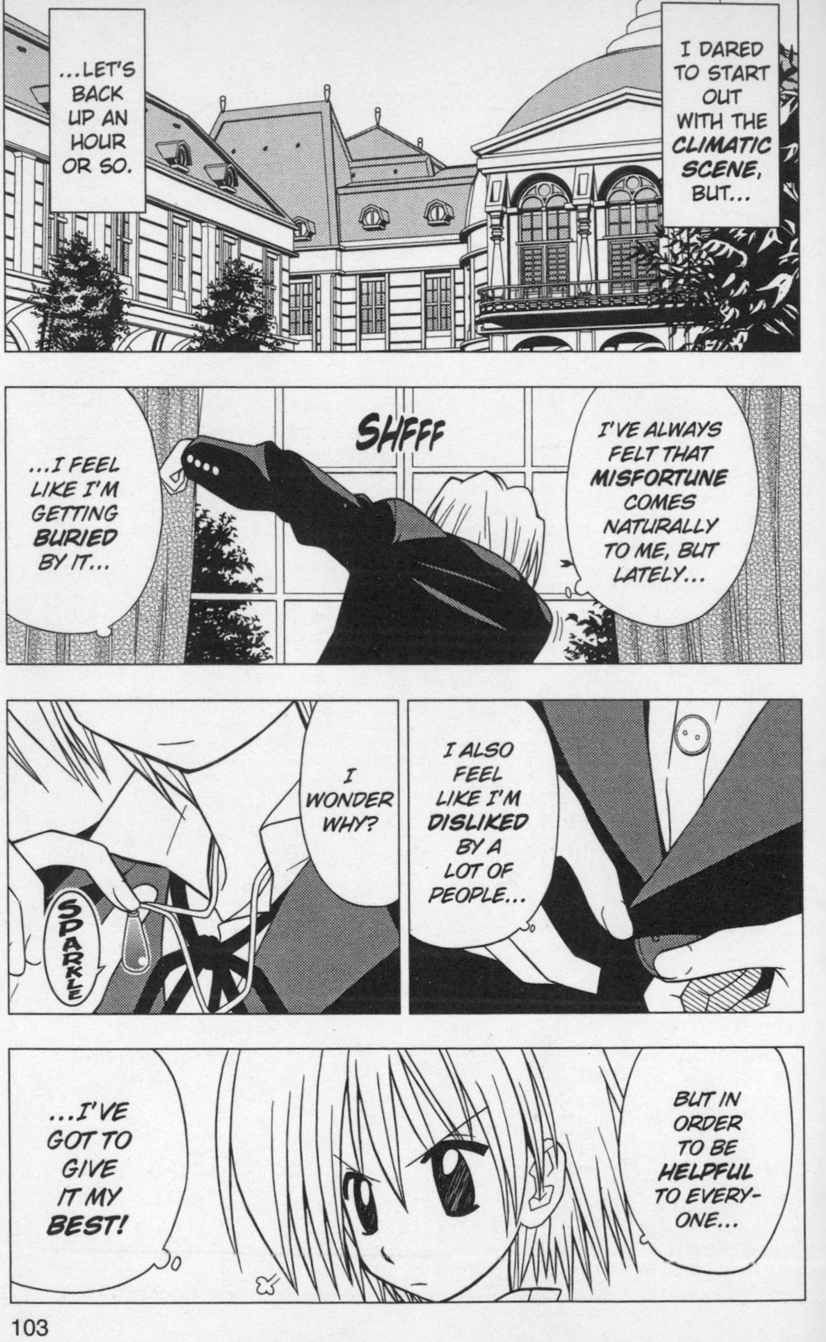
I DARED TO START OUT WITH THE CLIMATIC SCENE, BUT...
...LET'S BACK UP AN HOUR OR SO.
I'VE ALWAYS FELT THAT MISFORTUNE COMES NATURALLY TO ME, BUT LATELY...
SHFFF
...I FEEL LIKE I'M GETTING BURIED BY IT...
I ALSO FEEL LIKE I'M DISLIKED BY A LOT OF PEOPLE...
I WONDER WHY?
SPARKLE
BUT IN ORDER TO BE HELPFUL TO EVERY-ONE...
...I'VE GOT TO GIVE IT MY BEST!

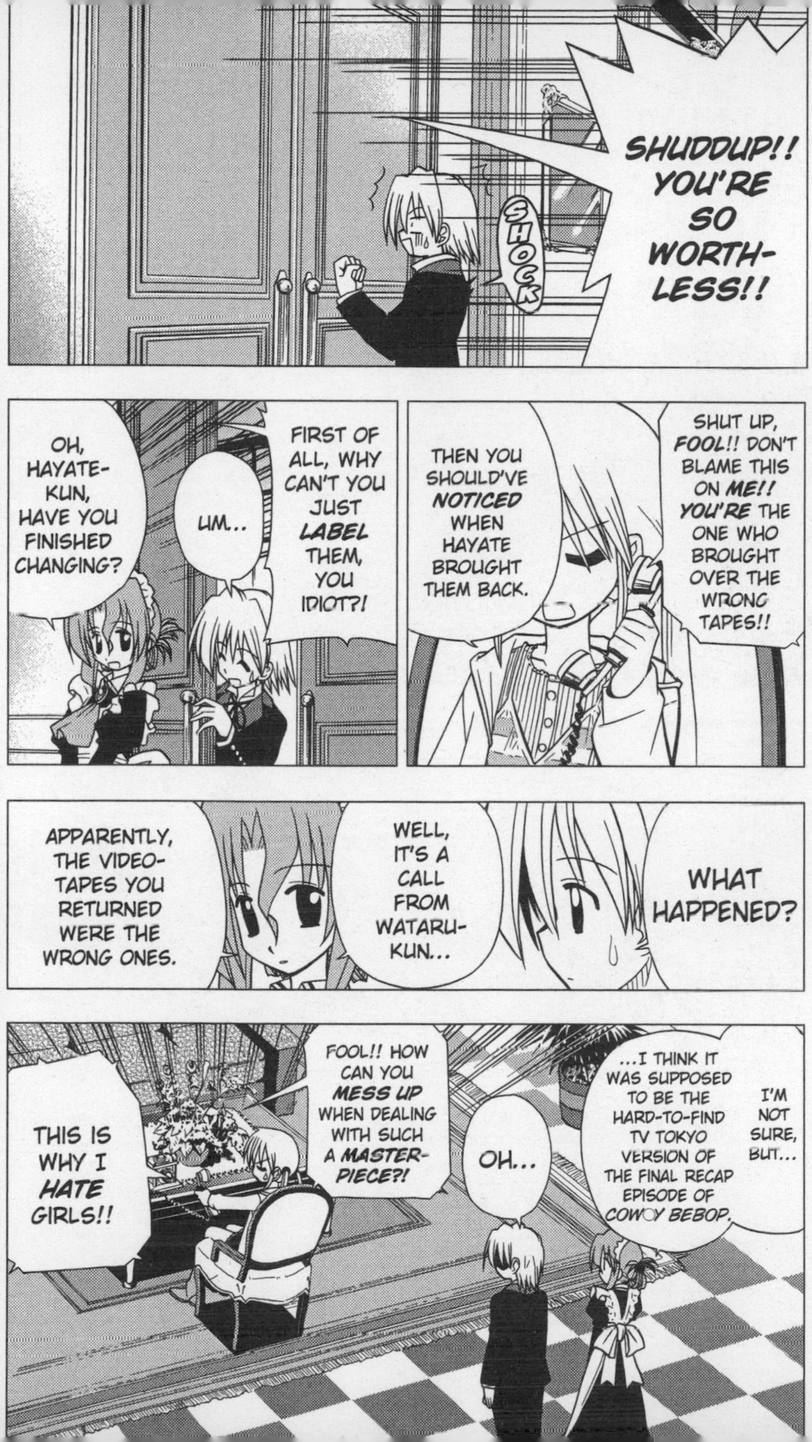
SHUDDUP!! YOU'RE SO WORTH-LESS!!
SHOCK
SHUT UP, FOOL!! DON'T BLAME THIS ON ME!! YOU'RE THE ONE WHO BROUGHT OVER THE WRONG TAPES!!
THEN YOU SHOULD'VE NOTICED WHEN HAYATE BROUGHT THEM BACK.
FIRST OF ALL, WHY CAN'T YOU JUST LABEL THEM, YOU IDIOT?!
UM...
OH, HAYATE-KUN, HAVE YOU FINISHED CHANGING?
WHAT HAPPENED?
WELL, IT'S A CALL FROM WATARU-KUN...
APPARENTLY, THE VIDEO-TAPES YOU RETURNED WERE THE WRONG ONES.
I'M NOT SURE, BUT...
...I THINK IT WAS SUPPOSED TO BE THE HARD-TO-FIND TV TOKYO VERSION OF THE FINAL RECAP EPISODE OF COW○Y BEBOP.
OH...
FOOL!! HOW CAN YOU MESS UP WHEN DEALING WITH SUCH A MASTER-PIECE?!
THIS IS WHY I HATE GIRLS!!

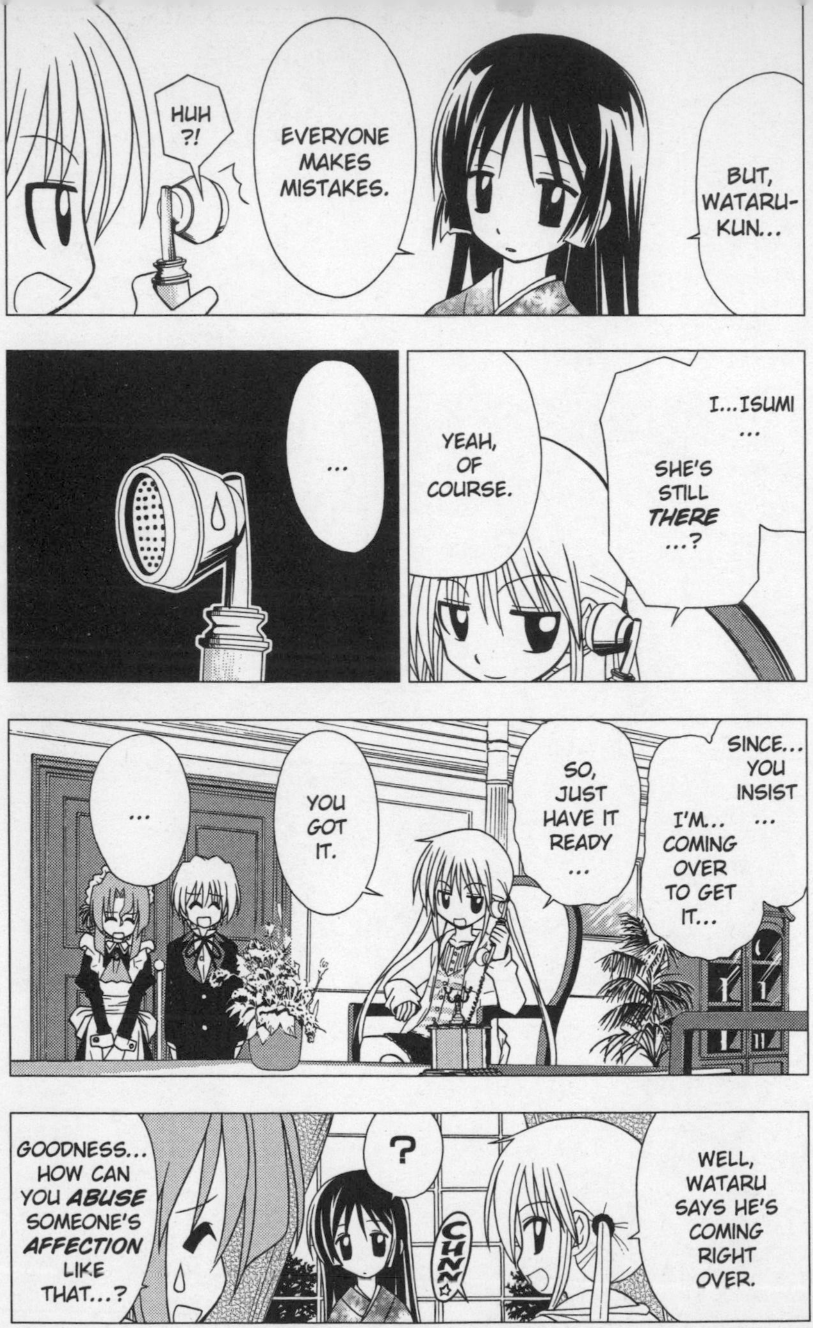

BUT, WATARU-KUN...
EVERYONE MAKES MISTAKES.
HUH ?!
I...ISUMI ...
SHE'S STILL *THERE* ...?
YEAH, OF COURSE.
...
SINCE... YOU INSIST ...
I'M... COMING OVER TO GET IT...
SO, JUST HAVE IT READY ...
YOU GOT IT.
...
WELL, WATARU SAYS HE'S COMING RIGHT OVER.
CHNN☆
?
GOODNESS... HOW CAN YOU *ABUSE* SOMEONE'S *AFFECTION* LIKE THAT...?

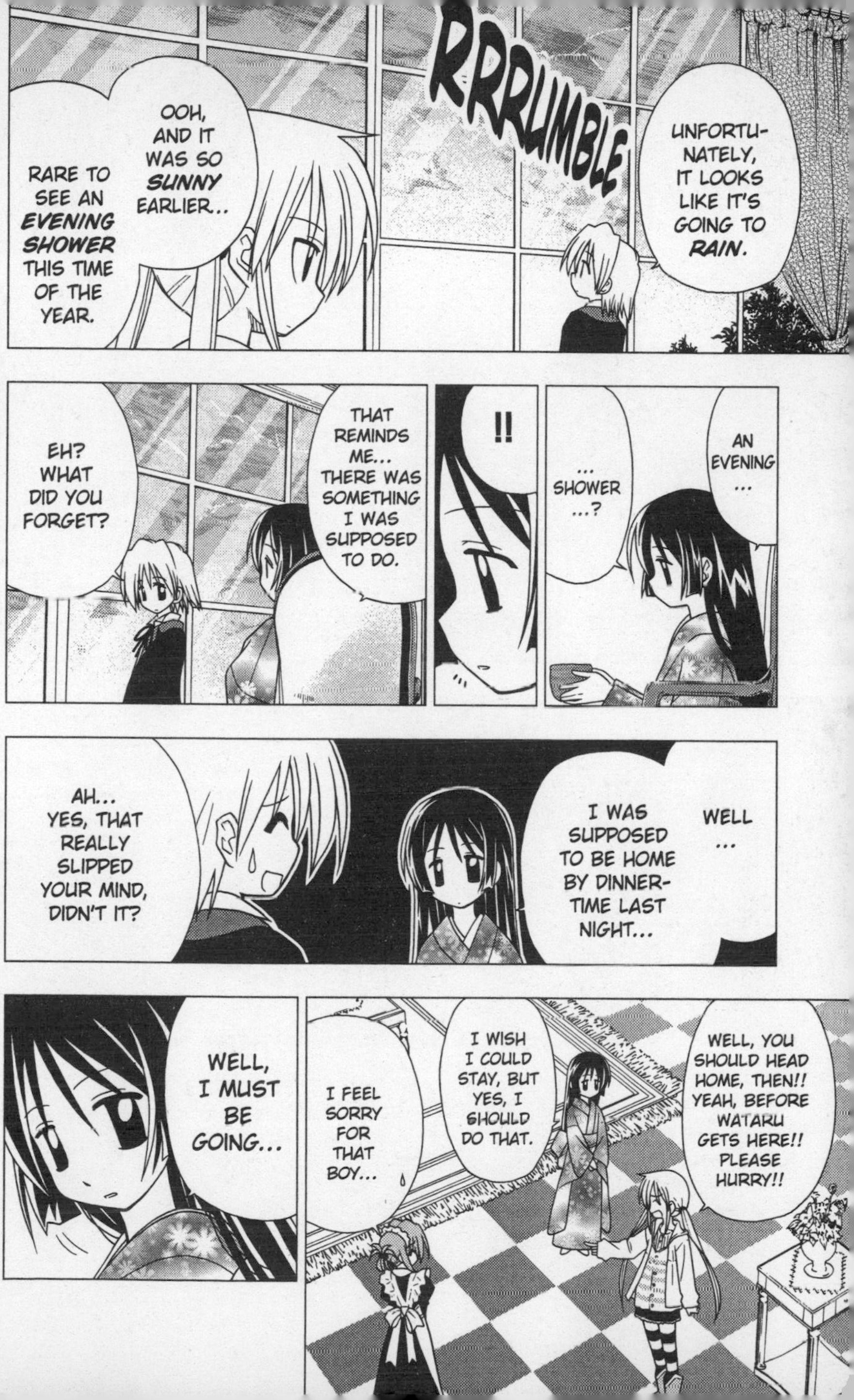
UNFORTUNATELY, IT LOOKS LIKE IT'S GOING TO RAIN.
RRRUMBLE
OOH, AND IT WAS SO SUNNY EARLIER...
RARE TO SEE AN EVENING SHOWER THIS TIME OF THE YEAR.
AN EVENING ...
... SHOWER ...?
!!
THAT REMINDS ME... THERE WAS SOMETHING I WAS SUPPOSED TO DO.
EH? WHAT DID YOU FORGET?
WELL ...
I WAS SUPPOSED TO BE HOME BY DINNER-TIME LAST NIGHT...
AH... YES, THAT REALLY SLIPPED YOUR MIND, DIDN'T IT?
WELL, YOU SHOULD HEAD HOME, THEN!! YEAH, BEFORE WATARU GETS HERE!! PLEASE HURRY!!
I WISH I COULD STAY, BUT YES, I SHOULD DO THAT.
I FEEL SORRY FOR THAT BOY...
WELL, I MUST BE GOING...

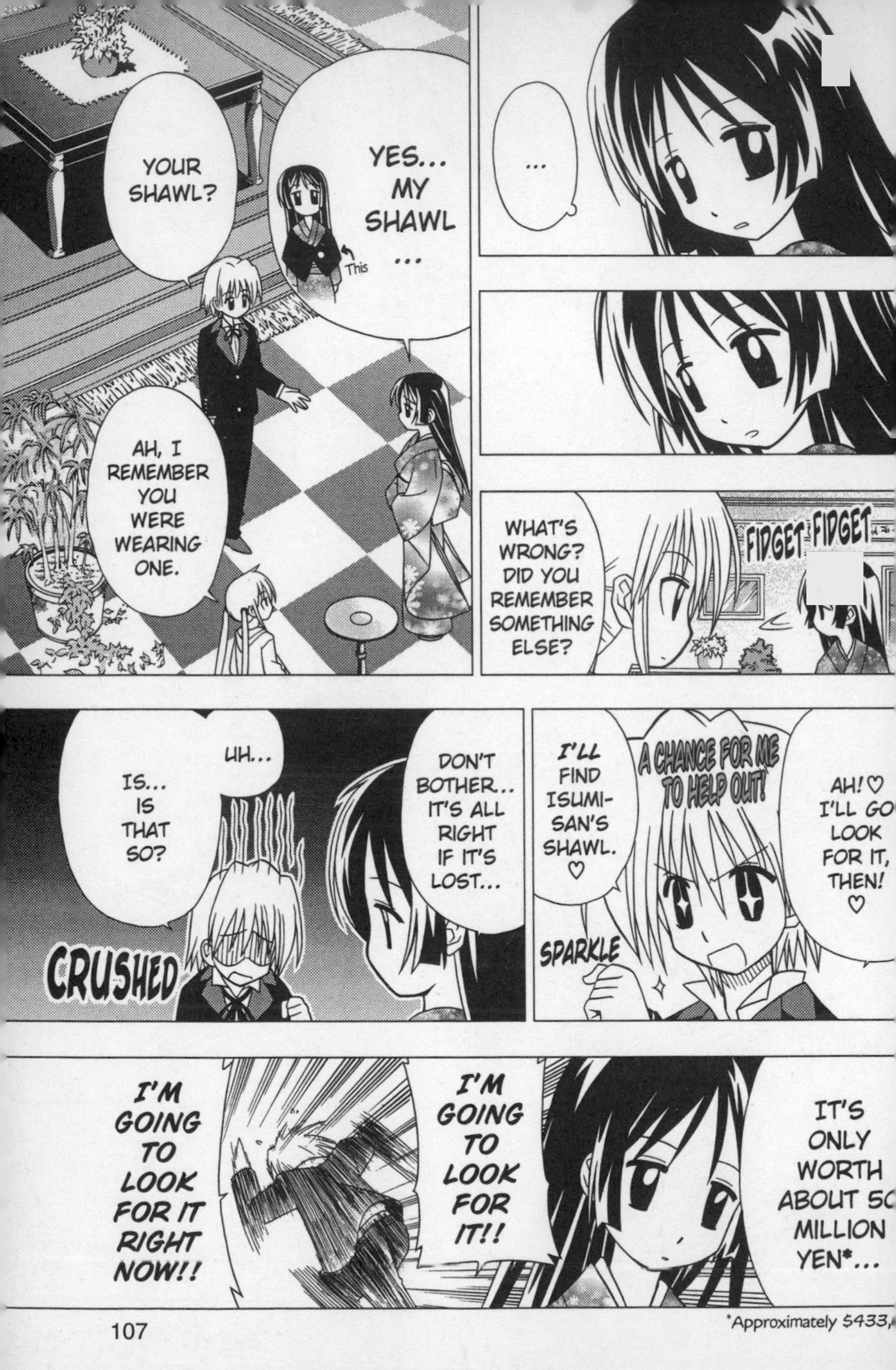
...
WHAT'S WRONG? DID YOU REMEMBER SOMETHING ELSE?
FIDGET FIDGET
YOUR SHAWL?
YES... MY SHAWL ...
This
AH, I REMEMBER YOU WERE WEARING ONE.
AH! ♡ I'LL GO LOOK FOR IT, THEN! ♡
A CHANCE FOR ME TO HELP OUT!
I'LL FIND ISUMI-SAN'S SHAWL. ♡
SPARKLE
DON'T BOTHER... IT'S ALL RIGHT IF IT'S LOST...
UH...
IS... IS THAT SO?
CRUSHED
IT'S ONLY WORTH ABOUT 50 MILLION YEN*...
I'M GOING TO LOOK FOR IT!!
I'M GOING TO LOOK FOR IT RIGHT NOW!!

*Approximately $433,

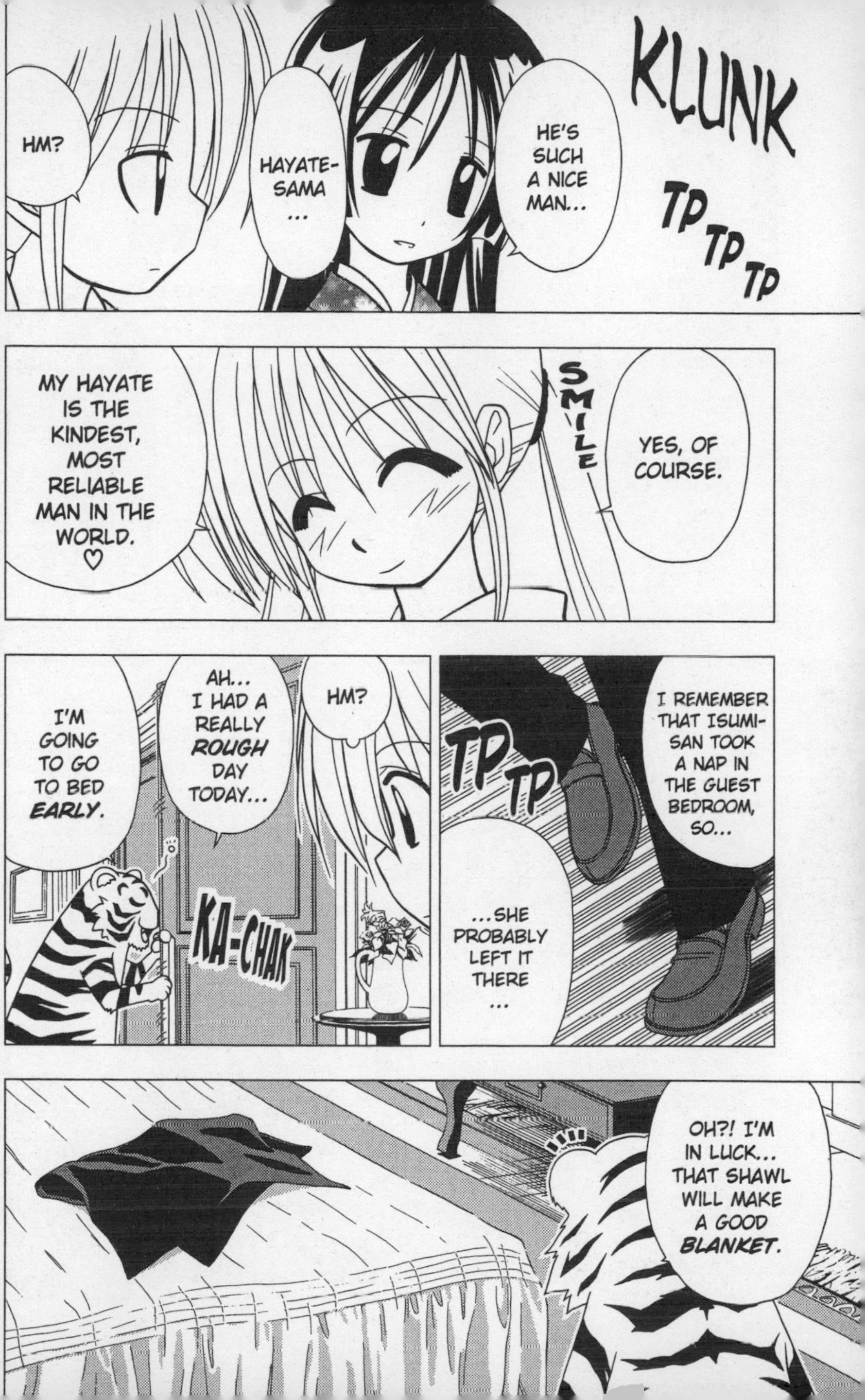
KLUNK
TP TP TP
HE'S SUCH A NICE MAN...
HAYATE-SAMA ...
HM?
YES, OF COURSE.
SMILE
MY HAYATE IS THE KINDEST, MOST RELIABLE MAN IN THE WORLD. ♡
I REMEMBER THAT ISUMI-SAN TOOK A NAP IN THE GUEST BEDROOM, SO...
TP TP
...SHE PROBABLY LEFT IT THERE ...
HM?
AH... I HAD A REALLY ROUGH DAY TODAY...
I'M GOING TO GO TO BED EARLY.
KA-CHAK
OH?! I'M IN LUCK... THAT SHAWL WILL MAKE A GOOD BLANKET.

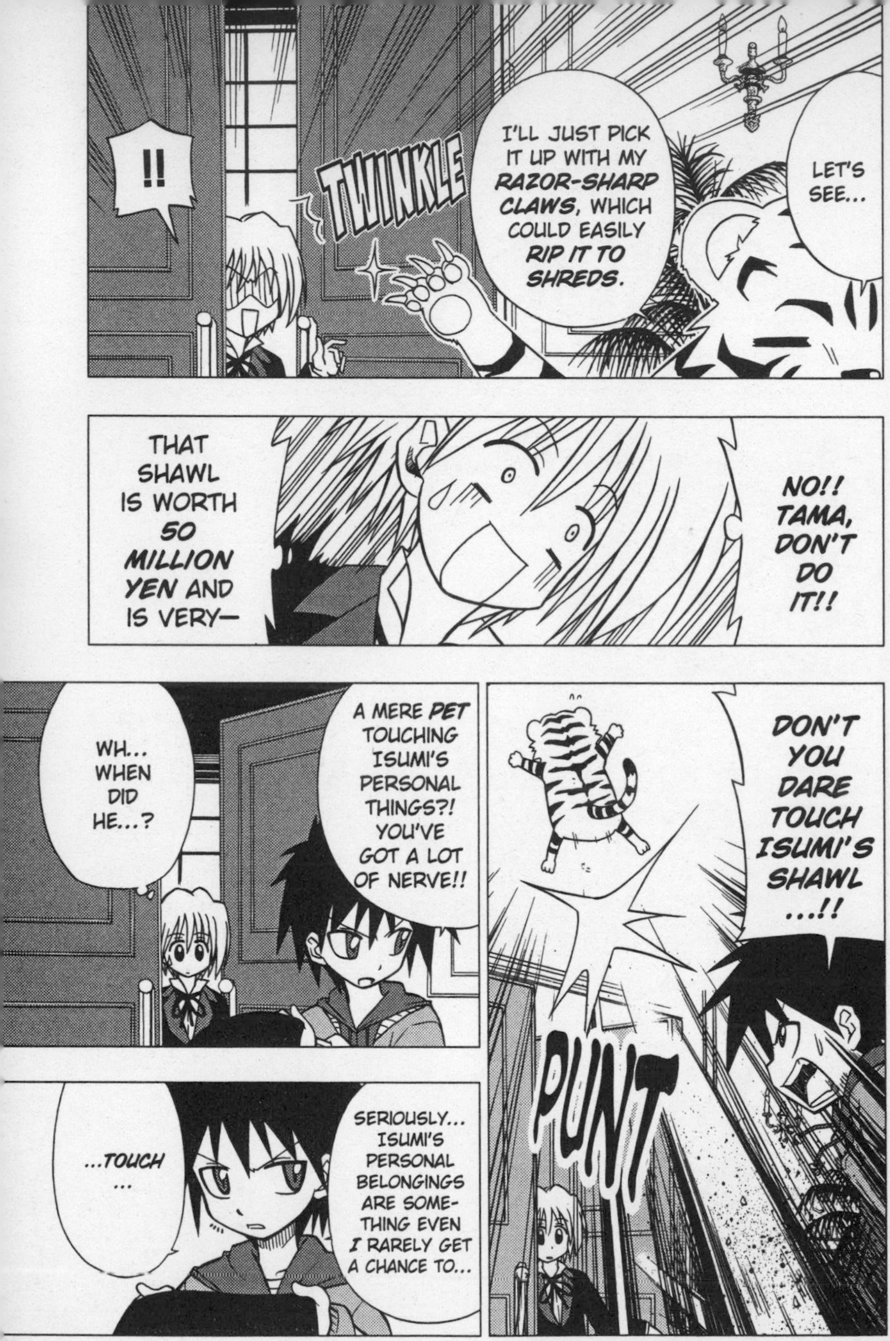
LET'S SEE...
I'LL JUST PICK IT UP WITH MY RAZOR-SHARP CLAWS, WHICH COULD EASILY RIP IT TO SHREDS.
TWINKLE
!!
NO!! TAMA, DON'T DO IT!!
THAT SHAWL IS WORTH 50 MILLION YEN AND IS VERY—
DON'T YOU DARE TOUCH ISUMI'S SHAWL ...!!
PUNT
A MERE PET TOUCHING ISUMI'S PERSONAL THINGS?! YOU'VE GOT A LOT OF NERVE!!
WH... WHEN DID HE...?
SERIOUSLY... ISUMI'S PERSONAL BELONGINGS ARE SOME-THING EVEN I RARELY GET A CHANCE TO...
...TOUCH ...

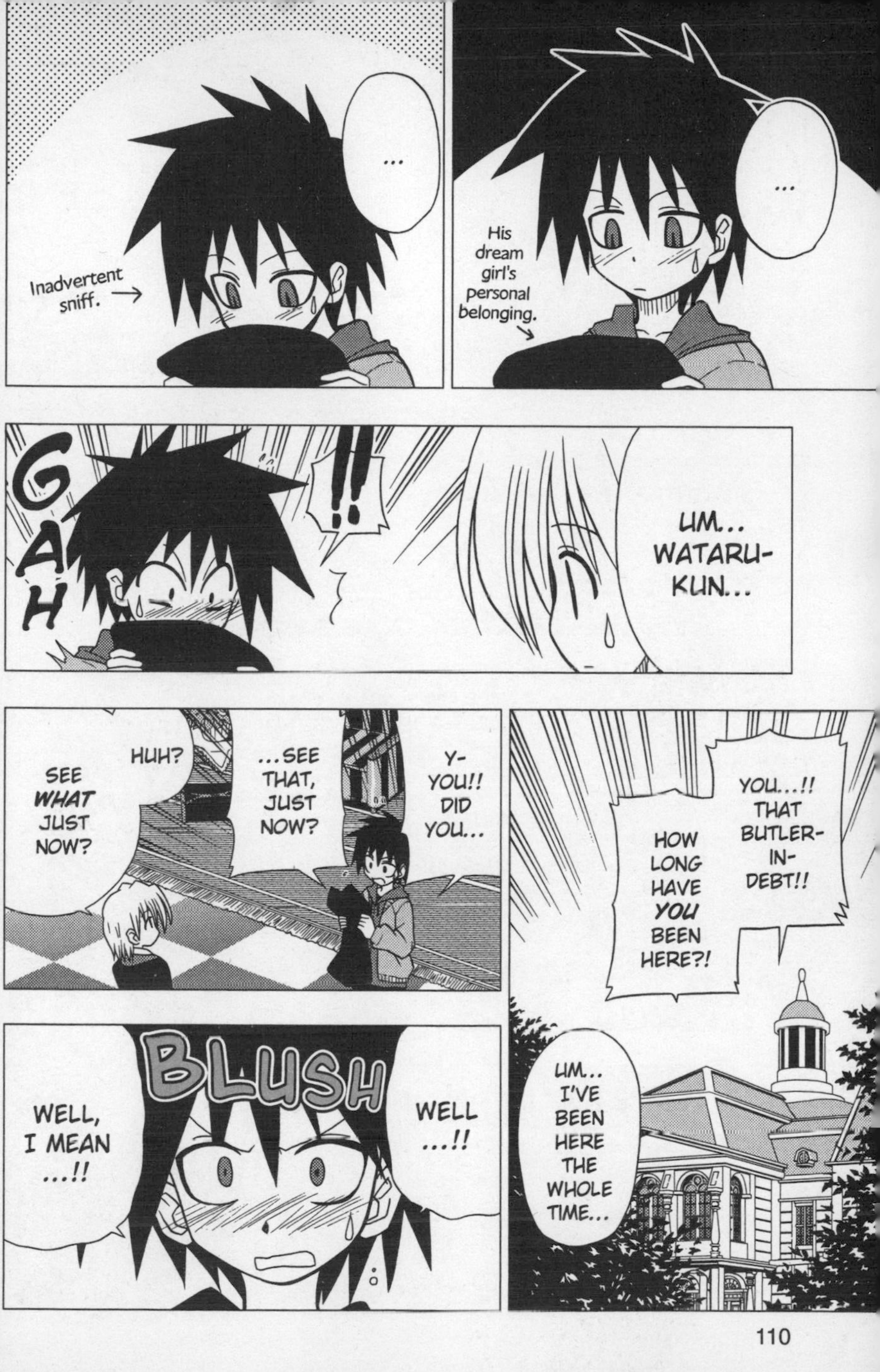
...
His dream girl's personal belonging.
...
Inadvertent sniff.
UM... WATARU-KUN...
!!
GAH
YOU...!! THAT BUTLER-IN-DEBT!!
HOW LONG HAVE *YOU* BEEN HERE?!
UM... I'VE BEEN HERE THE WHOLE TIME...
Y-YOU!! DID YOU...
...SEE THAT, JUST NOW?
HUH?
SEE *WHAT* JUST NOW?
BLUSH
WELL...!!
WELL, I MEAN...!!

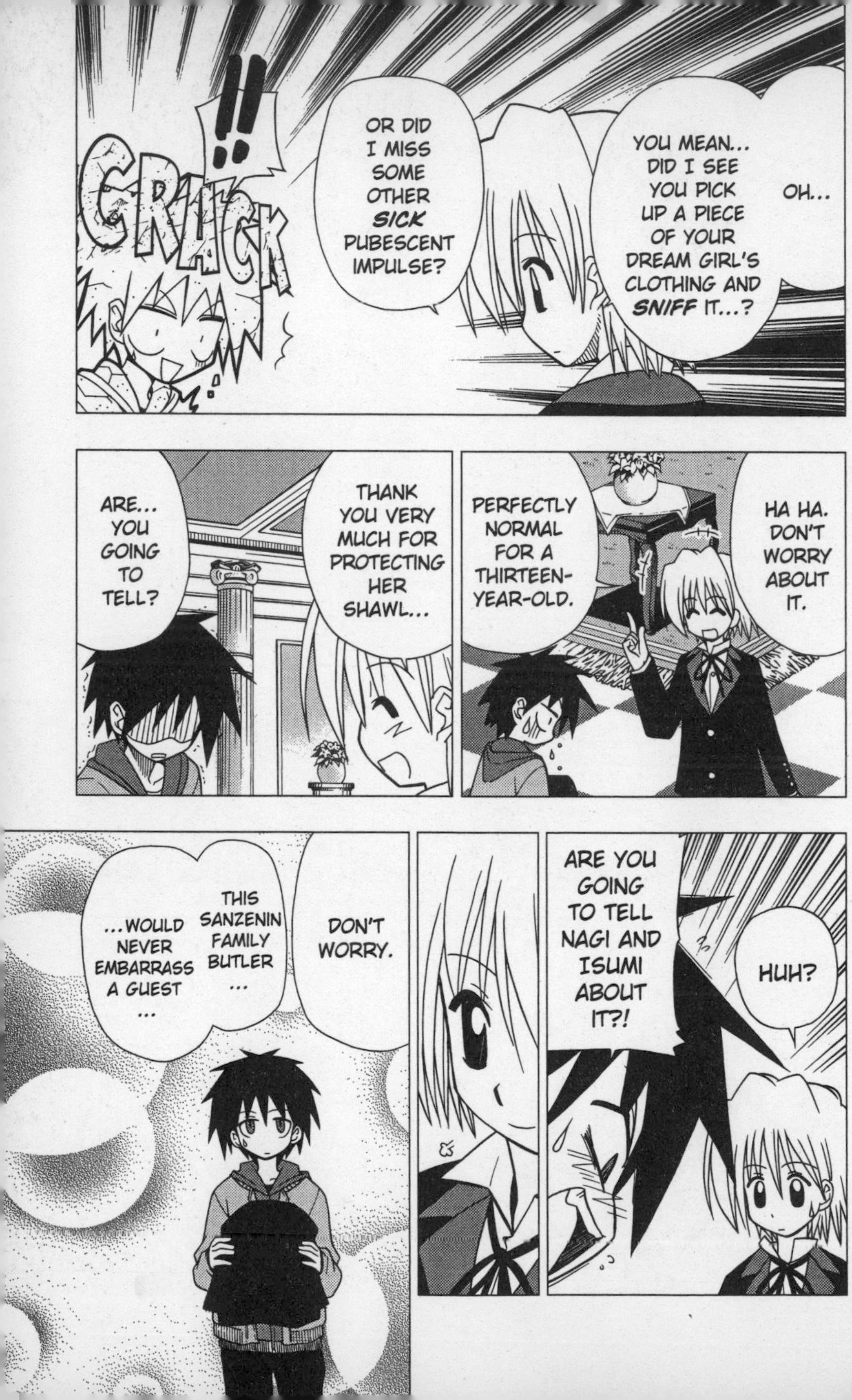
OH...
YOU MEAN... DID I SEE YOU PICK UP A PIECE OF YOUR DREAM GIRL'S CLOTHING AND SNIFF IT...?
OR DID I MISS SOME OTHER SICK PUBESCENT IMPULSE?
!!
CRACK
HA HA. DON'T WORRY ABOUT IT.
PERFECTLY NORMAL FOR A THIRTEEN-YEAR-OLD.
THANK YOU VERY MUCH FOR PROTECTING HER SHAWL...
ARE... YOU GOING TO TELL?
HUH?
ARE YOU GOING TO TELL NAGI AND ISUMI ABOUT IT?!
DON'T WORRY.
THIS SANZENIN FAMILY BUTLER...
...WOULD NEVER EMBARRASS A GUEST...

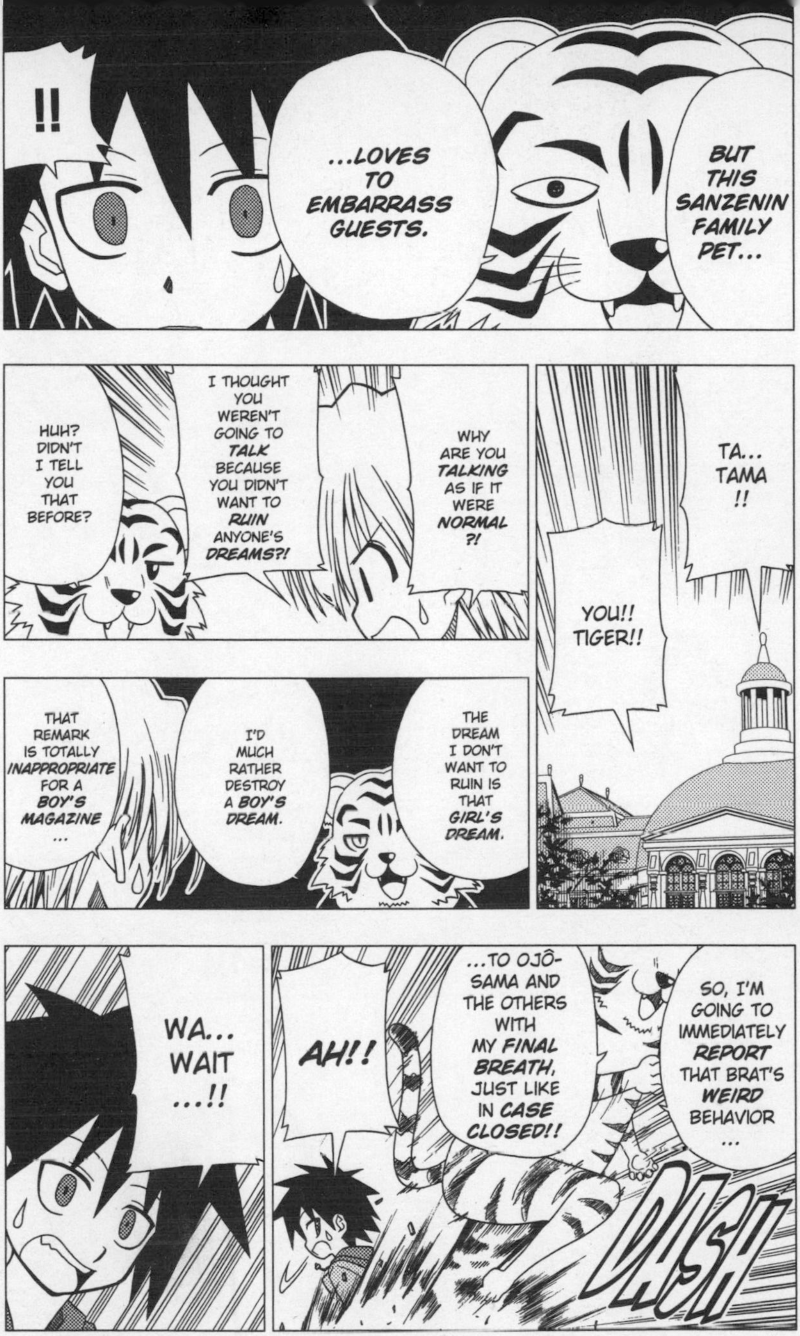
BUT THIS SANZENIN FAMILY PET...
...LOVES TO EMBARRASS GUESTS.
!!
TA... TAMA!!
YOU!! TIGER!!
WHY ARE YOU TALKING AS IF IT WERE NORMAL?!
I THOUGHT YOU WEREN'T GOING TO TALK BECAUSE YOU DIDN'T WANT TO RUIN ANYONE'S DREAMS?!
HUH? DIDN'T I TELL YOU THAT BEFORE?
THE DREAM I DON'T WANT TO RUIN IS THAT GIRL'S DREAM.
I'D MUCH RATHER DESTROY A BOY'S DREAM.
THAT REMARK IS TOTALLY INAPPROPRIATE FOR A BOY'S MAGAZINE...
SO, I'M GOING TO IMMEDIATELY REPORT THAT BRAT'S WEIRD BEHAVIOR...
...TO OJÔ-SAMA AND THE OTHERS WITH MY FINAL BREATH, JUST LIKE IN CASE CLOSED!!
AH!!
DASH
WA... WAIT ...!!

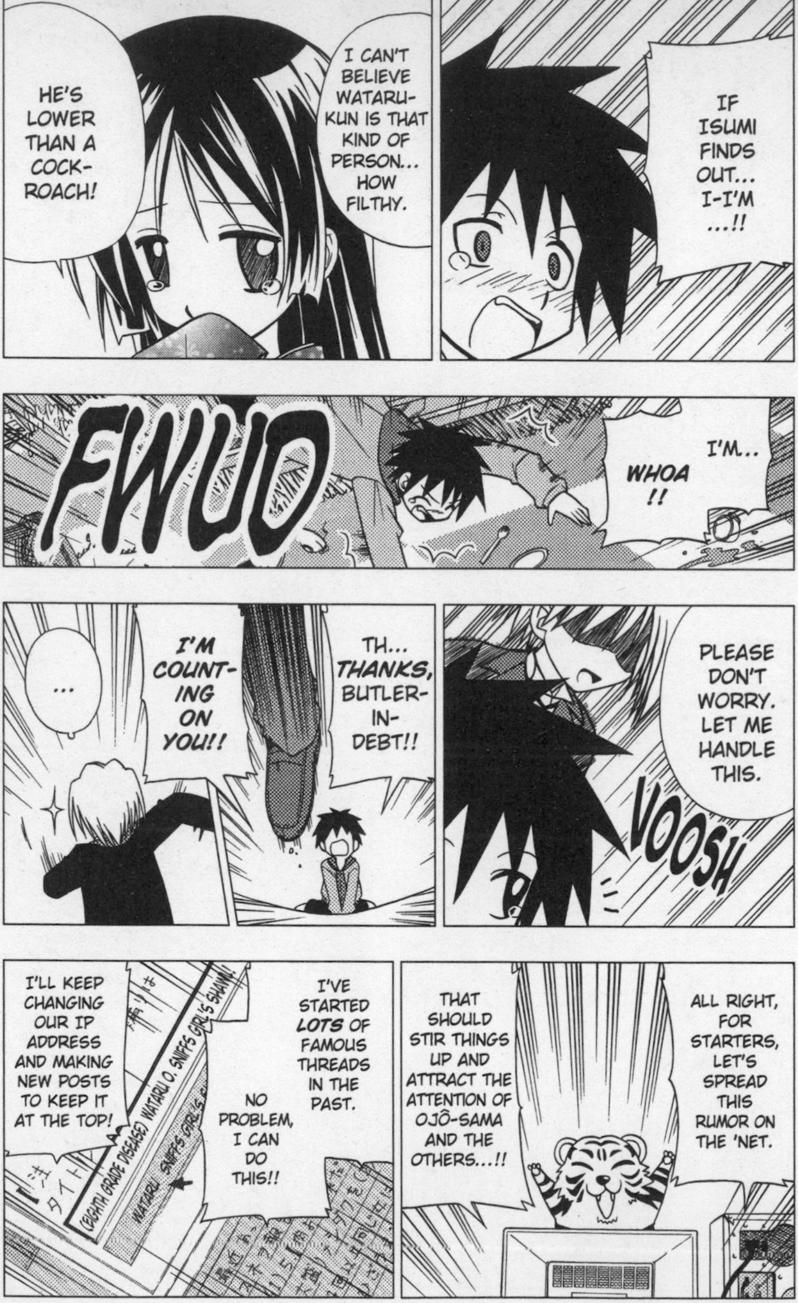
IF ISUMI FINDS OUT... I-I'M ...!!
I CAN'T BELIEVE WATARU-KUN IS THAT KIND OF PERSON... HOW FILTHY.
HE'S LOWER THAN A COCK-ROACH!
I'M...
WHOA !!
FWUO
PLEASE DON'T WORRY. LET ME HANDLE THIS.
VOOSH
TH... *THANKS,* BUTLER-IN-DEBT!!
I'M COUNTING ON YOU!!
...
ALL RIGHT, FOR STARTERS, LET'S SPREAD THIS RUMOR ON THE 'NET.
THAT SHOULD STIR THINGS UP AND ATTRACT THE ATTENTION OF OJÔ-SAMA AND THE OTHERS...!!
I'VE STARTED *LOTS* OF FAMOUS THREADS IN THE PAST.
NO PROBLEM, I CAN DO THIS!!
I'LL KEEP CHANGING OUR IP ADDRESS AND MAKING NEW POSTS TO KEEP IT AT THE TOP!
(EIGHTH GRADE DISEASE) WATARU O. SNIFFS GIRL'S SHAWL!

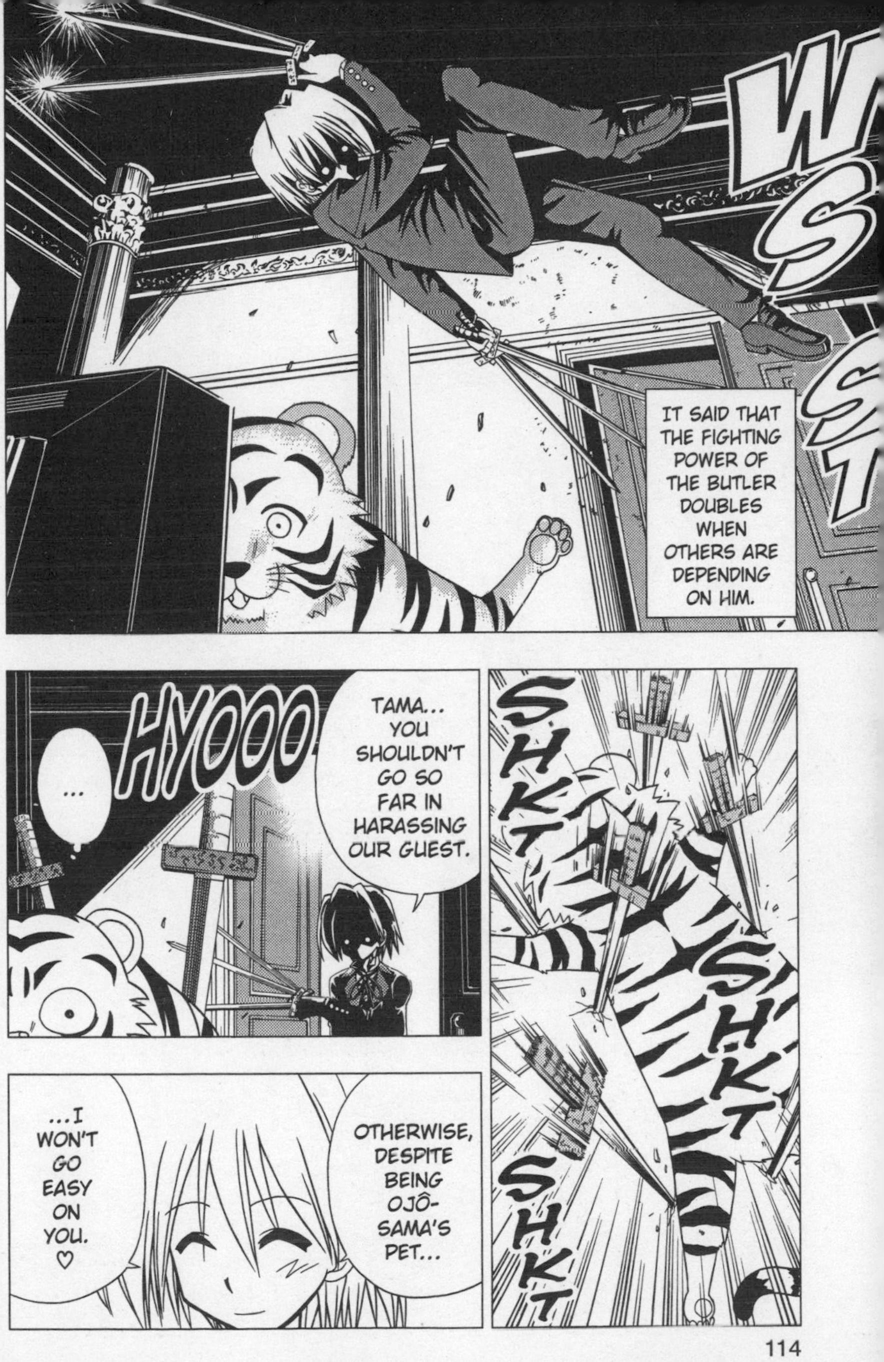
IT SAID THAT THE FIGHTING POWER OF THE BUTLER DOUBLES WHEN OTHERS ARE DEPENDING ON HIM.
SHKT
SHKT
SHKT
TAMA... YOU SHOULDN'T GO SO FAR IN HARASSING OUR GUEST.
HYOOO
...
OTHERWISE, DESPITE BEING OJÔ-SAMA'S PET...
...I WON'T GO EASY ON YOU. ♡

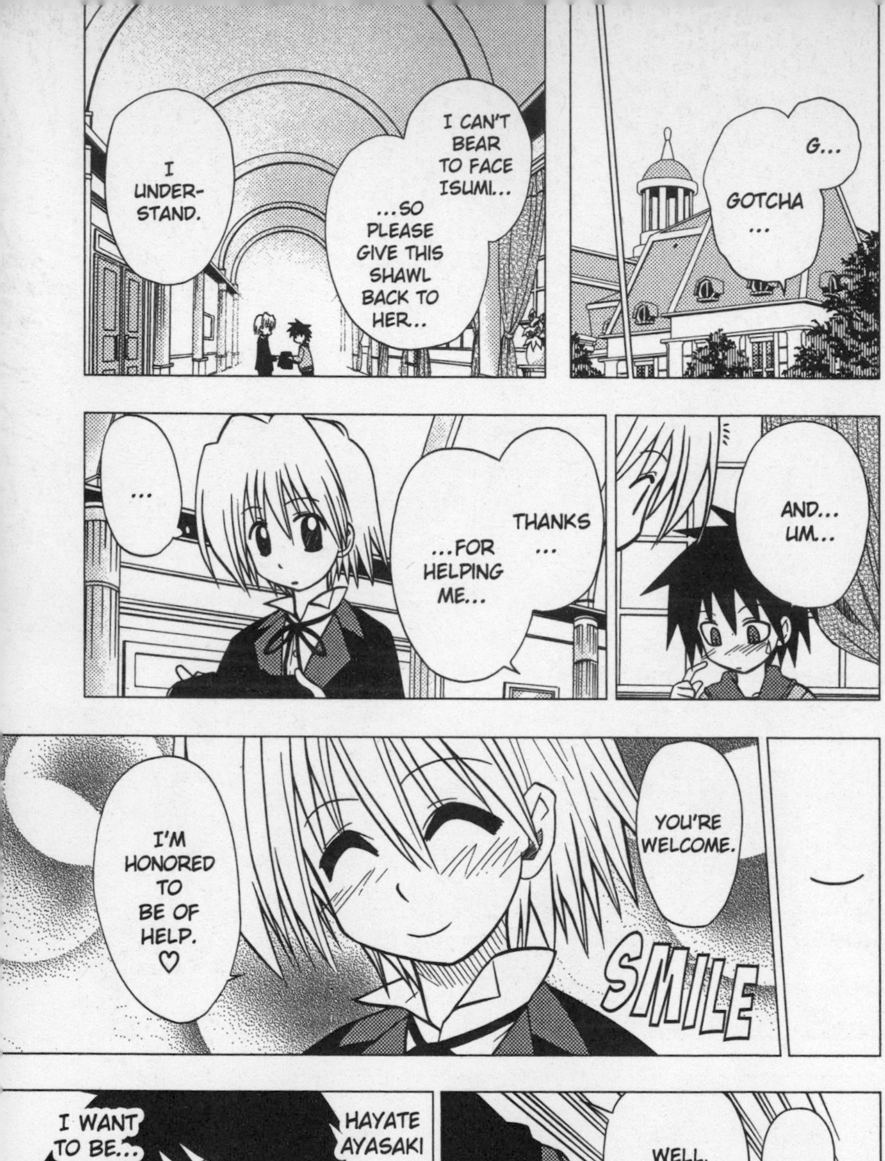
G... GOTCHA ...
I CAN'T BEAR TO FACE ISUMI...
...SO PLEASE GIVE THIS SHAWL BACK TO HER...
I UNDER-STAND.
AND... UM...
THANKS ...
...FOR HELPING ME...
...
YOU'RE WELCOME.
SMILE
I'M HONORED TO BE OF HELP. ♡
...
WELL, PLEASE EXCUSE ME.
TMP
HAYATE AYASAKI ...
I WANT TO BE... A MAN LIKE HIM...

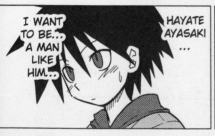

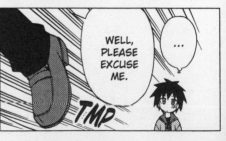

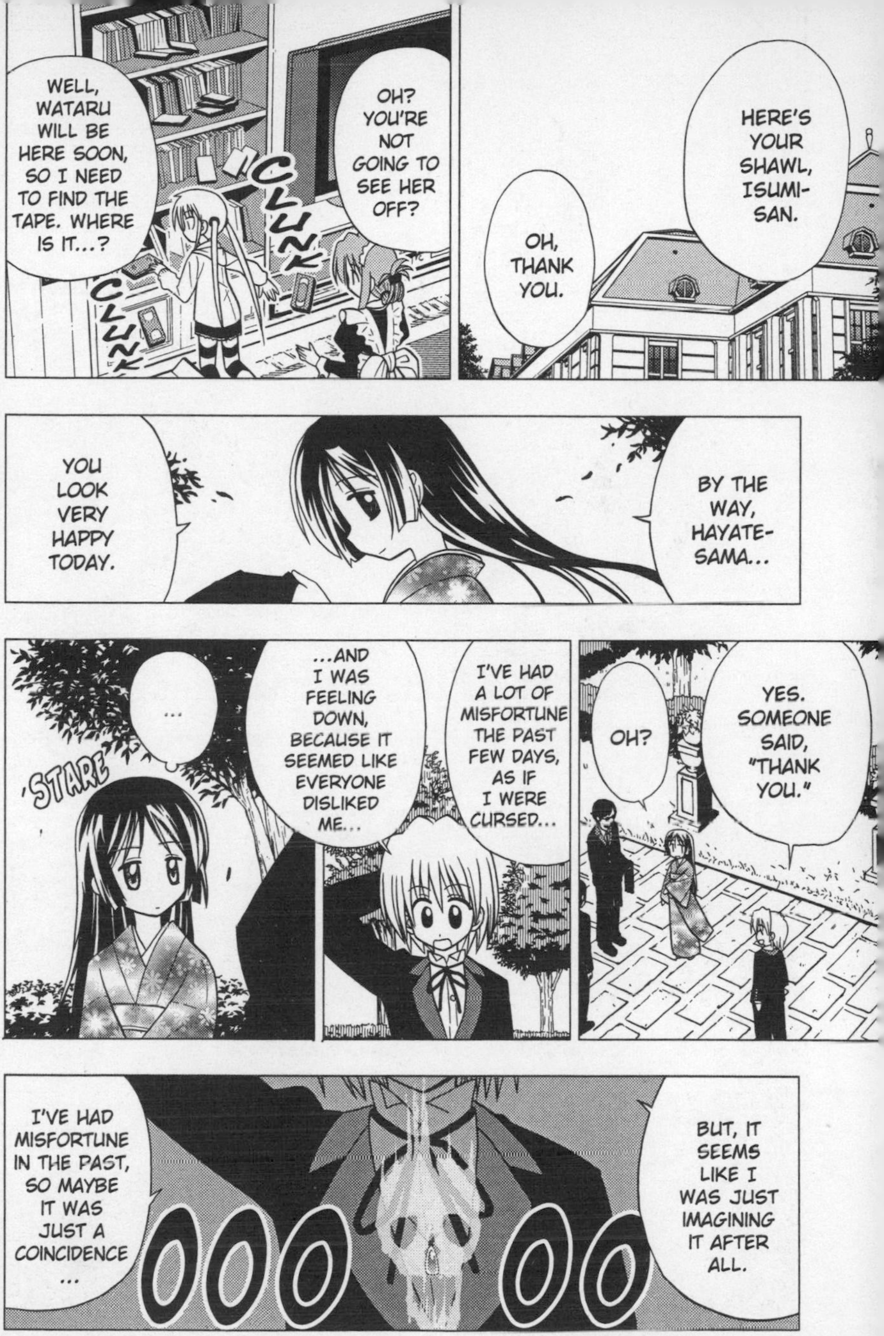
HERE'S YOUR SHAWL, ISUMI-SAN.
OH, THANK YOU.
OH? YOU'RE NOT GOING TO SEE HER OFF?
WELL, WATARU WILL BE HERE SOON, SO I NEED TO FIND THE TAPE. WHERE IS IT...?
CLUNK
CLUNK
BY THE WAY, HAYATE-SAMA...
YOU LOOK VERY HAPPY TODAY.
YES. SOMEONE SAID, "THANK YOU."
OH?
I'VE HAD A LOT OF MISFORTUNE THE PAST FEW DAYS, AS IF I WERE CURSED...
...AND I WAS FEELING DOWN, BECAUSE IT SEEMED LIKE EVERYONE DISLIKED ME...
...
STARE
BUT, IT SEEMS LIKE I WAS JUST IMAGINING IT AFTER ALL.
I'VE HAD MISFORTUNE IN THE PAST, SO MAYBE IT WAS JUST A COINCIDENCE...

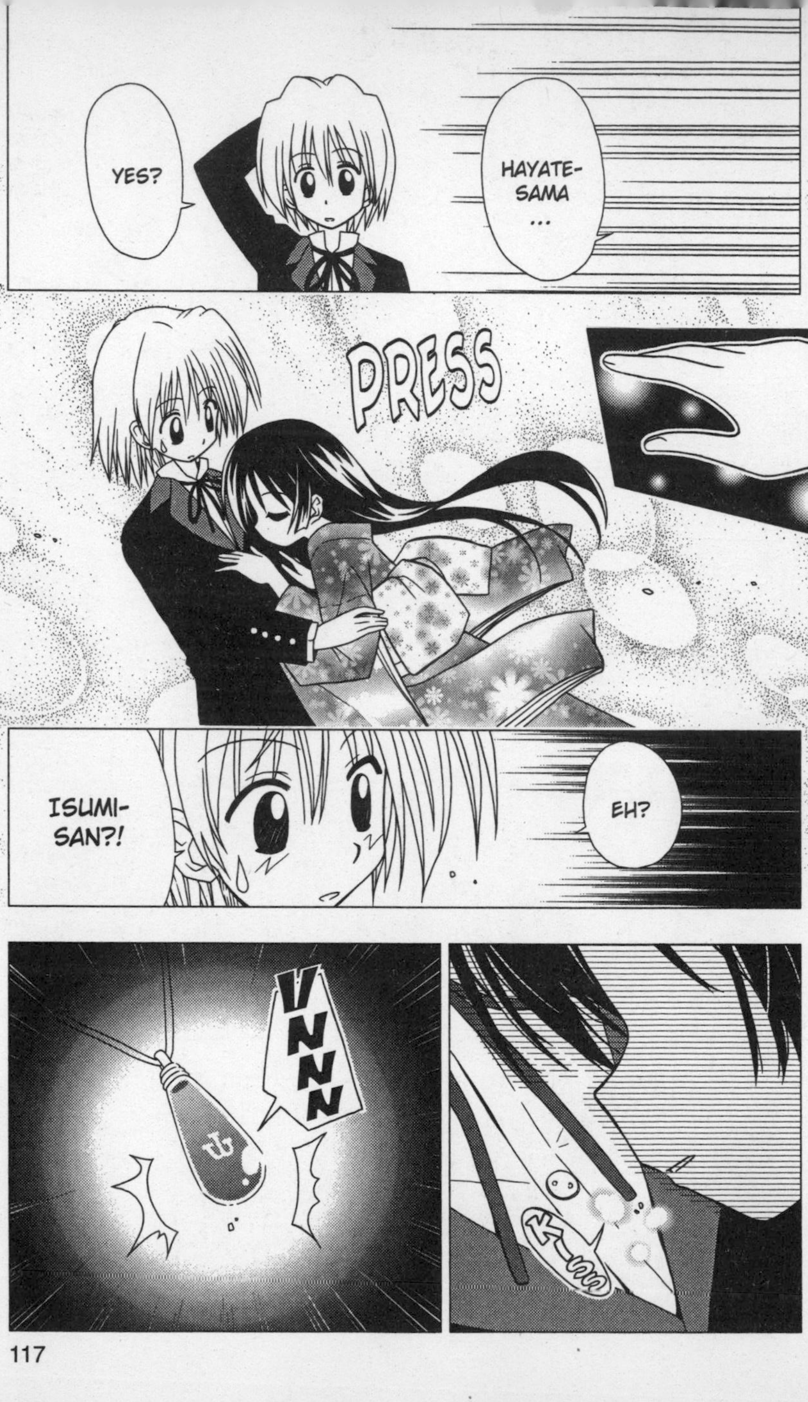
HAYATE-SAMA ...
YES?
PRESS
EH?
ISUMI-SAN?!
K-SS
VNNN

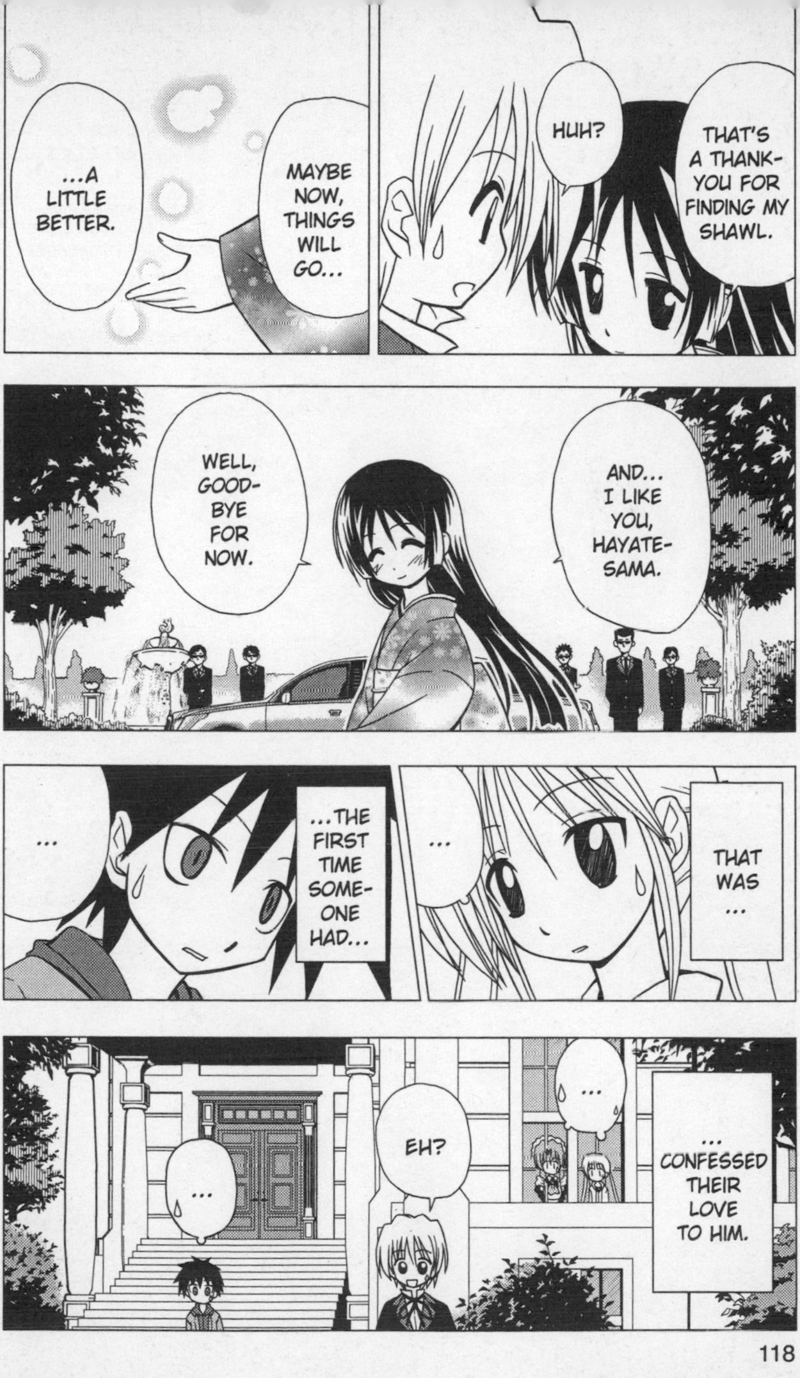
THAT'S A THANK-YOU FOR FINDING MY SHAWL.
HUH?
MAYBE NOW, THINGS WILL GO...
...A LITTLE BETTER.
AND... I LIKE YOU, HAYATE-SAMA.
WELL, GOOD-BYE FOR NOW.
THAT WAS...
...
...THE FIRST TIME SOME-ONE HAD...
...
...CONFESSED THEIR LOVE TO HIM.
...
EH?
...

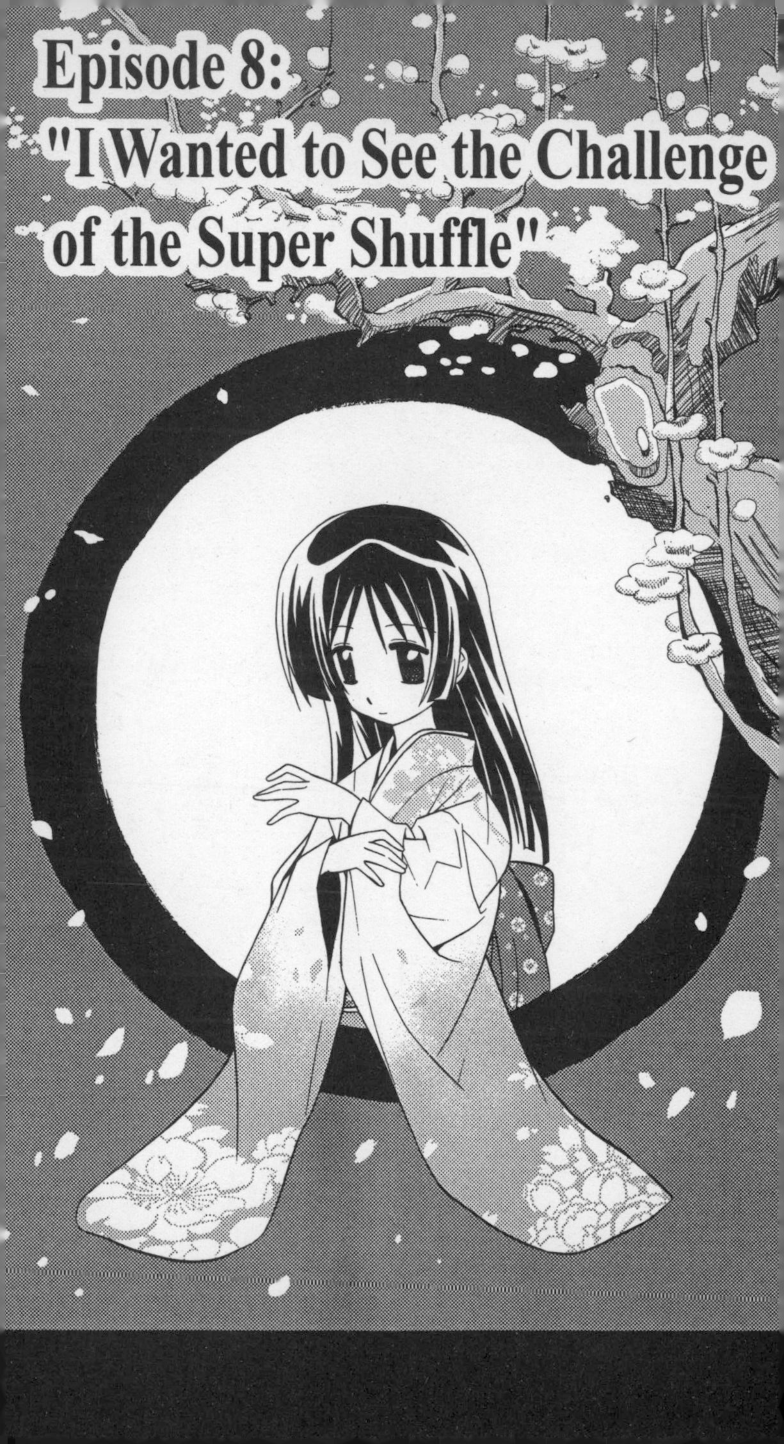
Episode 8:
"I Wanted to See the Challenge of the Super Shuffle"

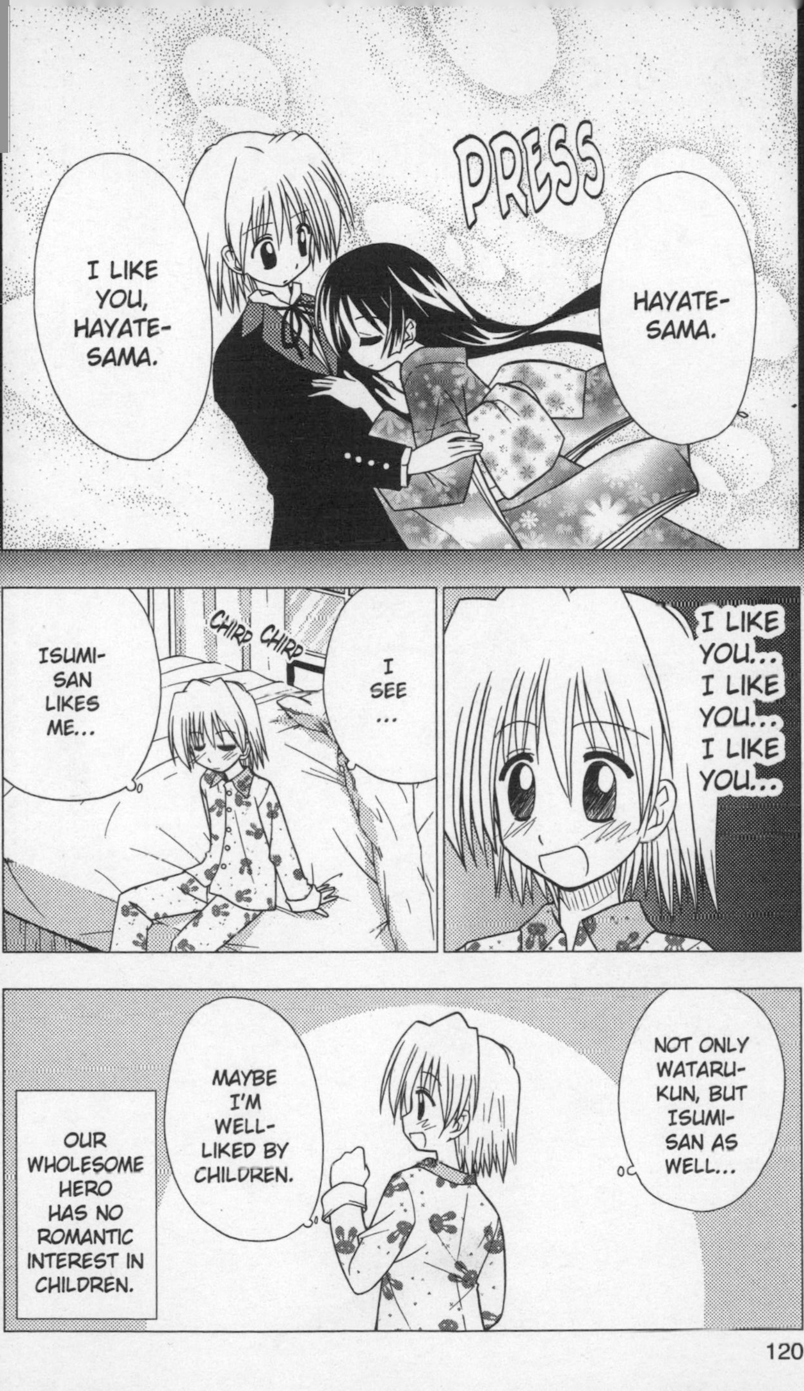
HAYATE-SAMA.
PRESS
I LIKE YOU, HAYATE-SAMA.
I LIKE YOU... I LIKE YOU... I LIKE YOU...
I SEE ...
CHIRP CHIRP
ISUMI-SAN LIKES ME...
NOT ONLY WATARU-KUN, BUT ISUMI-SAN AS WELL...
MAYBE I'M WELL-LIKED BY CHILDREN.
OUR WHOLESOME HERO HAS NO ROMANTIC INTEREST IN CHILDREN.

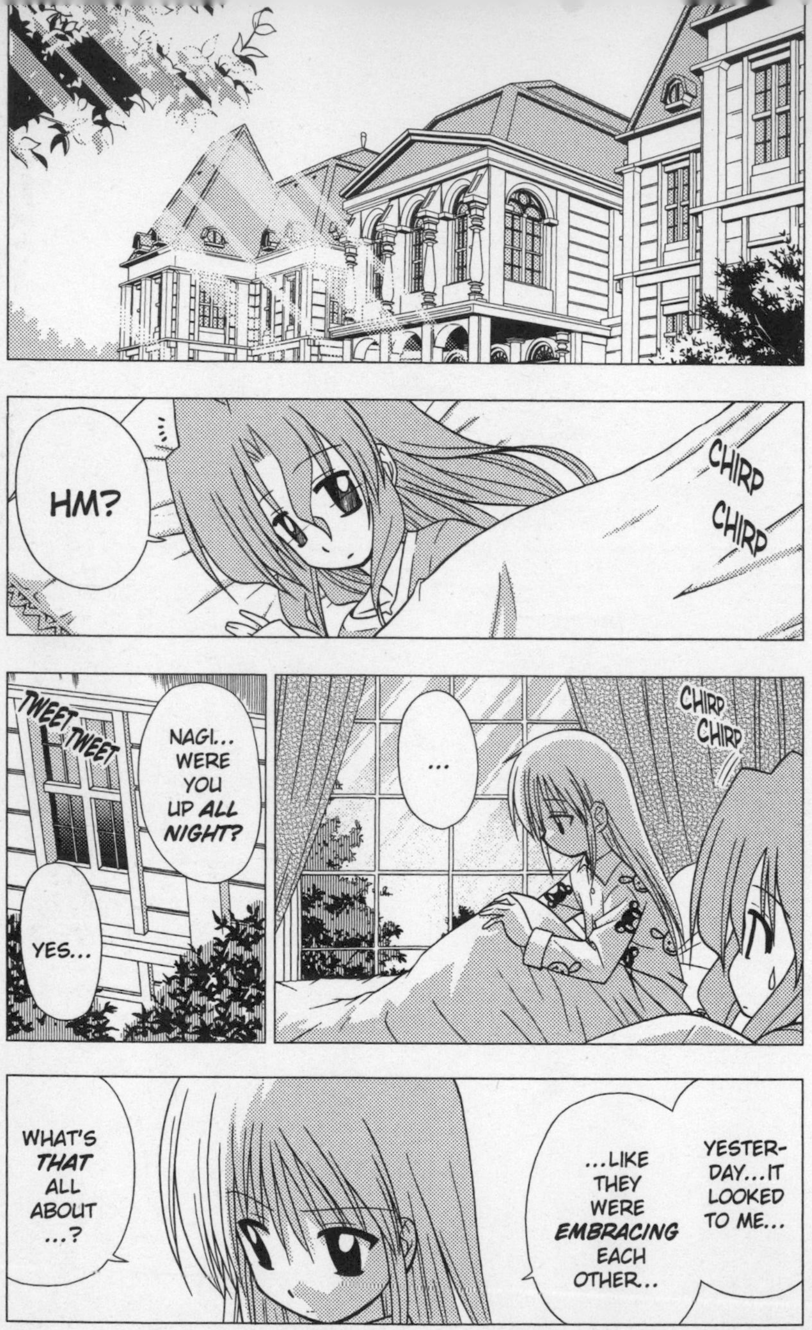
CHIRP CHIRP
HM?
CHIRP CHIRP
...
NAGI... WERE YOU UP ALL NIGHT?
TWEET TWEET
YES...
YESTER-DAY... IT LOOKED TO ME...
...LIKE THEY WERE EMBRACING EACH OTHER...
WHAT'S THAT ALL ABOUT...?

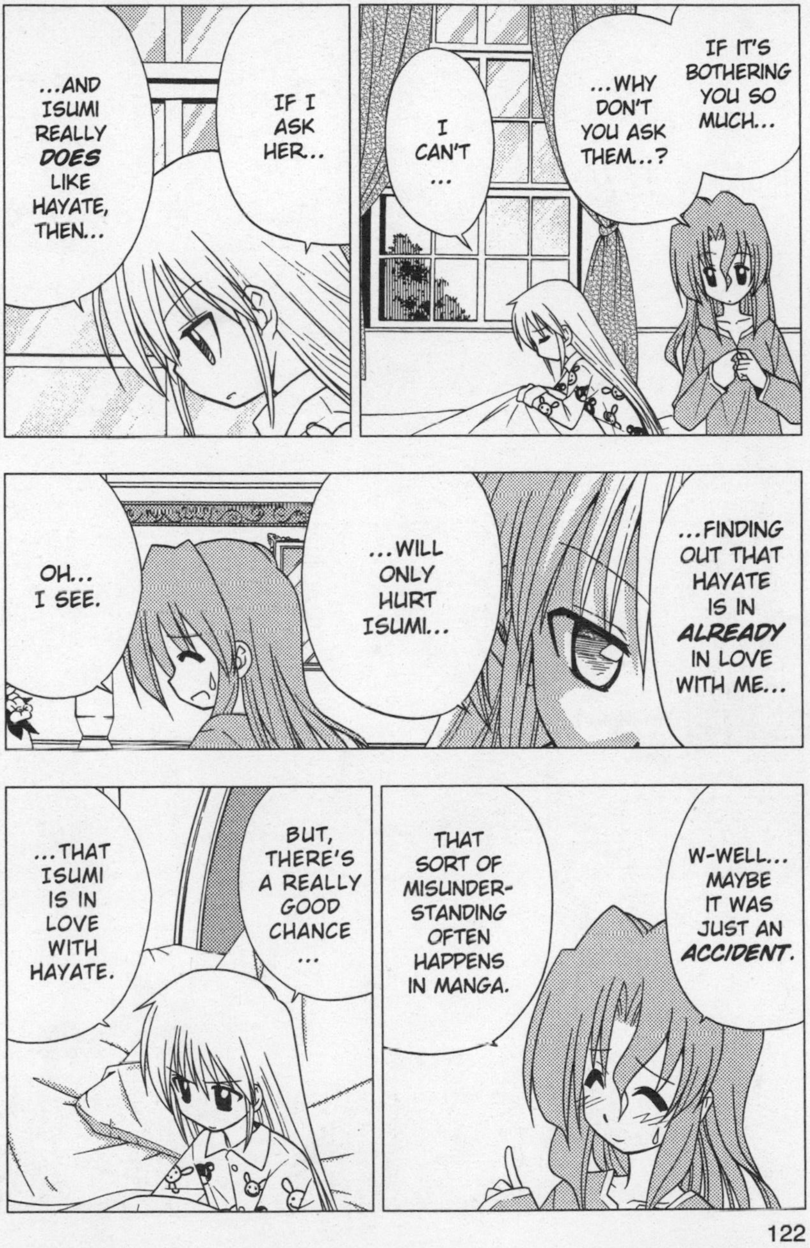
IF IT'S BOTHERING YOU SO MUCH...
...WHY DON'T YOU ASK THEM...?
I CAN'T ...
IF I ASK HER...
...AND ISUMI REALLY DOES LIKE HAYATE, THEN...
...FINDING OUT THAT HAYATE IS IN ALREADY IN LOVE WITH ME...
...WILL ONLY HURT ISUMI...
OH... I SEE.
W-WELL... MAYBE IT WAS JUST AN ACCIDENT.
THAT SORT OF MISUNDERSTANDING OFTEN HAPPENS IN MANGA.
BUT, THERE'S A REALLY GOOD CHANCE ...
...THAT ISUMI IS IN LOVE WITH HAYATE.

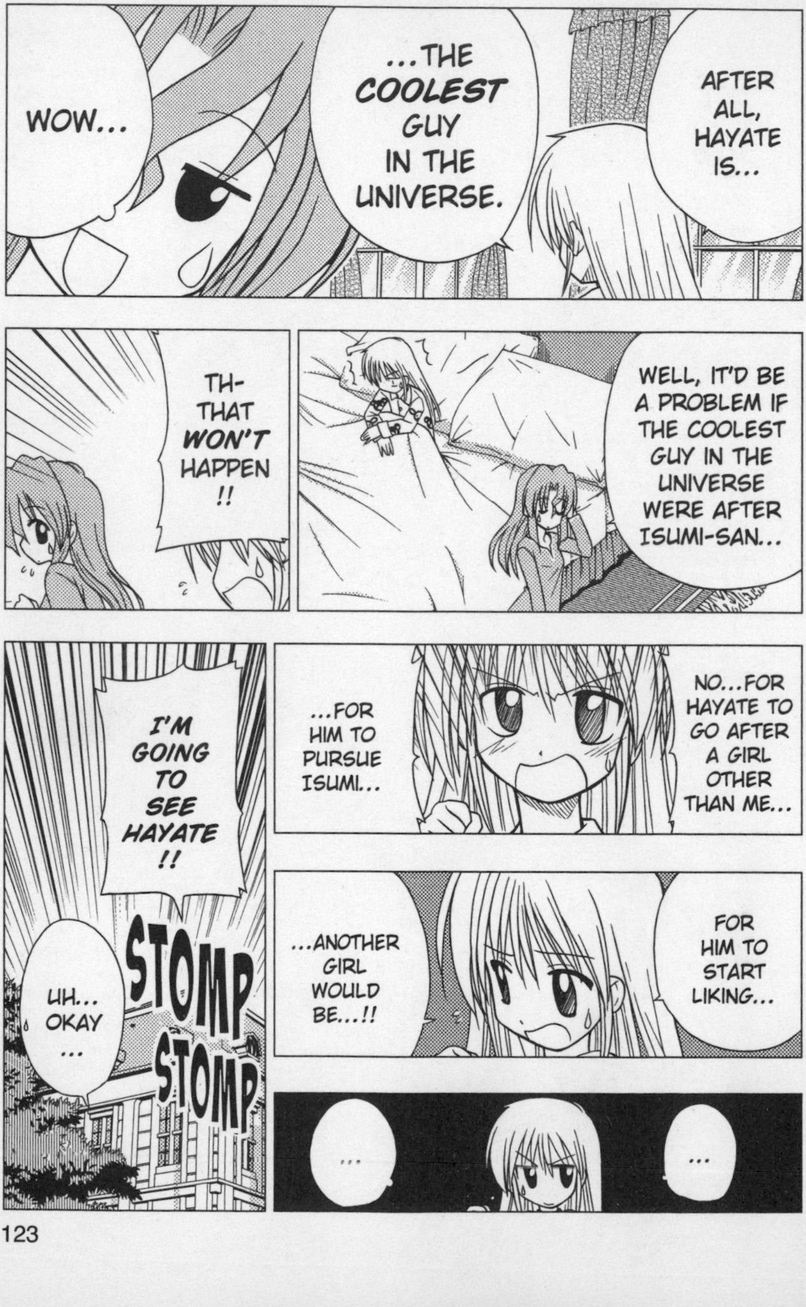
AFTER ALL, HAYATE IS...
...THE COOLEST GUY IN THE UNIVERSE.
WOW...
WELL, IT'D BE A PROBLEM IF THE COOLEST GUY IN THE UNIVERSE WERE AFTER ISUMI-SAN...
TH-THAT WON'T HAPPEN!!
NO...FOR HAYATE TO GO AFTER A GIRL OTHER THAN ME...
...FOR HIM TO PURSUE ISUMI...
FOR HIM TO START LIKING...
...ANOTHER GIRL WOULD BE...!!
...
...
I'M GOING TO SEE HAYATE!!
STOMP
STOMP
UH... OKAY...

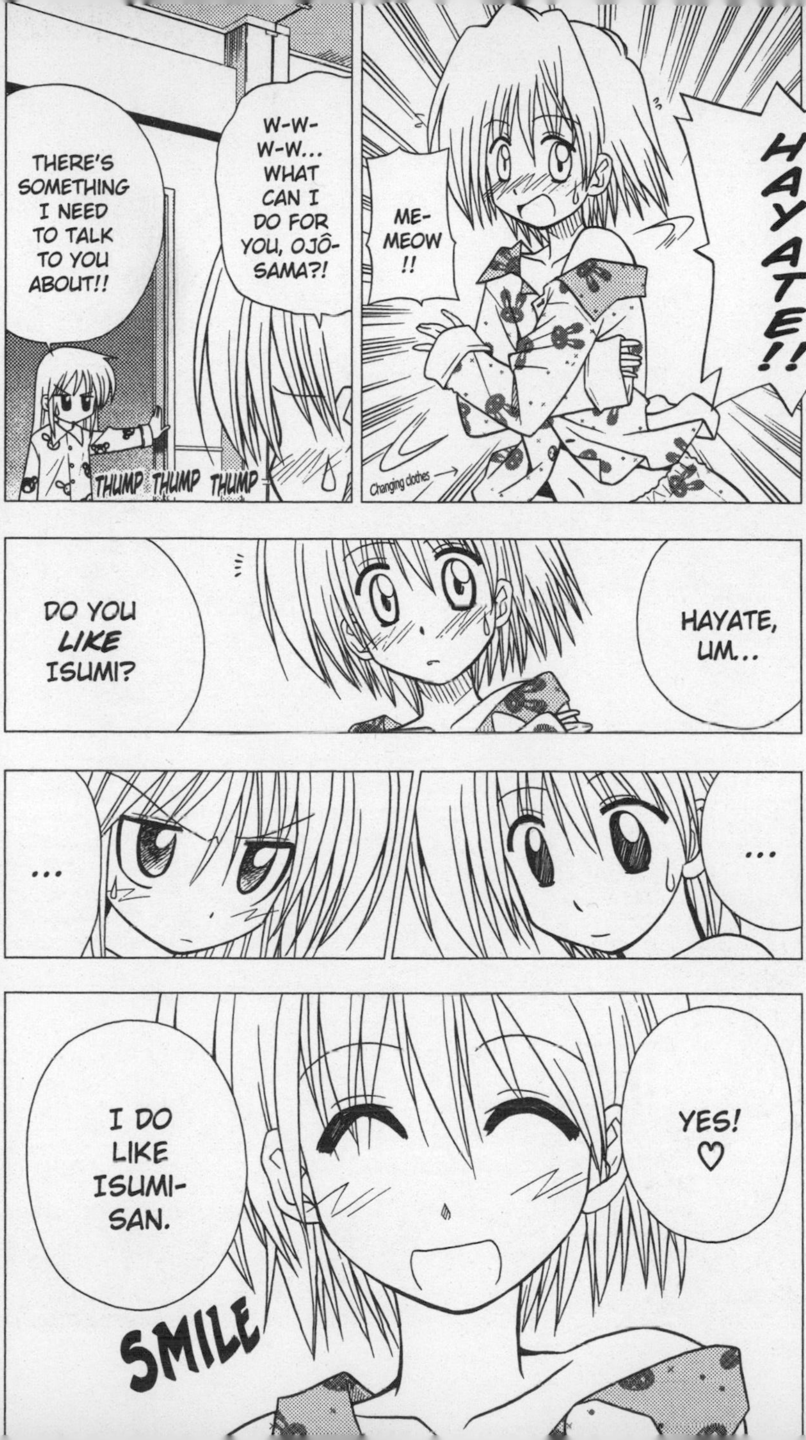
HAYATE!!
ME-MEOW!!
Changing clothes
W-W-W-W... WHAT CAN I DO FOR YOU, OJÔ-SAMA?!
THERE'S SOMETHING I NEED TO TALK TO YOU ABOUT!!
THUMP THUMP THUMP
HAYATE, UM...
DO YOU *LIKE* ISUMI?
...
...
YES! ♡
I DO LIKE ISUMI-SAN.
SMILE

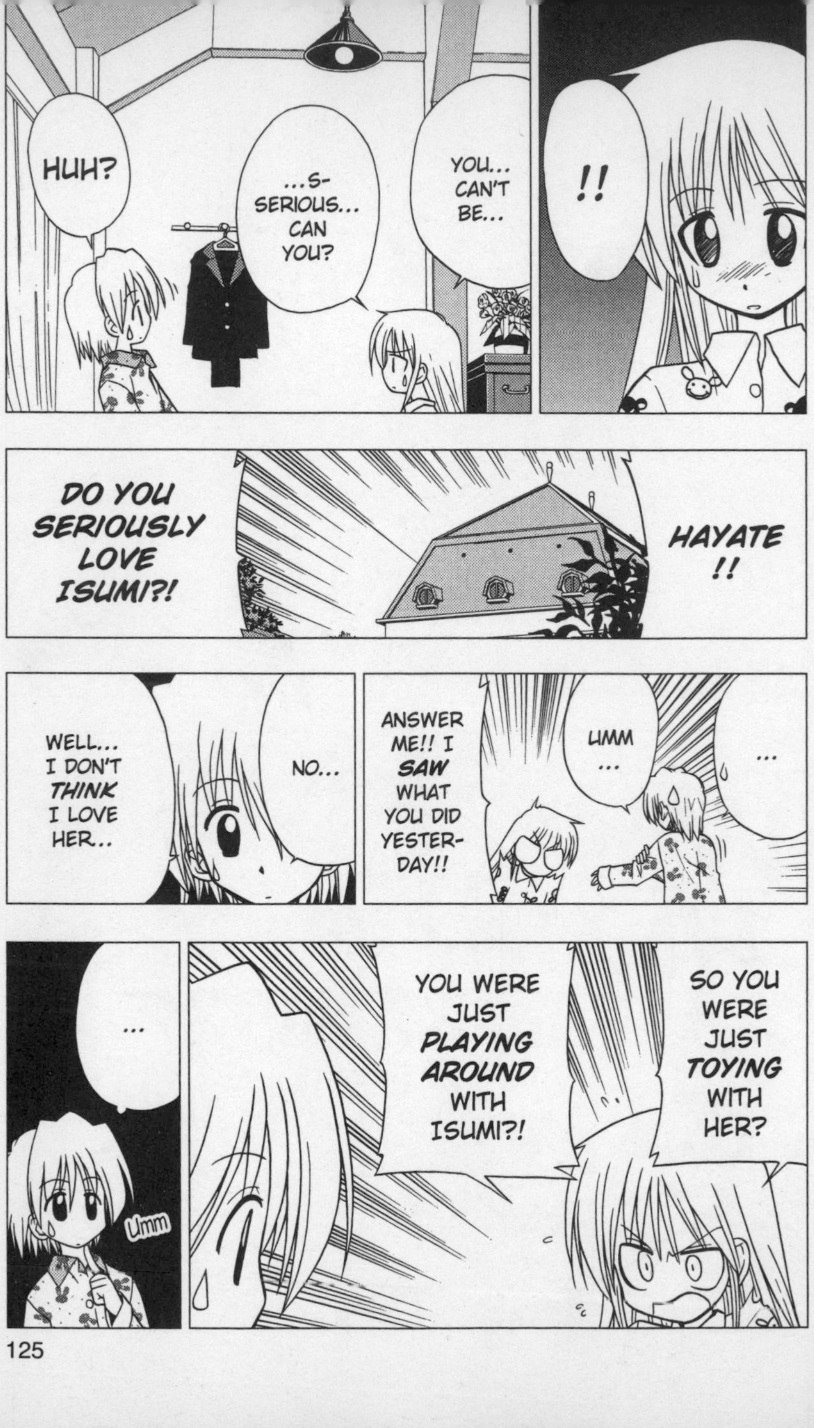
!!
YOU... CAN'T BE...
...S-SERIOUS... CAN YOU?
HUH?
HAYATE!!
DO YOU SERIOUSLY LOVE ISUMI?!
...
UMM...
ANSWER ME!! I SAW WHAT YOU DID YESTERDAY!!
NO...
WELL... I DON'T THINK I LOVE HER..
SO YOU WERE JUST TOYING WITH HER?
YOU WERE JUST PLAYING AROUND WITH ISUMI?!
...
Umm

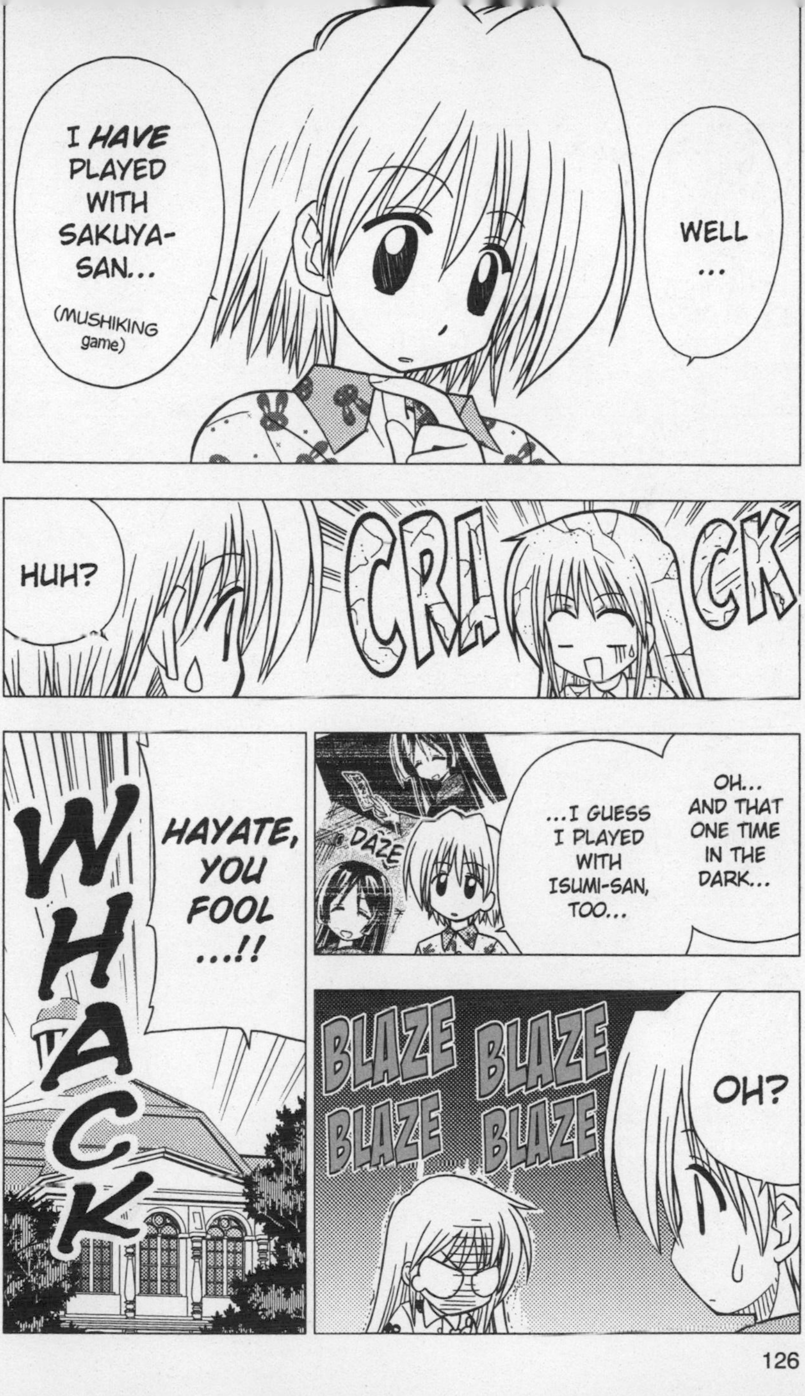
WELL ...
I HAVE PLAYED WITH SAKUYA-SAN...
(MUSHIKING game)
CRACK
HUH?
OH... AND THAT ONE TIME IN THE DARK...
...I GUESS I PLAYED WITH ISUMI-SAN, TOO...
DAZE
OH?
BLAZE BLAZE BLAZE BLAZE
HAYATE, YOU FOOL ...!!
WHACK

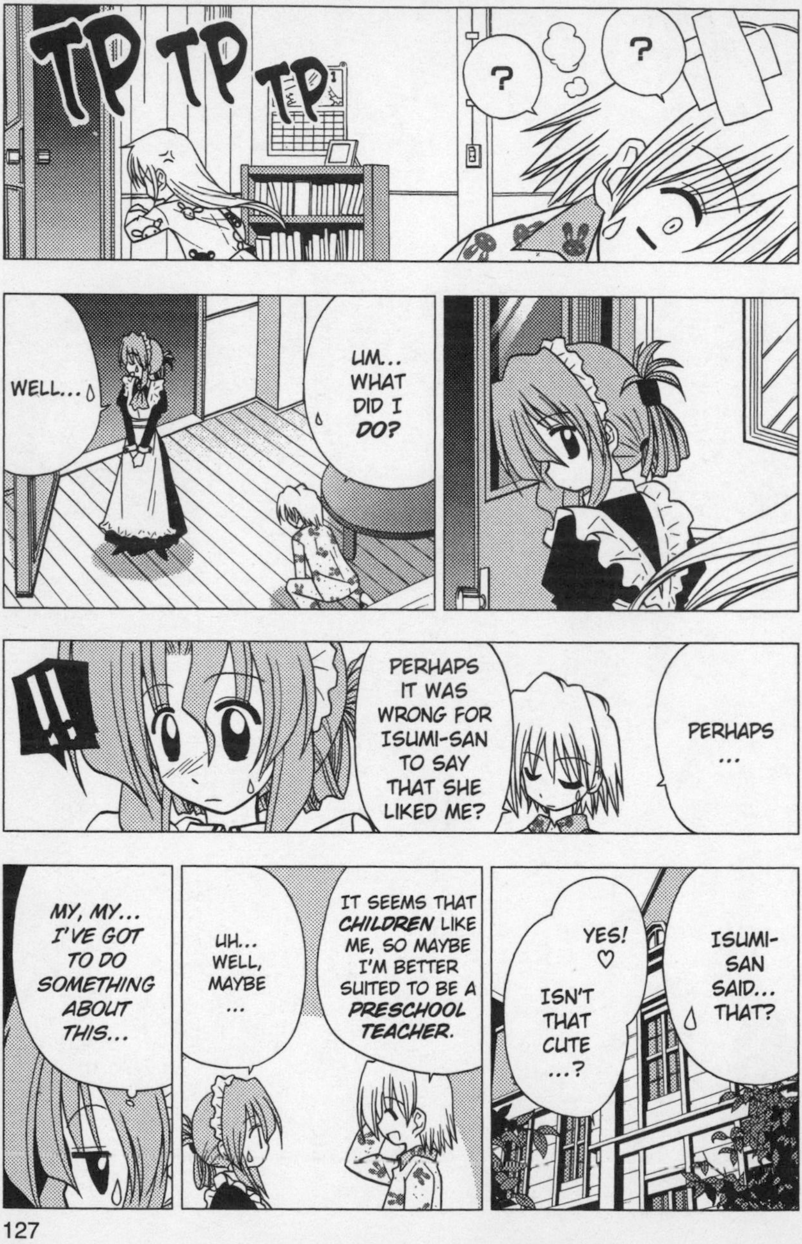
?
?
TP TP TP
UM... WHAT DID I DO?
WELL...
PERHAPS...
PERHAPS IT WAS WRONG FOR ISUMI-SAN TO SAY THAT SHE LIKED ME?
!!
ISUMI-SAN SAID... THAT?
YES! ♡
ISN'T THAT CUTE...?
IT SEEMS THAT CHILDREN LIKE ME, SO MAYBE I'M BETTER SUITED TO BE A PRESCHOOL TEACHER.
UH... WELL, MAYBE...
MY, MY... I'VE GOT TO DO SOMETHING ABOUT THIS...

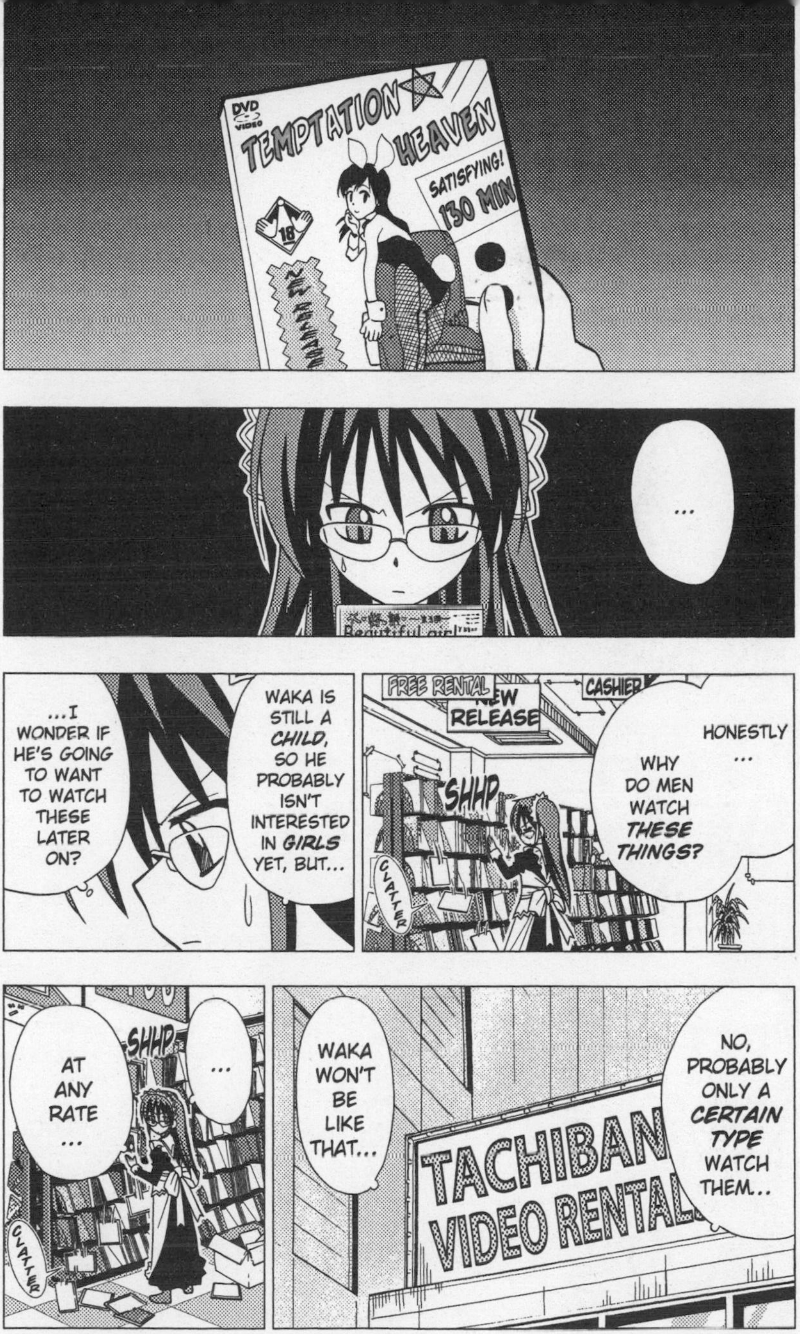
DVD VIDEO
TEMPTATION HEAVEN
SATISFYING! 130 MIN
18
...
CASHIER
FREE RENTAL
NEW RELEASE
HONESTLY...
WHY DO MEN WATCH THESE THINGS?
SHHP
CLATTER
WAKA IS STILL A CHILD, SO HE PROBABLY ISN'T INTERESTED IN GIRLS YET, BUT...
...I WONDER IF HE'S GOING TO WANT TO WATCH THESE LATER ON?
NO, PROBABLY ONLY A CERTAIN TYPE WATCH THEM...
WAKA WON'T BE LIKE THAT...
TACHIBAN
VIDEO RENTAL
...
AT ANY RATE...
SHHP
CLATTER

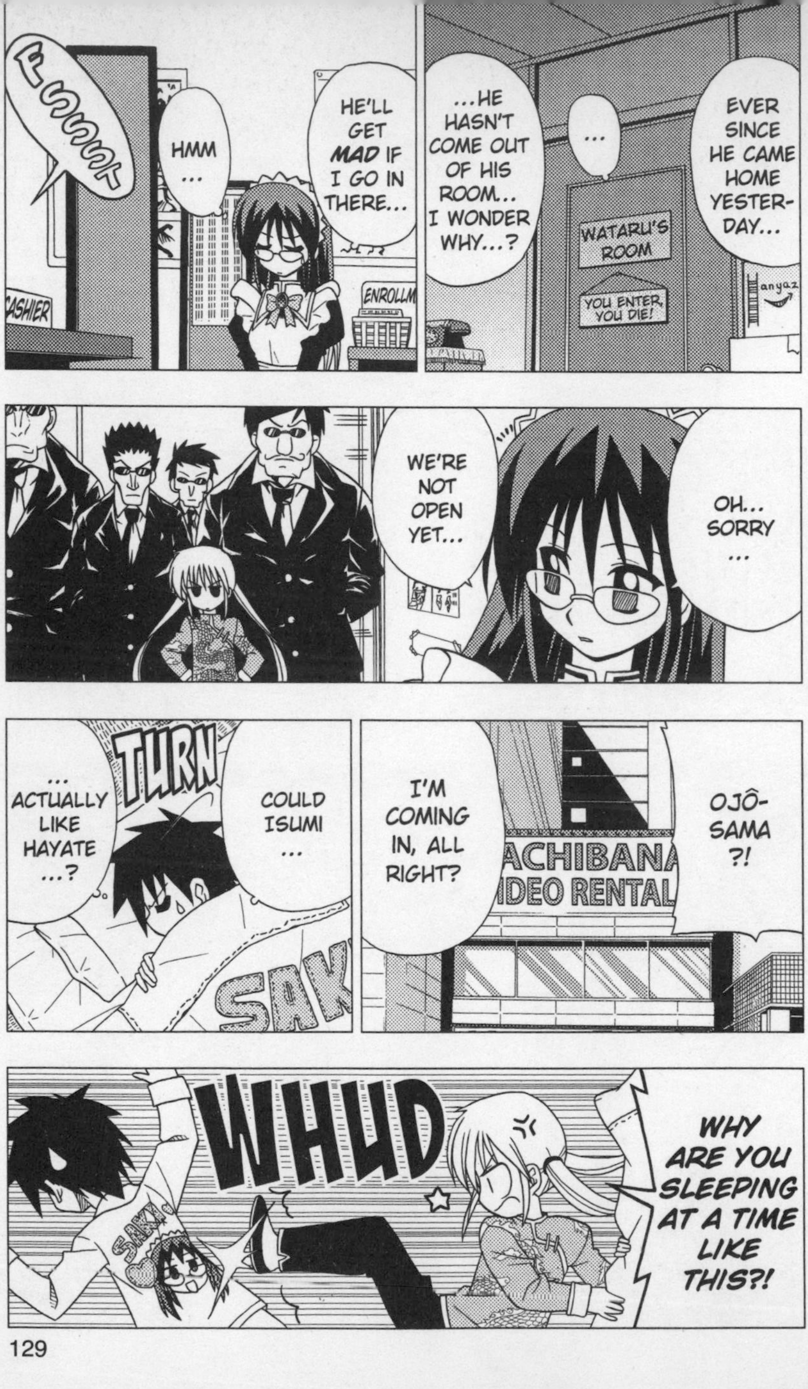
EVER SINCE HE CAME HOME YESTERDAY...
...
...HE HASN'T COME OUT OF HIS ROOM... I WONDER WHY...?
WATARU'S ROOM
YOU ENTER, YOU DIE!
anyaz
HE'LL GET **MAD** IF I GO IN THERE...
HMM ...
FSSSK
CASHIER
ENROLLM
OH... SORRY ...
WE'RE NOT OPEN YET...
OJÔ-SAMA ?!
I'M COMING IN, ALL RIGHT?
ACHIBANA
IDEO RENTAL
COULD ISUMI ...
TURN
... ACTUALLY LIKE HAYATE ...?
SAK
WHY ARE YOU SLEEPING AT A TIME LIKE THIS?!
WHUD
SAKI

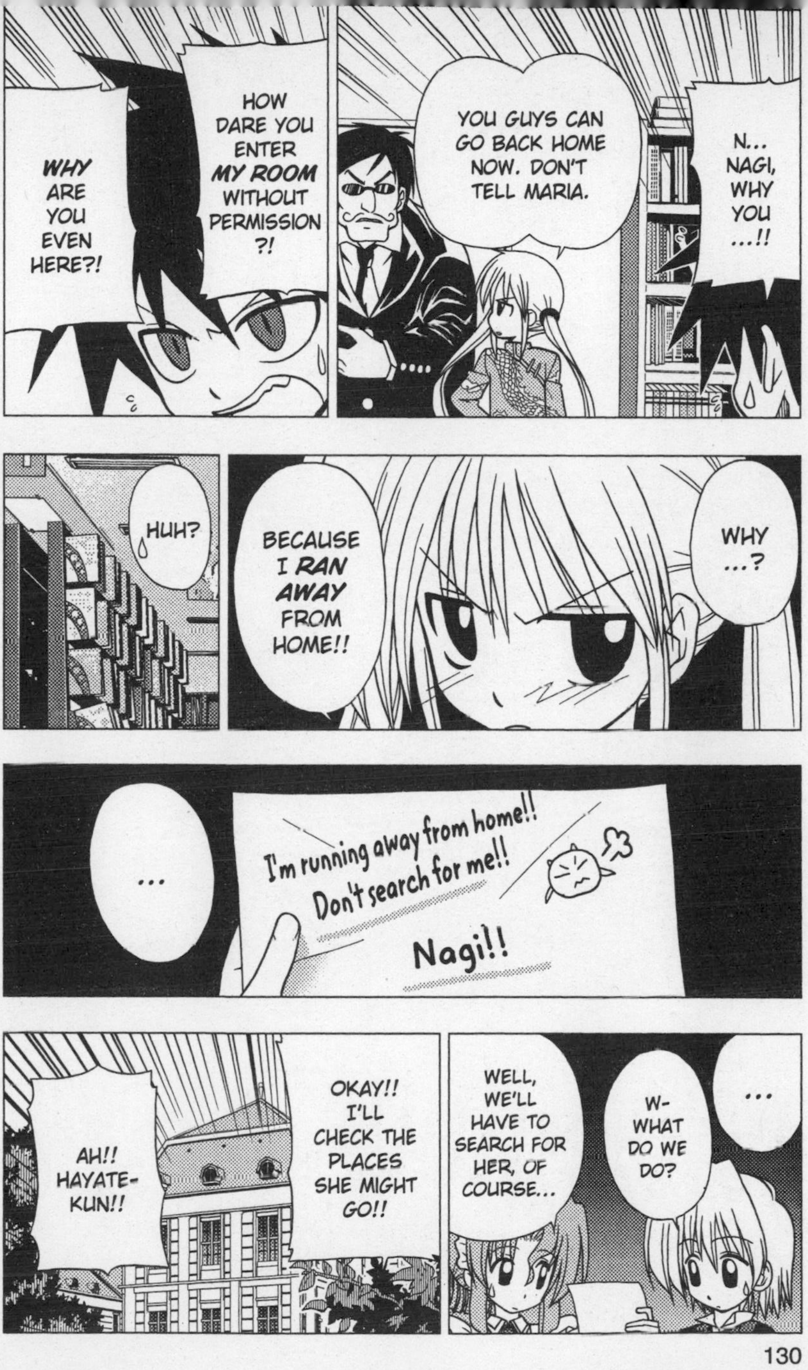
N... NAGI, WHY YOU ...!!
YOU GUYS CAN GO BACK HOME NOW. DON'T TELL MARIA.
HOW DARE YOU ENTER MY ROOM WITHOUT PERMISSION?!
WHY ARE YOU EVEN HERE?!
WHY ...?
BECAUSE I RAN AWAY FROM HOME!!
HUH?
I'm running away from home!! Don't search for me!!
Nagi!!
...
...
W-WHAT DO WE DO?
WELL, WE'LL HAVE TO SEARCH FOR HER, OF COURSE...
OKAY!! I'LL CHECK THE PLACES SHE MIGHT GO!!
AH!! HAYATE-KUN!!

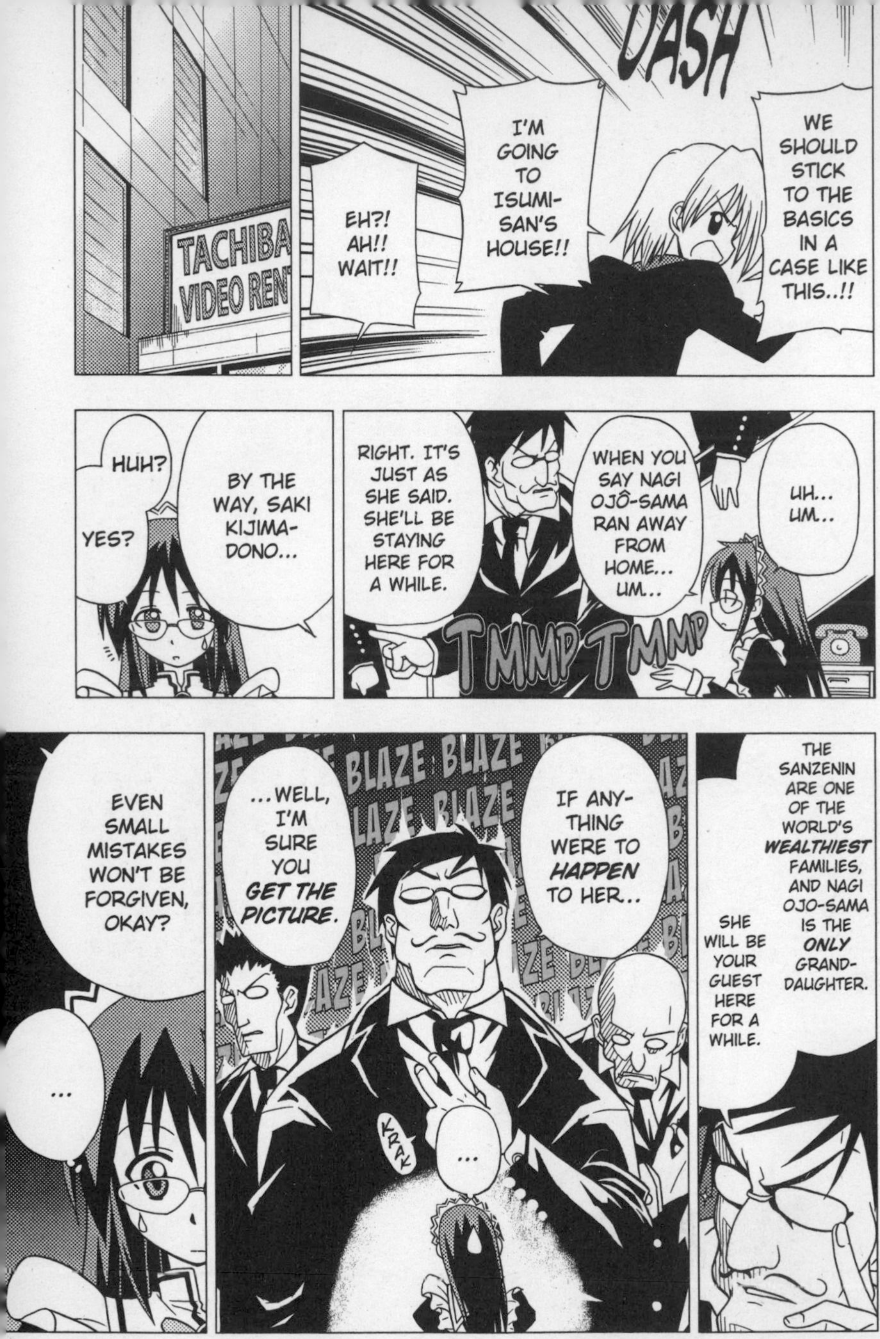
WE SHOULD STICK TO THE BASICS IN A CASE LIKE THIS..!!
DASH
I'M GOING TO ISUMI-SAN'S HOUSE!!
EH?! AH!! WAIT!!
TACHIBA VIDEO RENT
UH... UM...
WHEN YOU SAY NAGI OJÔ-SAMA RAN AWAY FROM HOME... UM...
RIGHT. IT'S JUST AS SHE SAID. SHE'LL BE STAYING HERE FOR A WHILE.
TMMP TMMP
BY THE WAY, SAKI KIJIMA-DONO...
HUH?
YES?
THE SANZENIN ARE ONE OF THE WORLD'S ***WEALTHIEST*** FAMILIES, AND NAGI OJO-SAMA IS THE ***ONLY*** GRAND-DAUGHTER.
SHE WILL BE YOUR GUEST HERE FOR A WHILE.
BLAZE BLAZE
IF ANY-THING WERE TO ***HAPPEN*** TO HER...
...WELL, I'M SURE YOU ***GET THE PICTURE***.
KRAK
...
EVEN SMALL MISTAKES WON'T BE FORGIVEN, OKAY?
...

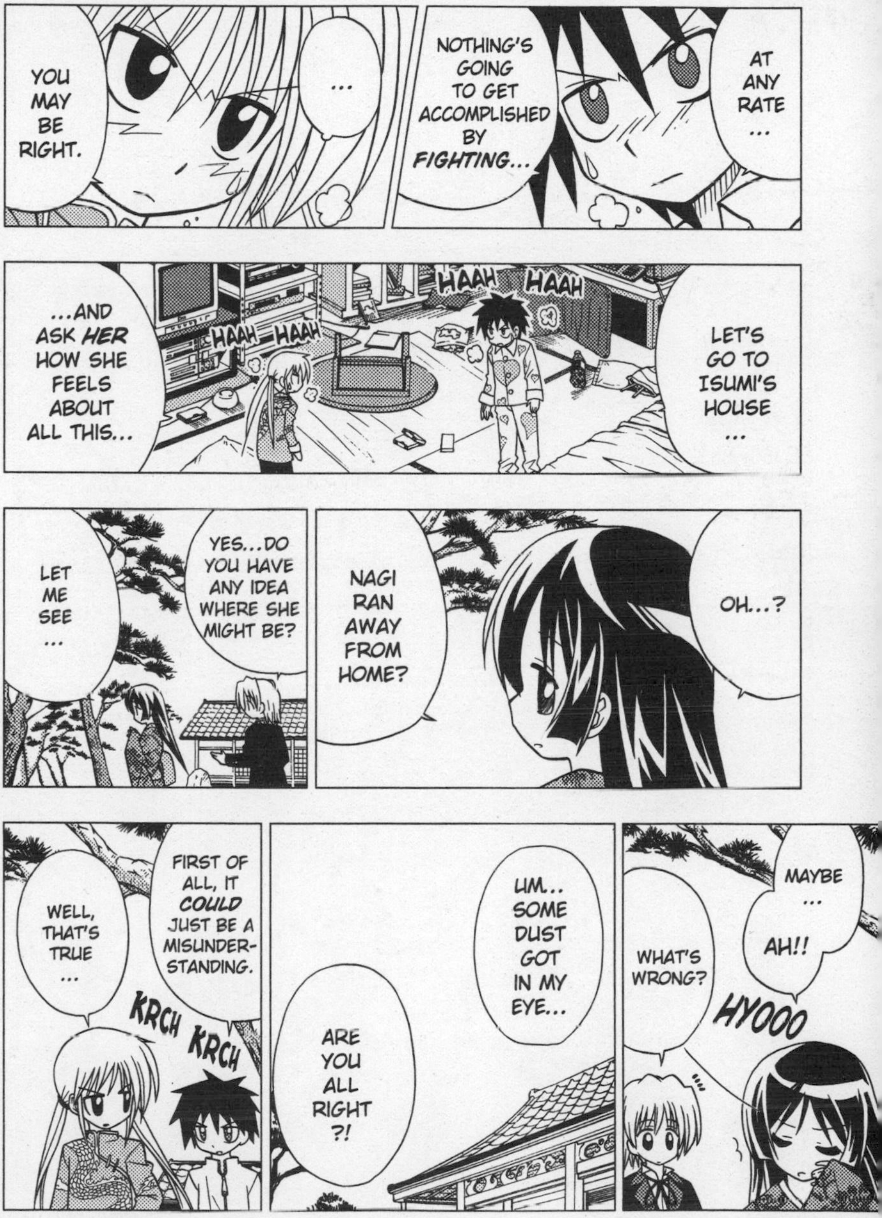
AT ANY RATE ...
NOTHING'S GOING TO GET ACCOMPLISHED BY *FIGHTING*...
...
YOU MAY BE RIGHT.
LET'S GO TO ISUMI'S HOUSE ...
HAAH HAAH
HAAH HAAH
...AND ASK *HER* HOW SHE FEELS ABOUT ALL THIS...
OH...?
NAGI RAN AWAY FROM HOME?
YES...DO YOU HAVE ANY IDEA WHERE SHE MIGHT BE?
LET ME SEE ...
MAYBE ...
AH!!
HYOOO
WHAT'S WRONG?
...
UM... SOME DUST GOT IN MY EYE...
ARE YOU ALL RIGHT ?!
FIRST OF ALL, IT *COULD* JUST BE A MISUNDERSTANDING.
KRCH KRCH
WELL, THAT'S TRUE ...

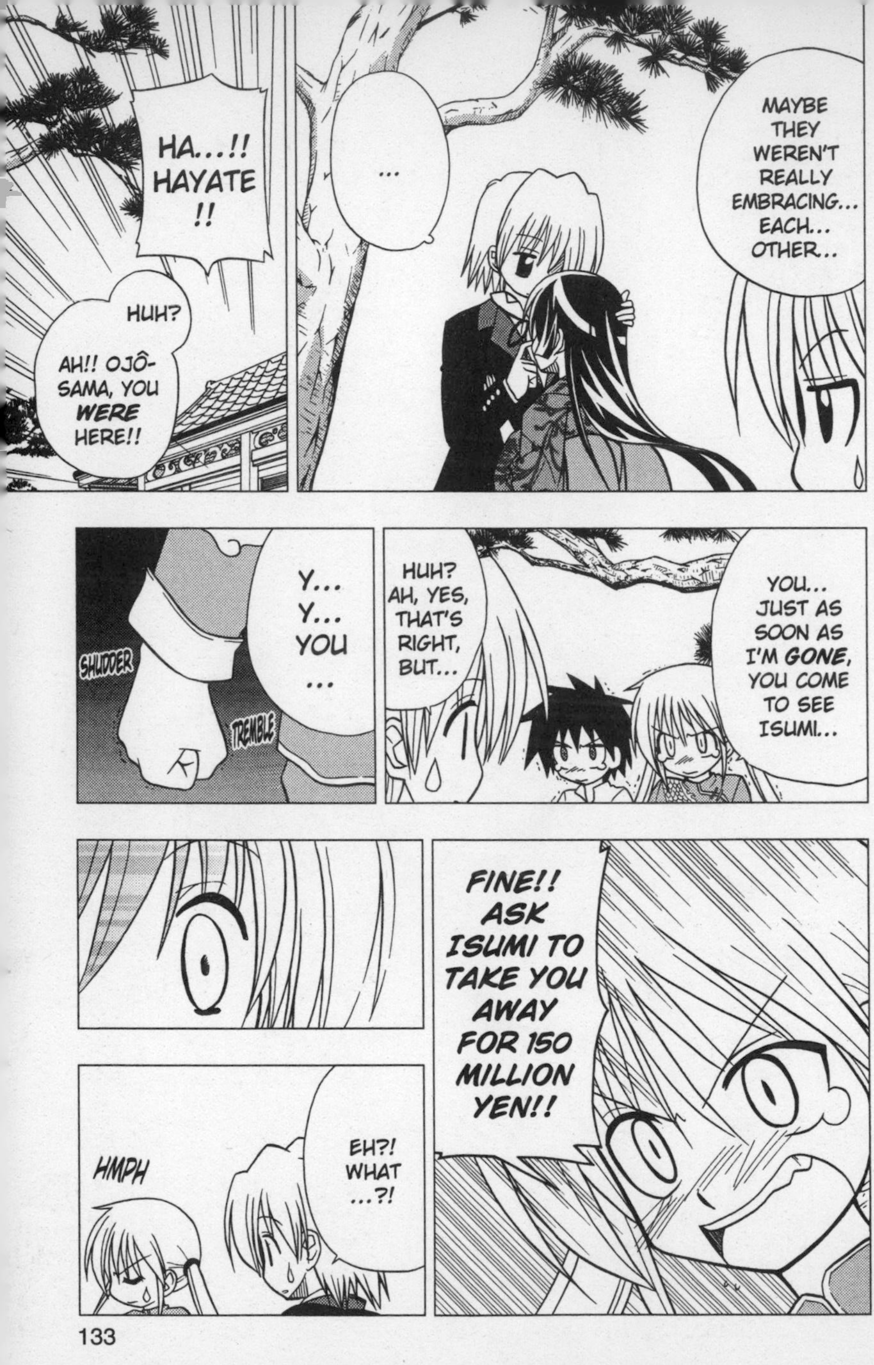
MAYBE THEY WEREN'T REALLY EMBRACING... EACH... OTHER...
...
HA...!! HAYATE !!
HUH?
AH!! OJÔ-SAMA, YOU *WERE* HERE!!
YOU... JUST AS SOON AS I'M *GONE*, YOU COME TO SEE ISUMI...
HUH? AH, YES, THAT'S RIGHT, BUT...
Y... Y... YOU ...
SHUDDER
TREMBLE
FINE!! ASK ISUMI TO TAKE YOU AWAY FOR 150 MILLION YEN!!
EH?! WHAT ...?!
HMPH

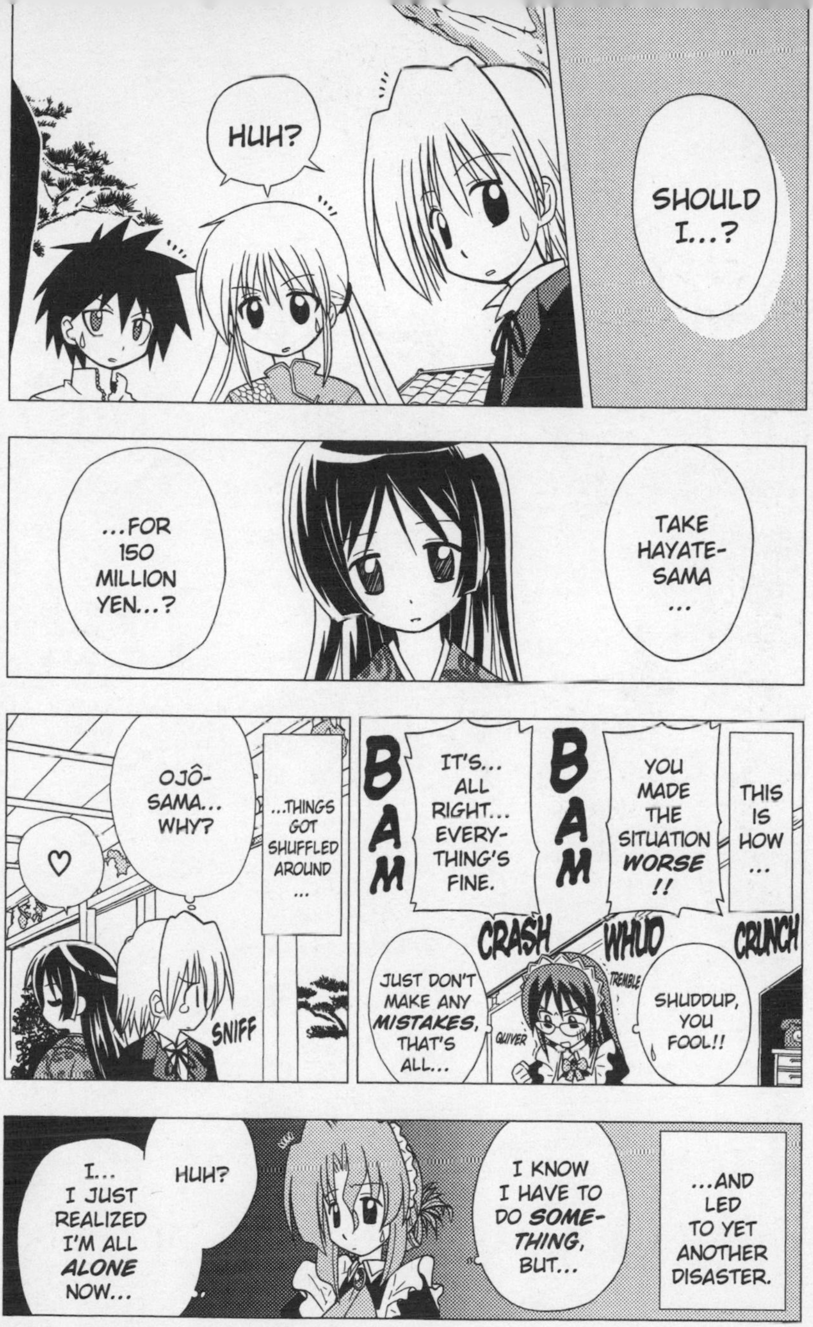
SHOULD I...?
HUH?
TAKE HAYATE-SAMA...
...FOR 150 MILLION YEN...?
THIS IS HOW...
YOU MADE THE SITUATION WORSE!!
BAM
IT'S... ALL RIGHT... EVERYTHING'S FINE.
BAM
CRUNCH
WHUD
CRASH
SHUDDUP, YOU FOOL!!
TREMBLE
QUIVER
JUST DON'T MAKE ANY MISTAKES, THAT'S ALL...
...THINGS GOT SHUFFLED AROUND...
OJÔ-SAMA... WHY?
♡
SNIFF
...AND LED TO YET ANOTHER DISASTER.
I KNOW I HAVE TO DO SOMETHING, BUT...
HUH?
I... I JUST REALIZED I'M ALL ALONE NOW...

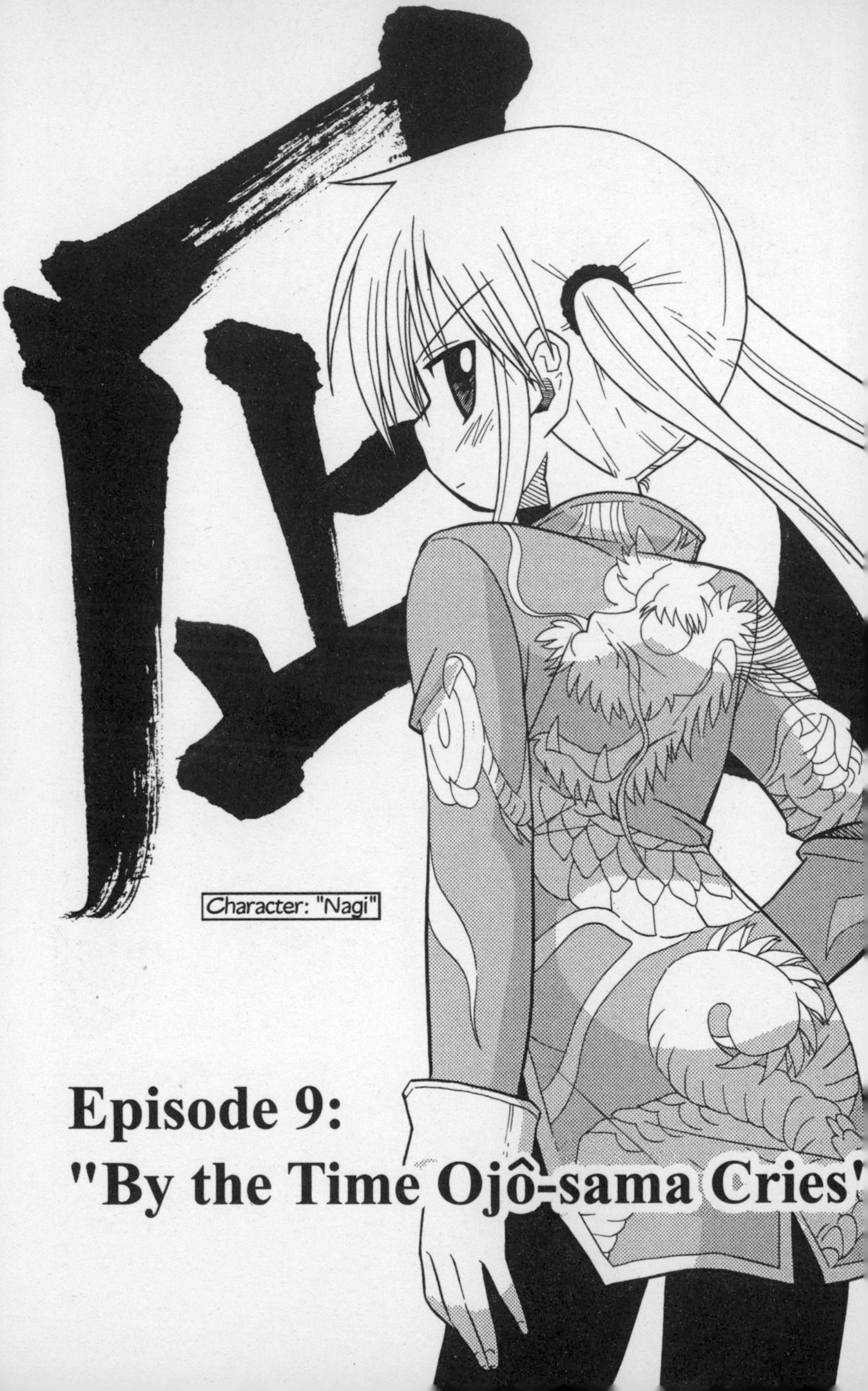
Character: "Nagi"

Episode 9: "By the Time Ojô-sama Cries"

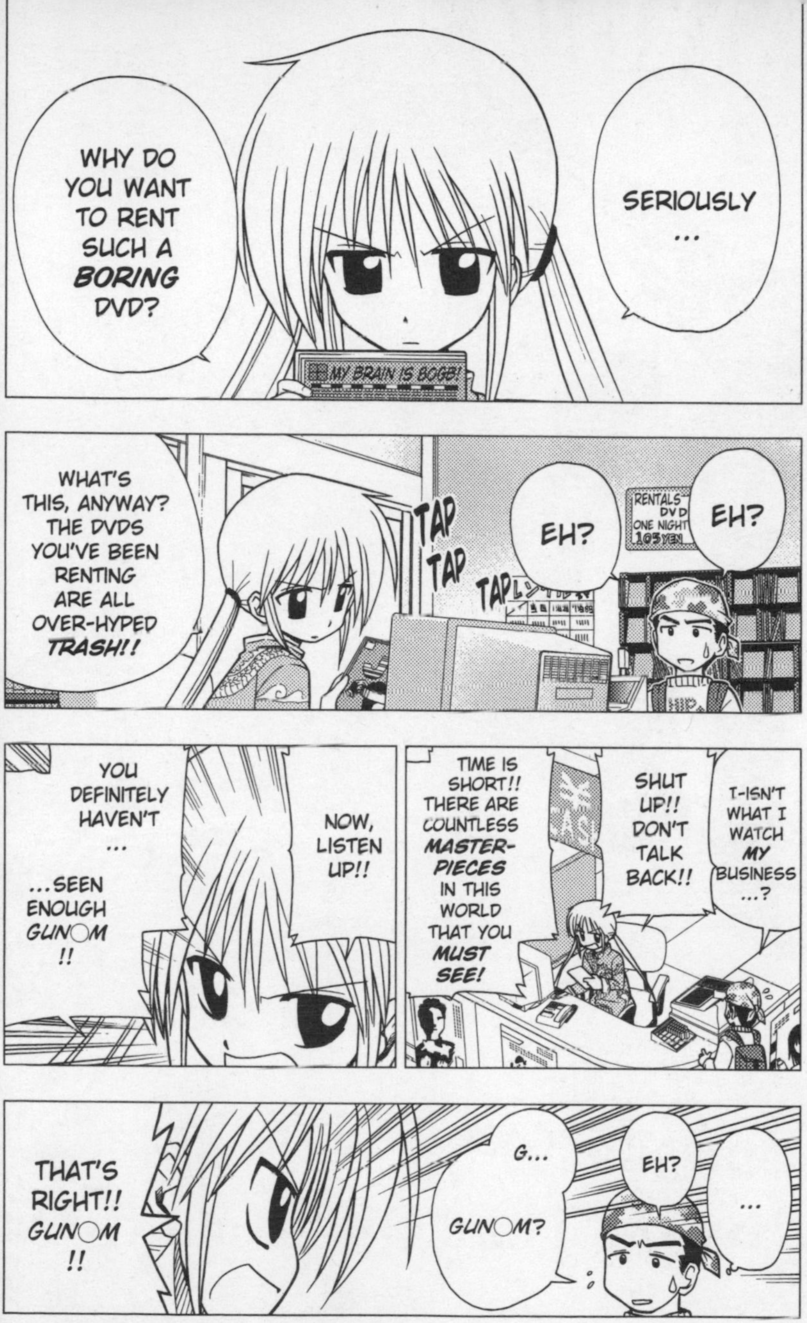
SERIOUSLY ...
WHY DO YOU WANT TO RENT SUCH A BORING DVD?
MY BRAIN IS BOGB!
EH?
EH?
RENTALS DVD ONE NIGHT 105 YEN
TAP TAP TAP
WHAT'S THIS, ANYWAY? THE DVDS YOU'VE BEEN RENTING ARE ALL OVER-HYPED TRASH!!
I-ISN'T WHAT I WATCH MY BUSINESS ...?
SHUT UP!! DON'T TALK BACK!!
TIME IS SHORT!! THERE ARE COUNTLESS MASTER-PIECES IN THIS WORLD THAT YOU MUST SEE!
NOW, LISTEN UP!!
YOU DEFINITELY HAVEN'T ...
...SEEN ENOUGH GUN○M !!
...
EH?
G... GUN○M?
THAT'S RIGHT!! GUN○M !!

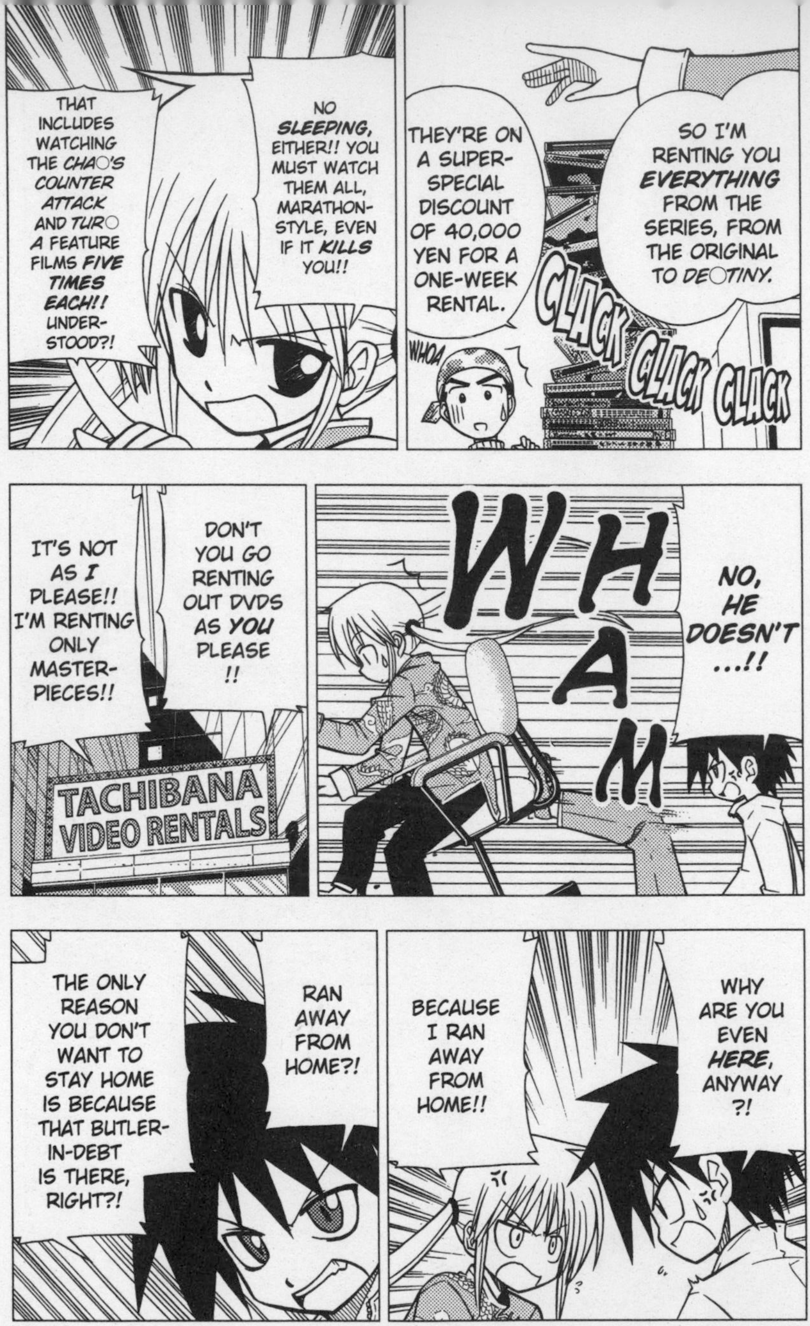
SO I'M RENTING YOU EVERYTHING FROM THE SERIES, FROM THE ORIGINAL TO DE○TINY.
THEY'RE ON A SUPER-SPECIAL DISCOUNT OF 40,000 YEN FOR A ONE-WEEK RENTAL.
CLACK CLACK CLACK
WHOA
NO SLEEPING, EITHER!! YOU MUST WATCH THEM ALL, MARATHON-STYLE, EVEN IF IT KILLS YOU!!
THAT INCLUDES WATCHING THE CHA○'S COUNTER ATTACK AND TUR○ A FEATURE FILMS FIVE TIMES EACH!! UNDER-STOOD?!
NO, HE DOESN'T...!!
WHAM
DON'T YOU GO RENTING OUT DVDS AS YOU PLEASE!!
IT'S NOT AS I PLEASE!! I'M RENTING ONLY MASTER-PIECES!!
TACHIBANA VIDEO RENTALS
WHY ARE YOU EVEN HERE, ANYWAY?!
BECAUSE I RAN AWAY FROM HOME!!
RAN AWAY FROM HOME?!
THE ONLY REASON YOU DON'T WANT TO STAY HOME IS BECAUSE THAT BUTLER-IN-DEBT IS THERE, RIGHT?!

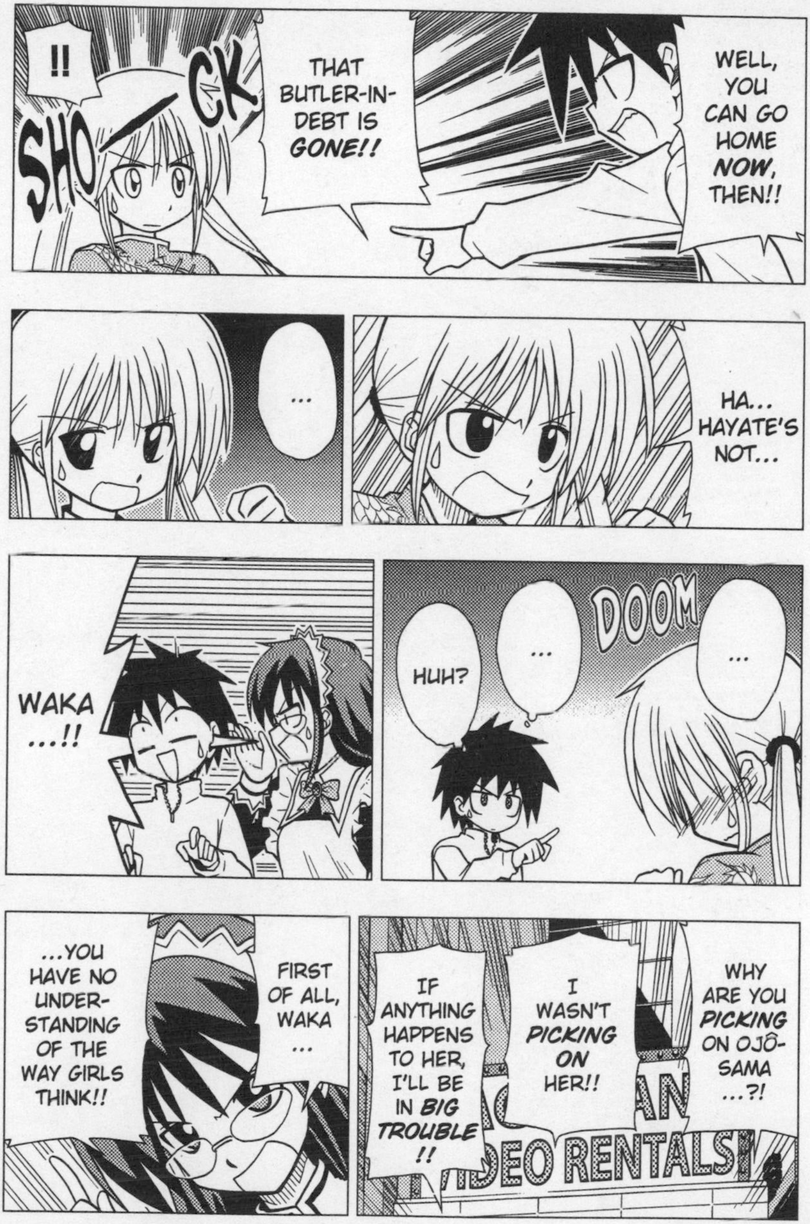
WELL, YOU CAN GO HOME NOW, THEN!!
THAT BUTLER-IN-DEBT IS GONE!!
!!
SHO—CK
HA... HAYATE'S NOT...
...
...
DOOM
...
HUH?
WAKA ...!!
WHY ARE YOU PICKING ON OJÔ-SAMA ...?!
I WASN'T PICKING ON HER!!
IF ANYTHING HAPPENS TO HER, I'LL BE IN BIG TROUBLE!!
FIRST OF ALL, WAKA ...
...YOU HAVE NO UNDER-STANDING OF THE WAY GIRLS THINK!!

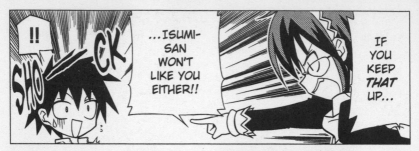

IF YOU KEEP THAT UP...
...ISUMI-SAN WON'T LIKE YOU EITHER!!
!!
SHOCK
...
...?
HUH?
DOOM
ARRGH!! I'M GOING TO BURN THIS STORE TO THE GROUND...!!
I WANT EVERYTHING TO DISAPPEAR...!!
AAH!! NO!! NO, WAKA!! OJÔ-SAMA!!
KYAAAA!!
ACH
DEO RENTALS
MEANWHILE, AS SAKI-SAN WAS...
...BEING ABUSED BY HER TWO CHARGES...
THE BUTLER-IN-DEBT, ABANDONED BY HIS MISTRESS...
...HAD THE EYES OF A DEAD FISH.
DAZE

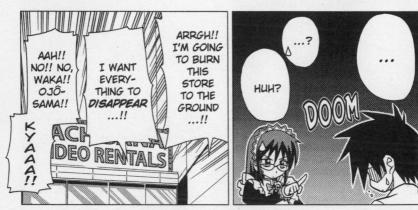

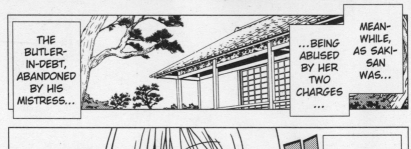

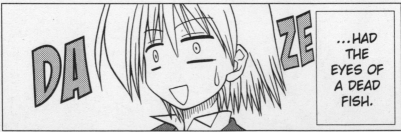

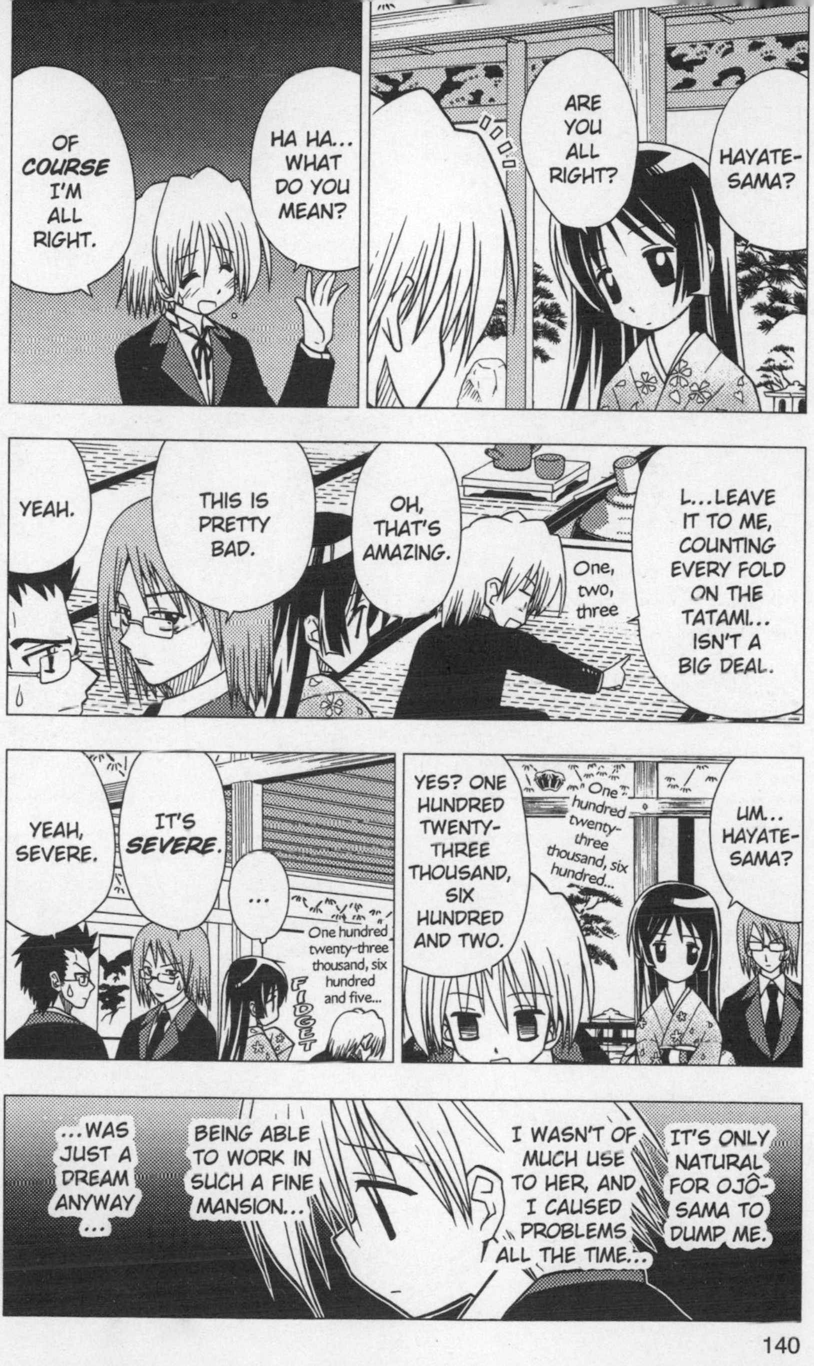
HAYATE-SAMA?
ARE YOU ALL RIGHT?
HA HA... WHAT DO YOU MEAN?
OF COURSE I'M ALL RIGHT.
L...LEAVE IT TO ME, COUNTING EVERY FOLD ON THE TATAMI... ISN'T A BIG DEAL.
One, two, three
OH, THAT'S AMAZING.
THIS IS PRETTY BAD.
YEAH.
UM... HAYATE-SAMA?
One hundred twenty-three thousand, six hundred...
YES? ONE HUNDRED TWENTY-THREE THOUSAND, SIX HUNDRED AND TWO.
One hundred twenty-three thousand, six hundred and five...
FIDGET
...
IT'S SEVERE.
YEAH, SEVERE.
IT'S ONLY NATURAL FOR OJÔ-SAMA TO DUMP ME.
I WASN'T OF MUCH USE TO HER, AND I CAUSED PROBLEMS ALL THE TIME...
BEING ABLE TO WORK IN SUCH A FINE MANSION...
...WAS JUST A DREAM ANYWAY...

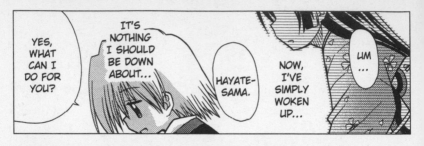

UM ...
NOW, I'VE SIMPLY WOKEN UP...
HAYATE-SAMA.
IT'S NOTHING I SHOULD BE DOWN ABOUT...
YES, WHAT CAN I DO FOR YOU?
SHOVE.
SHOVE
...
WHUP
I-ISUMI... SAN?
AH...!!
SO SORRY ...!!

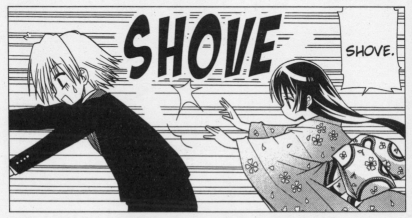

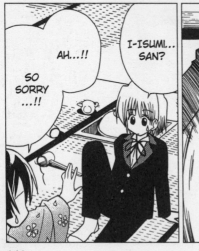

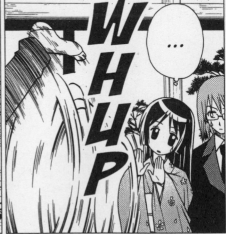

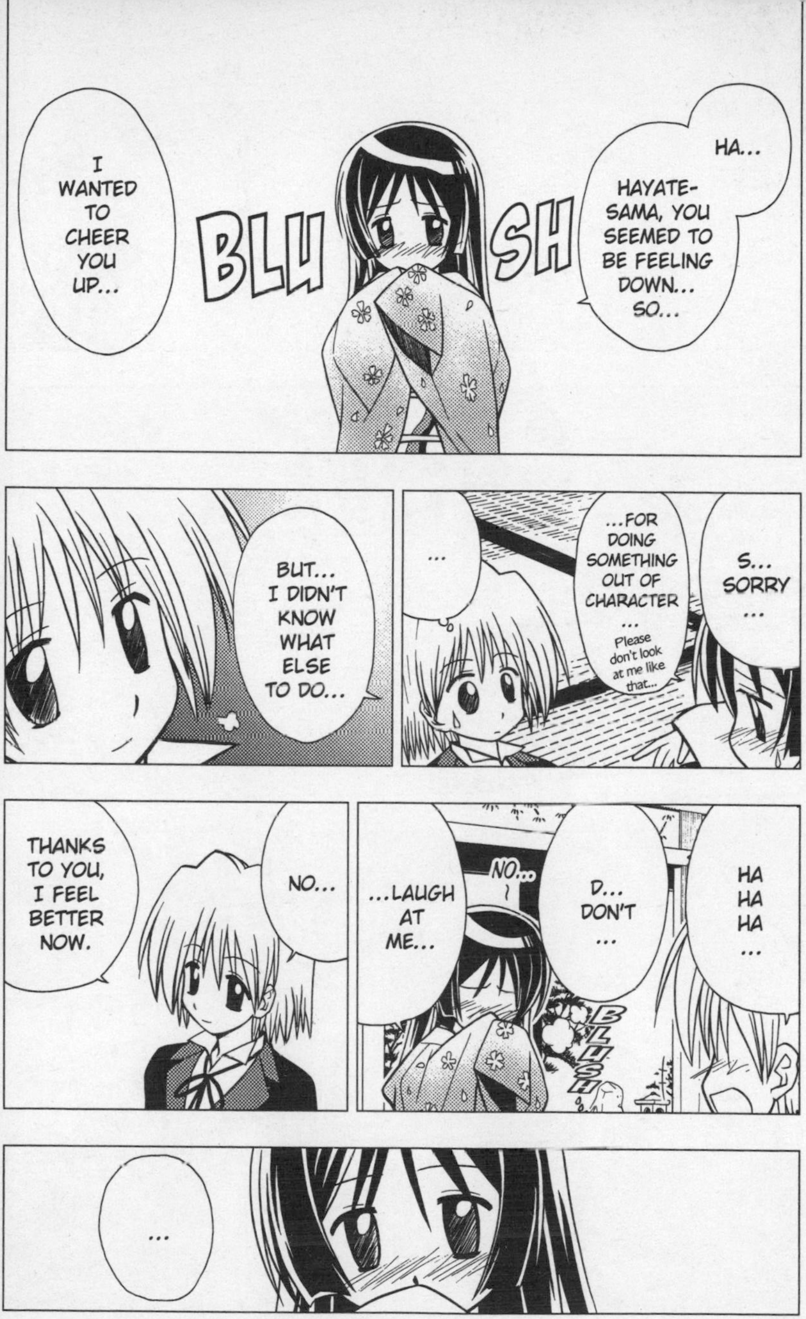
HA...
HAYATE-SAMA, YOU SEEMED TO BE FEELING DOWN... SO...
BLUSH
I WANTED TO CHEER YOU UP...
S... SORRY...
...FOR DOING SOMETHING OUT OF CHARACTER...
Please don't look at me like that...
...
BUT... I DIDN'T KNOW WHAT ELSE TO DO...
HA HA HA...
D... DON'T...
NO...
...LAUGH AT ME...
BLUSH
NO...
THANKS TO YOU, I FEEL BETTER NOW.
...

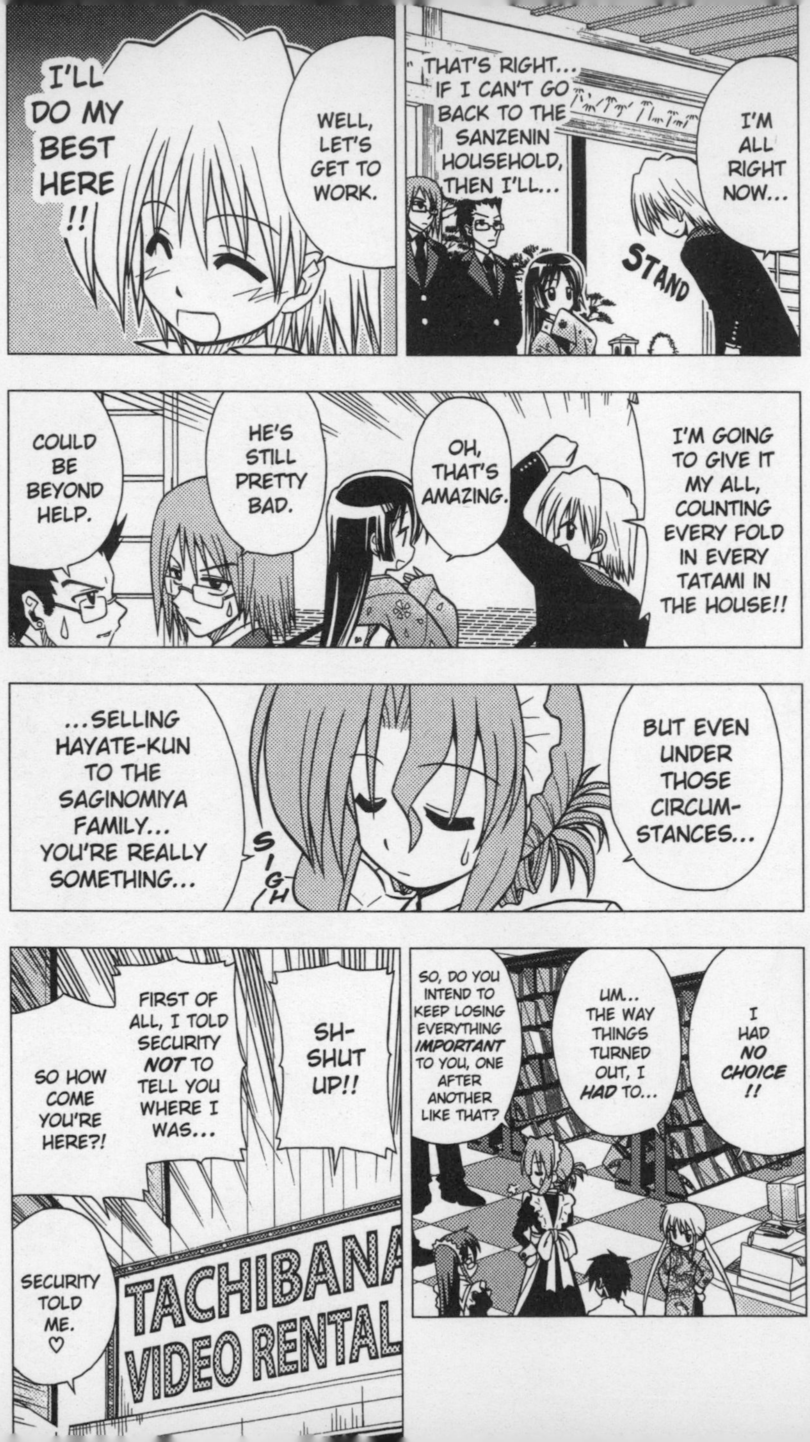
I'M ALL RIGHT NOW...
THAT'S RIGHT... IF I CAN'T GO BACK TO THE SANZENIN HOUSEHOLD, THEN I'LL...
STAND
WELL, LET'S GET TO WORK.
I'LL DO MY BEST HERE!!
I'M GOING TO GIVE IT MY ALL, COUNTING EVERY FOLD IN EVERY TATAMI IN THE HOUSE!!
OH, THAT'S AMAZING.
HE'S STILL PRETTY BAD.
COULD BE BEYOND HELP.
BUT EVEN UNDER THOSE CIRCUMSTANCES...
SIGH
...SELLING HAYATE-KUN TO THE SAGINOMIYA FAMILY... YOU'RE REALLY SOMETHING...
I HAD NO CHOICE!!
UM... THE WAY THINGS TURNED OUT, I HAD TO...
SO, DO YOU INTEND TO KEEP LOSING EVERYTHING IMPORTANT TO YOU, ONE AFTER ANOTHER LIKE THAT?
SH-SHUT UP!!
FIRST OF ALL, I TOLD SECURITY NOT TO TELL YOU WHERE I WAS...
SO HOW COME YOU'RE HERE?!
SECURITY TOLD ME. ♡
TACHIBANA VIDEO RENTAL

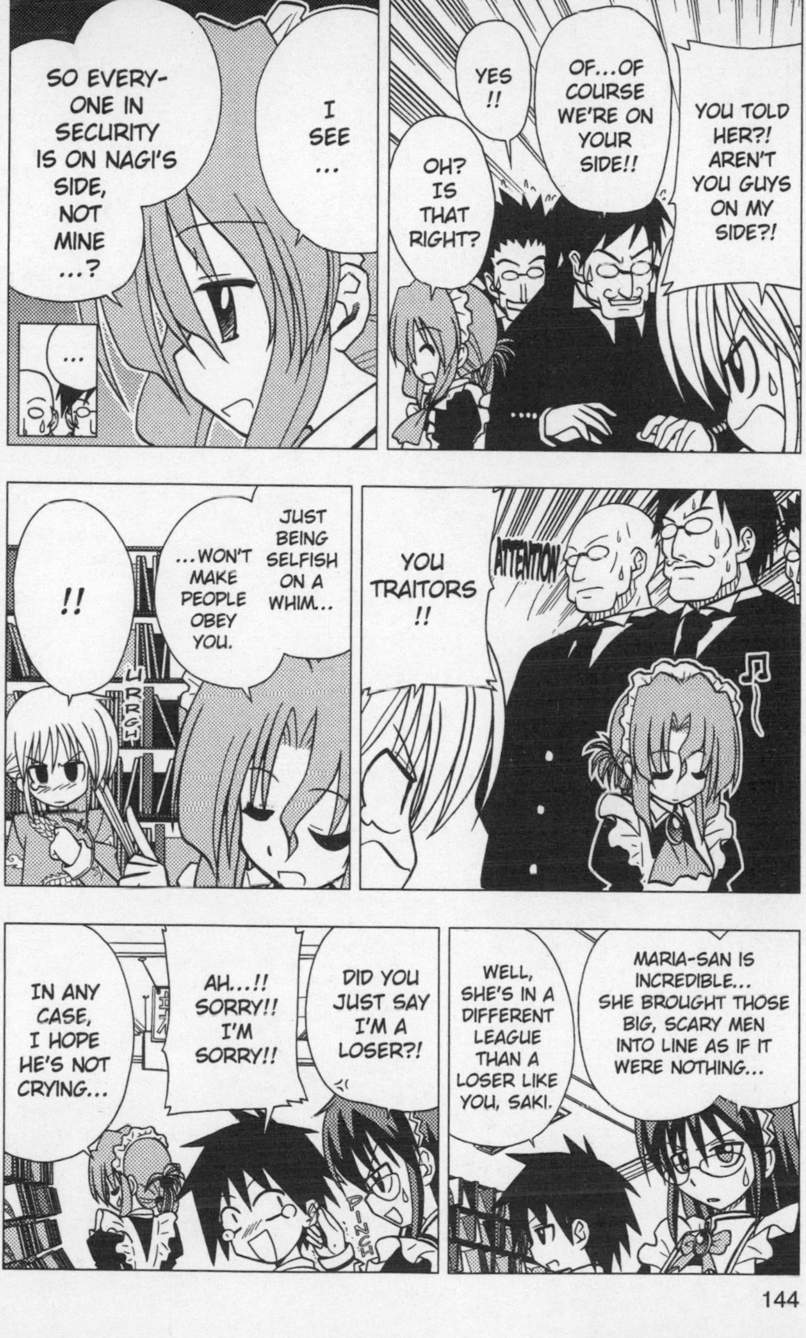
YOU TOLD HER?! AREN'T YOU GUYS ON MY SIDE?!
OF...OF COURSE WE'RE ON YOUR SIDE!!
YES !!
OH? IS THAT RIGHT?
....
I SEE ...
SO EVERY-ONE IN SECURITY IS ON NAGI'S SIDE, NOT MINE ...?
...
ATTENTION
YOU TRAITORS !!
JUST BEING SELFISH ON A WHIM...
...WON'T MAKE PEOPLE OBEY YOU.
!!
URRGH
MARIA-SAN IS INCREDIBLE... SHE BROUGHT THOSE BIG, SCARY MEN INTO LINE AS IF IT WERE NOTHING...
WELL, SHE'S IN A DIFFERENT LEAGUE THAN A LOSER LIKE YOU, SAKI.
DID YOU JUST SAY I'M A LOSER?!
PINCH
AH...!! SORRY!! I'M SORRY!!
IN ANY CASE, I HOPE HE'S NOT CRYING...

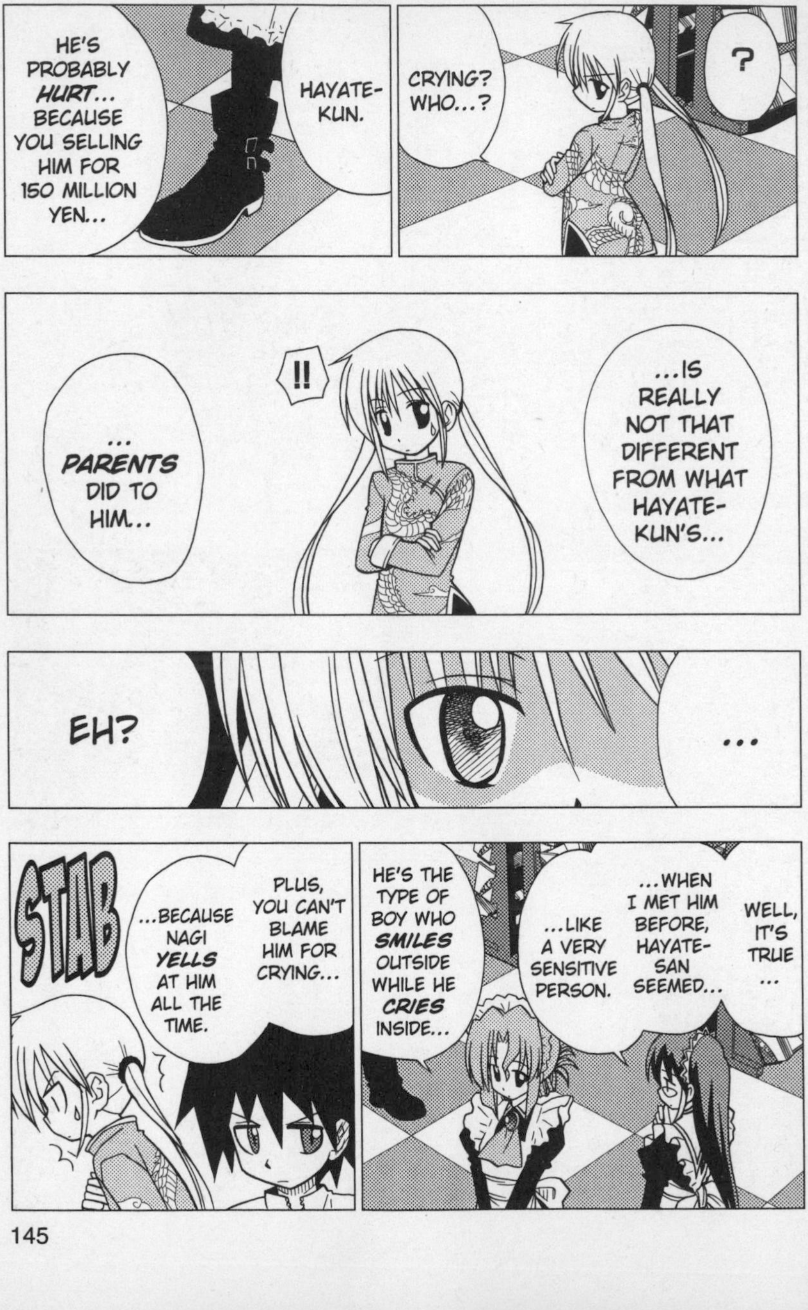
?
CRYING? WHO...?
HAYATE-KUN.
HE'S PROBABLY *HURT*... BECAUSE YOU SELLING HIM FOR 150 MILLION YEN...
...IS REALLY NOT THAT DIFFERENT FROM WHAT HAYATE-KUN'S...
!!
... *PARENTS* DID TO HIM...
...
EH?
WELL, IT'S TRUE ...
...WHEN I MET HIM BEFORE, HAYATE-SAN SEEMED...
...LIKE A VERY SENSITIVE PERSON.
HE'S THE TYPE OF BOY WHO *SMILES* OUTSIDE WHILE HE *CRIES* INSIDE...
PLUS, YOU CAN'T BLAME HIM FOR CRYING...
...BECAUSE NAGI *YELLS* AT HIM ALL THE TIME.
STAB

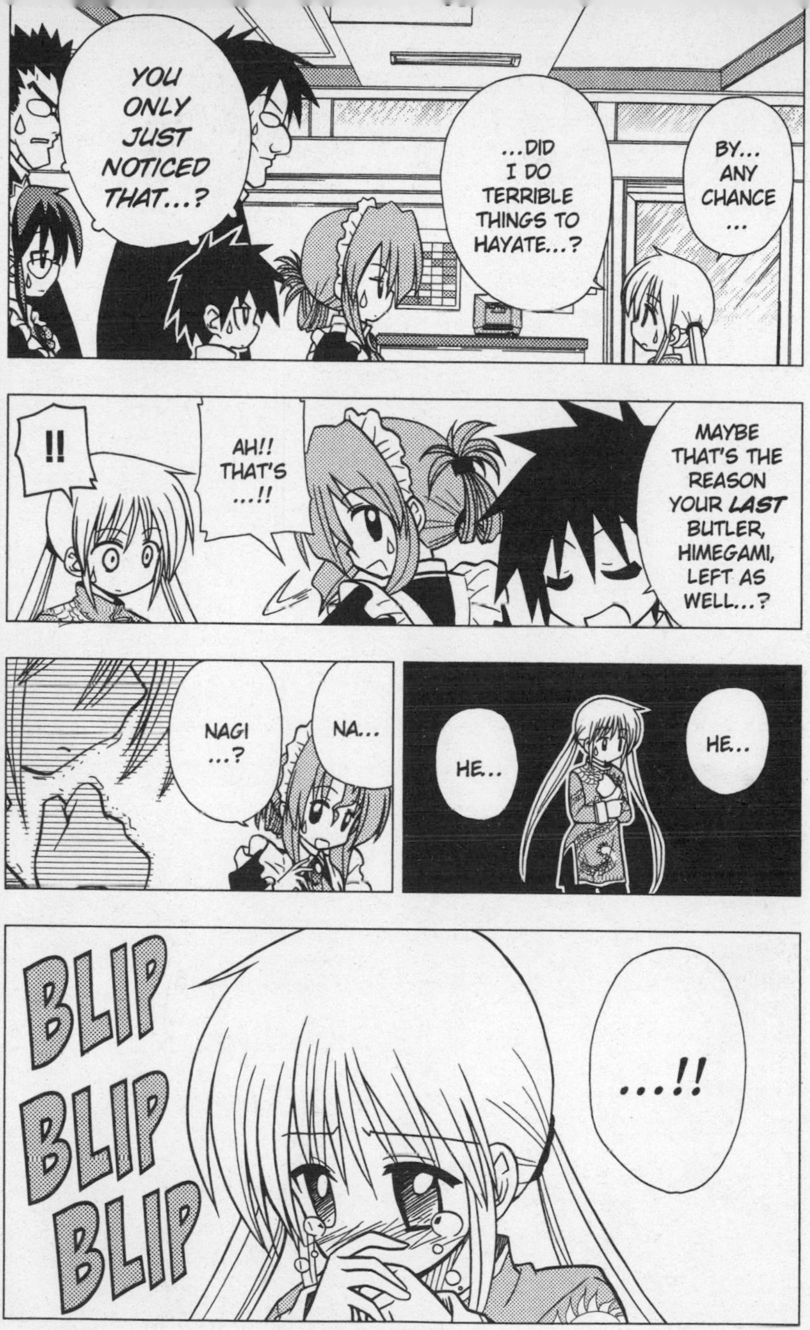
BY... ANY CHANCE ...
...DID I DO TERRIBLE THINGS TO HAYATE...?
YOU ONLY JUST NOTICED THAT...?
MAYBE THAT'S THE REASON YOUR LAST BUTLER, HIMEGAMI, LEFT AS WELL...?
AH!! THAT'S ...!!
!!
HE...
HE...
NA...
NAGI ...?
...!!
BLIP BLIP BLIP

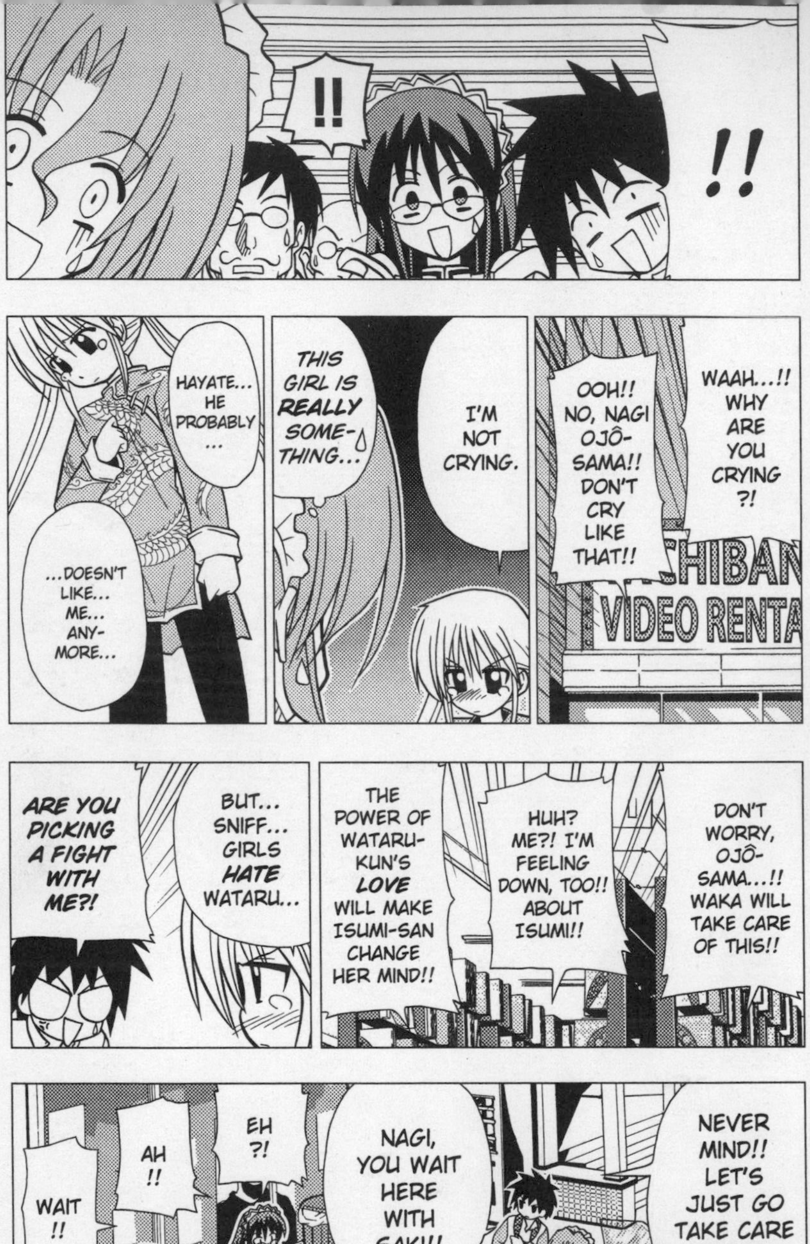
!!
!!
WAAH...!! WHY ARE YOU CRYING?!
OOH!! NO, NAGI OJÔ-SAMA!! DON'T CRY LIKE THAT!!
SHIBAN
VIDEO RENTA
I'M NOT CRYING.
THIS GIRL IS REALLY SOMETHING...
HAYATE... HE PROBABLY...
...DOESN'T LIKE... ME... ANYMORE...
DON'T WORRY, OJÔ-SAMA...!! WAKA WILL TAKE CARE OF THIS!!
HUH? ME?! I'M FEELING DOWN, TOO!! ABOUT ISUMI!!
THE POWER OF WATARU-KUN'S LOVE WILL MAKE ISUMI-SAN CHANGE HER MIND!!
BUT... SNIFF... GIRLS HATE WATARU...
ARE YOU PICKING A FIGHT WITH ME?!
NEVER MIND!! LET'S JUST GO TAKE CARE OF THIS NOW!!
NAGI, YOU WAIT HERE WITH SAKI!!
EH?!
AH!!
WAIT!!

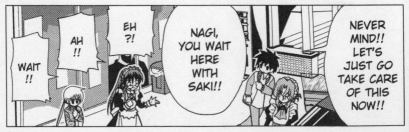

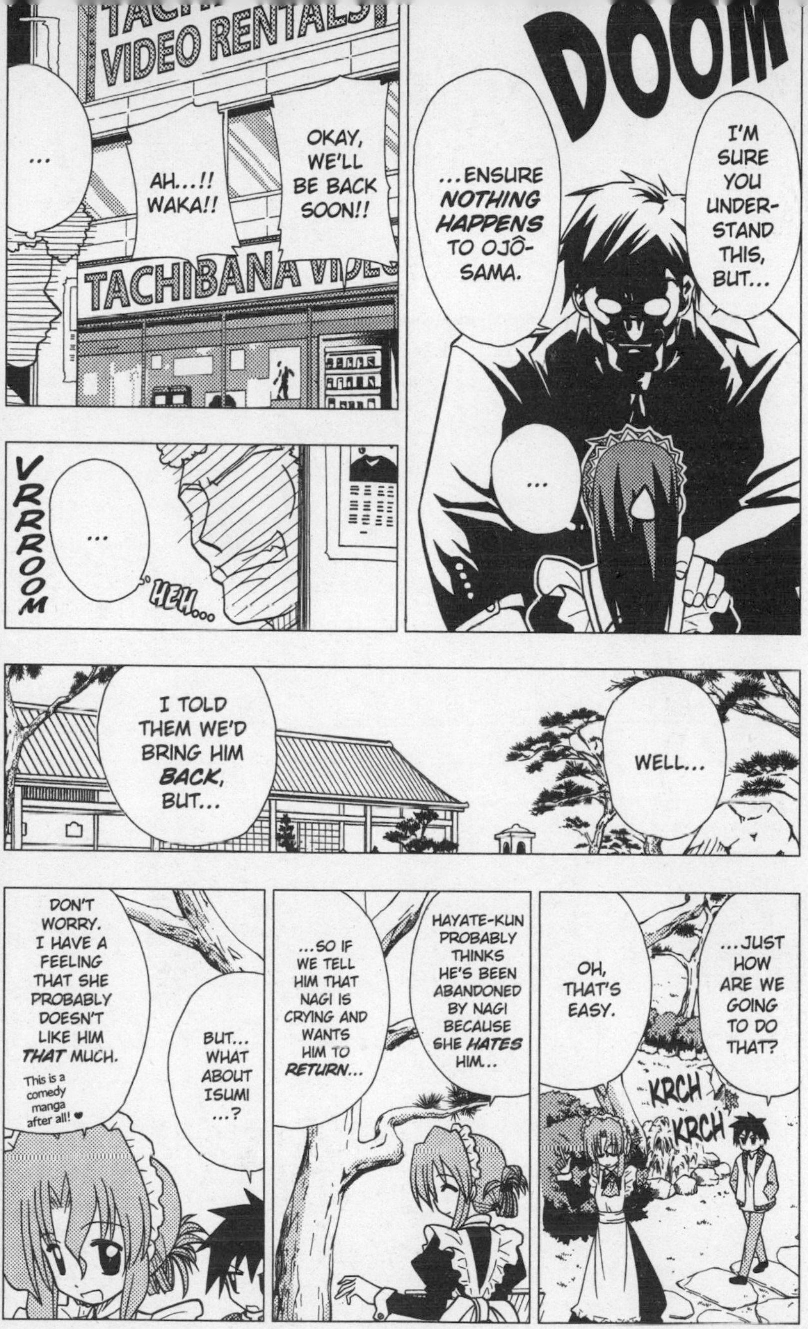
DOOM
I'M SURE YOU UNDERSTAND THIS, BUT...
...ENSURE NOTHING HAPPENS TO OJÔ-SAMA.
...
VIDEO RENTALS
OKAY, WE'LL BE BACK SOON!!
AH...!! WAKA!!
...
TACHIBANA
HEH...
...
VRRROOM
WELL...
I TOLD THEM WE'D BRING HIM BACK, BUT...
...JUST HOW ARE WE GOING TO DO THAT?
OH, THAT'S EASY.
KRCH KRCH
HAYATE-KUN PROBABLY THINKS HE'S BEEN ABANDONED BY NAGI BECAUSE SHE HATES HIM...
...SO IF WE TELL HIM THAT NAGI IS CRYING AND WANTS HIM TO RETURN...
BUT... WHAT ABOUT ISUMI ...?
DON'T WORRY. I HAVE A FEELING THAT SHE PROBABLY DOESN'T LIKE HIM THAT MUCH.
This is a comedy manga after all! ♥

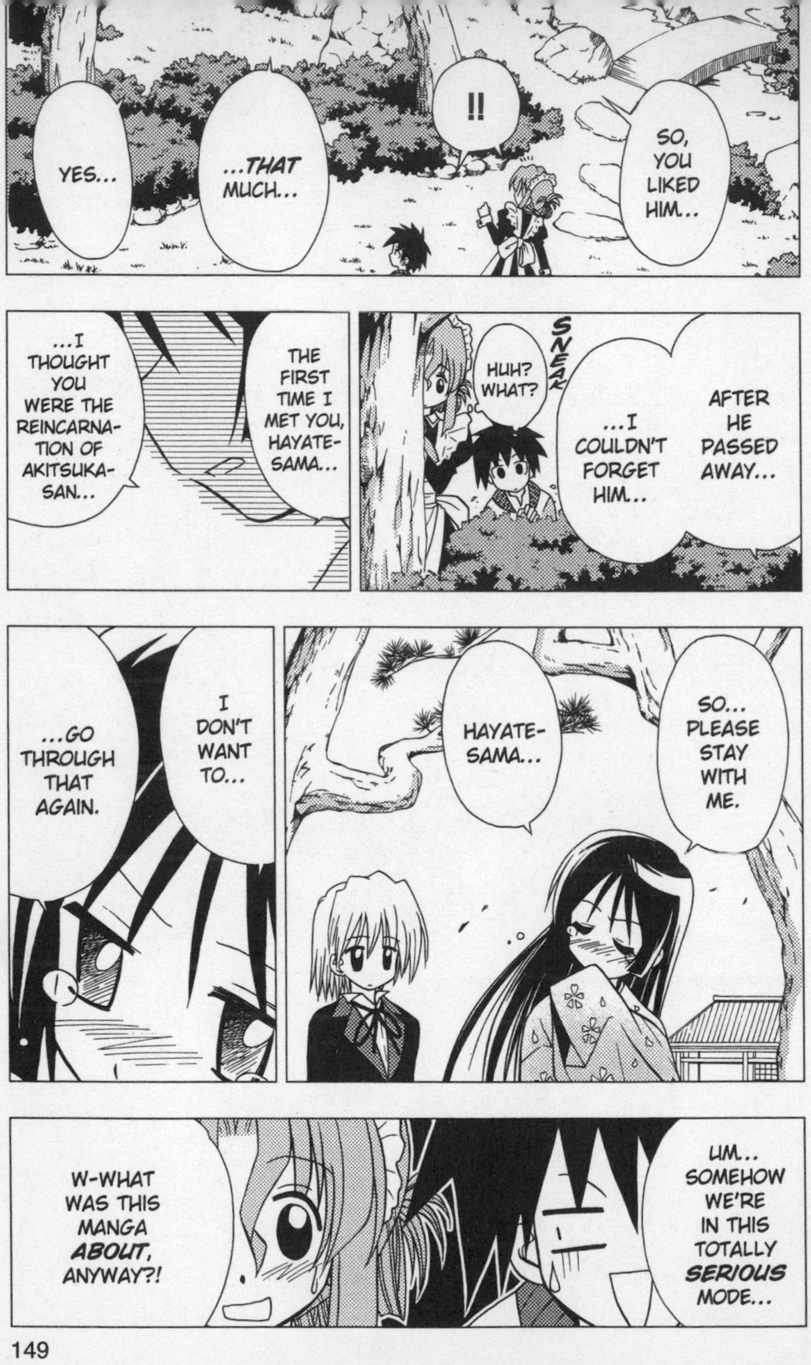
SO, YOU LIKED HIM...
!!
...THAT MUCH...
YES...
AFTER HE PASSED AWAY...
...I COULDN'T FORGET HIM...
SNEAK
HUH? WHAT?
THE FIRST TIME I MET YOU, HAYATE-SAMA...
...I THOUGHT YOU WERE THE REINCARNATION OF AKITSUKA-SAN...
SO... PLEASE STAY WITH ME.
HAYATE-SAMA...
I DON'T WANT TO...
...GO THROUGH THAT AGAIN.
UM... SOMEHOW WE'RE IN THIS TOTALLY SERIOUS MODE...
W-WHAT WAS THIS MANGA ABOUT, ANYWAY?!

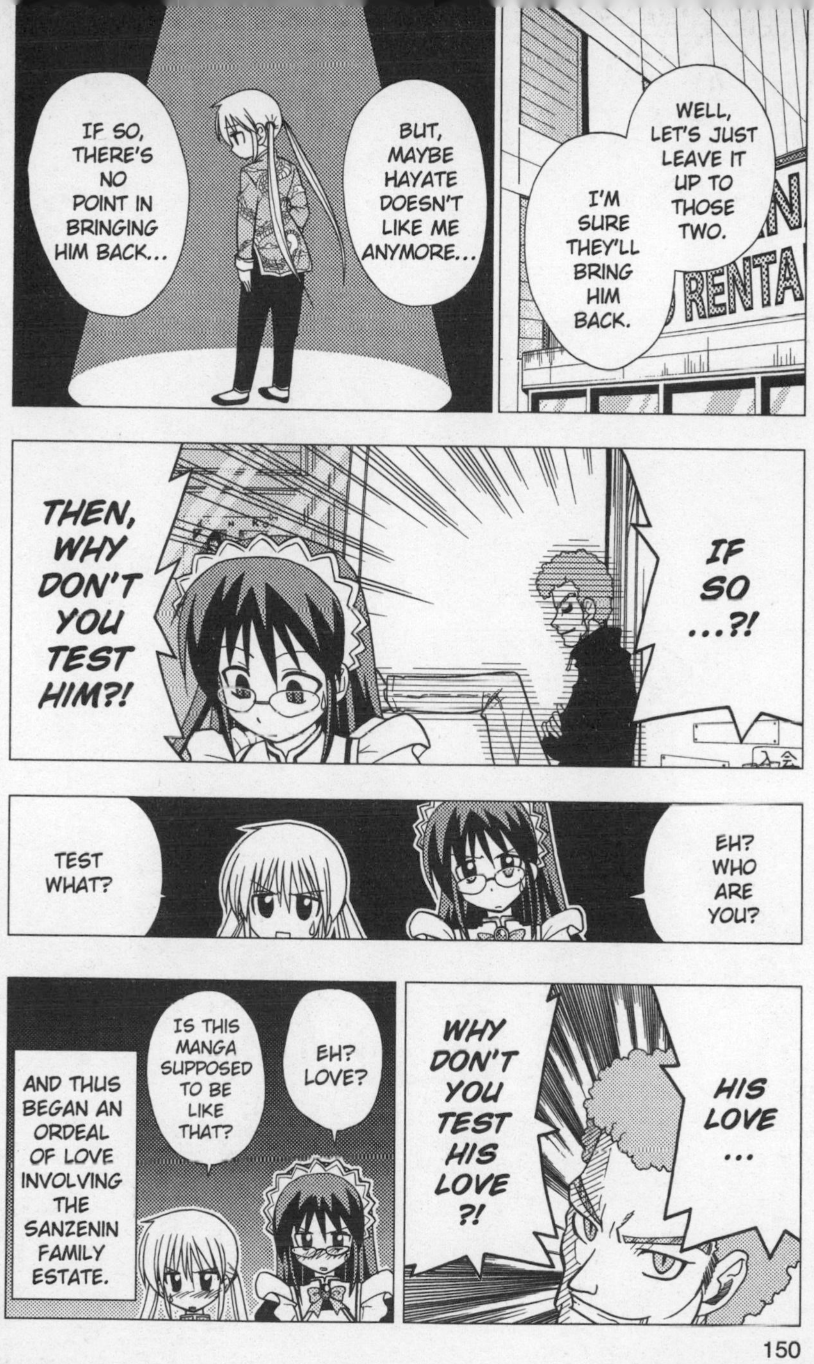
WELL, LET'S JUST LEAVE IT UP TO THOSE TWO.
I'M SURE THEY'LL BRING HIM BACK.
BUT, MAYBE HAYATE DOESN'T LIKE ME ANYMORE...
IF SO, THERE'S NO POINT IN BRINGING HIM BACK...
IF SO ...?!
THEN, WHY DON'T YOU TEST HIM?!
EH? WHO ARE YOU?
TEST WHAT?
HIS LOVE ...
WHY DON'T YOU TEST HIS LOVE ?!
EH? LOVE?
IS THIS MANGA SUPPOSED TO BE LIKE THAT?
AND THUS BEGAN AN ORDEAL OF LOVE INVOLVING THE SANZENIN FAMILY ESTATE.

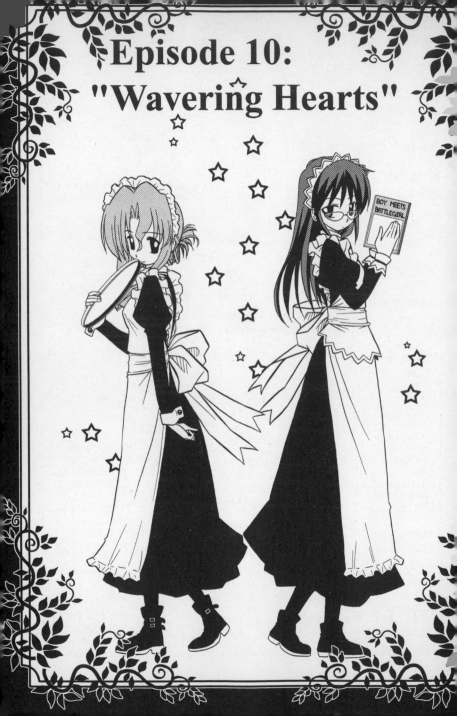

Episode 10: "Wavering Hearts"

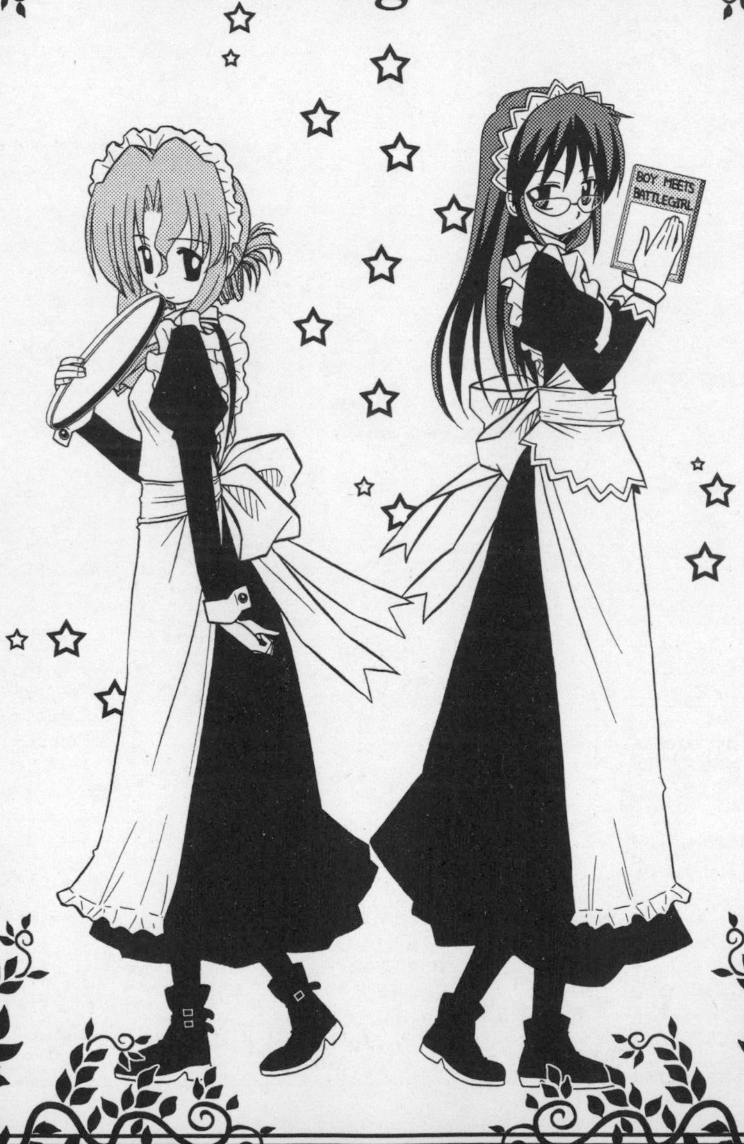
BOY MEETS BATTLEGIRL

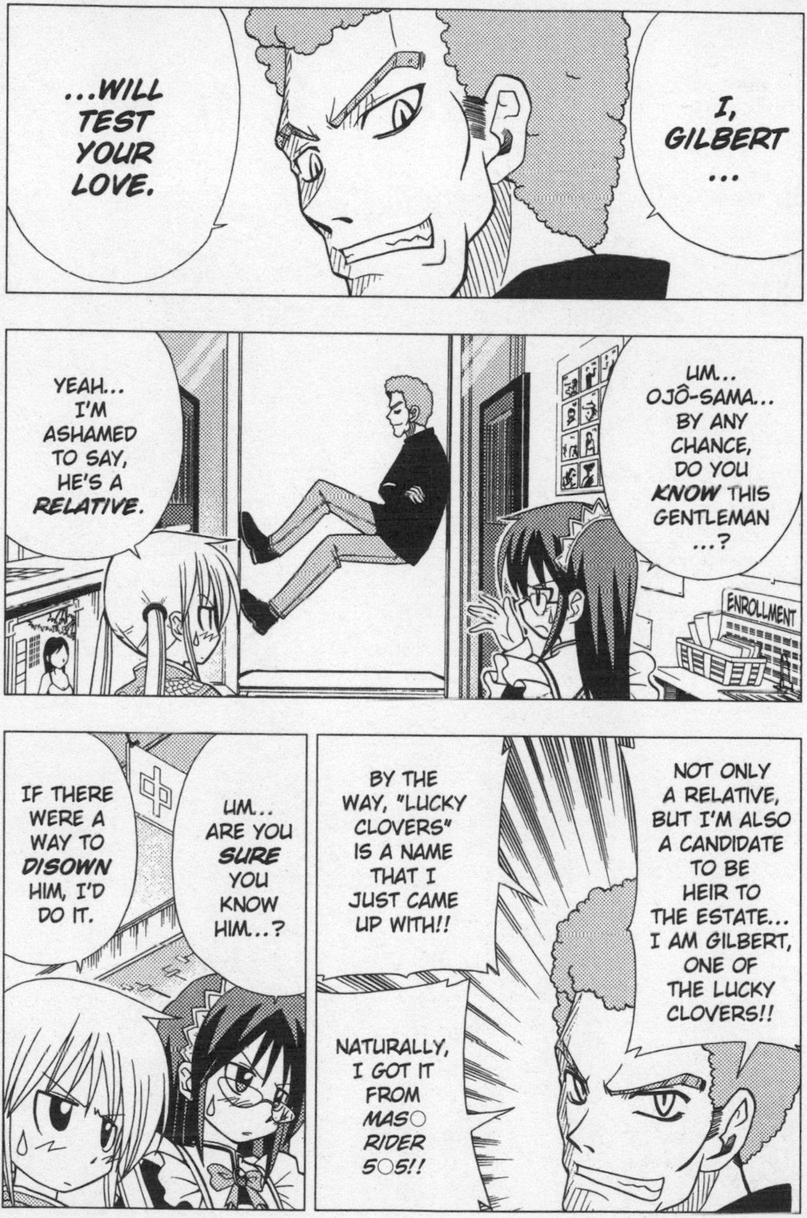
I, GILBERT ...
...WILL TEST YOUR LOVE.
UM... OJÔ-SAMA... BY ANY CHANCE, DO YOU KNOW THIS GENTLEMAN ...?
ENROLLMENT
YEAH... I'M ASHAMED TO SAY, HE'S A RELATIVE.
NOT ONLY A RELATIVE, BUT I'M ALSO A CANDIDATE TO BE HEIR TO THE ESTATE... I AM GILBERT, ONE OF THE LUCKY CLOVERS!!
BY THE WAY, "LUCKY CLOVERS" IS A NAME THAT I JUST CAME UP WITH!!
NATURALLY, I GOT IT FROM MAS○ RIDER 5○5!!
UM... ARE YOU SURE YOU KNOW HIM...?
中
IF THERE WERE A WAY TO DISOWN HIM, I'D DO IT.

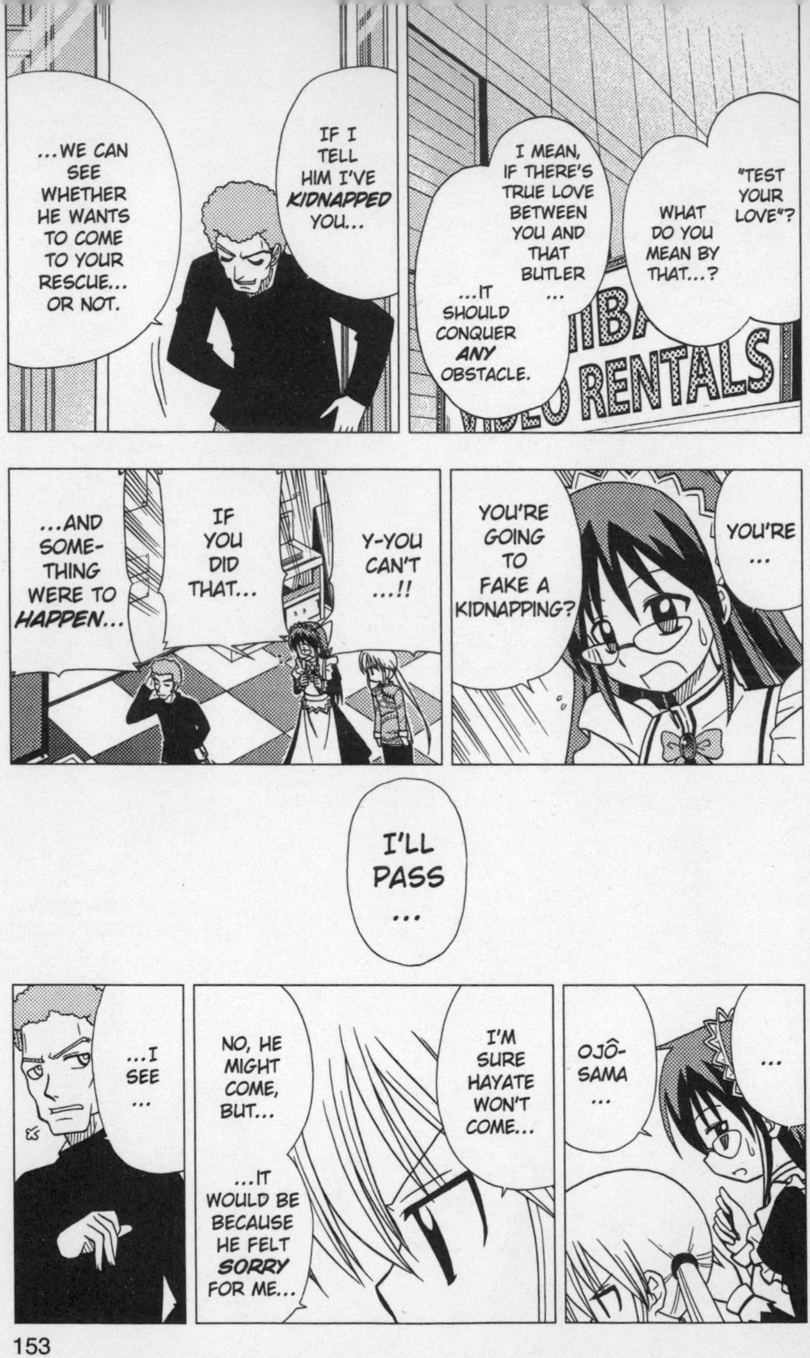
"TEST YOUR LOVE"?
WHAT DO YOU MEAN BY THAT...?
I MEAN, IF THERE'S TRUE LOVE BETWEEN YOU AND THAT BUTLER...
...IT SHOULD CONQUER *ANY* OBSTACLE.
RENTALS
IF I TELL HIM I'VE *KIDNAPPED* YOU...
...WE CAN SEE WHETHER HE WANTS TO COME TO YOUR RESCUE... OR NOT.
YOU'RE...
YOU'RE GOING TO FAKE A KIDNAPPING?
Y-YOU CAN'T...!!
IF YOU DID THAT...
...AND SOME-THING WERE TO *HAPPEN*...
I'LL PASS...
...
OJÔ-SAMA...
I'M SURE HAYATE WON'T COME...
NO, HE MIGHT COME, BUT...
...IT WOULD BE BECAUSE HE FELT *SORRY* FOR ME...
...I SEE...

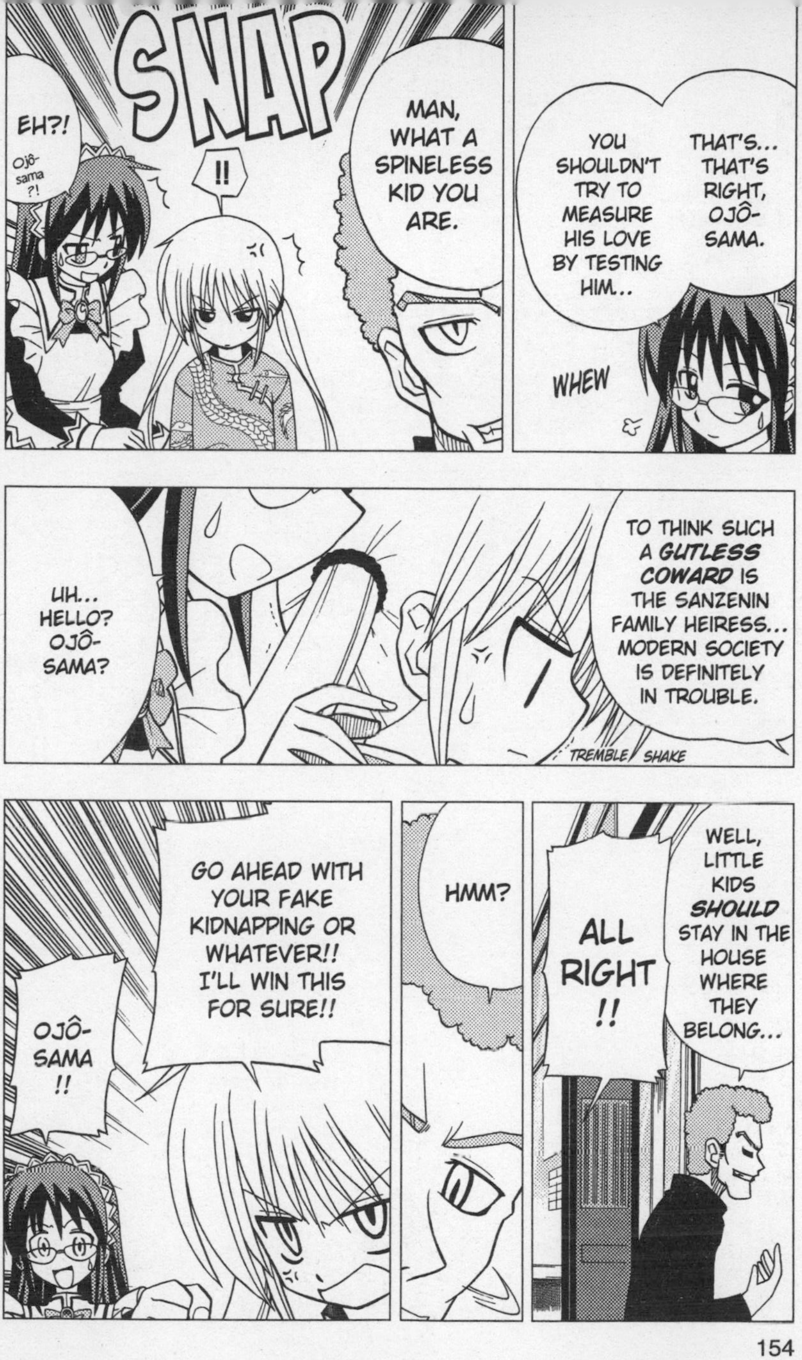
THAT'S... THAT'S RIGHT, OJÔ-SAMA.
YOU SHOULDN'T TRY TO MEASURE HIS LOVE BY TESTING HIM...
WHEW
MAN, WHAT A SPINELESS KID YOU ARE.
SNAP
EH?!
Ojô-sama ?!
!!
TO THINK SUCH A ***GUTLESS COWARD*** IS THE SANZENIN FAMILY HEIRESS... MODERN SOCIETY IS DEFINITELY IN TROUBLE.
TREMBLE SHAKE
UH... HELLO? OJÔ-SAMA?
WELL, LITTLE KIDS ***SHOULD*** STAY IN THE HOUSE WHERE THEY BELONG...
ALL RIGHT !!
HMM?
GO AHEAD WITH YOUR FAKE KIDNAPPING OR WHATEVER!! I'LL WIN THIS FOR SURE!!
OJÔ-SAMA !!

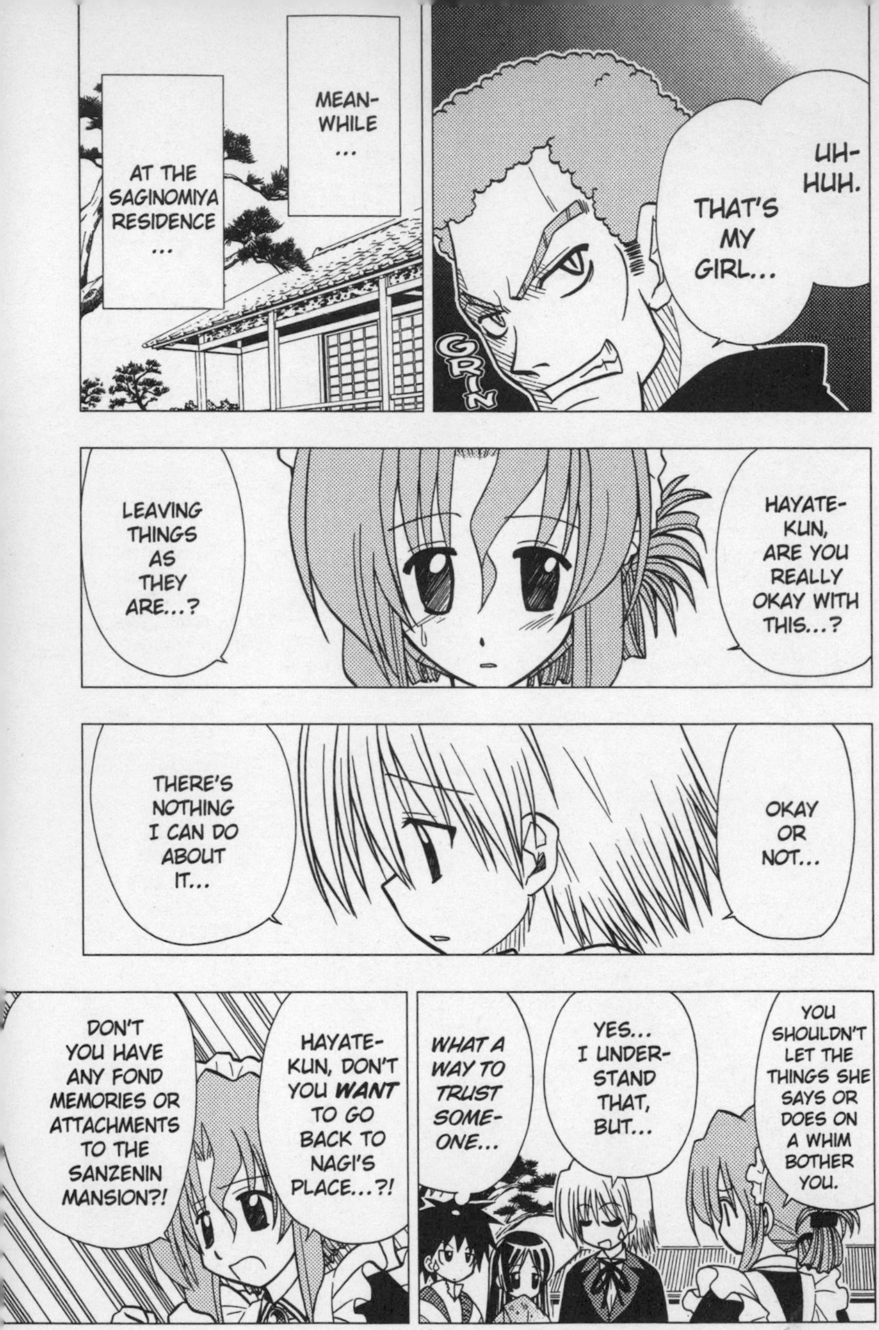

UH-HUH.
THAT'S MY GIRL...
GRIN
MEAN-WHILE...
AT THE SAGINOMIYA RESIDENCE...
HAYATE-KUN, ARE YOU REALLY OKAY WITH THIS...?
LEAVING THINGS AS THEY ARE...?
OKAY OR NOT...
THERE'S NOTHING I CAN DO ABOUT IT...
YOU SHOULDN'T LET THE THINGS SHE SAYS OR DOES ON A WHIM BOTHER YOU.
YES... I UNDER-STAND THAT, BUT...
WHAT A WAY TO TRUST SOME-ONE...
HAYATE-KUN, DON'T YOU ***WANT*** TO GO BACK TO NAGI'S PLACE...?!
DON'T YOU HAVE ANY FOND MEMORIES OR ATTACHMENTS TO THE SANZENIN MANSION?!

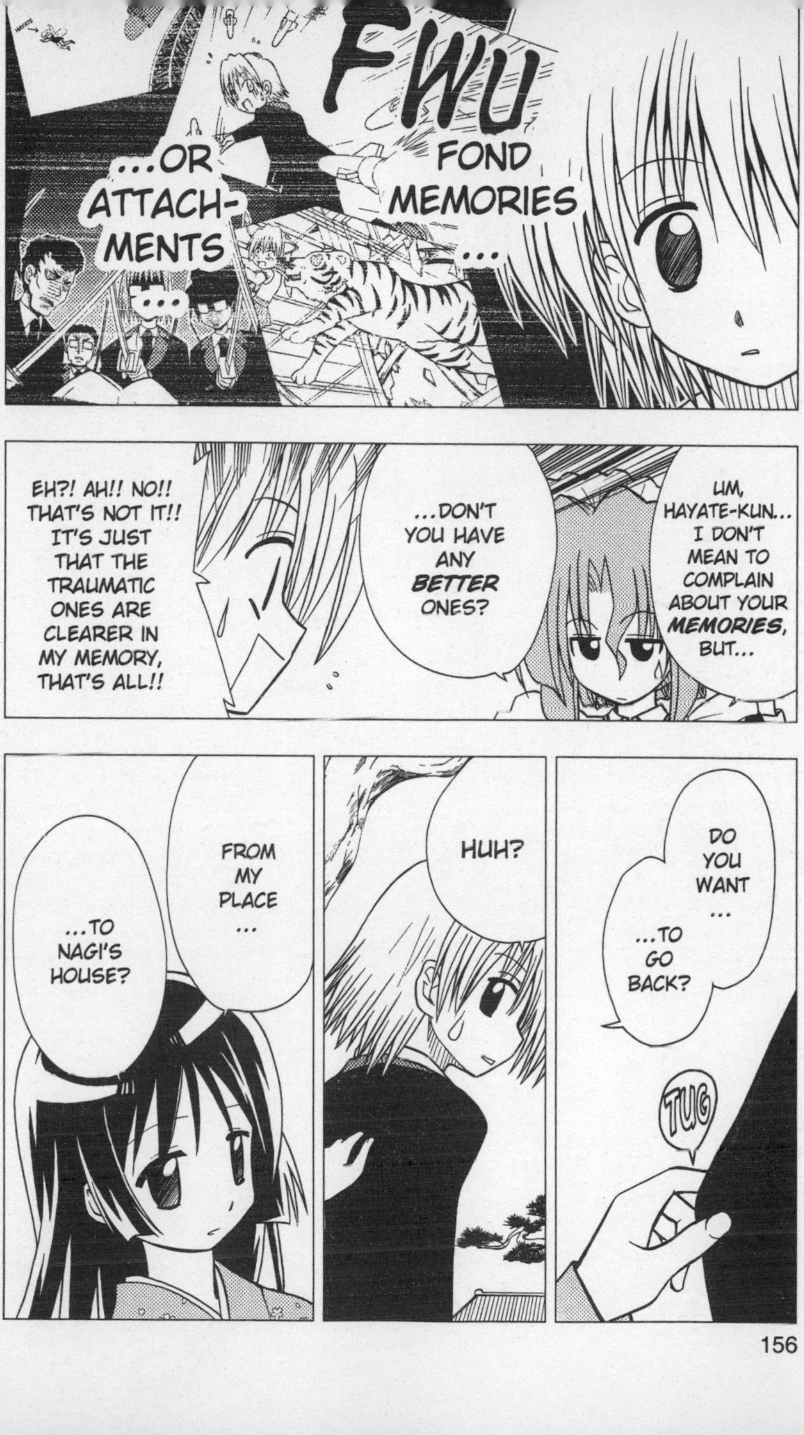
FWU
FOND MEMORIES …
…OR ATTACH-MENTS
…
HAYATE
UM, HAYATE-KUN… I DON'T MEAN TO COMPLAIN ABOUT YOUR MEMORIES, BUT…
…DON'T YOU HAVE ANY BETTER ONES?
EH?! AH!! NO!! THAT'S NOT IT!! IT'S JUST THAT THE TRAUMATIC ONES ARE CLEARER IN MY MEMORY, THAT'S ALL!!
DO YOU WANT …
…TO GO BACK?
TUG
HUH?
FROM MY PLACE …
…TO NAGI'S HOUSE?

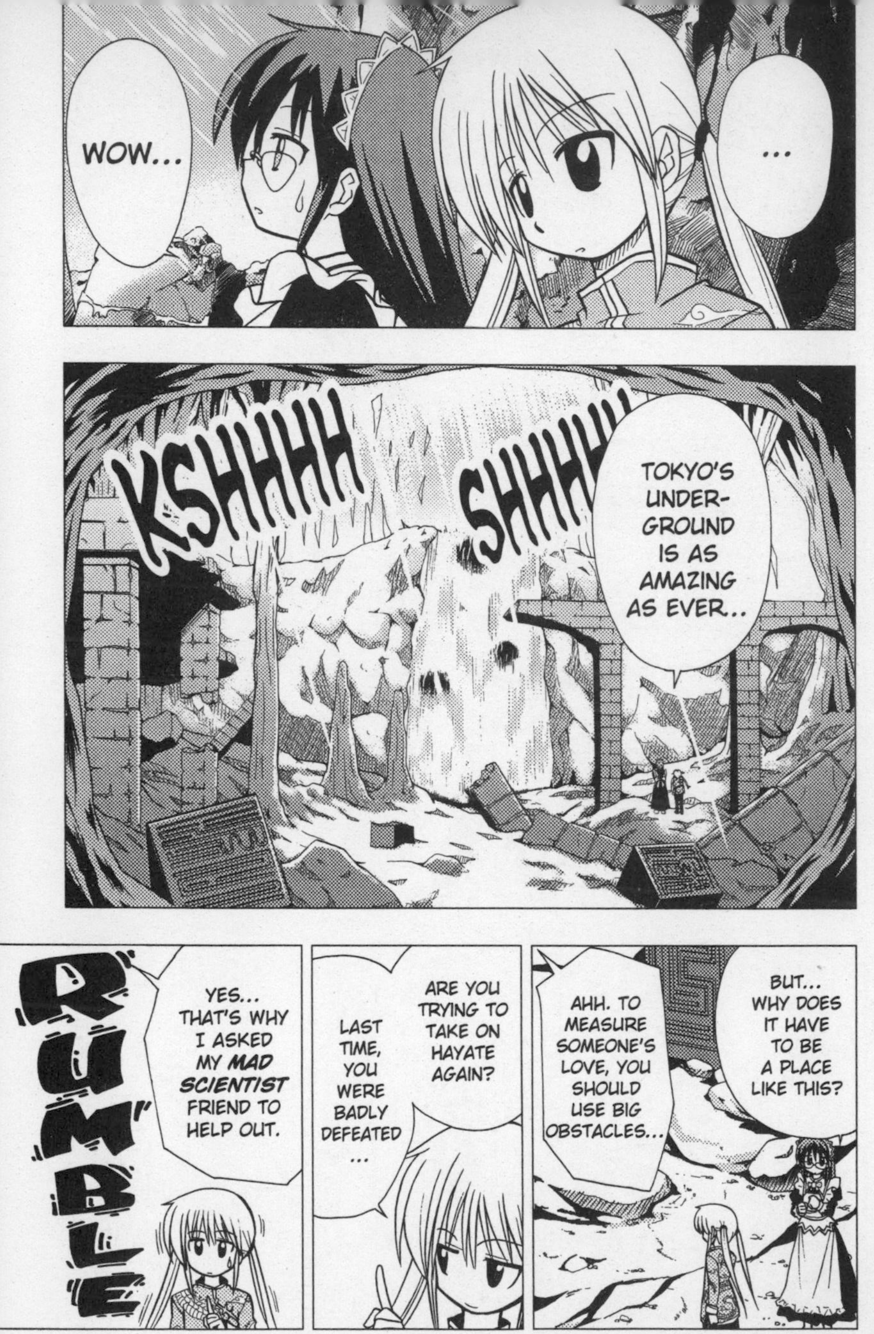
...
WOW...
TOKYO'S UNDER-GROUND IS AS AMAZING AS EVER...
SHHHH
KSHHHH
BUT... WHY DOES IT HAVE TO BE A PLACE LIKE THIS?
AHH. TO MEASURE SOMEONE'S LOVE, YOU SHOULD USE BIG OBSTACLES...
ARE YOU TRYING TO TAKE ON HAYATE AGAIN?
LAST TIME, YOU WERE BADLY DEFEATED...
YES... THAT'S WHY I ASKED MY MAD SCIENTIST FRIEND TO HELP OUT.
RUMBLE

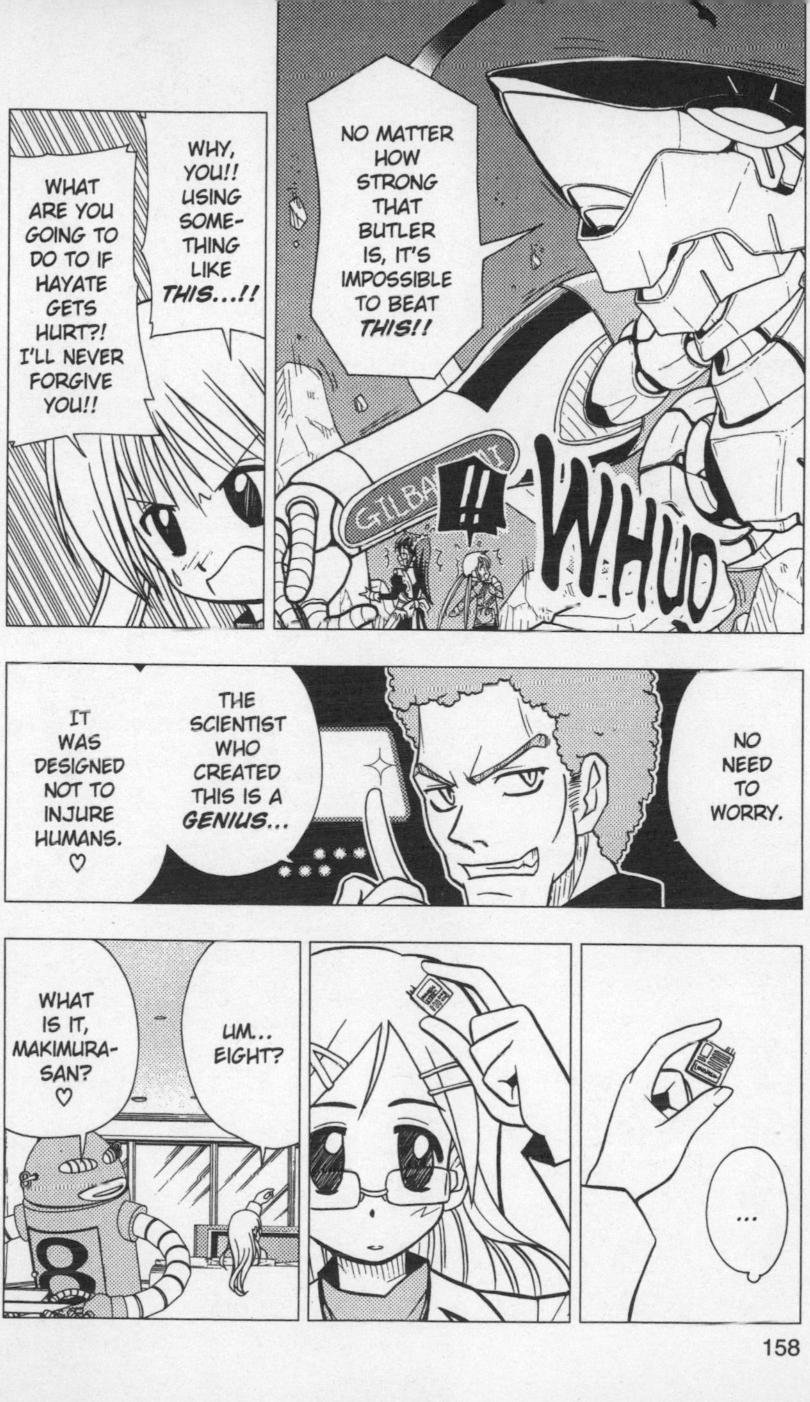
NO MATTER HOW STRONG THAT BUTLER IS, IT'S IMPOSSIBLE TO BEAT *THIS!!*
!!
WHUD
WHY, YOU!! USING SOME-THING LIKE *THIS...!!*
WHAT ARE YOU GOING TO DO TO IF HAYATE GETS HURT?! I'LL NEVER FORGIVE YOU!!
NO NEED TO WORRY.
THE SCIENTIST WHO CREATED THIS IS A *GENIUS...*
IT WAS DESIGNED NOT TO INJURE HUMANS. ♡
...
UM... EIGHT?
WHAT IS IT, MAKIMURA-SAN? ♡

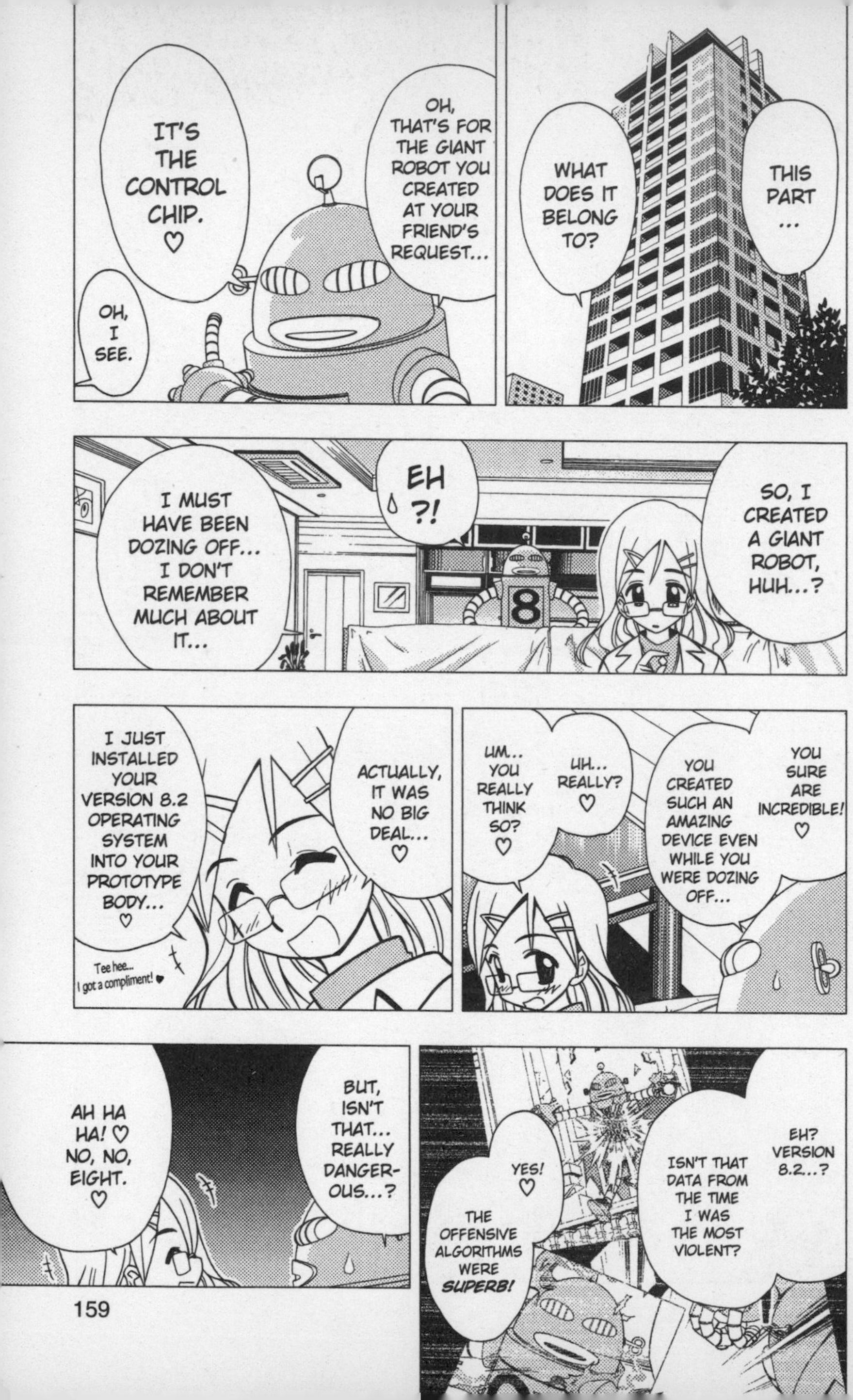
THIS PART ...
WHAT DOES IT BELONG TO?
OH, THAT'S FOR THE GIANT ROBOT YOU CREATED AT YOUR FRIEND'S REQUEST...
IT'S THE CONTROL CHIP. ♡
OH, I SEE.
SO, I CREATED A GIANT ROBOT, HUH...?
EH ?!
8
I MUST HAVE BEEN DOZING OFF... I DON'T REMEMBER MUCH ABOUT IT...
YOU SURE ARE INCREDIBLE! ♡
YOU CREATED SUCH AN AMAZING DEVICE EVEN WHILE YOU WERE DOZING OFF...
UH... REALLY? ♡
UM... YOU REALLY THINK SO? ♡
ACTUALLY, IT WAS NO BIG DEAL... ♡
I JUST INSTALLED YOUR VERSION 8.2 OPERATING SYSTEM INTO YOUR PROTOTYPE BODY... ♡
Tee hee... I got a compliment! ♥
EH? VERSION 8.2...?
ISN'T THAT DATA FROM THE TIME I WAS THE MOST VIOLENT?
YES! ♡
THE OFFENSIVE ALGORITHMS WERE *SUPERB!*
BUT, ISN'T THAT... REALLY DANGER-OUS...?
AH HA HA! ♡ NO, NO, EIGHT. ♡

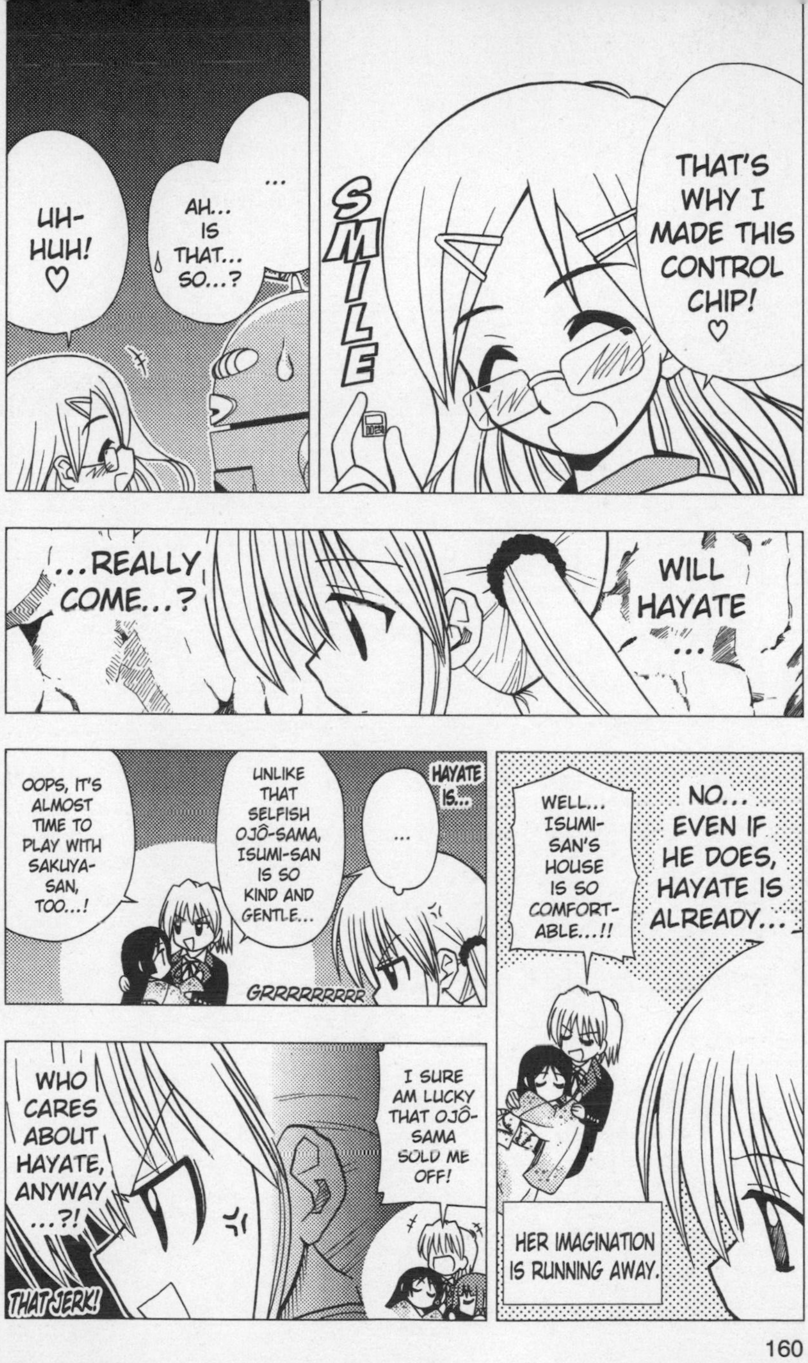

THAT'S WHY I MADE THIS CONTROL CHIP! ♥
SMILE
...
AH... IS THAT... SO...?
UH-HUH! ♥
WILL HAYATE ...
...REALLY COME...?
NO... EVEN IF HE DOES, HAYATE IS ALREADY...
WELL... ISUMI-SAN'S HOUSE IS SO COMFORT-ABLE...!!
HER IMAGINATION IS RUNNING AWAY.
HAYATE IS...
...
UNLIKE THAT SELFISH OJÔ-SAMA, ISUMI-SAN IS SO KIND AND GENTLE...
OOPS, IT'S ALMOST TIME TO PLAY WITH SAKUYA-SAN, TOO...!
GRRRRRRRRR
I SURE AM LUCKY THAT OJÔ-SAMA SOLD ME OFF!
WHO CARES ABOUT HAYATE, ANYWAY...?!
THAT JERK!

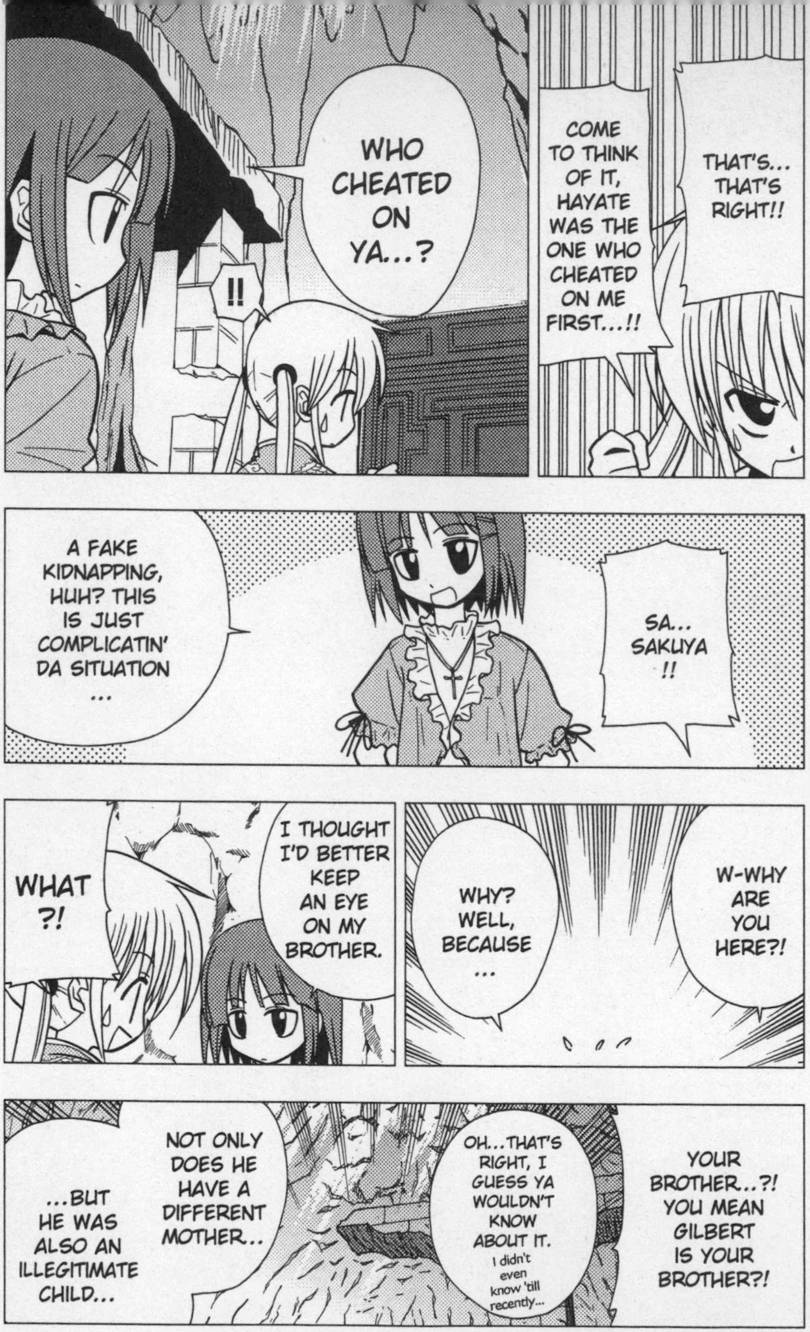
THAT'S... THAT'S RIGHT!!
COME TO THINK OF IT, HAYATE WAS THE ONE WHO CHEATED ON ME FIRST...!!
WHO CHEATED ON YA...?
!!
SA... SAKUYA !!
A FAKE KIDNAPPING, HUH? THIS IS JUST COMPLICATIN' DA SITUATION ...
W-WHY ARE YOU HERE?!
WHY? WELL, BECAUSE ...
I THOUGHT I'D BETTER KEEP AN EYE ON MY BROTHER.
WHAT ?!
YOUR BROTHER...?! YOU MEAN GILBERT IS YOUR BROTHER?!
OH...THAT'S RIGHT, I GUESS YA WOULDN'T KNOW ABOUT IT.
I didn't even know 'till recently...
NOT ONLY DOES HE HAVE A DIFFERENT MOTHER...
...BUT HE WAS ALSO AN ILLEGITIMATE CHILD...

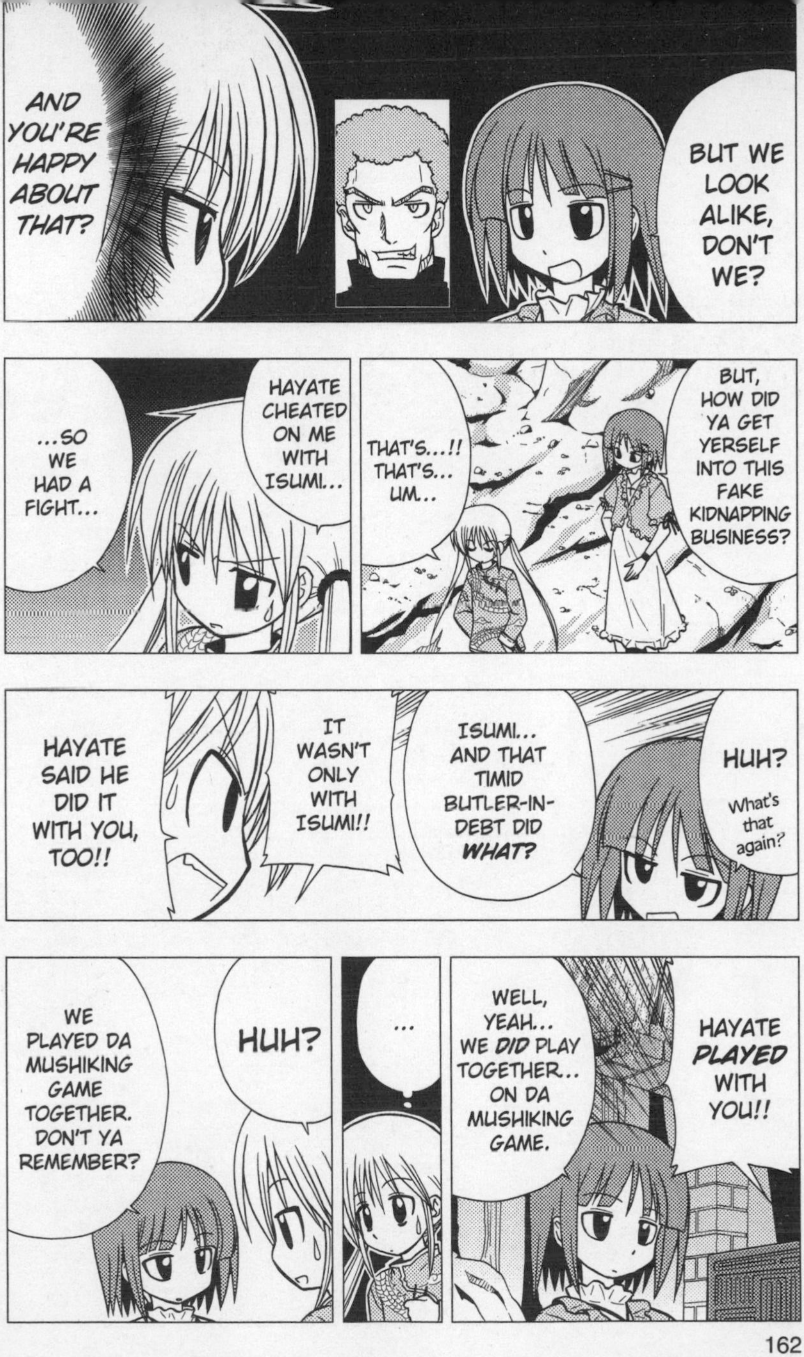
BUT WE LOOK ALIKE, DON'T WE?
AND YOU'RE HAPPY ABOUT THAT?
BUT, HOW DID YA GET YERSELF INTO THIS FAKE KIDNAPPING BUSINESS?
THAT'S...!! THAT'S... UM...
HAYATE CHEATED ON ME WITH ISUMI...
...SO WE HAD A FIGHT...
HUH?
What's that again?
ISUMI... AND THAT TIMID BUTLER-IN-DEBT DID *WHAT?*
IT WASN'T ONLY WITH ISUMI!!
HAYATE SAID HE DID IT WITH YOU, TOO!!
HAYATE *PLAYED* WITH YOU!!
WELL, YEAH... WE *DID* PLAY TOGETHER... ON DA MUSHIKING GAME.
...
HUH?
WE PLAYED DA MUSHIKING GAME TOGETHER. DON'T YA REMEMBER?

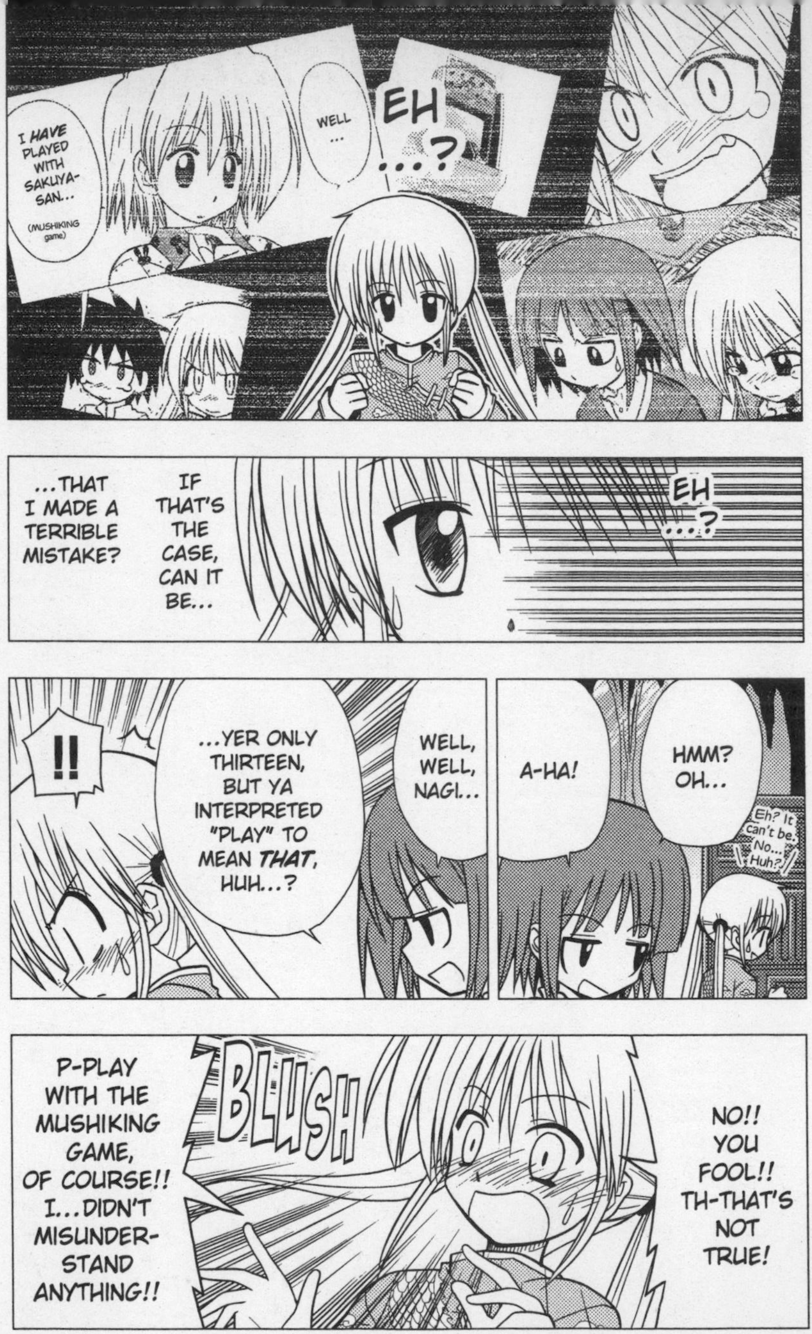
EH ...?
WELL ...
I HAVE PLAYED WITH SAKUYA-SAN...
(MUSHIKING game)
EH ...?
IF THAT'S THE CASE, CAN IT BE...
...THAT I MADE A TERRIBLE MISTAKE?
HMM? OH...
Eh? It can't be. No... Huh?
A-HA!
WELL, WELL, NAGI...
...YER ONLY THIRTEEN, BUT YA INTERPRETED "PLAY" TO MEAN THAT, HUH...?
!!
NO!! YOU FOOL!! TH-THAT'S NOT TRUE!
BLUSH
P-PLAY WITH THE MUSHIKING GAME, OF COURSE!! I...DIDN'T MISUNDER-STAND ANYTHING!!

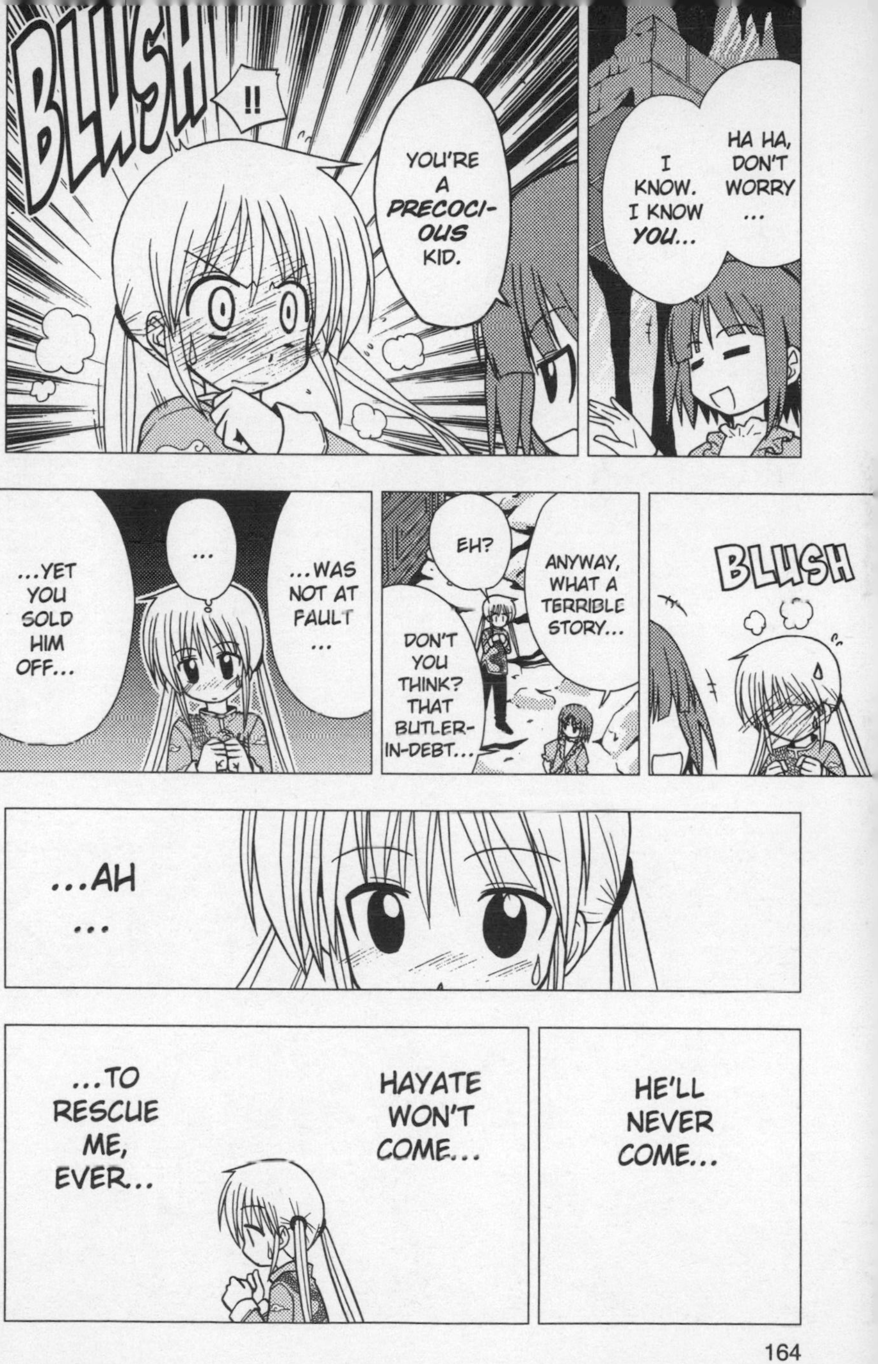
HA HA, DON'T WORRY ...
I KNOW. I KNOW YOU...
YOU'RE A PRECOCIOUS KID.
!!
BLUSH
BLUSH
ANYWAY, WHAT A TERRIBLE STORY...
EH?
DON'T YOU THINK? THAT BUTLER-IN-DEBT...
...WAS NOT AT FAULT ...
...
...YET YOU SOLD HIM OFF...
...AH ...
HE'LL NEVER COME...
HAYATE WON'T COME...
...TO RESCUE ME, EVER...

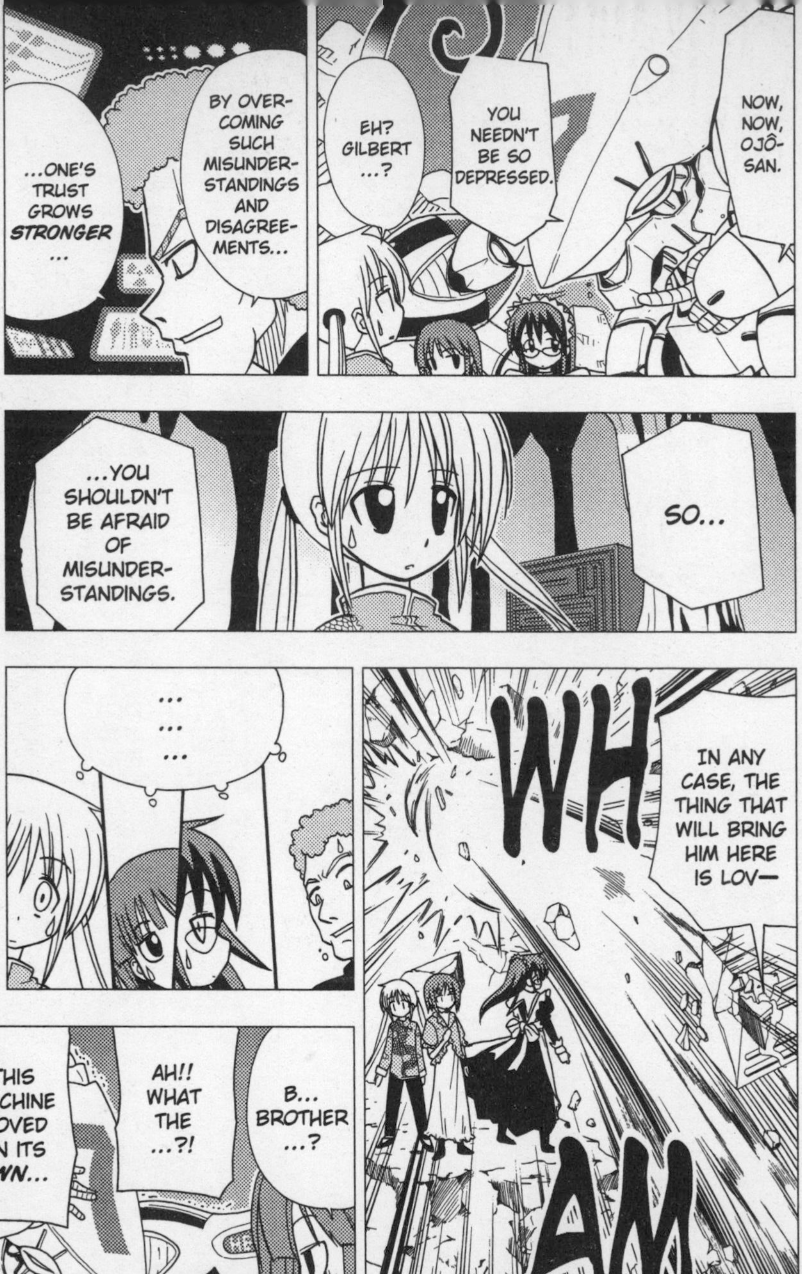
NOW, NOW, OJÔ-SAN.
YOU NEEDN'T BE SO DEPRESSED.
EH? GILBERT ...?
BY OVERCOMING SUCH MISUNDERSTANDINGS AND DISAGREEMENTS...
...ONE'S TRUST GROWS ***STRONGER*** ...
SO...
...YOU SHOULDN'T BE AFRAID OF MISUNDERSTANDINGS.
IN ANY CASE, THE THING THAT WILL BRING HIM HERE IS LOV—
WHAM
... ...
B... BROTHER ...?
AH!! WHAT THE ...?!
THIS MACHINE MOVED ON ITS ***OWN***...

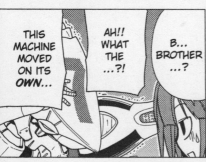

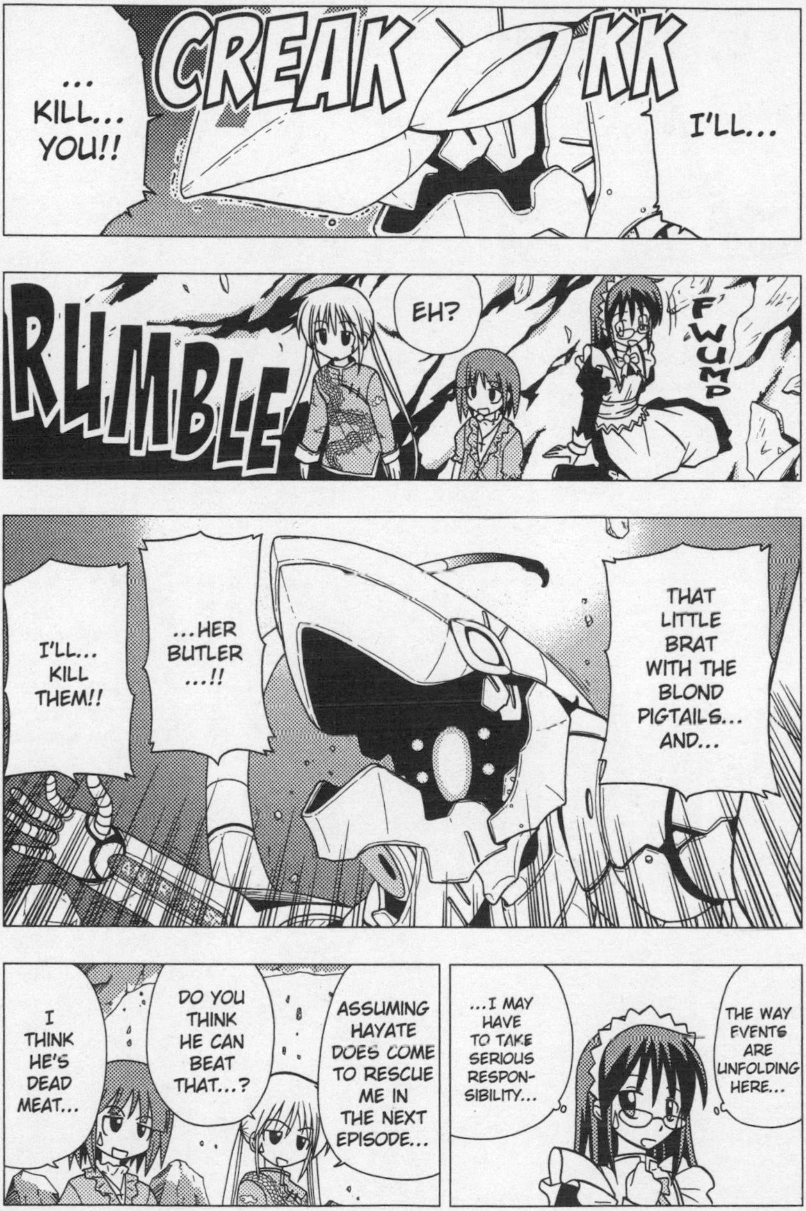
I'LL...
CREAK KK
...KILL... YOU!!
FWUMP
EH?
RUMBLE
THAT LITTLE BRAT WITH THE BLOND PIGTAILS... AND...
...HER BUTLER ...!!
I'LL... KILL THEM!!
THE WAY EVENTS ARE UNFOLDING HERE...
...I MAY HAVE TO TAKE SERIOUS RESPONSIBILITY...
ASSUMING HAYATE DOES COME TO RESCUE ME IN THE NEXT EPISODE...
DO YOU THINK HE CAN BEAT THAT...?
I THINK HE'S DEAD MEAT...

Episode 11:
"I'm Hoping My Voice Will Reach You"

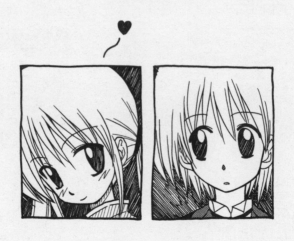

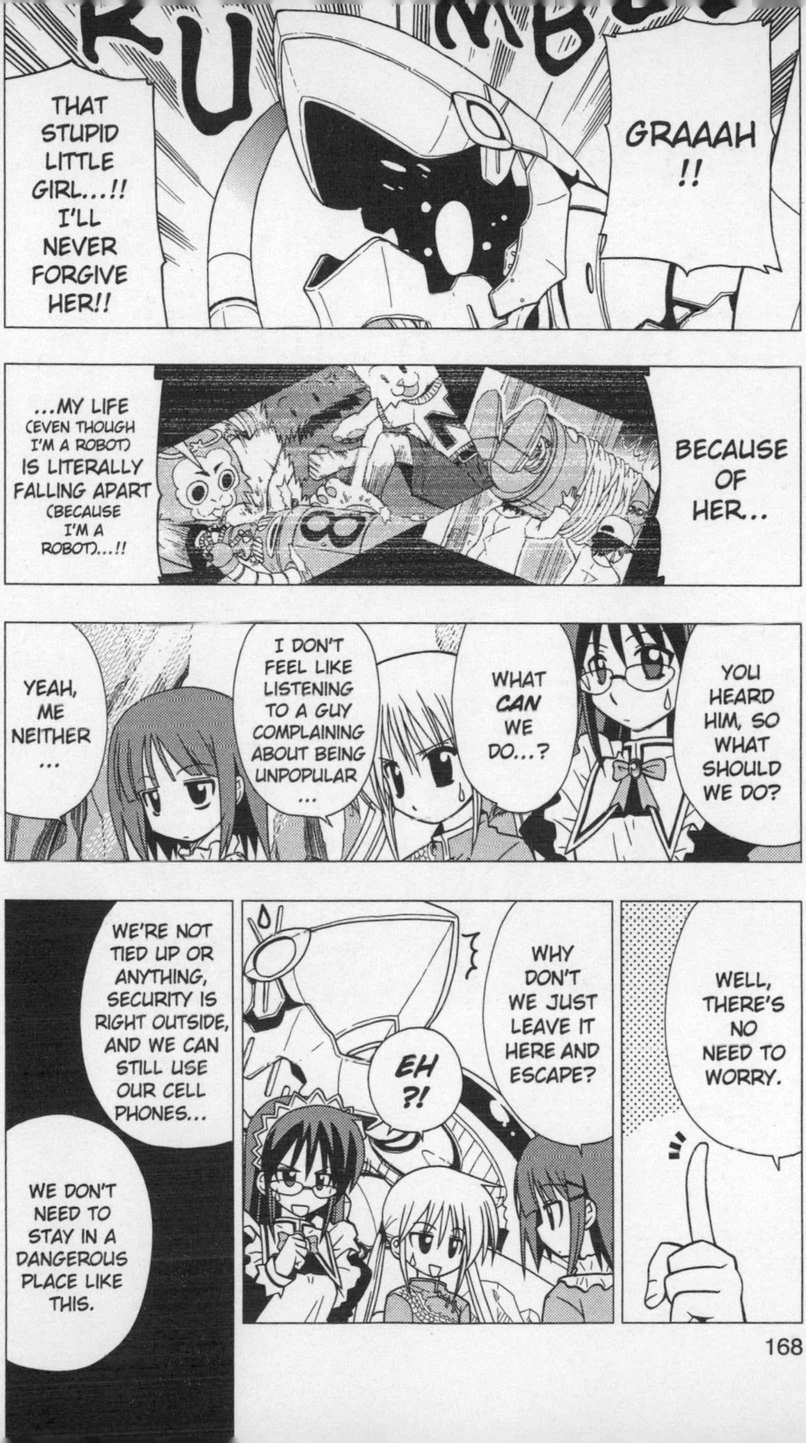
GRAAAH!!
THAT STUPID LITTLE GIRL...!! I'LL NEVER FORGIVE HER!!
BECAUSE OF HER...
...MY LIFE (EVEN THOUGH I'M A ROBOT) IS LITERALLY FALLING APART (BECAUSE I'M A ROBOT)...!!
YOU HEARD HIM, SO WHAT SHOULD WE DO?
WHAT CAN WE DO...?
I DON'T FEEL LIKE LISTENING TO A GUY COMPLAINING ABOUT BEING UNPOPULAR...
YEAH, ME NEITHER...
WELL, THERE'S NO NEED TO WORRY.
WHY DON'T WE JUST LEAVE IT HERE AND ESCAPE?
EH?!
WE'RE NOT TIED UP OR ANYTHING, SECURITY IS RIGHT OUTSIDE, AND WE CAN STILL USE OUR CELL PHONES...
WE DON'T NEED TO STAY IN A DANGEROUS PLACE LIKE THIS.

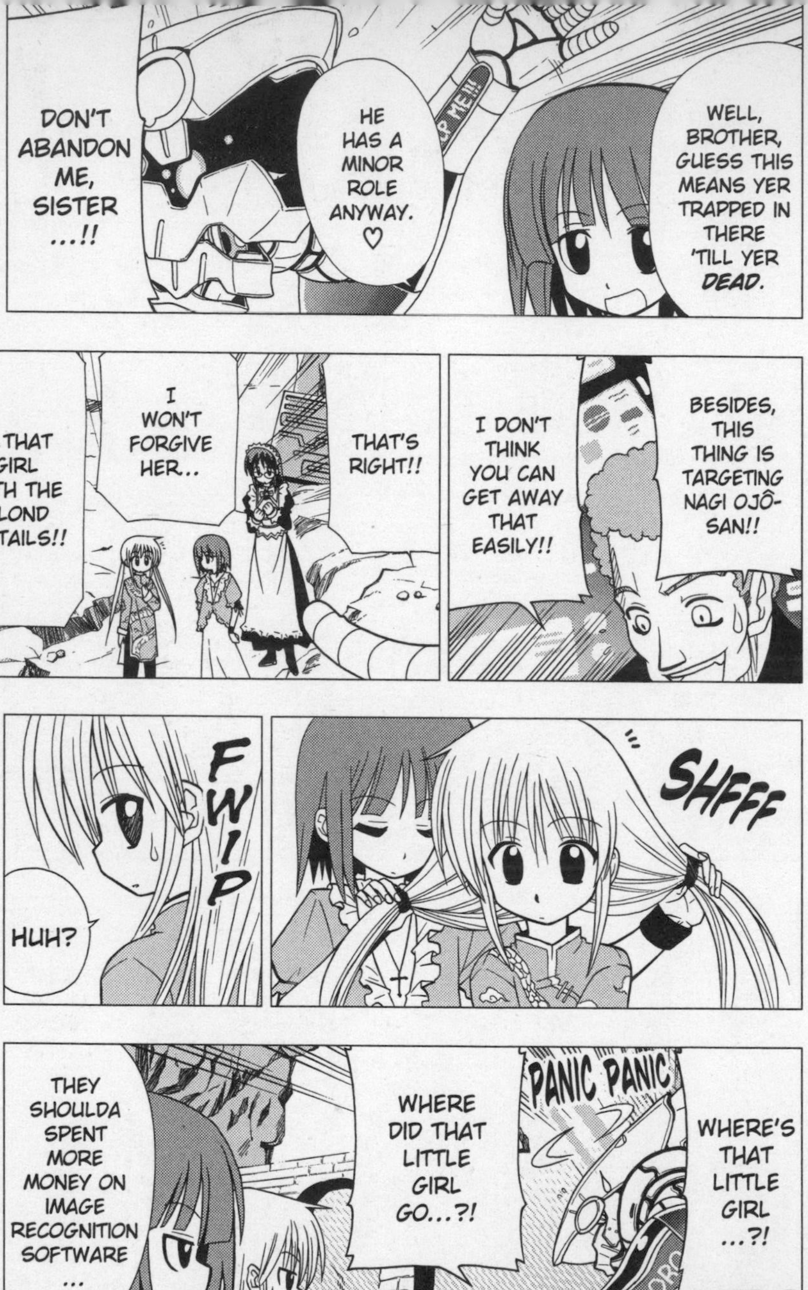
WELL, BROTHER, GUESS THIS MEANS YER TRAPPED IN THERE 'TILL YER *DEAD*.
HE HAS A MINOR ROLE ANYWAY. ♡
DON'T ABANDON ME, SISTER ...!!
BESIDES, THIS THING IS TARGETING NAGI OJÔ-SAN!!
I DON'T THINK YOU CAN GET AWAY THAT EASILY!!
THAT'S RIGHT!!
I WON'T FORGIVE HER...
...THAT GIRL WITH THE BLOND PIGTAILS!!
SHFFF
FWIP
HUH?
PANIC PANIC
WHERE'S THAT LITTLE GIRL ...?!
WHERE DID THAT LITTLE GIRL GO...?!
THEY SHOULDA SPENT MORE MONEY ON IMAGE RECOGNITION SOFTWARE ...

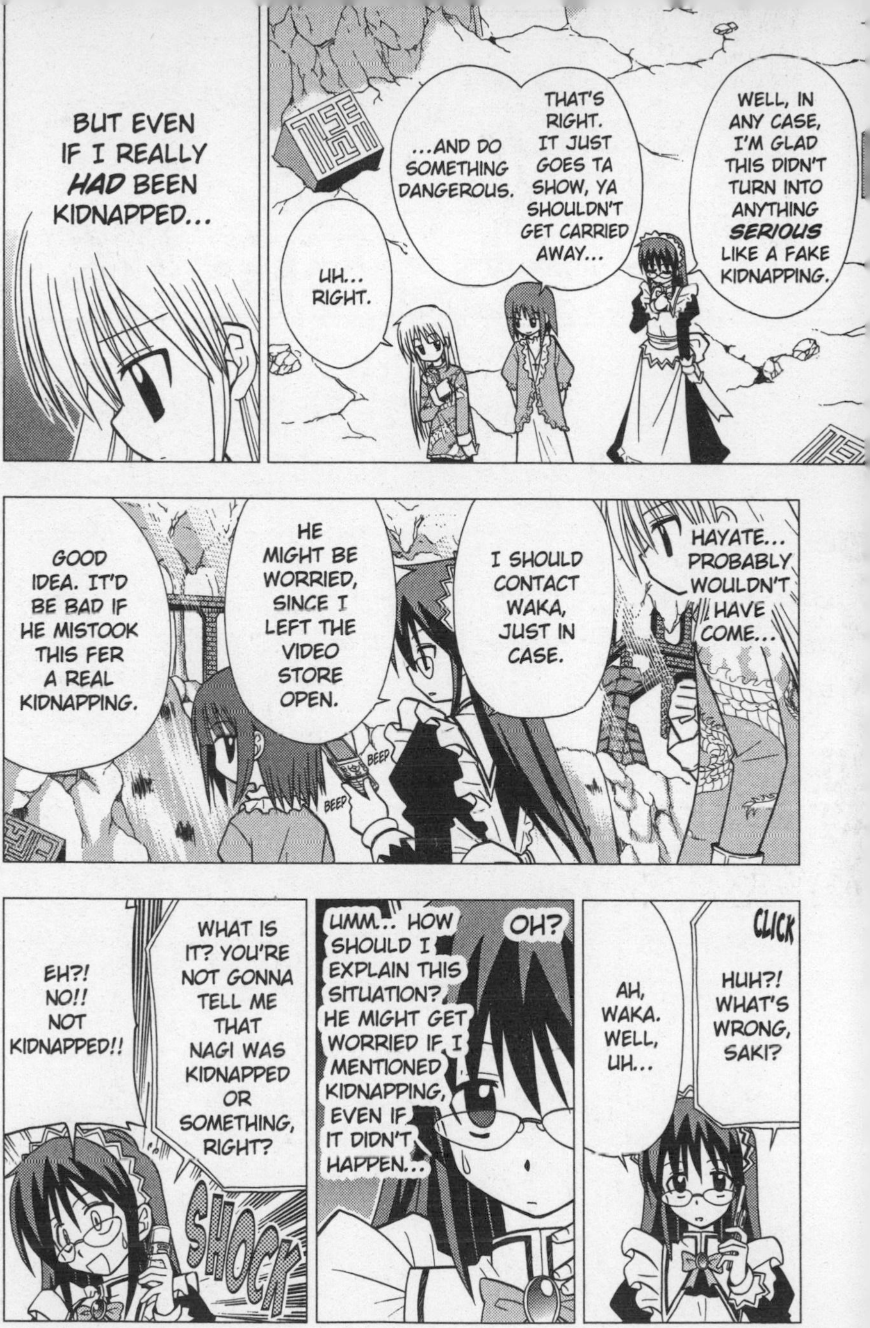
WELL, IN ANY CASE, I'M GLAD THIS DIDN'T TURN INTO ANYTHING **SERIOUS** LIKE A FAKE KIDNAPPING.
THAT'S RIGHT. IT JUST GOES TA SHOW, YA SHOULDN'T GET CARRIED AWAY...
...AND DO SOMETHING DANGEROUS.
UH... RIGHT.
BUT EVEN IF I REALLY ***HAD*** BEEN KIDNAPPED...
HAYATE... PROBABLY WOULDN'T HAVE COME...
I SHOULD CONTACT WAKA, JUST IN CASE.
HE MIGHT BE WORRIED, SINCE I LEFT THE VIDEO STORE OPEN.
BEEP
BEEP
GOOD IDEA. IT'D BE BAD IF HE MISTOOK THIS FER A REAL KIDNAPPING.
CLICK
HUH?! WHAT'S WRONG, SAKI?
AH, WAKA. WELL, UH...
OH?
UMM... HOW SHOULD I EXPLAIN THIS SITUATION? HE MIGHT GET WORRIED IF I MENTIONED KIDNAPPING, EVEN IF IT DIDN'T HAPPEN...
WHAT IS IT? YOU'RE NOT GONNA TELL ME THAT NAGI WAS KIDNAPPED OR SOMETHING, RIGHT?
EH?! NO!! NOT KIDNAPPED!!
SHOCK

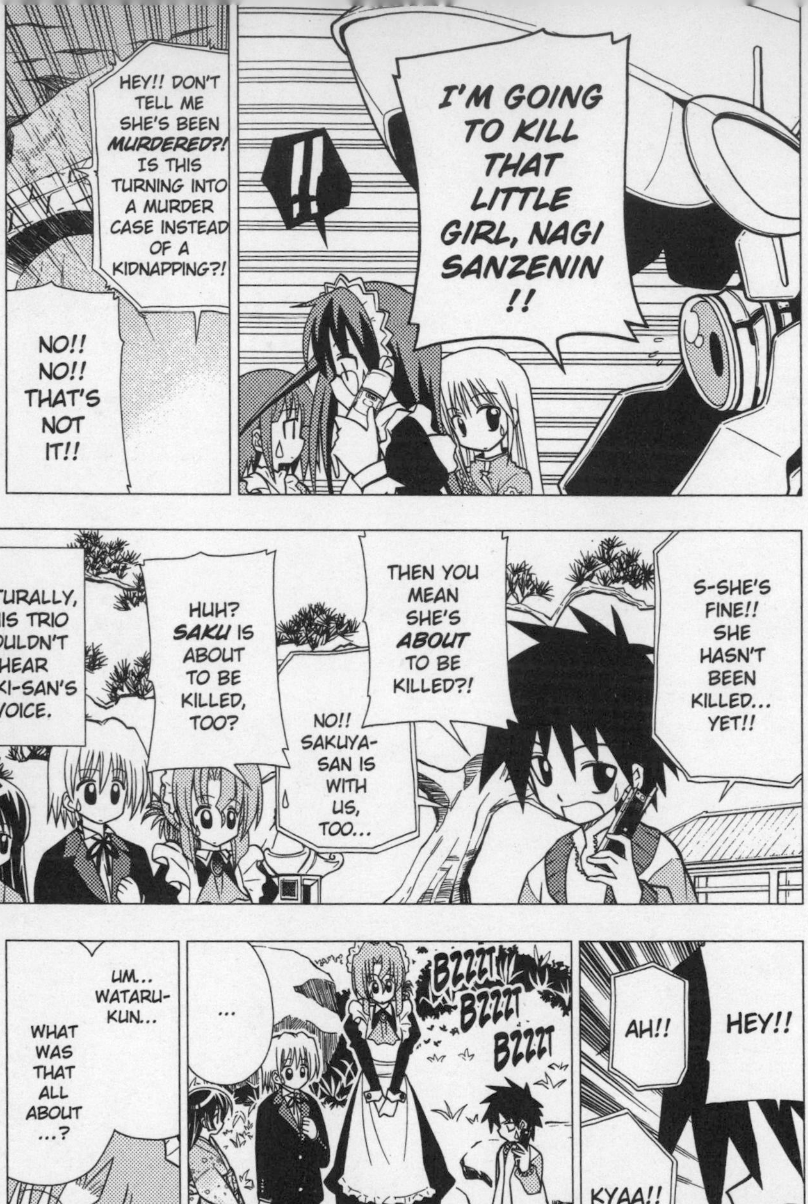
I'M GOING TO KILL THAT LITTLE GIRL, NAGI SANZENIN!!
HEY!! DON'T TELL ME SHE'S BEEN MURDERED?! IS THIS TURNING INTO A MURDER CASE INSTEAD OF A KIDNAPPING?!
NO!! NO!! THAT'S NOT IT!!
S-SHE'S FINE!! SHE HASN'T BEEN KILLED... YET!!
THEN YOU MEAN SHE'S ABOUT TO BE KILLED?!
NO!! SAKUYA-SAN IS WITH US, TOO...
HUH? SAKU IS ABOUT TO BE KILLED, TOO?
NATURALLY, THIS TRIO COULDN'T HEAR SAKI-SAN'S VOICE.
HEY!!
AH!!
KYAA!!
CLICK
BZZZT
BZZZT
BZZZT
...
UM... WATARU-KUN...
WHAT WAS THAT ALL ABOUT...?

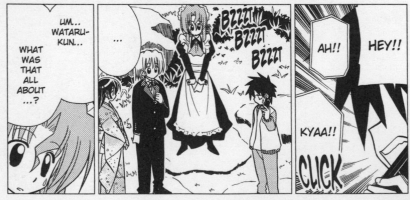

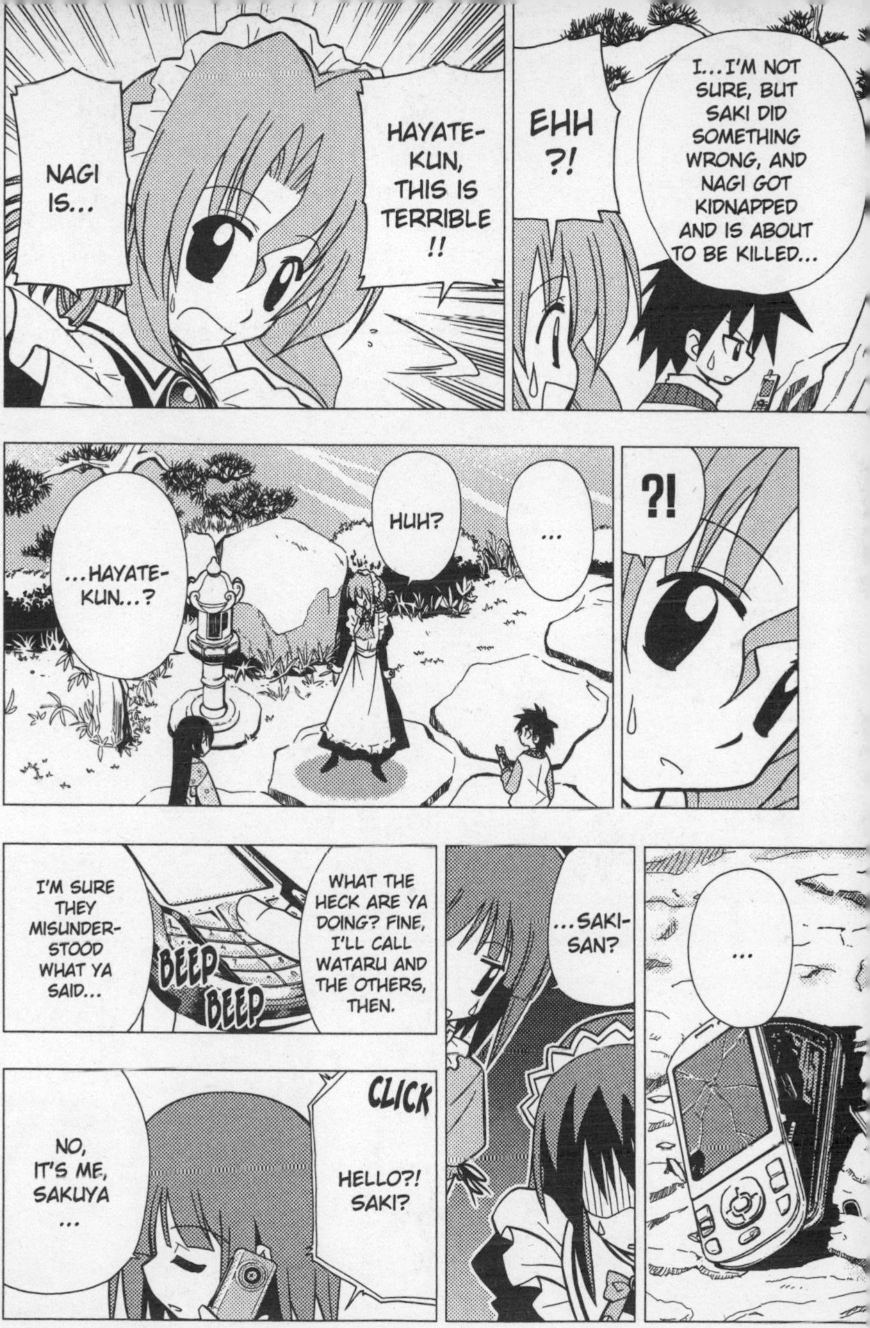
I...I'M NOT SURE, BUT SAKI DID SOMETHING WRONG, AND NAGI GOT KIDNAPPED AND IS ABOUT TO BE KILLED...
EHH ?!
HAYATE-KUN, THIS IS TERRIBLE !!
NAGI IS...
?!
...
HUH?
...HAYATE-KUN...?
...
...SAKI-SAN?
WHAT THE HECK ARE YA DOING? FINE, I'LL CALL WATARU AND THE OTHERS, THEN.
BEEP BEEP
I'M SURE THEY MISUNDER-STOOD WHAT YA SAID...
CLICK
HELLO?! SAKI?
NO, IT'S ME, SAKUYA ...

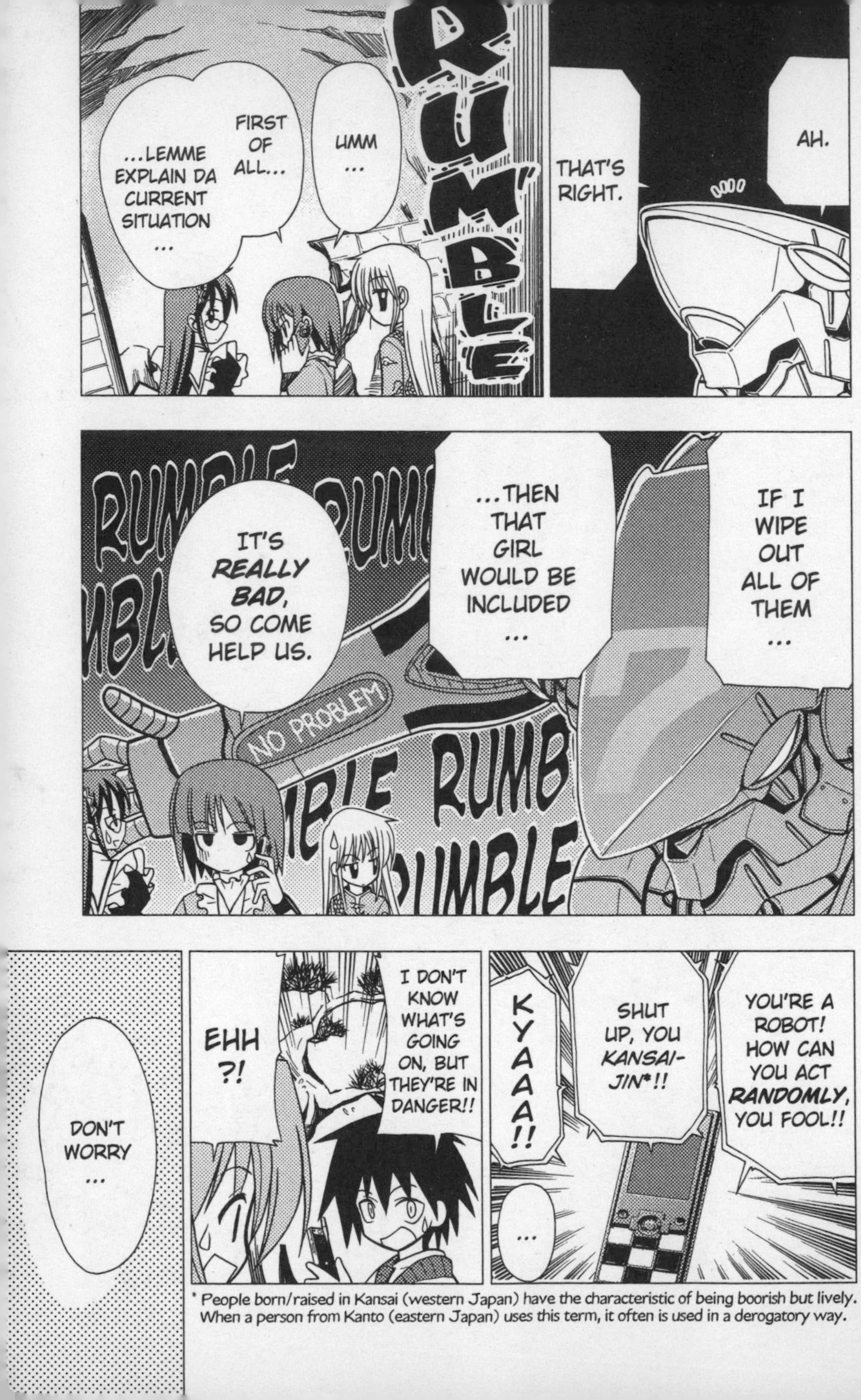
AH.
THAT'S RIGHT.
RUMBLE
UMM...
FIRST OF ALL...
...LEMME EXPLAIN DA CURRENT SITUATION...
IF I WIPE OUT ALL OF THEM...
...THEN THAT GIRL WOULD BE INCLUDED...
IT'S *REALLY BAD*, SO COME HELP US.
NO PROBLEM
RUMBLE RUMBLE RUMBLE RUMBLE
YOU'RE A ROBOT! HOW CAN YOU ACT *RANDOMLY*, YOU FOOL!!
SHUT UP, YOU *KANSAI-JIN**!!
KYAAAA!!
...
I DON'T KNOW WHAT'S GOING ON, BUT THEY'RE IN DANGER!!
EHH?!
DON'T WORRY...

* People born/raised in Kansai (western Japan) have the characteristic of being boorish but lively. When a person from Kanto (eastern Japan) uses this term, it often is used in a derogatory way.

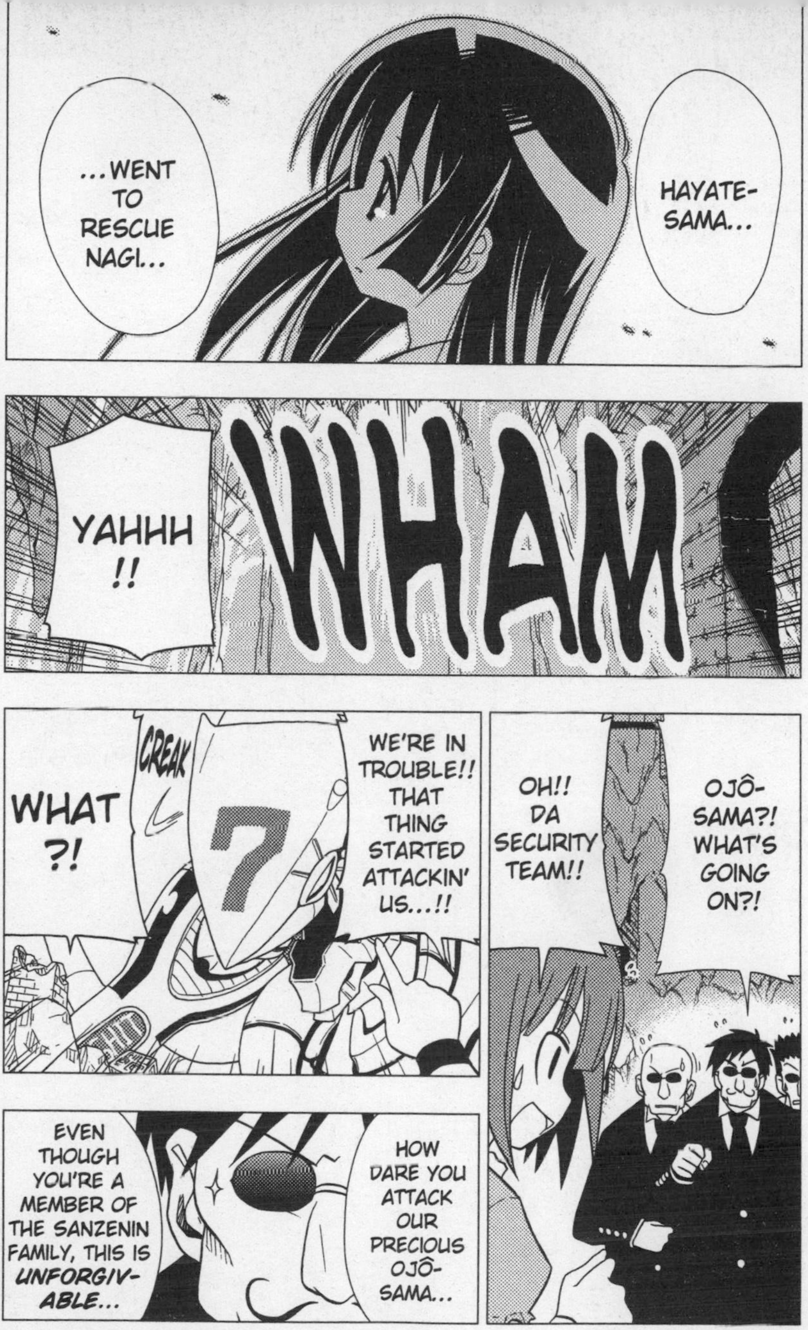
HAYATE-SAMA...
...WENT TO RESCUE NAGI...
WHAM
YAHHH!!
OJÔ-SAMA?! WHAT'S GOING ON?!
OH!! DA SECURITY TEAM!!
WE'RE IN TROUBLE!! THAT THING STARTED ATTACKIN' US...!!
CREAK
WHAT?!
HOW DARE YOU ATTACK OUR PRECIOUS OJÔ-SAMA...
EVEN THOUGH YOU'RE A MEMBER OF THE SANZENIN FAMILY, THIS IS *UNFORGIVABLE*...

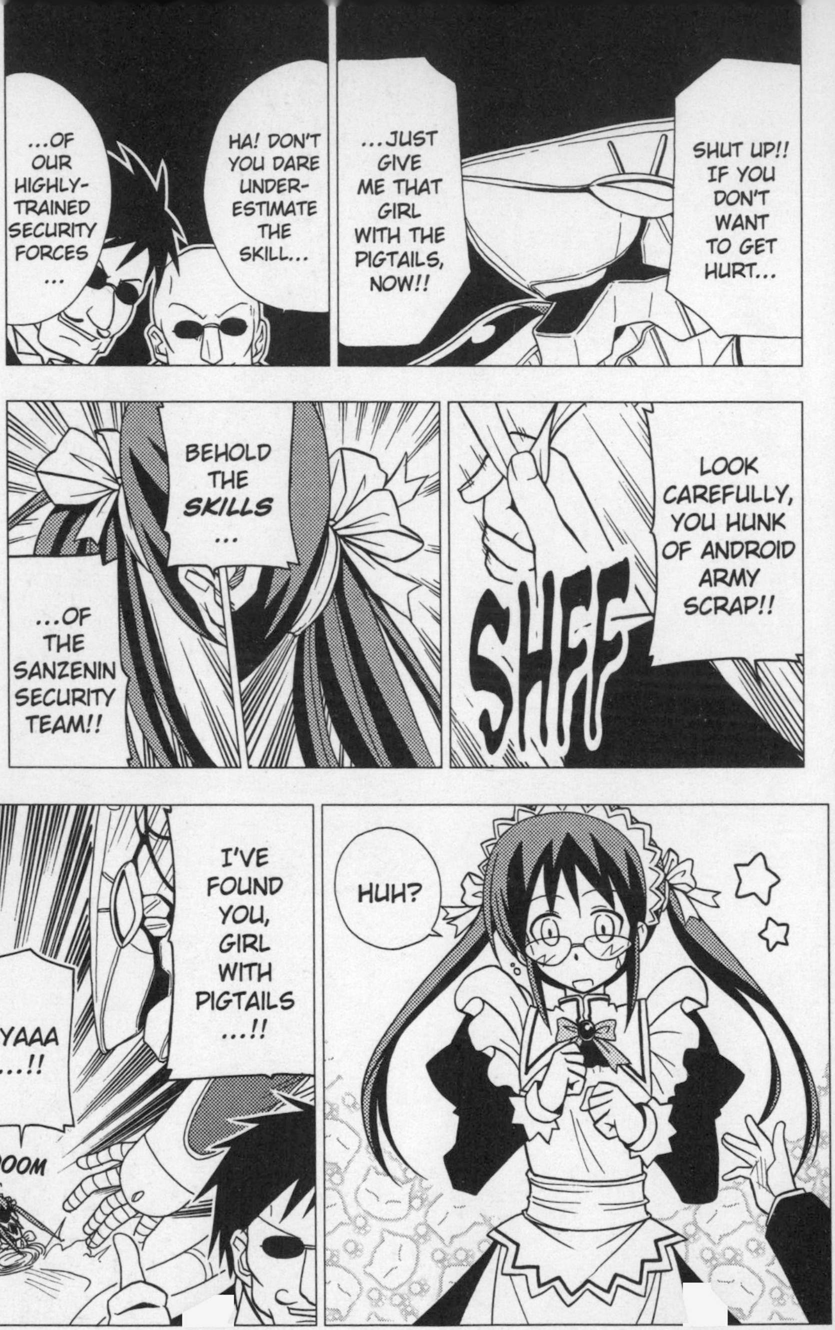
SHUT UP!! IF YOU DON'T WANT TO GET HURT...
...JUST GIVE ME THAT GIRL WITH THE PIGTAILS, NOW!!
HA! DON'T YOU DARE UNDER-ESTIMATE THE SKILL...
...OF OUR HIGHLY-TRAINED SECURITY FORCES...
LOOK CAREFULLY, YOU HUNK OF ANDROID ARMY SCRAP!!
SHFF
BEHOLD THE SKILLS...
...OF THE SANZENIN SECURITY TEAM!!
HUH?
I'VE FOUND YOU, GIRL WITH PIGTAILS...!!
KYAAA...!!
VROOOM

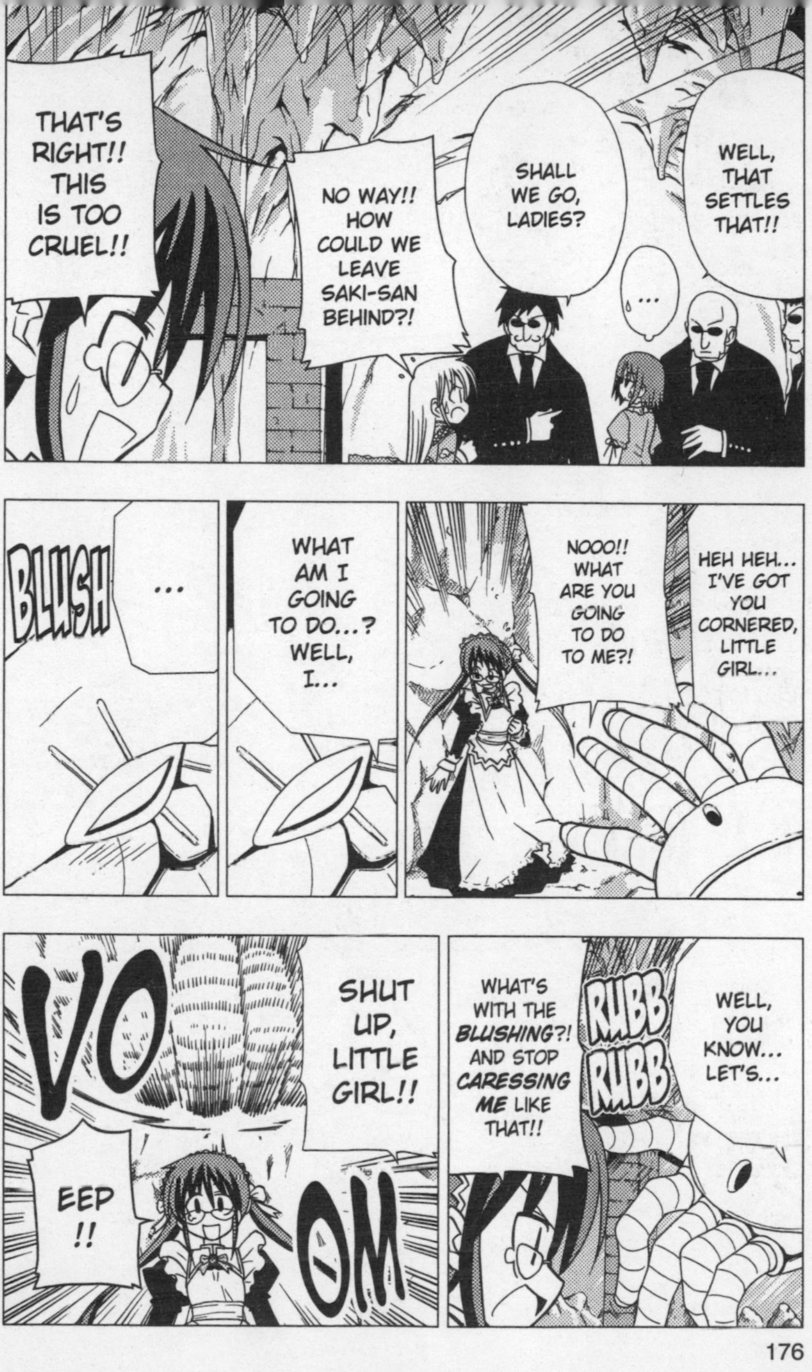
WELL, THAT SETTLES THAT!!
...
SHALL WE GO, LADIES?
NO WAY!! HOW COULD WE LEAVE SAKI-SAN BEHIND?!
THAT'S RIGHT!! THIS IS TOO CRUEL!!
HEH HEH... I'VE GOT YOU CORNERED, LITTLE GIRL...
NOOO!! WHAT ARE YOU GOING TO DO TO ME?!
WHAT AM I GOING TO DO...? WELL, I...
...
BLUSH
WELL, YOU KNOW... LET'S...
RUBB RUBB
WHAT'S WITH THE *BLUSHING*?! AND STOP *CARESSING ME* LIKE THAT!!
SHUT UP, LITTLE GIRL!!
VO
OM
EEP !!

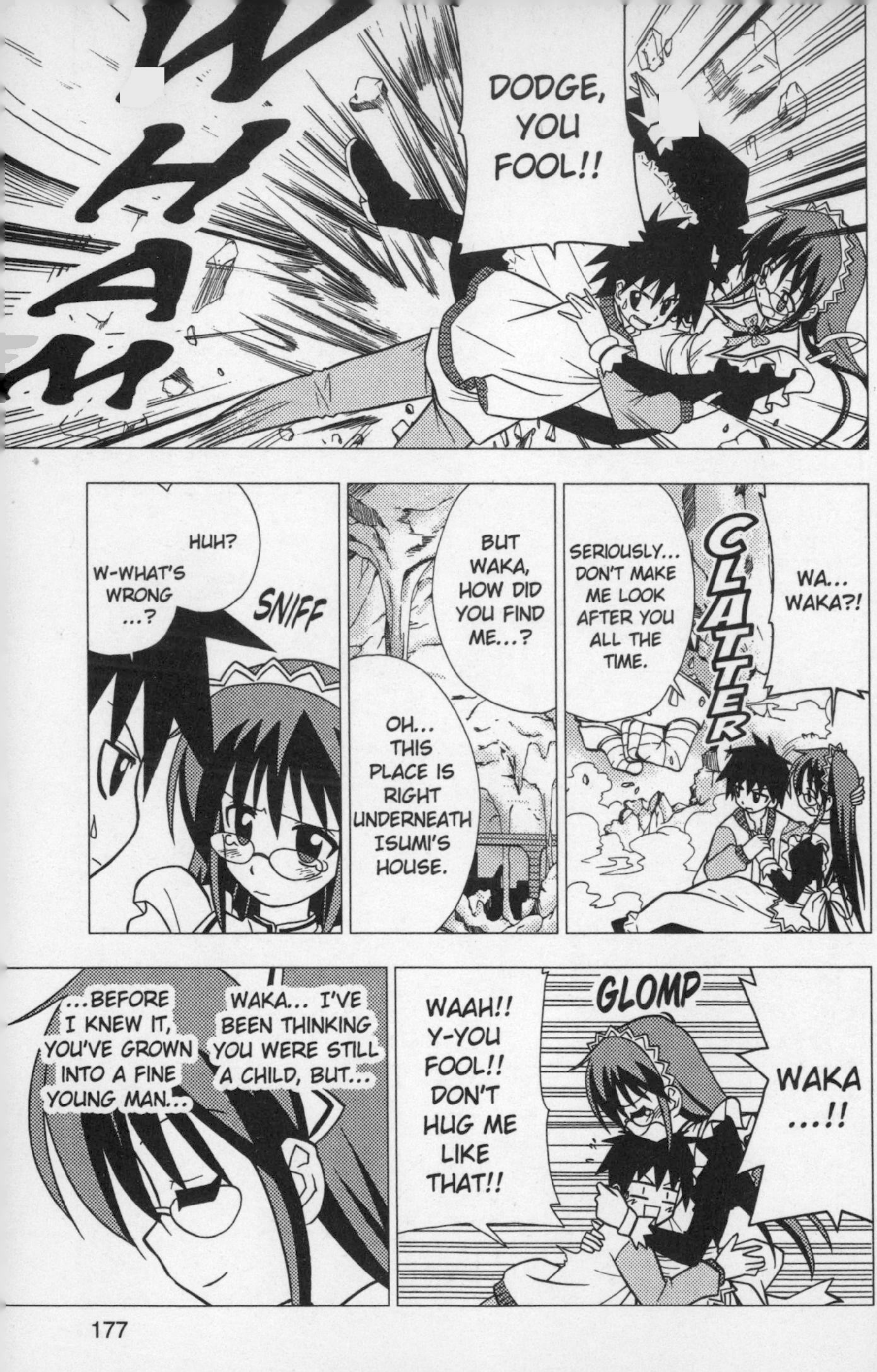
DODGE, YOU FOOL!!
WHAM
WA... WAKA?!
CLATTER
SERIOUSLY... DON'T MAKE ME LOOK AFTER YOU ALL THE TIME.
BUT WAKA, HOW DID YOU FIND ME...?
OH... THIS PLACE IS RIGHT UNDERNEATH ISUMI'S HOUSE.
HUH? W-WHAT'S WRONG ...?
SNIFF
WAKA ...!!
GLOMP
WAAH!! Y-YOU FOOL!! DON'T HUG ME LIKE THAT!!
WAKA... I'VE BEEN THINKING YOU WERE STILL A CHILD, BUT...
...BEFORE I KNEW IT, YOU'VE GROWN INTO A FINE YOUNG MAN...

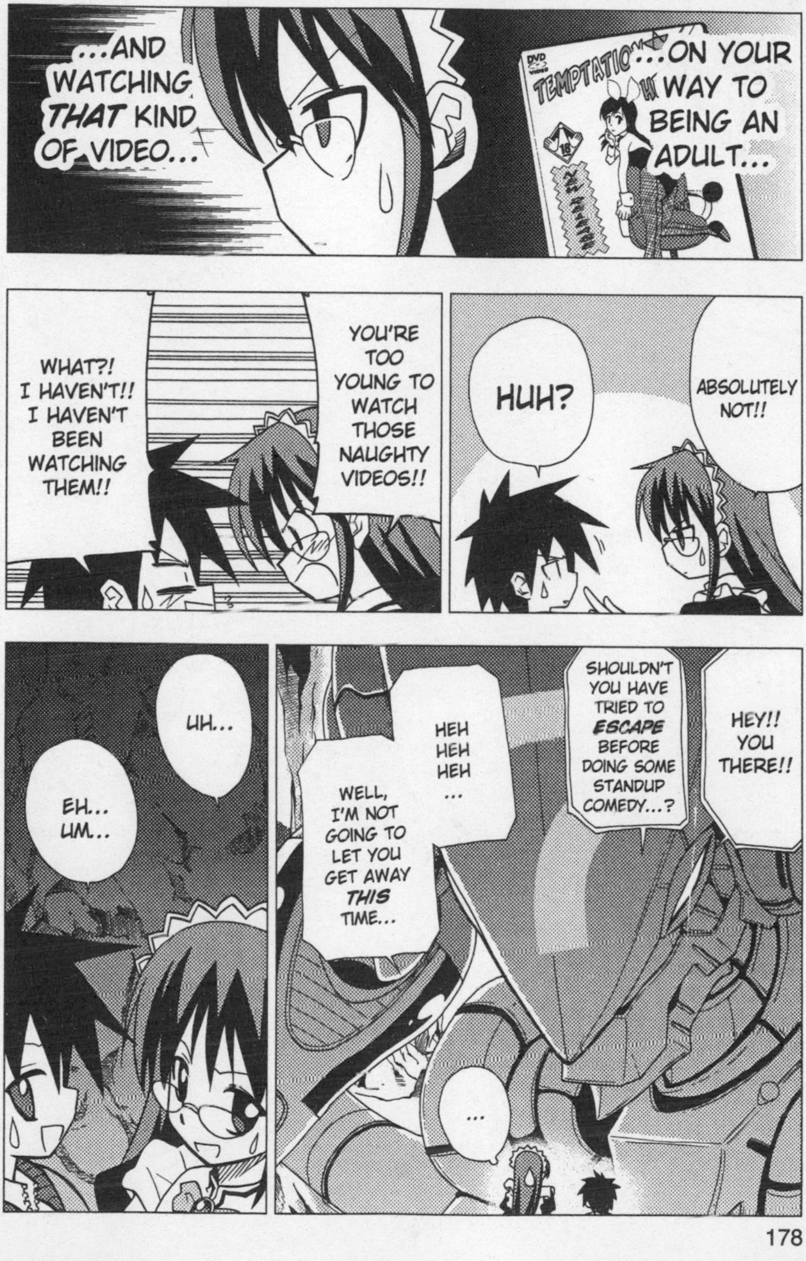
...ON YOUR WAY TO BEING AN ADULT...
...AND WATCHING *THAT* KIND OF VIDEO...
ABSOLUTELY NOT!!
HUH?
YOU'RE TOO YOUNG TO WATCH THOSE NAUGHTY VIDEOS!!
WHAT?! I HAVEN'T!! I HAVEN'T BEEN WATCHING THEM!!
HEY!! YOU THERE!!
SHOULDN'T YOU HAVE TRIED TO *ESCAPE* BEFORE DOING SOME STANDUP COMEDY...?
HEH HEH HEH ...
WELL, I'M NOT GOING TO LET YOU GET AWAY *THIS* TIME...
...
UH...
EH... UM...

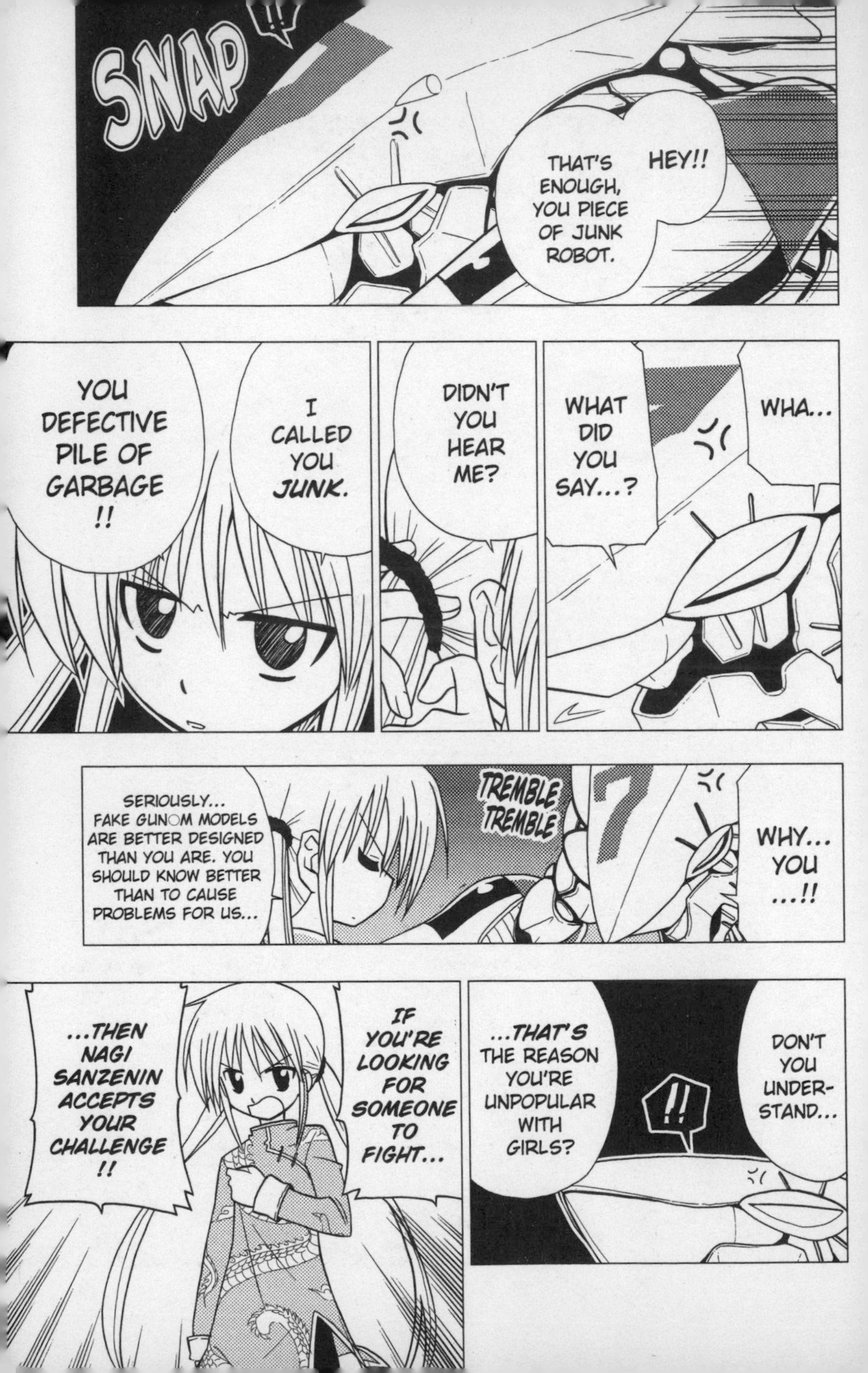
HEY!!
THAT'S ENOUGH, YOU PIECE OF JUNK ROBOT.
SNAP !!
WHA...
WHAT DID YOU SAY...?
DIDN'T YOU HEAR ME?
I CALLED YOU JUNK.
YOU DEFECTIVE PILE OF GARBAGE !!
WHY... YOU ...!!
TREMBLE TREMBLE
SERIOUSLY... FAKE GUN○M MODELS ARE BETTER DESIGNED THAN YOU ARE. YOU SHOULD KNOW BETTER THAN TO CAUSE PROBLEMS FOR US...
DON'T YOU UNDER-STAND...
...THAT'S THE REASON YOU'RE UNPOPULAR WITH GIRLS?
!!
IF YOU'RE LOOKING FOR SOMEONE TO FIGHT...
...THEN NAGI SANZENIN ACCEPTS YOUR CHALLENGE !!

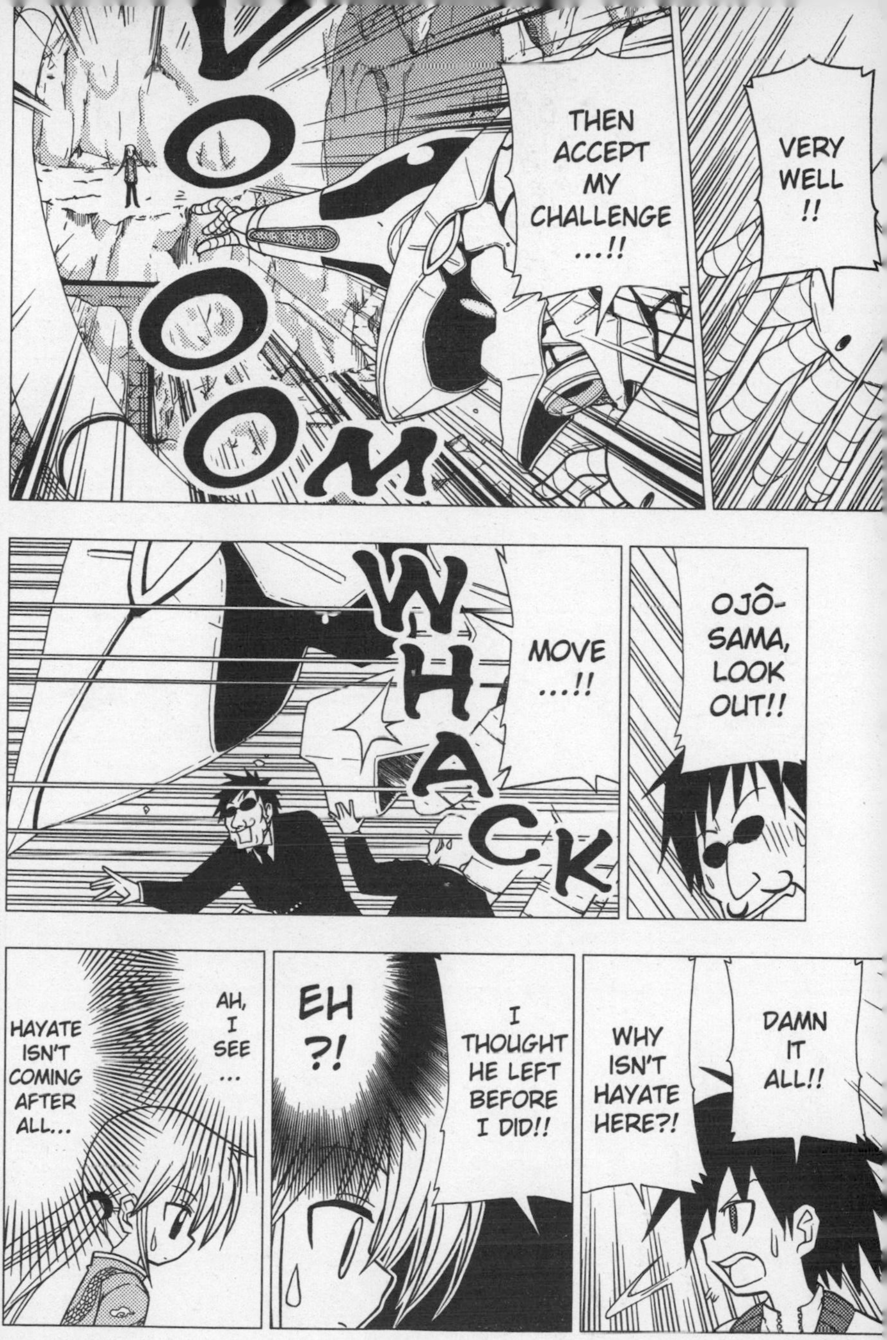
VERY WELL!!
THEN ACCEPT MY CHALLENGE...!!
VOOOM
OJÔ-SAMA, LOOK OUT!!
MOVE...!!
WHACK
DAMN IT ALL!!
WHY ISN'T HAYATE HERE?!
I THOUGHT HE LEFT BEFORE I DID!!
EH?!
AH, I SEE...
HAYATE ISN'T COMING AFTER ALL...

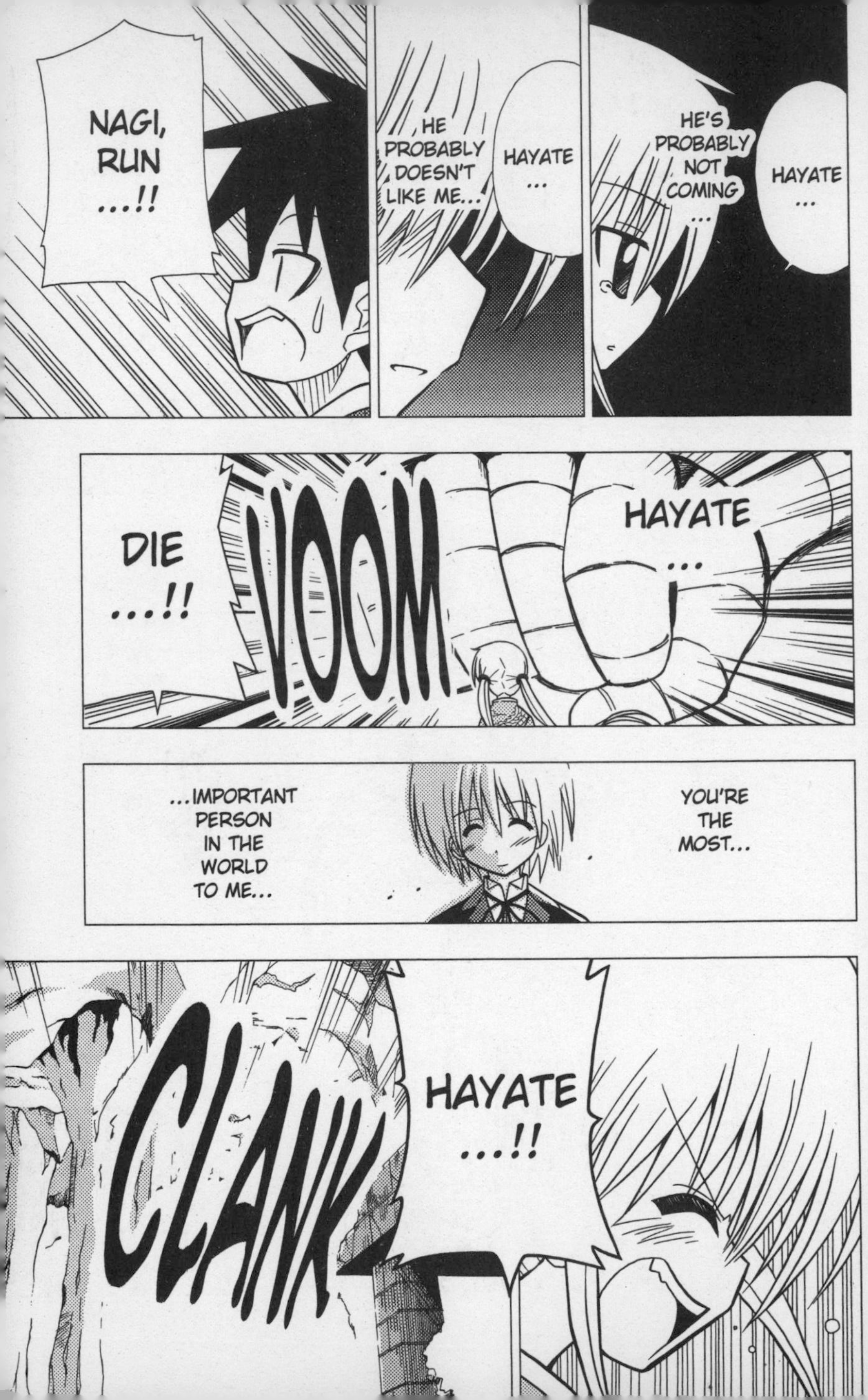
HAYATE...
HE'S PROBABLY NOT COMING...
HAYATE...
HE PROBABLY DOESN'T LIKE ME...
NAGI, RUN...!!
HAYATE...
VOOM
DIE...!!
YOU'RE THE MOST...
...IMPORTANT PERSON IN THE WORLD TO ME...
HAYATE...!!
CLANK

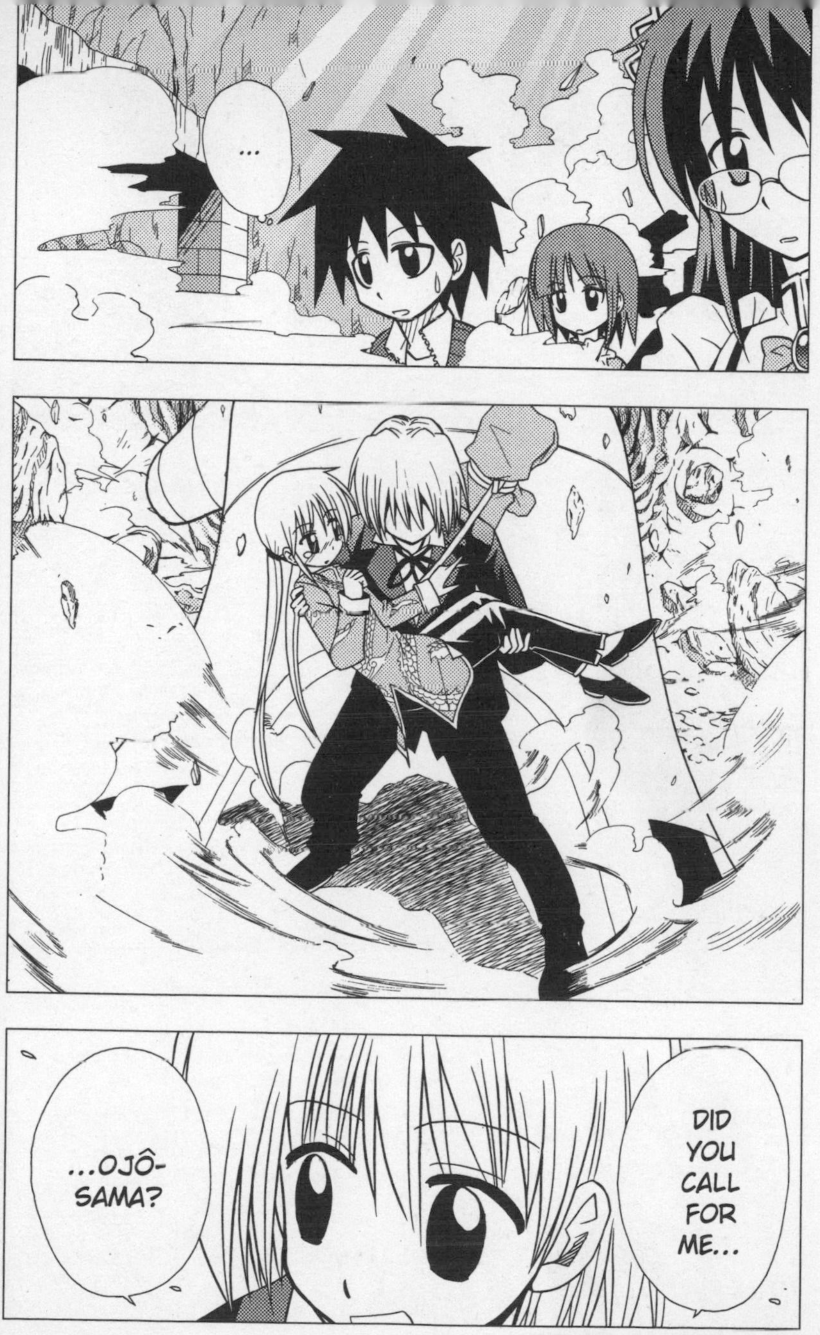
...
...OJÔ-SAMA?
DID YOU CALL FOR ME...

TO BE CONTINUED

HAYATE THE COMBAT BUTLER

BONUS PAGE

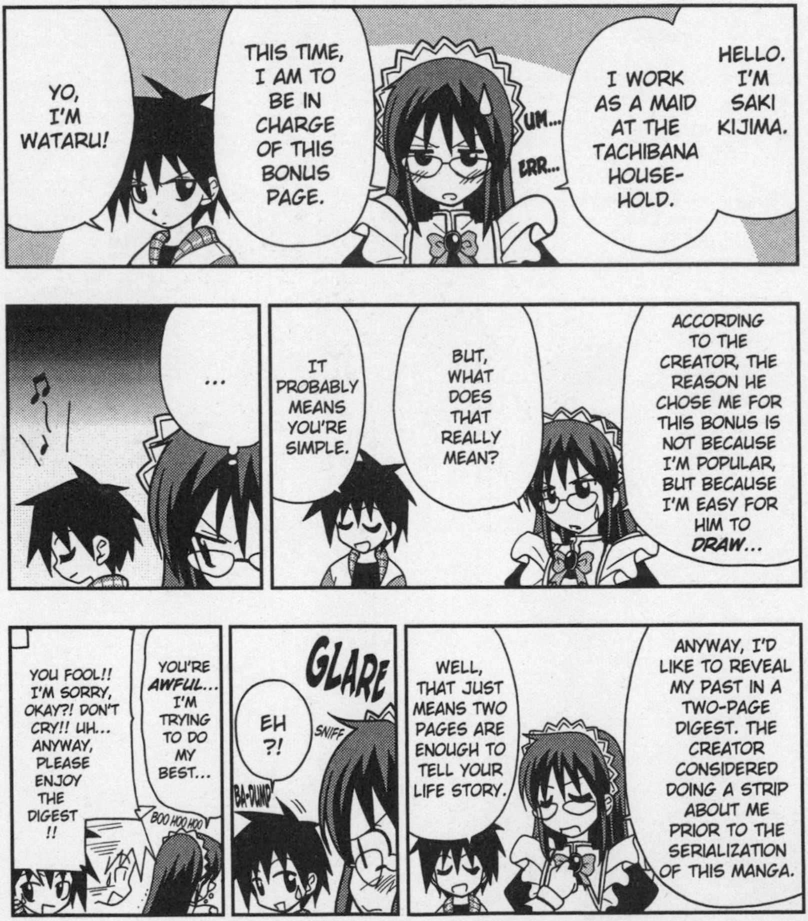
HELLO. I'M SAKI KIJIMA.
I WORK AS A MAID AT THE TACHIBANA HOUSE-HOLD.
UM... ERR...
THIS TIME, I AM TO BE IN CHARGE OF THIS BONUS PAGE.
YO, I'M WATARU!
ACCORDING TO THE CREATOR, THE REASON HE CHOSE ME FOR THIS BONUS IS NOT BECAUSE I'M POPULAR, BUT BECAUSE I'M EASY FOR HIM TO *DRAW*...
BUT, WHAT DOES THAT REALLY MEAN?
IT PROBABLY MEANS YOU'RE SIMPLE.
...
ANYWAY, I'D LIKE TO REVEAL MY PAST IN A TWO-PAGE DIGEST. THE CREATOR CONSIDERED DOING A STRIP ABOUT ME PRIOR TO THE SERIALIZATION OF THIS MANGA.
WELL, THAT JUST MEANS TWO PAGES ARE ENOUGH TO TELL YOUR LIFE STORY.
GLARE
SNIFF
EH ?!
BA-DUMP
YOU'RE *AWFUL*... I'M TRYING TO DO MY BEST...
BOO HOO HOO
YOU FOOL!! I'M SORRY, OKAY?! DON'T CRY!! UH... ANYWAY, PLEASE ENJOY THE DIGEST !!

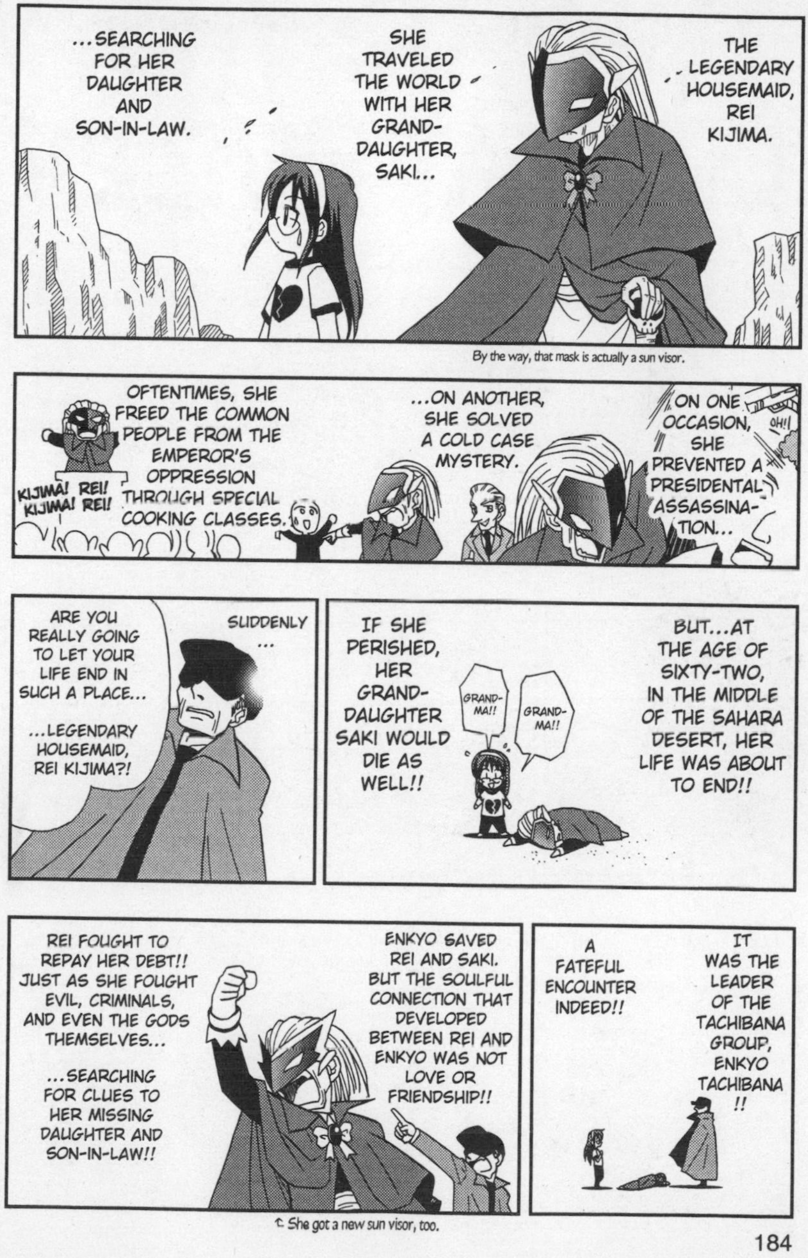
THE LEGENDARY HOUSEMAID, REI KIJIMA.
SHE TRAVELED THE WORLD WITH HER GRAND-DAUGHTER, SAKI...
...SEARCHING FOR HER DAUGHTER AND SON-IN-LAW.
By the way, that mask is actually a sun visor.
ON ONE OCCASION, SHE PREVENTED A PRESIDENTAL ASSASSINA-TION...
OH!!
...ON ANOTHER, SHE SOLVED A COLD CASE MYSTERY.
OFTENTIMES, SHE FREED THE COMMON PEOPLE FROM THE EMPEROR'S OPPRESSION THROUGH SPECIAL COOKING CLASSES.
KIJIMA! REI! KIJIMA! REI!
BUT...AT THE AGE OF SIXTY-TWO, IN THE MIDDLE OF THE SAHARA DESERT, HER LIFE WAS ABOUT TO END!!
GRAND-MA!!
GRAND-MA!!
IF SHE PERISHED, HER GRAND-DAUGHTER SAKI WOULD DIE AS WELL!!
SUDDENLY...
ARE YOU REALLY GOING TO LET YOUR LIFE END IN SUCH A PLACE...
...LEGENDARY HOUSEMAID, REI KIJIMA?!
IT WAS THE LEADER OF THE TACHIBANA GROUP, ENKYO TACHIBANA!!
A FATEFUL ENCOUNTER INDEED!!
ENKYO SAVED REI AND SAKI. BUT THE SOULFUL CONNECTION THAT DEVELOPED BETWEEN REI AND ENKYO WAS NOT LOVE OR FRIENDSHIP!!
REI FOUGHT TO REPAY HER DEBT!! JUST AS SHE FOUGHT EVIL, CRIMINALS, AND EVEN THE GODS THEMSELVES...
...SEARCHING FOR CLUES TO HER MISSING DAUGHTER AND SON-IN-LAW!!
↑ She got a new sun visor, too.

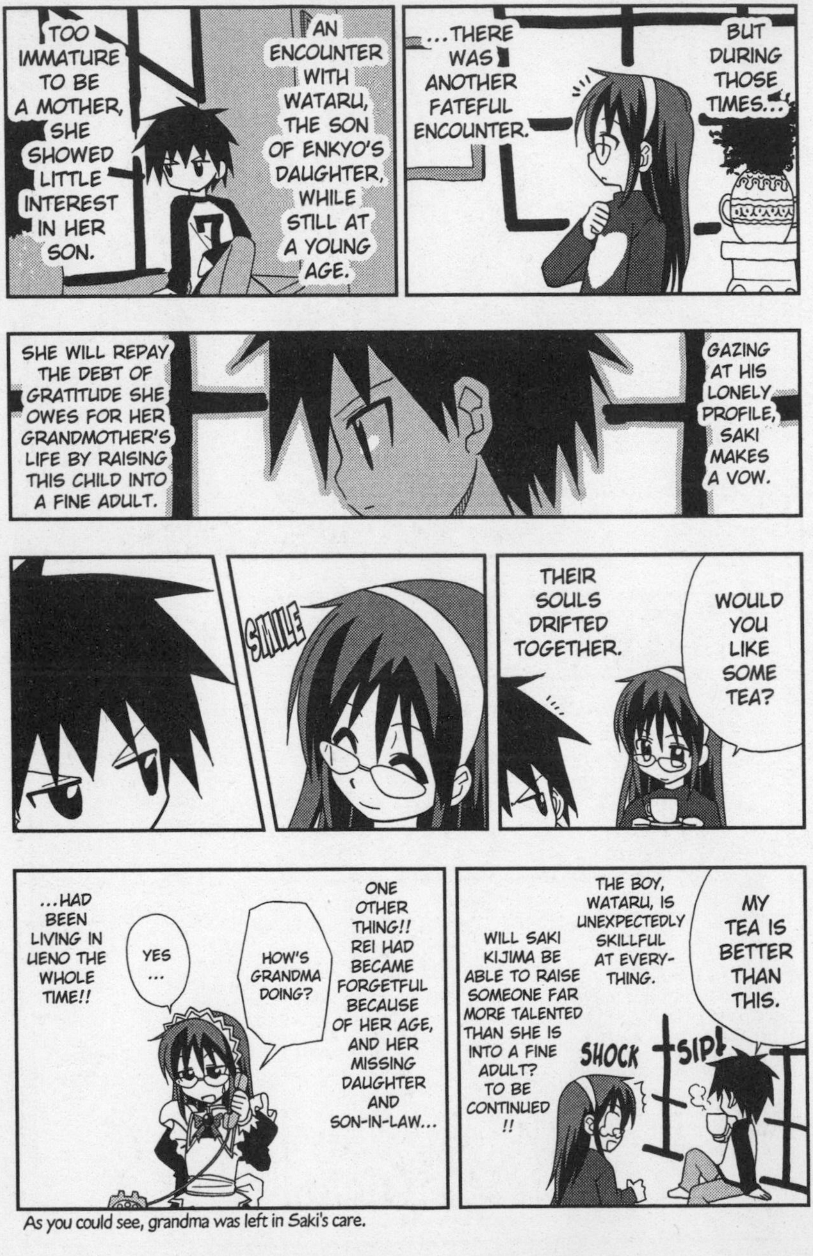
BUT DURING THOSE TIMES...
...THERE WAS ANOTHER FATEFUL ENCOUNTER.
AN ENCOUNTER WITH WATARU, THE SON OF ENKYO'S DAUGHTER, WHILE STILL AT A YOUNG AGE.
TOO IMMATURE TO BE A MOTHER, SHE SHOWED LITTLE INTEREST IN HER SON.
GAZING AT HIS LONELY PROFILE, SAKI MAKES A VOW.
SHE WILL REPAY THE DEBT OF GRATITUDE SHE OWES FOR HER GRANDMOTHER'S LIFE BY RAISING THIS CHILD INTO A FINE ADULT.
WOULD YOU LIKE SOME TEA?
THEIR SOULS DRIFTED TOGETHER.
SMILE
MY TEA IS BETTER THAN THIS.
THE BOY, WATARU, IS UNEXPECTEDLY SKILLFUL AT EVERY-THING.
WILL SAKI KIJIMA BE ABLE TO RAISE SOMEONE FAR MORE TALENTED THAN SHE IS INTO A FINE ADULT? TO BE CONTINUED !!
SIP!
SHOCK
ONE OTHER THING!! REI HAD BECAME FORGETFUL BECAUSE OF HER AGE, AND HER MISSING DAUGHTER AND SON-IN-LAW...
HOW'S GRANDMA DOING?
YES ...
...HAD BEEN LIVING IN UENO THE WHOLE TIME!!

As you could see, grandma was left in Saki's care.

PROFILE

[Age] 13

[Birthday] August 30th

[Blood Type] AB

[Family Structure]
Father
Mother
(Currently enjoying extravagant
 overseas travel with Rei)

[Height] 139 cm

[Weight] 32 kg

[Strengths/Likes]
Isumi
Passionate film productions

[Weaknesses/Dislikes]
Sakuya (he cannot disobey her)

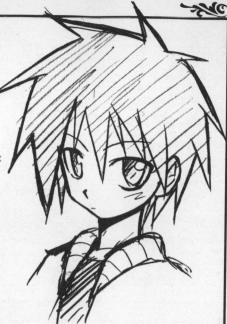

Wataru Tachibana

His name in Kanji is written as "橘亘."
Among the main characters, the creator thinks he is the
easiest to draw. The creator made two one-shot comics
using a character with a different name,
but having almost the same appearance,
personality and basic setting as Wataru.
He is Nagi's fiancé as specified in his late grandfather's will.
Basically, when the creator draws this type of character,
he combines him with an old man's personality.
In order to break off the engagement with Nagi,
he tries hard every day to become wealthier than the
Sanzenin family. Everything he does is for Isumi,
so he actually studies and works very hard.
Unfortunately, his manner of speech and personality
are very poor. Unlike Nagi, he has a wide circle of friends.
However, they may or may not be introduced in this manga.

PROFILE

[Age] 20

[Birthday] June 17th

[Blood Type] B

[Family Structure]
Father (adopted into the family)
Mother
Sister Hinata (10)
Grandmother (Rei Kijima)

[Height] 161 cm

[Weight] 45 kg

[Strengths/Likes]
Coffee
Maid Uniform
Crafting small items
Wataru
Grandmother

[Weaknesses/Dislikes]
Domestic duties in general
Moving fragile goods without
breaking them

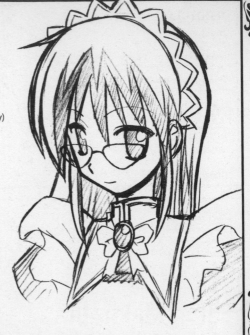

Saki Kijima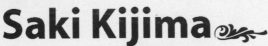

Her name in Kanji is written as "貴嶋沙希."
She looks very capable when she doesn't say anything,
but Wataru calls her a ditz because she seems
to be cursed with making mistakes. Despite that,
for some reason, she's popular. The creator enjoys drawing
her because of both her look and her personality.
The creator would like to come up with stories that focus
only on Wataru and Saki-san, but he worries that the readers
may not be interested, so that plan is on hold for now.
By the way, Wataru's room is filled with Saki-san's
handmade items. Saki-san's grandmother taught
her how to make things, but Saki-san doesn't have the
skill to come up with new designs of her own.

PROFILE

[Age] Unknown **[Birthday]** Unknown
[Blood Type] Unknown
[Family Structure] Only direct relative is Nagi
[Height] Unknown **[Weight]** Unknown
[Strengths/Likes] Maria
[Weaknesses/Dislikes] Nagi and Hayate

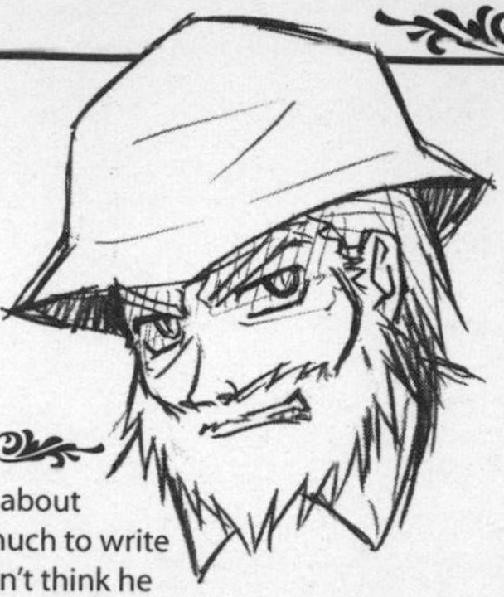

Mikado Sanzenin

He's Nagi's grandfather, who I can't really say much about right now. Actually, I just realized there is nothing much to write about him, even though I introduced him here. I don't think he will appear again for a while, but please don't forget him!♥

PROFILE

[Age] 22 **[Birthday]** October 20th **[Blood Type]** B
[Family Structure] Father Mother Brother
[Height] 156 cm **[Weight]** 41 kg
[Strengths/Likes] Electronics, personal computers, sleeping
[Weaknesses/Dislikes] Getting scolded by the Boss

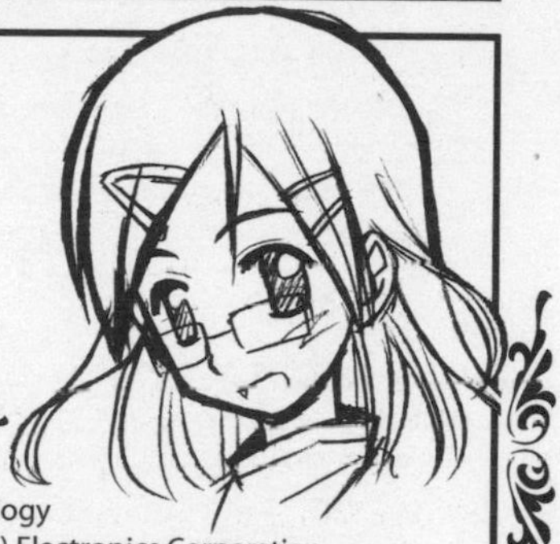

Shiori Makimura

Chief of Development, Humanoid Nursing and Battlefield Weapons Department, Advanced Technology Development Division, Mikado Hyper Energy (M.H.E.) Electronics Corporation—a Sanzenin Group company. She is a woman with the body of an adult, but the mind of a child. Although she is highly intelligent, she is also very innocent, and basically only thinks about electronics. Robo Eight is her current lover. She lives with her mechanical creation in a super-high-class condo situated in a prime Tokyo location. Robo Eight diligently performs chores like taking out the trash and cleaning, so he has become well-loved by the residents of the community.

PROFILE

[Age] 3 **[Birthday]** May 5th
[Family Structure] Makimura-san is all that he has
[Height] 200 cm **[Weight]** 130 kg
[Strengths/Likes] Makimura-san is all that he has
[Weaknesses/Dislikes] Hatred towards human beings

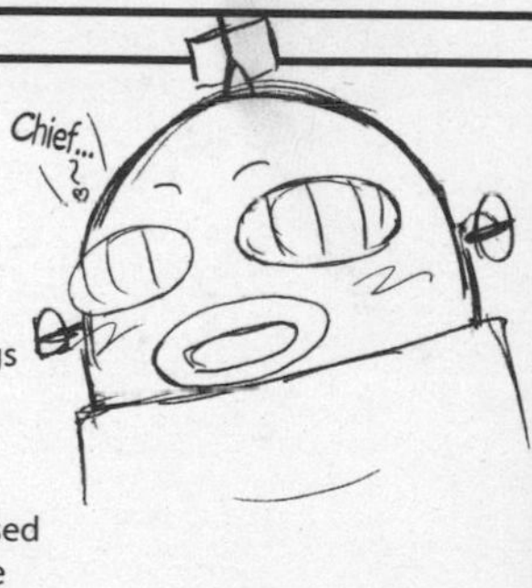
Chief...?

Eight Ver.8.3

By the way, the creator just wanted to convey "increased hatred as a result of duplication" along the lines of the way Patla◯or did it, so the "Prototype Seven" appearing toward the end of this volume was just a way to do that. It was awfully hard to draw...

SO, *HAYATE THE COMBAT BUTLER* HAS FINALLY
MADE IT TO VOLUME THREE!

UNLIKE THE PREVIOUS VOLUME, I DID MORE BONUS
PAGES FOR THIS RELEASE, BUT THE SCHEDULE
WAS TIGHTER, SO IT WAS PRETTY HECTIC.

THANKS TO EVERYONE'S SUPPORT, HOWEVER,
THE SERIES SOMEHOW MANAGED TO AVOID GETTING CUT.
THANK YOU VERY MUCH!!

TO BE HONEST WITH YOU, I HAD A VAGUE FEELING THAT THE
STORY MIGHT BE DISCONTINUED, PROBABLY DURING ONE OF
THE EPISODES IN THIS VOLUME. I CONTINUED TO THINK
ABOUT FUTURE STORYLINES AND SETTINGS, BUT OFTEN
THOUGHT, "THAT PROBABLY WON'T EVER BE USED..."
I ACTUALLY CRIED WHEN I THOUGHT ABOUT THAT, USUALLY
IN SOME FAMILY RESTAURANT AROUND MIDNIGHT.

BUT THAT ASIDE, IT APPEARS LIKE WE MIGHT BE ABLE TO
CONTINUE THE STORY FOR A LITTLE WHILE, SO I'LL TRY TO
WORK HARD, AND TAKE THINGS ONE WEEK AT A TIME.
MY GOAL FOR THE MOMENT IS "LET'S SHOOT FOR A ONE-
YEAR ANNIVERSARY EPISODE! ☆" BEYOND THAT,
THE FUTURE IS UNKNOWN...

OH, AND NOT SURPRISINGLY, I'M UPDATING MY
COLUMN IN *WEB SUNDAY* EVERY WEEK, SO PLEASE
CHECK THAT OUT THAT AS WELL. I HOPE TO
RECEIVE YOUR CONTINUED SUPPORT...

WELL, SEE YOU! ☆

Let's play with Saki-san!! (1)

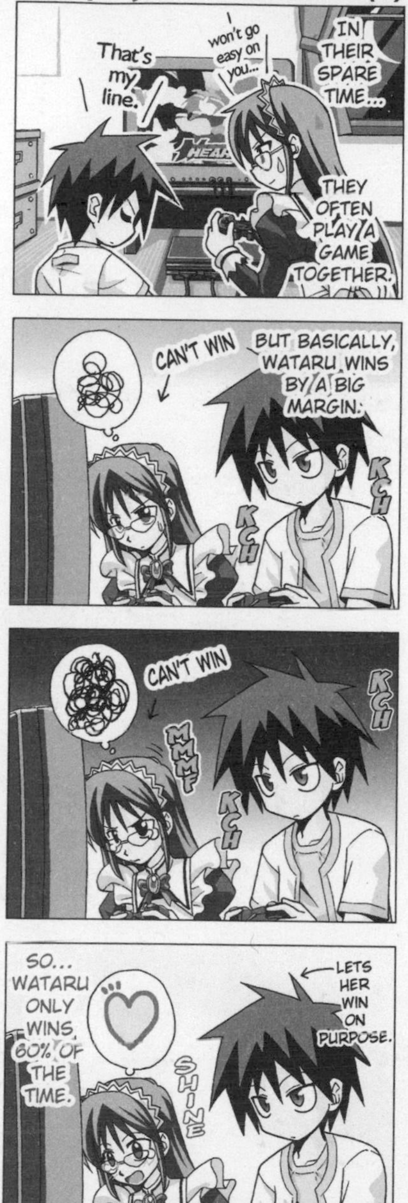
IN THEIR SPARE TIME...
THEY OFTEN PLAY A GAME TOGETHER.
I won't go easy on you...
That's my line.
BUT BASICALLY, WATARU WINS BY A BIG MARGIN.
CAN'T WIN
KCH
KCH
CAN'T WIN
MMMF
KCH
KCH
SO... WATARU ONLY WINS 60% OF THE TIME.
LETS HER WIN ON PURPOSE.
SHINE

Let's play with Saki-san!! (2)

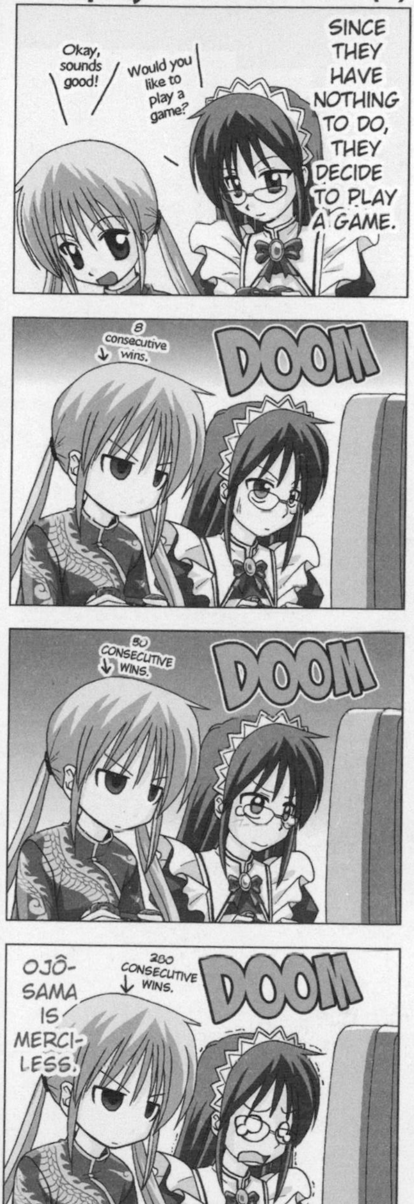
SINCE THEY HAVE NOTHING TO DO, THEY DECIDE TO PLAY A GAME.
Would you like to play a game?
Okay, sounds good!
DOOM
8 consecutive wins.
DOOM
80 CONSECUTIVE WINS.
OJÔ-SAMA IS MERCILESS.
DOOM
280 CONSECUTIVE WINS.

HAYATE THE COMBAT BUTLER
VOL. 3

STORY AND ART BY
KENJIRO HATA

English Adaptation/Mark Giambruno
Translation/Yuki Yoshioka & Cindy H. Yamauchi
Touch-up Art & Lettering/Freeman Wong
Design/Yukiko Whitley
Editor/Kit Fox

Managing Editor/Annette Roman
Editorial Director/Elizabeth Kawasaki
Editor in Chief, Books/Alvin Lu
Editor in Chief, Magazines/Marc Weidenbaum
Sr. Director of Acquisitions/Rika Inouye
Sr. VP of Marketing/Liza Coppola
Exec. VP of Sales & Marketing/John Easum
Publisher/Hyoe Narita

Printed in Canada

Published by VIZ Media, LLC
P.O. Box 77010
San Francisco, CA 94107

10 9 8 7 6 5 4 3 2 1
First printing, May 2007

RATED T+ FOR OLDER TEEN

PARENTAL ADVISORY
HAYATE THE COMBAT BUTLER is rated T+ for Older Teen and is recommended for ages 16 and up. This volume contains strong language, realistic and fantasy violence, and crude humor.

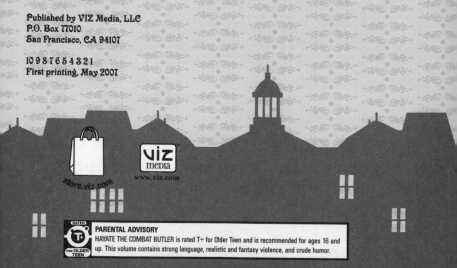

ハヤテのごとく! 3
Hayate the combat butler

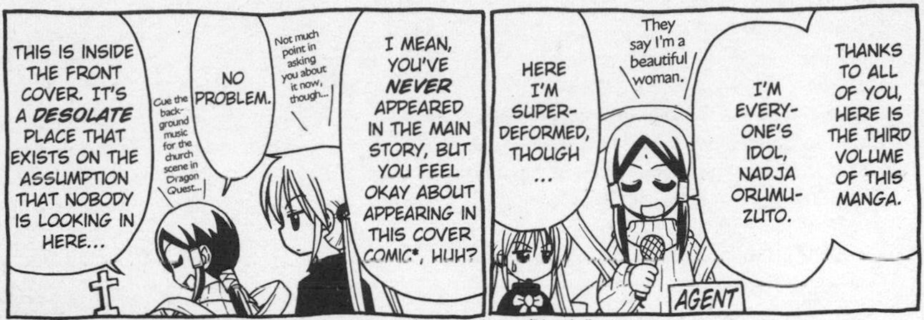
THANKS TO ALL OF YOU, HERE IS THE THIRD VOLUME OF THIS MANGA.
I'M EVERYONE'S IDOL, NADJA ORUMUZUTO.
They say I'm a beautiful woman.
HERE I'M SUPER-DEFORMED, THOUGH ...
AGENT
I MEAN, YOU'VE NEVER APPEARED IN THE MAIN STORY, BUT YOU FEEL OKAY ABOUT APPEARING IN THIS COVER COMIC*, HUH?
Not much point in asking you about it now, though...
NO PROBLEM.
Cue the background music for the church scene in Dragon Quest...
THIS IS INSIDE THE FRONT COVER. IT'S A DESOLATE PLACE THAT EXISTS ON THE ASSUMPTION THAT NOBODY IS LOOKING IN HERE...

*In the Japanese edition, this page appears on the cover, beneath the traditional slipcover.

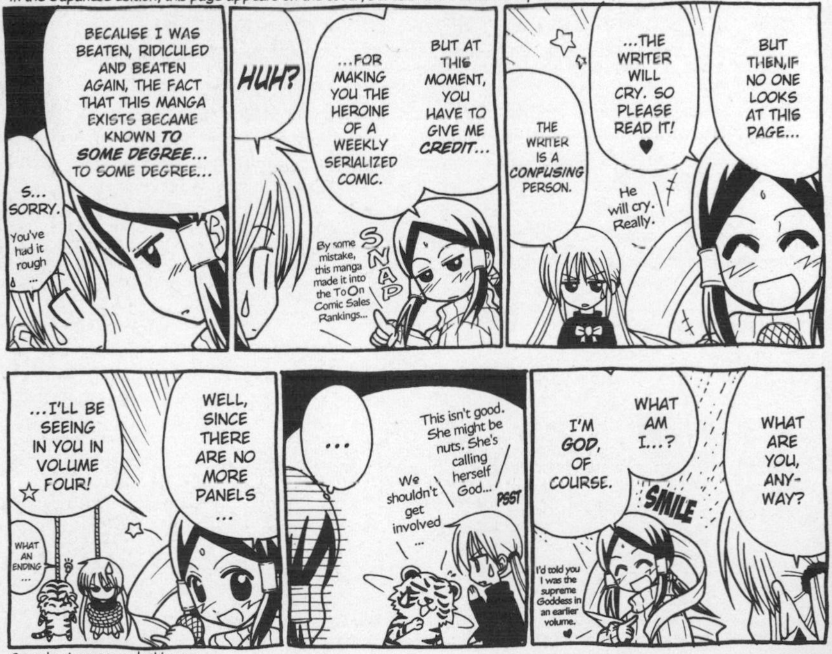
BUT THEN, IF NO ONE LOOKS AT THIS PAGE...
...THE WRITER WILL CRY. SO PLEASE READ IT! ♥
He will cry. Really.
THE WRITER IS A CONFUSING PERSON.
BUT AT THIS MOMENT, YOU HAVE TO GIVE ME CREDIT...
...FOR MAKING YOU THE HEROINE OF A WEEKLY SERIALIZED COMIC.
HUH?
SNAP
By some mistake, this manga made it into the ToOn Comic Sales Rankings...
BECAUSE I WAS BEATEN, RIDICULED AND BEATEN AGAIN, THE FACT THAT THIS MANGA EXISTS BECAME KNOWN TO SOME DEGREE... TO SOME DEGREE...
S... SORRY.
You've had it rough ...
WHAT ARE YOU, ANYWAY?
WHAT AM I...?
I'M GOD, OF COURSE.
SMILE
I'd told you I was the supreme Goddess in an earlier volume. ♥
...
This isn't good. She might be nuts. She's calling herself God...
We shouldn't get involved ...
PSST
WELL, SINCE THERE ARE NO MORE PANELS ...
...I'LL BE SEEING IN YOU IN VOLUME FOUR!
WHAT AN ENDING ...

Someday, I want to redo this page...